The
Autocratic
Academy

The Autocratic Academy

Timothy V. Kaufman-Osborn

Reenvisioning Rule within America's Universities

DUKE UNIVERSITY PRESS   DURHAM AND LONDON   2023

© 2023 DUKE UNIVERSITY PRESS

All rights reserved

Printed and bound by CPI Group (UK) Ltd, Croydon, CR0 4YY

Project Editor: Liz Smith

Designed by Matthew Tauch

Typeset in Portrait Text, Helvetica LT Std Ultra Compressed, and
Alegreya Sans by Westchester Publishing Services

Library of Congress Cataloging-in-Publication Data
Names: Kaufman-Osborn, Timothy V. (Timothy Vance),
[date] author.
Title: The autocratic academy : reenvisioning rule within America's
universities / Timothy V. Kaufman-Osborn.
Description: Durham : Duke University Press, 2023. |
Includes bibliographical references and index.
Identifiers: LCCN 2022043226 (print)
LCCN 2022043227 (ebook)
ISBN 9781478019824 (paperback)
ISBN 9781478017127 (hardcover)
ISBN 9781478024392 (ebook)
Subjects: LCSH: Universities and colleges—United States—
Administration. | Education, Higher—Aims and objectives—United
States. | Education, Higher—United States—History. | Education and
state—United States—History. | BISAC: EDUCATION / Schools / Levels /
Higher | EDUCATION / Educational Policy & Reform / General
Classification: LCC LB2341 .K3635 2023 (print) | LCC LB2341 (ebook) | DDC
378.73—dc23/eng/20221206
LC recordavailableathttps:/ /lccn.loc.gov/2022043226
LC ebookrec ordavailableathttps:/ /lccn.loc.gov/2022043227

Cover art: Partial text from a sign located on the perimeter of the
University of California at Berkeley.

Contents

Acknowledgments

Under the best of circumstances, writing a book is a solitary affair, and that is all the more so when that writing takes place in a windowless basement cell. Throw in a pandemic, and the line separating solitude from isolation thins considerably. I therefore am and will remain forever grateful to my partner of half a century, Sharon Kaufman-Osborn, who tolerated my occasional (?) grumpiness, my everyday fixation on this project, and my often clumsy exposition of arguments that I hope are now more clearly presented here.

I am also deeply appreciative of those whose work informs this book. Worthy of special mention is David Ciepley, who for the better part of two years patiently showed me why my uncritical understanding of corporations was just that and, in doing so, left an indelible mark on this book's main argument. I also want to thank Charlie Eaton and Bob Shireman, both of whom made materials available to me that proved central to its later chapters. Finally, in addition to the manuscript's anonymous reviewers, I am indebted to a host of scholars I will never meet but whose imprint on my argument is considerable. Rather than name those persons here, I direct readers to my endnotes as well as the list of references located toward this book's end.

For their invaluable assistance in tracking down obscure sources, I thank Jen Pope and Lee Keene, staff members at Whitman College's Penrose Library. Equally indispensable to this project are those with whom I have worked at Duke University Press. That includes Elizabeth Ault, my always gracious editor, as well as Benjamin Kossak, Liz Smith, Christi Stanforth, and Jessica Ryan. I know there are many others at Duke whose names I will never learn but who played key roles in this book's production, and to them I also offer my gratitude.

Although not expressly discussed within these pages, in thinking about how the constitution of rule within US colleges and universities might be differently fashioned, I draw inspiration from my 2019 visit to Spain's Mondragón University, where Ander Exteberria and Jon Altuna acted as my splendid hosts. Likewise, I gleaned much from my visit in 2018 to the University of Lincoln and the Co-operative College in Manchester, where Joss Winn, Mike Neary, and Cilla Ross taught me about the struggle to found the United Kingdom's first cooperative university.

For what it's worth (and I think it's a great deal), I dedicate this book to the students of Whitman College, who, for nearly four decades, kept me curious.

A Prologue in the Form of a Puzzle

The coronavirus pandemic has exposed deeply rooted structural defects within the American polity. To cite but a few, consider the paucity of affordable childcare for working parents, the impossibility of separating law enforcement from its racist past, the inequities of a health-care system whose benefits are available to some but denied to others, the disgraceful situation of seniors warehoused in facilities that abuse their claim to care, and the disposability of our most "essential" workers. None of these causes for collective outrage are new, but all are now harder to hide.

Were we to extend this list to other institutional spheres, might we ask whether the pandemic has also disclosed hitherto veiled truths about higher education in the United States and, specifically, how its colleges and universities are ruled? To help answer this question, consider a 2021 report issued by the American Association of University Professors (AAUP). In *Special Report: COVID-19 and Academic Governance*, the AAUP details egregious violations of what it calls "shared governance" at eight institutions of higher education. These include the termination of tenured as well as nontenured appointments, the suspension of faculty handbooks, the elimination of entire academic programs, the abolition of established bodies of governance, the invocation of force-majeure clauses to nullify collective bargaining agreements, and more.

College and university officials, the report notes, presented these actions as unfortunate but unavoidable responses to the financial fallout occasioned by COVID-19. The AAUP hints at a more cynical explanation when it quotes an interim dean at the University of Colorado at Boulder: "Never waste a good pandemic." Following this lead, the AAUP argues that many if not most of these top-down transgressions against shared governance were "prompted largely by opportunistic exploitations of catastrophic events." The pandemic, in other words, is not the original cause of these violations. Rather, COVID-19 merely "served as an accelerant, turning the gradual erosion of shared governance on some campuses into a landslide."[1]

The AAUP's report explains this attrition by pointing to the academy's "corporatization," which involves the treatment of colleges and universities by governing boards "as if" they "were businesses whose CEOs suddenly decided to stop making widgets or shut down the steelworks." The fruits of this misrepresentation are exemplified but hardly exhausted by "the expansion of areas of university administration, from the financial office to the office of the general counsel to the offices of risk management, in which the faculty have no involvement" as well as "the casualization of the faculty workforce entailed in the decades-long transition from a majority tenured to a majority nontenured faculty."[2] The academy, on this account, is run by those who confuse it with a for-profit business and who rule over a labor force defined by its insecure employment and hence its marginal capacity to counter the misguided designs of those who no longer know, if ever they did, what higher education is truly about.

From these findings the report draws an italicized conclusion: "*The COVID-19 pandemic has presented the most serious challenges to academic governance in the last fifty years.*" Peering into the future, its authors express their fear that rule by "unilateral" fiat may soon become a "permanent" element of institutional governance and so "acquire an unfortunate veneer of legitimacy." Whether this end can be averted is uncertain at best: "It remains to be seen whether such norms, once shattered, can be pieced back together or whether we are now in the domain of Humpty Dumpty, where what is broken cannot be mended and words can have any meaning that anyone wishes to attribute to them."[3]

To arrest this slide into academic authoritarianism, the AAUP offers a plea in the form of a platitude: "Governing boards, administrations, and faculties must make a conscious, concerted, and sustained effort to ensure that all parties are conversant with, and cultivate respect for, the norms of shared governance."[4] Given the report's account of the forces that now enfeeble faculty participation in institutional rule, this admonition is unconvincing if not incredible. Here the AAUP urges the very trustees and senior managers who have abetted the academy's insidious "corporatization" and, more recently, demonstrated their penchant for ruling by high-handed edict to concede the error of their misguided ways and affirm unswerving allegiance to norms they have undermined for decades.

How are we to make sense of the disjuncture between the AAUP's bleak account of the academy's current plight and this Pollyannaish prescription for its recovery? On my reading, the AAUP's incoherence stems from its failure to call into question the academy's essential constitution of rule. No matter how vociferously critics bemoan the "corporatization" of America's colleges and universities, the fact remains that they are almost always organized in the legal form that is a corporation.[5] More precisely, the American academy is fashioned as a historically specific type of corporation; and it is this type that authorizes and enables the governing boards and administrators censured by the AAUP to do what they will. Until this way of structuring the power of rule within the academy is criticized, contested, and ultimately repudiated, the AAUP's impasse will be ours as well.

This book attempts to do what the AAUP does not and thereby suggest a way to forestall a fall into Humpty Dumpty's dystopia. My aim is to challenge and, if I am successful, to modify the familiar ways we now frame debates about how the academy is and should be governed. This is easier said than done because, as the gulf between the AAUP's ominous analysis of our present situation and its anodyne remedy intimates, the academy's current constitution of rule is so often taken, uncritically if not unwittingly, as an obdurate given that demands accommodation rather than reconstitution as a very different kind of corporate body.

The principal purpose of part I, therefore, is to accomplish a task that John Dewey once ascribed to all critical inquiry: "to break through the crust of conventionalized and routine consciousness."[6] Today, that crust renders it difficult for us to see the American academy for what it is and hence to imagine alternatives to what we do not properly understand. This part's first chapter, accordingly, opens and closes with two recent incidents that reveal much about how rule is organized and exercised within US colleges and universities. Extrapolating from these tales, I invite readers to entertain the possibility that these enterprises are best characterized not as sanctuaries violated by the venal agents of "corporatization" but as corporations organized in autocratic form.

We cannot stop there, though, because much about our contemporary understanding of the corporation is itself defective. Today, when we employ the term *corporation*, we most often think of the for-profit behemoths that first emerged around the turn of the twentieth century and that now dominate the capitalist political economy of the twenty-first. On this account, and chiefly because economists of neoliberal disposition have secured an effective monopoly over our conception of what corporations are, we identify them as economic entities fashioned by means of contractual exchanges, located within the free market, and owned by their shareholders.[7] This representation, I maintain in part I's second chapter, is insidious, ideological, and incoherent. For reasons that neoliberal economists cannot afford to concede, corporations cannot be fashioned by means of contract alone, are owned by no one, and are essentially political in nature. To hold otherwise is to mystify the corporation and thereby bolster its contributions to local, national, and global projects of domination and exploitation.

In the third and final chapter of part I, closing my effort to fulfill Dewey's exhortation, I offer a historical overview of the European and more particularly the Anglo-American corporation. This inquiry reveals that the power of rule within the corporation has assumed two quite different forms, which I call the "autocratic" and the "republican." The autocratic character of the US academy, therefore, is not inherent within the corporate form per se but, instead, is a contingent feature that emerges out of struggles about which of these two forms will prevail. Accordingly, I suggest that we ask not how to decorporatize the academy, as the AAUP does, but rather whether American colleges and universities should now be reincorporated in republican form.

In part II, I put the corporate types elaborated in chapter 3 to work via an inquiry into the constitution of rule within America's earliest colleges. Specifically, in chapter 4, I examine contests over how and by whom William & Mary should be governed; and, in chapter 5, I do the same for Harvard. I focus on these two colleges not because they indicate the shape of collegiate constitutions to come, but because they do not. In each, one finds institutionalized traces of autocratic as well as republican corporate forms; and it is this disparity that opens up and indeed invites controversies that will diminish once the former comes to prevail over the latter.

Part II closes with a reading of the 1819 US Supreme Court case *Trustees of Dartmouth College v. Woodward*, which, on my account, signals the effective end of colonial and post-Revolutionary controversies about the academy's corporate constitution. Chief Justice Marshall's opinion in *Dartmouth* is this book's hinge in the sense that it marks the moment when republican understandings of the corporation lost much of their power to persuade as they were displaced by those that will eventually culminate in today's neoliberal variant (or mutant, if you prefer). To accomplish this end, Marshall joins a justification of autocratic rule to a capitalist conception of property, thereby dispossessing all but trustees of any claim to govern disposition of the academy's assets; and that is the conception of the academic corporation that is presupposed by the sign that appears at the beginning of chapter 9.

The triumph marked by *Dartmouth* did not, however, foreclose all future conflict about the corporate constitution of the American academy. To illustrate, in the first chapter of part III, I elaborate arguments advanced by the now mostly forgotten contributors to what one dubbed the "professors' literature of protest."[8] Writing during the two decades before and after the turn of the twentieth century and chiefly in response to the encroachments of industrial tycoons on newly minted research universities, this diverse group offered a critique that is often strikingly prescient in its anticipation of the "corporatized" academy (and sometimes quite funny as well). Like their colonial and post-Revolutionary predecessors, however, they asked not whether the academy should discard its corporate form, but rather how that corporation might be rendered something other than an autocratic anomaly within a nation committed to the ideal of republican self-governance.

These aspirations were quashed, I show in part III's second chapter, when the AAUP accepted as a fait accompli the academy's formation as an autocratic corporation but sought to secure some measure of power within these confines by affirming the prerogatives of professional expertise held exclusively by faculty members. However unwittingly, the consequence was to intensify the academy's standing as an antidemocratic order that joins unaccountable rule to the exploitation inherent within a capitalist economy. This unhappy result is the banal but harsh truth disclosed by the widget makers' authoritarian response to the coronavirus pandemic, and it is this same truth that reveals the hollowness of the AAUP's appeal for all constituencies within the academy, ruler as well as ruled, to recommit to the principles of shared governance.

In the two chapters that comprise part IV, I argue that today we are witnessing the academy's thoroughgoing incorporation within a political economy whose survival requires relentless maximization of capital accumulation and hence commodification of practices that once stood, at least in part, outside the marketplace. The results are twofold: First, we witness an erosion of the never absolute but considerable powers that, historically, have defined the unique institutional form that is the incorporated college or university. Second, this attrition undoes the capacity of the academy to accomplish purposes that distinguish the practice of education from what one wag has labeled "eduployment"[9] as well as the fruits of scholarship from what we now call "cognitive capital." In chapter 9, I explain how this vanishing act is playing out at Montana State, Princeton, and, in its most revealing form, at Purdue Global University. In chapter 10, using Michigan State as my primary example, I show how the contemporary university is now enmeshed in and ultimately subordinate to the networks of financialized power that define a neoliberal political economy.

In each of these cases, I argue, we are witnessing the cunning of history at work: as governing board members and their managerial minions preside over the academy's neoliberalization, they simultaneously sow the seeds of their own disempowerment. Ironically (but also rather deliciously), the academy's anachronistic boards are actively engaged in confirming my characterization of them as obsolescent relics whose autocratic pretensions are just that. True, in the short run, they remain capable of doing considerable harm as they press colleges and universities to become engines of capital accumulation. That very work, though, engenders a loss of institutional autonomy that cannot help but compromise the capacity of trustees to govern the realms they claim to rule.

In the epilogue, I suggest that the task before us is not to repudiate the academy's "corporatization" but to *reaffirm* its identity as a corporation capable of pursuing purposes and sustaining practices that are not reducible to those of a capitalist political economy. To do so, I argue against the academy's autocratic constitution and in favor of its incorporation on the model of a republican commonwealth. Rather than present a detailed characterization of Commonwealth University, which is beyond my ken, I offer two principles of institutional design that define this academy. First, the members of this corporation must retain the authority to select those who are to rule, and those who govern must in turn remain accountable to these same members. Second, the assets of Commonwealth University must be corporately owned and so subject to expropriation in the service of capital accumulation by no one. Stitched together, these principles recover certain elements of the corporate form that have been suppressed but also radicalize those that are peculiarly well suited to nurture the collective good that is free inquiry.

That, in a nutshell, is the gist of the argument I advance here. I suspect that more than a few readers will be inclined to endorse this argument's representation of the American academy as an autocracy that, today, is becoming little more than a handmaiden of capital accumulation. I am less confident that these same readers will find agreeable my call to reconstruct the academy in the form of a remodeled corporation.

It is not without reason that many, especially on the political left, now recoil at the very mention of the term *corporation*. That knee-jerk reaction, however, is predicated on a reductionist view of the corporation, one that equates this entity with the for-profit variant that prevails within contemporary capitalist political economies.[10] That type is indeed inseparable from reproduction of the forms of expropriation and exploitation that Bernie Sanders condemns when he wags his forefinger at the "1 percent"; and the antidemocratic inequalities of wealth and power Sanders rightly castigates have a history that is bound up in turn with the projects of settler colonialism and slavery. To those who consider this history inseparable from that of the corporation that afforded these projects institutionalized form, my argument will appear counterintuitive at best.

That argument will appear still more problematic when we recall that many nonprofit corporations in the United States are also bathed in blood, and that includes its colleges and universities. Organized in the form of autocratic corporations, America's institutions of higher education are implicated in producing and perpetuating the forms of systemic violence that have haunted this nation since Harvard was founded in 1636. For this understanding, we owe a considerable debt to those who in recent years have begun to uncover higher education's complicity in this deplorable history. To cite but two examples, consider Craig Wilder's *Ebony and Ivy: Race, Slavery, and the Troubled History of America's Universities*, which demonstrates that many of our earliest colleges were built on the backs of slave labor. So, too, consider the work of Tristan Ahtone and Robert Lee, who show how the universities enabled by the Morrill Act of 1862 presupposed the massive dislocation and dispossession of Indigenous peoples.[11]

Nevertheless, I persist. As a contingent creature of history, the corporation is a fraught artifact whose several manifestations fashion the accumulation and exercise of power, internally as well as externally, in diverse ways. To hold that this institutional form is inherently or necessarily bound up with the cause of domination is to lose sight of its ambiguous promise. Constituted one way, the corporation was and remains implicated in certain of America's worst crimes at home and abroad. Constituted in a different way, the corporation offers an exemplar of republican self-governance that harbors the potential to ground a critique of its autocratic alter ego and, equally important, to counter privatized appropriation of the academy's assets in the service of neoliberal capitalism. The corporate form, in short, deserves something other than the visceral rejection it so often elicits today, and higher education deserves something better than the kind of incorporation that now malforms its conduct. If these claims appear implausible or even incredible, the most I can do is to request a generous suspension of disbelief, at least for the moment.

To close this prologue, let me say this: Although this is a conceit I no doubt share with other critics of contemporary higher education in the United States, I am convinced that the issue I explore in this book is especially urgent at this particular moment in American history. As the United States slides into authoritarianism, as antidemocratic forces gain in muscle and vitriol, the sector of our political economy called "higher education" may contest or it may expedite this fate. What colleges and universities cannot do is remain aloof from this struggle over America's future, for they represent a key battleground on which this conflict is now being and will continue to be fought.

The role played by colleges and universities will turn not just on what students and scholars do in the classroom, the library, and the lab, but also on who rules the academy. How colleges and universities in the United States are governed is therefore hardly an academic question. This book, accordingly, seeks to clarify the constitution of rule within US colleges and universities, to inquire into that constitution's implications for the capacity of colleges and universities to cultivate the free inquiry that is their purpose, and, finally, to ask whether some other constitutional form might better nurture an end that is indispensable to any democracy worthy of the name.

In 1913, a scholar whose name we do not know insisted that it is not merely self-contradictory but dangerous to believe that "a country committed to democracy in its entire governmental system could be very successful politically so long as the institutions of first importance to its intellectual life should be the very antithesis of democratic."[12] In response, another asked how the academy might be reconstituted as a "democracy of scholars serving the larger democracy of which it is a part."[13] At bottom, this book is an attempt to elaborate the concern that animated the first of these two students of higher education and to answer the question posed by the second.

Nibbling at the Crust of Convention

1

Imperious Regents and Disposable Custodians

An Exemplary Tale

"We can terminate everybody, even down to the janitor, if it's the will of the board."[1] So declared Wesley G. Terrell moments before the governing body of Texas Southern, a public university, amended its bylaws and so gave this fiat official form: the Board of Regents shall "remove any professor, instructor, tutor, or other officer or employee connected with the institution when, in its judgment, the best interests and proper operation of the institution requires it."[2] This revision, reported the *Chronicle of Higher Education*, came on the heels of a public meeting in which Ronald J. Price, another regent, complained of indignities he had recently suffered at the hands of staff members. For one, he had been seated in the back row at a Democratic presidential debate. Still more egregious, a university employee had dropped him off, along with several other board members, more than a block away from the site of Texas Southern's homecoming celebration as if "we were a bunch of homeless people."[3] Like a petulant prima donna, Price informed the president, "That is unacceptable, and that can never happen again, or heads need to roll."[4]

Those troubled by this amendment to Texas Southern's bylaws raised doubts about the capacity of a nine-member board to pass informed judgment on each of the university's fourteen hundred faculty and staff members.

The regents' right to make this change, however, was not challenged, and it is not clear on what grounds one might do so. The university's enabling statute declares that the "government of the university is vested in a board of nine regents appointed by the governor with the advice and consent of the Senate."[5] Once appointed, Texas Southern's bylaws indicate, the board enjoys "wide discretion in exercising the power and authority granted by the State Legislature, including discretion in what action it takes directly and in what authority it delegates to other bodies within the University."[6] While the board may, for example, cede to senior administrators the authority to fire rank-and-file staff members, it "retains the unilateral right to temporarily or permanently repeal, rescind, suspend or waive" this power "whenever it is determined that such action is in the best interest of the institution."[7] In sum, the board of regents is authorized to establish the rules that govern Texas Southern, to modify those rules as it sees fit, and to contravene them at will.

The Academy as an Incorporated Autocracy

It is tempting to dismiss the example of Texas Southern University as an aberrant and even egregious case that tells us little about the structure of governance at other American colleges and universities. Before we jump to that reassuring conclusion, imagine that we were to put the following question to someone who is reasonably conversant with American higher education: Who rules the American academy?

Given the diverse forms taken by postsecondary institutions in the United States (to cite but a few, consider tribal colleges, research universities, community colleges, technical institutes, professional schools, and liberal arts colleges), especially when crisscrossed by the distinction between public and private, any generalization about their governance is subject to qualification.[8] That noted, no matter what type is under consideration, our hypothetical respondent might say something like this:

Final legal authority is vested in a governing board whose fiduciary duty is to advance the mission of the college or university over which it presides. One of the principal responsibilities of a governing board is to hire a president to whom significant powers are delegated (although, as the bylaws of Texas Southern indicate, that which is ceded can always be repossessed). The president in turn employs a handful of senior officers (for example, a provost, a chief financial officer, a vice president for alumni relations) who, like the president, also participate in governance via the exercise of delegated powers. (These of course are the managers whom faculty members reify and then vilify as "the administration.")

Next, we encounter faculty who, especially if eligible for tenure, are granted some measure of authority over domains pertaining to their specialized expertise (for example, the curriculum) and, sometimes, the right to consult about matters that impinge on these domains (for example, the academic program budget). This is what we call "shared governance." These parties are ranked above contingent faculty members who, as a rule, command few if any of the perquisites granted to those more fortunate, including the right to take part in institutional governance, but nonetheless enjoy the cultural capital that accompanies designation as college instructors.

Beneath the faculty, we find a diverse group of employees lumped together in the undifferentiated category we call "staff." Its members are subordinate to senior administrators, inferior to faculty members in status, and have no rightful claim to participate in institutional governance. Within this category, to mention but a few, we locate custodians, buildings and grounds workers, data-processing officers, administrative assistants, sponsored program coordinators, health center nurses, security officers, web designers, print production specialists, rental shop managers, interfaith chaplains, media relations strategists, financial aid counselors, athletic trainers, and many more.

What our hypothetical respondent has just described in broad strokes is a constitution of rule whose shape is akin to that of a pyramid. If we were to depict this structure in graphic form, it might look something like the diagram in figure 1.1 (see below).

Were we to do justice to this diagram, of course, we would need to consider each layer separately and complicate all so as to take into account their internal stratifications. Only if we were then to relocate each of these individual pecking orders within its appropriate stratum would we capture a constitution of rule whose graded complexity appears downright feudal.

So depicted, what shall we call the formal constitution of the American academy? For their help answering this question, we owe the regents of Texas Southern a debt of gratitude. By their words and deeds they have pierced the veil that enables the AAUP to represent the academy's slide into authoritarianism as a lamentable aberration. That claim will not do if the American academy is, as I maintain, structurally constituted as an autocracy.

At least for now, my use of this tendentious term must stand as something akin to a promissory note because, in large part, the purpose of this

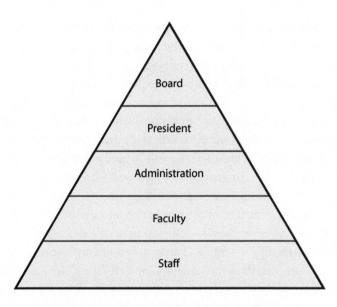

FIGURE 1.1 The Constitution of the Academy

book is to explicate its sense, defend its adequacy, and, most important, show how the character of the autocratic academy has evolved over time, culminating in the AAUP's recent nightmare featuring Humpty Dumpty. At present, suffice it to say that with this term I mean to highlight two features of the academy's constitutional form that are so familiar that they often disappear from view. First, as William A. Kaplan and Barbara A. Lee explain in *The Law of Higher Education*, this form is hierarchically organized and finds its apex in an identifiable head:

> Internal governance structures and processes may differ among institutions depending on their status as public, private secular, or private religious, and also depending on their size and the degree programs that they offer. The internal governance of a large research university, for instance, may differ from that of a small liberal arts college, which in turn may differ from that of a community college. Regardless of the type of institution, however, there is substantial commonality among the internal structures of U.S. institutions of higher education. In general, every institution has, at its head, a governing board that is usually called a board of trustees or (for some public institutions) a board of regents.[9]

Second, as the example of Texas Southern illustrates, the power of rule is concentrated in a body whose members are neither selected by nor formally accountable to those over whom they rule; and, for this reason, American colleges and universities are inherently antidemocratic. When we combine these two features, we see that institutions of higher education in the United States are ruled by a monocratic power that affirms its unilateral authority to govern over those who have no lawful title to participate in the exercise of that power and, as such, are its subjects (or, to use more familiar terminology to which I will turn in a moment, its employees).

Some, I realize, may dismiss my representation of the American academy as an autocracy on the ground that nonprofit colleges and universities in the United States do not possess the autonomy that they consider a necessary condition of such rule. To make this point, my critics might point to specifically public institutions of higher education and note that they are dependent on state legislatures for the funding that keeps them afloat; that the members of their governing boards are not self-perpetuating usurpers but, instead, are chosen by legislatures, governors, or, in a few cases, by popular vote; and, finally, that we are now witnessing a troubling enthusiasm on the part of certain elected representatives to encroach on the academy's internal affairs. (Think, for example, of Idaho's House Bill 377, which was signed into law by its governor in April 2021 and which bans the teaching of "critical race theory" on the ground that it "exacerbate[s] and inflame[s] divisions on the basis of sex, race, ethnicity, religion, color, [and] national origin.")[10] For these reasons, my detractors may contend, colleges and universities are ever less able to manage matters within their own institutional homes and so their governing boards are better characterized not as autocrats but as heteronomous pawns.

One way to respond to this criticism is to note that no autocracy, academic or otherwise, is ever perfectly autonomous or absolutely sovereign. All must take into account external powers that constrain their actions in this way or that as well as the possibility that certain deeds may provoke resistance within. It is false, moreover, to maintain that private colleges and universities, unlike public institutions, are exemplars of autonomy because they are free from state regulation (think of their legal obligation to obey occupational safety and health codes) or because they derive no financial benefit from state policy (think of their tax-exempt status). Whether public or private, the capacity of the academy's rulers to exercise the powers granted to them by law absent intervention or challenge is never absolute but always a contingent matter of degree.

That said, should the academy's autonomy one day evaporate altogether, my argument will no longer stand; for, on that day, colleges and universities will become nothing but administrative branches of the state, much like the gambling commission, the department of licensing, or the state patrol. Until that time comes, however, I will maintain my representation of the American academy as an autocracy. I will do so not because colleges and universities in the United States are perfectly autonomous but, rather, because they are constituted as corporations of a historically contingent type. Indeed, even those few that are not formally constituted *as* corporations are nonetheless organized in the form *of* corporations, again of a very specific sort. Whether public or private, the academy's governing boards are exclusively granted certain general powers, including, for example, the power to own property, to sue and be sued, to grant degrees, and, most important for my purposes, to govern the academy's internal affairs. That their monopolistic possession of these powers is sometimes subject to legislative modification, especially within public universities, does not render their exercise accountable to those they rule; and it is for this reason that higher education's governing boards in the United States qualify as autocrats and the institutions they rule as incorporated autocracies.

Nor does it undermine my characterization to concede that the academy's autocrats often rule not by unilateral fiat but in accordance with and conformity to rules codified in governing board bylaws and faculty handbooks. This, too, is true of any autocracy that seeks to rule by something other than brute force by giving its orders a patina of legitimacy. What renders American colleges and universities autocracies, again, is not their rule by so many iron fists but the categorical exclusion of their subjects from any guaranteed title to participate in the exercise of that rule. Yes, this right may sometimes be delegated to the ruled with respect to specific domains (for example, the curriculum controlled by the faculty). But should that right be summarily and arbitrarily withdrawn, as has happened at several colleges and universities since the onset of the pandemic, its losers will be hard pressed to find any conclusive basis for complaint. The possibility of rule by fiat, in short, always lurks behind governance in accordance with established rules, and this too qualifies the academy as an autocracy.

The Academy as a Capitalist Autocracy

To represent the academy as an autocracy is to regard the corporate law of higher education as a subspecies of "constitutional law," which, as I use the term here, refers to how power is formally marshaled, distributed, exercised, and legitimated within colleges and universities.[11] No account of this constitution will be complete, however, unless we also recognize that in large part the academy's power is deployed via economic devices. The power of rule may be exercised in the form of command, whether or not codified in institutional bylaws and statutes, but that power derives much of its bite from the contractual agreements that specify the terms of employment.

Were we to incorporate this sort of power within our diagram, we would need to show how contracts and the relations of domination and subordination inherent within them intersect and complement the work done by hierarchical relations of rule. To suggest what this might look like, I find helpful Elizabeth Anderson's seemingly oxymoronic concept of "private government." Too well schooled in classical liberalism, we tend to equate government with state power and so miss its presence in other arenas and especially the workplace. To rectify this omission, Anderson argues that government "exists wherever some have the authority to issue orders to others, backed by sanctions, in one or more domains of life." These sites are places of unfreedom when this power's exercise is joined to a denial to subjects of any "standing to demand that their interests be taken into account" and "no voice other than what their employers care to give them (which is often none at all)."[12]

The form of private government that defines a specifically capitalist economy is inherent within its default form of employment. "At-will" employment amplifies the vertical relationship of domination and subordination between employer and employee by rendering the continuity of employment radically precarious. To modify the term *contract* by labeling it "at-will" is to render that agreement one that denies an employee any measure of security because, strictly speaking, that contract has no temporal duration. Insofar as an employer may terminate employment at any time (just as, in principle, an employee can quit at any time), this contract only truly exists in the present moment at which point it may be renewed for another moment or it may not, in which case this contractual agreement immediately ends. So, too, all capitalist employment agreements are defined by what economists call "contractual incompleteness." This phrase effectively acknowledges that no job description ever specifies in complete detail the responsibilities an employee has agreed to or may be asked to perform. The right to modify those responsibilities is restricted to the employer, but never the employee who is legally obligated to obey or face termination. Positions held within these "private governments," in other words, are defined by the perpetual modifiability of their terms and hence the inherently arbitrary power of employer over employee.

This is why Anderson insists that "under the employment-at-will baseline, workers, in effect, cede *all* of their rights to their employers, except those specifically guaranteed to them by law, for the duration of the employment relationship."[13] Yes, this stark relationship may be tempered within the industrial work site via concessions extracted by unions (for example, seniority rules that stipulate who gets axed first); or, within government agencies, via civil service regulations that require performance reviews as a preface to termination; or, within the academy, via the due process rights afforded the lucky few who are tenured. But these are exceptions that do no more than prove the rule; and that rule is precisely what the AAUP fears is now coming to define academic employment in the land of Humpty Dumpty. In short, the wholesale evisceration of tenure in recent decades and the displacement of tenured positions by those that are contingent and hence at-will are now doing much to shatter the sentimental claptrap that encourages us to consider the academy more like an ivory tower than an iron cage.

That we do not typically identify colleges and universities as autocratic private governments testifies to our will to forget a truth that, if accepted, will have the unflattering effect of positioning most readers of this book not as agents but as objects of power exercised by others. This reluctance also testifies to our desire to believe that the autocratic character of college and universities in the United States can be explained not by its formal constitutional structure but by the proliferation of petty tyrants like those found at Texas Southern. The temptation to find this hypothesis credible is seductive, especially for faculty, because it furnishes readily identifiable targets for our beefs of the day. No matter how much satisfaction the blame game may bring, however, it distracts us from seeing that the antidemocratic constitution of the American academy is not an incidental feature that turns on who resides at the top. Rather, the origins of the American academy qua incorporated autocracy can be traced to colonial America, as I will show in part II, and the specific form that corporation assumes today reveals capitalism's relentless drive to render all employment contingent and hence precarious, as I will show in part IV.

Justifying the Academic Autocracy?

If I have successfully established a prima facie case for representing the American academy as an order that weds autocratic political power to the form of domination inherent within capitalist economic contracts, a problem arises in the form of a question: On what grounds should we believe that this structure is anything other than a historical accident whose appearance of legitimacy is rooted in nothing but ossified convention? In a nation that celebrates the American Revolution because it threw off the fetters of monocratic rule, does not an academy so constituted contradict its founding principles? And, most important, why should we believe that a hierarchical organization of power that vests final authority within a body granted a monopoly over the power of rule is peculiarly well suited to the free inquiry that defines higher education?

Given its anomalous character, we might anticipate that fans of the American academy as currently organized would pay substantial attention to justifying its constitution of power. This, though, is a question that has gone mostly unasked and unanswered; and that too testifies to the status of the academy's basic architecture of rule as an unexamined given that begs to be debunked.

A rare exception to this general neglect appears in a report issued more than half a century ago by an ad hoc committee under the title "The Governing of Princeton University." This committee was created in 1968, chiefly in response to protests over Princeton's complicity in the Vietnam War via its support of research conducted on behalf of the Department of Defense. Students challenged not just that support but also the authority of the trustees who, in virtue of their final responsibility for the university, had approved that work. Indeed, some brazenly called for outright abolition of Princeton's governing board: "The issue is not whether the trustees are doing their job well. The issue is that there is no justification for such a group of men controlling the destiny of an institution and a community in which they have no legitimate place. The University is a community of students and faculty, not businessmen."[14]

In response, the committee acknowledged, first, that "the Trustees are legally responsible for seeing that the University pursues the purposes for which it was chartered and that its assets are used to further these purposes"; second, that the authority of Princeton's trustees to do so "is commensurate with their responsibility, that is, it is substantially complete"; and, third, that the university's governance "implies the existence of *some* group of persons legally responsible for the actions of the corporation and with the authority to speak in its name."[15]

To its credit, the committee then conceded that "what has just been said does not necessarily mean that legal authority over the affairs of the university need be located in a board of the usual sort, that is, a board of non-resident members." To justify entrusting final authority to a board so constituted, the committee advanced five reasons: Unlike Princeton's employees and students, outside trustees can be expected (1) to "approach certain kinds of decisions, particularly budget decisions, more disinterestedly than a university's faculty, staff or students"; (2) to "make an important contribution to the welfare of a university by explaining its needs and policies to others," which includes "defending it against efforts to infringe freedom of discussion and inquiry," and "resisting undue interference in the affairs of the university by other 'outsiders'"; (3) to "help to insure a better definition of the public interest in the affairs of a university" by bringing "a variety of views to bear on the issues of university policy"; (4) to "aid a university in raising funds"; and (5) to "bring to a university various kinds of expert knowledge," which it illustrates by citing the presence on Princeton's board of lawyers, doctors, bankers, and financiers.[16] According to this report, in sum, the trustees' singular possession of these virtues warrants vesting ultimate legal authority in Princeton's governing board and hence denying others the right to take part in governance unless that board's members decide otherwise.

Yet the committee gives us substantial reason to doubt its own rationale. For example, it is not at all obvious that the special expertise of board members will be deployed in furtherance of Princeton's mission given that the "non-resident trustee carries out his duties in addition to those of his principal occupation" and hence is in a "poor position to evaluate the particular contexts in which many issues of policy arise in a university." Nor is it clear that these trustees are well suited to serve as champions of free inquiry given the committee's citation of a survey indicating how many governing board members at Princeton and elsewhere are "hostile to academic freedom or have a very narrow conception of what it implies."[17] Nor, finally, is it evident that Princeton's governing board is well positioned to articulate and incorporate the diverse viewpoints the report's authors consider essential to determining how best to promote higher education. At the time, the report tells us, nearly two out of every three board members were occupied in banking, finance, business, industry, law or medicine; just under half "were 60 years of age or more and none were younger than 40"; and "all were men; all were white; all were alumni of Princeton, and almost all were Protestant."[18]

Unless Princeton University's mission is to reproduce an economic, political, and cultural elite composed of elderly white male Protestant graduates, it is not clear why we should consider this board better suited to advance its educational purposes than the constituencies this report's authors consider short-sighted and self-serving (i.e., students, staff, and faculty). But perhaps that was then and this is now. Perhaps, today, the composition and qualifications of governing boards have changed such that we can now be more confident about their unique capacity to rule the academy well.

To test this hypothesis, let's look not at a private university but at the University of South Carolina System, which includes eight campuses and enrolls about fifty thousand students. In a scathing report issued in 2020, consultants retained by the Association of Governing Boards of Universities and Colleges (AGB) condemned the system's "entrenched" and "fundamentally misguided governance structure."[19]

The system's board, the AGB's experts explained, includes the governor of South Carolina, the state education superintendent, and the president of the alumni association, each of whom serves in an ex officio capacity, as well as sixteen board members elected by the state legislature. Given this mode of appointment, we should not be surprised to learn that many of South Carolina's elected officials believe trustees owe them "special responsiveness and loyalty" and should prove amenable to "requests for favors." The capacity of board members to resist these partisan pleadings and so defend the university's distinctive educational purposes is next to nil because their "expertise and experience" in matters academic is "extremely limited."[20] That ignorance is compounded, the report continues, by the parochialism of their occupations. Other than the two government officials, all are white-collar professionals who make their living in law, finance, health care, or real estate. That seventeen of its nineteen members are men and eighteen are white is perhaps not irrelevant to this board's ability to rule well in a state where women constitute a majority of a population that is itself about a third Black.

Princeton and the University of South Carolina System are hardly anomalous. In 2020, McKinsey and Company reported that 70 percent of higher education board members are men and nearly three-quarters are white.[21] Robert Scott, moreover, tells us that "under 10 percent of American college and university trustees have any professional experience in higher education."[22] And, finally, in *How to Run a College*, Brian Mitchell and W. Joseph King, each of whom has served as a college president, declare that academic governing boards in the United States are "uninformed, oversubscribed, and heavily dependent on alumni members who often view a college as a personal fiefdom."[23] Given this composition, what is remarkable is not that American higher education reproduces and indeed aggravates existing class, race, and gender-based structures of domination but that we continue to be taken aback by that fact.[24]

Making a Necessity of Virtue

The AGB's consultants to South Carolina close their broadside by noting that engagement in academic governance "is unlike any other role most trustees have ever taken on."[25] How so? All nonprofit colleges and universities in the United States are ruled by what are sometimes called "external lay" governing boards (which Richard Hofstadter and Walter Metzger once labeled "the great anomaly of American higher education").[26] The AGB explains: "Although the culture and process of governance varies widely among institutions, the presence of lay citizen governing boards distinguishes American higher education from most of the rest of the world, where universities ultimately are dependencies of the state. America's public and private institutions also depend on government, but they historically have been accorded autonomy in carrying out their educational functions through the medium of independent governing boards, working collaboratively with presidents, senior administrators and faculty leaders."[27] By "lay," the AGB means that expertise in higher education is neither a requirement nor an expectation of membership; and by "citizen" the AGB appears to indicate that board members are not employees of and hence derive no compensation from the institutions over which they rule, and so in that sense are "external."

External lay governing board members, the AGB continues, are "fiduciaries," and their duties are threefold: First, the duty of *care* enjoins "governing board members to carry out their responsibilities in good-faith and using that degree of diligence, care, and skill which ordinarily prudent persons would reasonably exercise under similar circumstances in like position." Second, the duty of *loyalty* requires "board members to act in good-faith and in a manner that is reasonably believed to be in the interests of the college or university and its nonprofit or public purposes rather than their own interests or the interests of another person or organization." And, finally, the duty of *obedience* affirms "the obligation of board members to ensure that the college or university is operating in the furtherance of its stated purposes (as set forth in its governing documents)."[28]

Fulfillment of these duties, which presupposes possession of the virtues necessary to do so, is the indispensable condition of the capacity of trustees to rule well, for they "require board members to make careful good-faith decisions in the best interest of the institution consistent with its public or charitable mission, independent of undue influence from any party or from financial interests." Moreover, and echoing the Princeton report, the AGB insists that external lay board members are not merely qualified but singularly qualified to act in accordance with these categorical imperatives: they "hold a *unique* position with regard to stewardship of the institutions they serve, a position *not shared* with students, faculty, alumni, donors, regulators, or others in the community."[29] So construed, these duties are the source of the self-limitation that constrains authority that is otherwise effectively unbound. As the AGB's South Carolina consultants conclude, echoing the motto of *Spider-Man*: "With the privilege of near-ultimate authority comes extraordinary responsibility."[30]

Leaving aside the question of whether this "near-ultimate authority" can be justified, this quotation poses another: On what grounds should we expect that board members will in fact possess the virtues necessary to act in accordance with this "extraordinary responsibility"? For those drawn from the for-profit corporate sector, as so many are, the self-abnegating virtues demanded of them as fiduciaries are not merely different from but at odds with the aptitudes and abilities required to succeed in a capitalist economy. Indeed, it is precisely because the academy's trustees are *not* subject to the market's disciplinary mechanisms that any behavioral economist would be quick to raise skeptical questions about the wisdom of vesting "near-ultimate authority" in these unaccountable bodies. Because their work is unremunerated, for example, governing board members are neither motivated by the incentives nor checked by the constraints that apply to the directors and chief executive officers of for-profit corporations. Unlike for-profit corporations that are publicly traded, moreover, academic governing boards are not accountable to their shareholders. Nor, finally, need trustees issue profit and loss statements every quarter to demonstrate in quantitative terms the success of their work. Rather than relying on virtues whose acquisition remains unexplained, our behavioral economist might therefore conclude, the academy would be better served if board members were in fact compensated employees whose salaries turn on measurable metrics that gauge their performance and reward or penalize them accordingly.

But perhaps the nondistribution rule, which prohibits governing board members from deriving personal pecuniary gain from any surplus revenue generated by a nonprofit college, will eliminate a temptation that might otherwise deflect them from their appointed duties. As Adam Smith understood, however, this same constraint removes the incentive that might tether the pursuit of private gain to the accomplishment of collective goods: "The directors of such companies, however, being the managers rather of other people's money than their own, it cannot well be expected that they should watch over it with the same anxious vigilance with which the partners in a private co-partnery frequently watch over their own. . . . Negligence and profusion, therefore must always prevail, more or less, in the management of the affairs of such a company."[31] In other words, from the vantage point of capitalism, it is precisely because American universities and colleges are nonprofit corporations that we should wonder what can possibly induce their rulers to sacrifice self-interest on behalf of a good from which they draw no tangible benefit.

To sum up, if the American academy is as I have characterized it, the authority of its rulers cannot help but prove suspect. Indeed, their very status as external lay boards denies them two sources of legitimacy they might otherwise call on. Because they are lay, they cannot claim the authority that, however problematically these days, accrues to professional expertise. Because they are external, they cannot claim the legitimacy that would follow if they were selected by those they govern. Nor, finally, is it clear why we should conclude that these rulers, unlike the ruled, are uniquely disposed to fulfill the duties that define their positions. A brief orientation to nonprofit governance, provided at the beginning of a member's term, is a sorry substitute for the virtues that, as Aristotle taught, can only be the fruits of habits practiced and perfected over the course of a lifetime.[32]

Tulsa's "True Commitment"

As a bookend to the story with which this chapter began, I offer a second exemplary tale. This tale reaffirms my representation of the American academy as an autocratic corporation but illustrated in this instance by a private rather than a public university. This story is chiefly important for my purposes because it comes with a twist in the form of a legal challenge that its faculty protagonists prepared but never ultimately filed. That challenge hints at a critique of the autocratic academy that turns not on a rejection of its status as a corporation but on an exploitation of the critical possibilities inherent within the corporate form when freed from the woebegone characterization that prevails today.

So, here goes: Only the credulous were caught off guard when, on November 7, 2019, the governing board of the University of Tulsa (TU) declared that it would move forward with a draconian restructuring of the school's academic program: "While we welcome suggestions for improvement through established pathways, there will be no 'repeal' or 'rollback' of *True Commitment*."[33] That plan reduced the number of degree programs from sixty-eight to thirty-six, chiefly by eliminating or consolidating programs in the humanities, arts, and natural sciences, but also dramatically expanded preprofessional training programs, especially those that "serve the rapidly growing technology and knowledge economy."[34] By refusing to relent or ever reconsider, the *Chronicle of Higher Education* observed, the board dealt what many considered a "fatal blow" to those faculty and students who had fought to forestall what they considered TU's betrayal of its educational mission.[35]

In a campus communication "written in the spirit of bringing us together and moving forward as the headwinds facing all higher education institutions increase," Tulsa's president, Gerard Clancy, explained why he and the board had concluded that they had no choice but to "reallocate" the university's resources. A decline in the number of high school graduates, rapid transformation of workforce skills required of graduates, and emergence of "a host of alternative avenues for education," including credentials, certificates, and corporate training programs, all represent "external factors" that are "beyond our control" but to which we "have a responsibility to respond swiftly and objectively."[36] The board's refusal to yield in response to internal opponents is thereby justified by citing its status as a victim of external circumstances beyond its control.

Several months prior to Clancy's edict, Tulsa's provost and executive vice president for academic affairs had announced to the faculty the recommendations that would eventually become the plan dubbed "True Commitment." The faculty's response was as predictable as the president's message was banal. First, its members charged the board and senior administrators with violating the principle of "shared governance," and, second, with aiding and abetting the university's "corporatization."

The provost responded to the first of these charges by noting that the recommendations in question emerged from the Provost's Program Review Committee (PPRC). Because this body included ten faculty members nominated by the deans of TU's several colleges, Janet Levin insisted that the PPRC's counsel emerged from a process that "models what well-informed shared governance looks like."[37] She did not, however, see fit to recall that the constitution of the faculty senate had been amended in 2018, with the board's endorsement, to include this provision: "Except in emergencies, major decisions and plans of the administration that significantly affect the academic affairs of the University should be discussed with the Faculty Senate for an expression of views *prior* to implementation or submission to the Board of Trustees."[38] Because this consultation had not taken place, in August 2019, the senate adopted a resolution condemning this procedural breach. That statement proved toothless, and when the board announced its refusal to conciliate, the newly formed chapter of the American Association of University Professors initiated and helped secure passage of resolutions of no confidence in the provost as well as the president. These censures had no apparent effect either, and so "True Commitment" marched onward.

Supplementing the shared governance charge, more than a few faculty members employed the epithet *corporatization* to explain why the university had launched this misbegotten venture. Most notably, in articles published in *The Nation* and elsewhere, Jacob Howland contended that the University of Tulsa has been "hit by a perfect storm of trends currently tearing through the American academy: the confident ignorance of administrators, the infantilization of students, the policing of faculty, the replacement of thinking by ideological jargon, and the corporatization of education."[39]

To make his case, Howland noted that the University of Tulsa's board of trustees at that time was composed exclusively of business executives and lawyers, and that none have backgrounds in higher education. Therefore, he posited, we should not be surprised that the board seems to think of the university's academic program as a market-driven enterprise that caters to students in the guise of consumers and cuts its losses when sales drop off. Nor should we be surprised that senior administrators responded to faculty members who resisted these disruptive innovations by playing what Howland labeled "administrative hardball,"[40] as they allegedly did when they "persuaded" the campus National Public Radio affiliate to deep-six an interview with him.

This tale of "autocratic corporatism" took a seamier turn as Howland traced the links between the university and certain of Tulsa's major corporate and philanthropic powers.[41] What are we to make, Howland asked, of the fact that the husband of the university's provost is the executive director of the George Kaiser Family Foundation, which is a major benefactor of TU as well as the city of Tulsa? And what are we to make of the fact that George Kaiser owns 54 percent of shares in the Bank of Oklahoma's parent company, BOK Financial (BOKF), which in turn is the corporate trustee of TU's $1 billion endowment? And what are we to make of the fact that the Kaiser Foundation's 2011 tax returns revealed that roughly a third of this nonprofit's $1.25 billion in assets was invested in ways that benefit Kaiser's for-profit enterprises? Weaving these threads together, Howland concluded that what was once an academic institution had now fallen prey to "a hostile takeover that appears to have made TU a subsidiary of Tulsa's biggest charitable foundation and an agent of the city's corporate interests."[42]

To this point, nothing about the faculty response to "True Commitment" is especially noteworthy. The possibility of a more intriguing challenge was intimated when a TU student attending a demonstration held aloft a sign that would make any good grammarian wince: "True Commitment to Who?"[43] This question was given formal legal articulation when a group calling itself the Concerned Faculty of TU drafted a complaint seeking injunctive relief from Michael Hunter, Oklahoma's attorney general, aimed at bringing "True Commitment" to an immediate halt. To the best of my knowledge, this complaint was never filed, but that does not lessen its import for my larger argument. Here the Concerned Faculty of TU departed from an attack on the university's "corporatization," which draws its sense from our conventional conception of the corporation as a private for-profit entity located in the sphere we reify as "the economy." Instead, although not framing their claims in these terms, the group effectively made a first stab at identifying the critical possibilities inherent within the corporate form.

To understand this challenge requires a bit of background. Emerging out of the Presbyterian School for Indian Girls, which was founded in 1882 as an instrument of settler colonialism, the University of Tulsa secured standing as a corporation in 1920 when the state of Oklahoma issued a certificate to that effect.[44] This document provided for establishment of "an educational corporation" whose "mission is to provide undergraduate, graduate and professional education of the highest quality." The sole members of this corporation are those who sit on its governing board, and it is to this body that Oklahoma granted the power "to do any and all other things necessary and appropriate to carry out the educational mission of the University" so long as its actions are "not inconsistent" with the provisions of this certificate or with Oklahoma and/or US law.[45] What distinguishes this board from that at Texas Southern, then, is not the extent of its powers but the fact that its trustees are appointed not by state officials but by its own members. The University of Tulsa is therefore the more perfect of these two autocracies because its ruling body is self-perpetuating and so accountable for its composition only to itself.

The powers conferred on the University of Tulsa's board by the state include the exclusive power to govern TU's affairs. This political power is exercised via the board's adoption of the internal statutes that it alone may amend, repeal, or suspend. True, the bylaws authorize the board to delegate certain of its powers to any officers it appoints. But this authority is an affirmation rather than a qualification of its power since, as noted earlier, any power delegated by a superior to a subordinate can always be qualified or withdrawn. Moreover, as at Texas Southern, TU's bylaws state that any or all employees, whether staff, faculty, or administrative, "may be removed in the Board's sole and absolute discretion, with or without cause, at any time."[46] In the last analysis, then, all who do compensated work for the university are at-will employees whose continued tenure in office is contingent on the forbearance of those who, as trustees, are exempt from this same prerogative power.

With respect to the faculty, the bylaws authorize its members to recommend, for example, the "procedures and standards" that are to govern instructional appointments, promotions, and dismissals as well as to establish the faculty's own mechanisms of self-governance (for example, a senate and designated committees). Every action taken by these bodies, however, is "subject at all times to the review and approval, modification, or disapproval, of the Provost/Vice President of Academic Affairs, the President, and the Board, in that order."[47] In short, because the faculty possesses no enforceable right to participate in institutional rule, should push come to shove, as it did when "True Commitment" was announced, its members can be no more than supplicants.

Perhaps recognizing that this is so, a group of enterprising faculty prepared a novel challenge to the board's plenary authority that reached beyond those rooted in appeals to shared governance. The gist of that complaint goes as follows: The University of Tulsa was granted corporate status by the state so that it could better advance Oklahoma's collective interest in an educated citizenry. This purpose, the university website stated in 2020, incorporates commitments to "excellence in scholarship, dedication to free inquiry, integrity of character, and commitment to humanity."[48] These ends, the complaint alleged, would suffer "irreparably injury," as would the "best interests of the University and all of its constituents, including the people of Oklahoma," if "True Commitment" were to be implemented. Specifically, because "True Commitment" guts the humanities and the natural sciences while expanding programs that "are almost exclusively technical and professional," its adoption threatens to transform "a major national research university" into "an overpriced technical and vocational school."[49] Should the board and its administrative agents get their way, in short, TU will become something other than what its articles of incorporation require that it remain.

As the state's highest law enforcement official, the complaint concluded, the attorney general possesses the authority to take action designed to ensure the board's fidelity to the purpose for which it was granted corporate status. That is so because the board's authority to govern, including its power to compose and enforce the rules applicable to everyone subject to its jurisdiction, is not self-generating. Rather, the board derives its authority to rule from the state-issued articles that afford it legal existence as, in this case, a private nonprofit corporation.[50] Should TU's rulers violate their fiduciary duty to uphold the purposes for which their powers were granted, the state may intervene to halt this betrayal and, if need be, to dissolve this corporation. What qualifies as the accomplishment of TU's mission is, therefore, not whatever its board declares it is; and, for that reason, the AAUP's dystopian depiction of an academy ruled by Humpty Dumpty, whose mandates are true because he says they are, is open to challenge.

That this suit was never filed does not compromise its utility for my purposes. Its rationale teaches us much about corporations that we are unlikely to appreciate so long as our understanding remains confined to that implicit in the term of abuse that is "corporatization." To restrict our understanding to that sense is in effect to allow neoliberal economists to dictate what we take corporations to be. That would be a mistake, and chapter 2 explains why this is so.

2

The Neoliberal Corporation Debunked

Against "Corporatization"

When we bemoan the academy's "corporatization," although rarely elaborated, we take for granted a specific understanding of what the corporation is. The AAUP, recall, hints at this conception when, in *Special Report: COVID-19 and Academic Governance*, it condemns those who treat colleges and universities "as if" they "were businesses whose CEOs suddenly decided to stop making widgets or shut down the steelworks."[1] Were we to press this report's authors to elaborate what they presuppose, no doubt they would explain that the corporation is an economic entity that is located within the capitalist marketplace and that pursues profit for the sake of private advantage. "Corporatization," on this account, is a deformation that has gained considerable momentum in recent decades as this entity has aggressively extended its tentacles into places, including the academy, that were once immune to the rationality of capitalism.

Is it possible, however, that the abstraction of this epithet falsely universalizes a historically specific and hence contingent form of the corporation? Is it possible, in other words, that this invective signals the success of neoliberal ideologues in securing a monopoly over our understanding of what the corporation is? And, if that is so, is it possible that we unwittingly reinforce "corporatization's" grip on the academy when we take this understanding as something given rather than exposing the neoliberal corporation as the contestable artifact that it is?

Historically speaking, representation of the corporation as a privately owned engine of capital accumulation is a creature of the nineteenth and early twentieth centuries. The specifically neoliberal account of this entity is not given proper theoretical articulation until we near the turn of the twenty-first. That account is incoherent insofar as it cannot acknowledge certain essential conditions and characteristics of the neoliberal corporation without undermining its own representation of this entity. To identify these features, as I do here, is to encourage us to think twice before we summon the charge of "corporatization," for that charge is parasitic on a conception of the corporation that is itself deeply flawed. To shake off the shackles of that representation is in turn to open up the possibility of asking how the academy might be re-formed as a very different sort of incorporated endeavor.[2]

What Is the Neoliberal Corporation?

In 1970, Milton Friedman famously declared that the only "social responsibility of business is to increase its profits."[3] While antecedents of this view can be found earlier in the twentieth century,[4] it only acquired hegemonic status in the decades following Friedman's attack on woolly-headed do-gooders who maintain that corporations, besides securing the mercenary ends of their investors, should advance specifically public purposes. "There is no longer any serious competitor," announced Henry Hansmann and Reinier Kraakman in 2001, "to the view that corporate law should principally strive to increase long-term shareholder value."[5] This view, as we will see, is predicated on two untenable tenets: (1) the corporation is constituted as a "nexus of contracts"; and (2) its purpose is to maximize the profit of shareholders because they are the corporation's owners. Braided together, these postulates form the crux of the neoliberal (mis)construction of the unique institutional formation that is a corporation.

To represent the corporation as a nexus of contracts is to regard "it" as nothing but a site where self-interested suppliers of key factors of production, including capital, labor, materials, and services, enter into voluntary contractual relations with one another: The *"legal fiction"* we call the "corporation," write Michael Jensen and William Meckling, is a *"nexus for a set of contracting relationships among individuals."*[6] Or, rather, to quote Frank Easterbrook and Daniel Fischel: "The corporation is a complex set of explicit and implicit contracts and corporate law enables the participants to select the optimal arrangement for the many different sets of risks and opportunities that are available in a large economy."[7]

Corporations, on this account, are constituted by multiple market exchanges that in principle could be accomplished by agents absent their institutionalization in the form of a firm. The corporate firm, therefore, is nothing but a convenient device that reduces the transactions costs that would otherwise be borne by the several parties to these exchanges were they not so organized. So, too, corporate law is nothing but a branch of contract law and, specifically, a set of generic rules that formalize what individual participants in production could craft on their own but need not do so because they are made available by the state at far less cost. In sum, the neoliberal corporation is a private creature of the free market; and its sole purpose is to facilitate the propensity of human beings, quoting Adam Smith, to "truck, barter, and exchange" via consensual entry into bargains that benefit all only because they profit each.[8]

This representation anticipates the second key tenet of neoliberalism's theory of the corporation: its commitment to "shareholder primacy." Multiple parties play a role in the process of production, including workers, managers, suppliers, vendors, customers, and others. Of these participants, the neoliberal account holds that shareholders hold a privileged position and, indeed, that the foremost priority of a corporation is and should be to boost their gains, as paid in the form of dividends. In part, this obligation follows from the status of shareholders as sources of the capital without which a corporation could not exist. More fundamentally, though, it stems from their standing as risk-takers who, unlike a corporation's compensated employees, are guaranteed no share of its profits. Instead, shareholders can only lay claim to whatever revenue may (or may not) remain after a corporation has made good on all its fixed obligations to employees, the providers of raw materials, commercial lenders, and so on. Perhaps counterintuitively, it is precisely because the claims of shareholders are "residual" in this sense that a capitalist economy organized to maximize their benefit offers the best of all possible worlds. Because their pecuniary gains are contingent rather than contractually specified, shareholders have the greatest incentive to ensure that corporations do in fact aggrandize their profits; and, according to neoclassical economic theory, this is the carrot that stimulates the productivity that improves the lot of everyone.

Because investors qua shareholders are the principal sources of corporate capital, the neoliberal account conventionally regards them as the owners of any given corporation. (To see the point, ask your preferred search engine who owns Facebook, and you will find that the answer is Mark Zuckerberg in his capacity as controlling shareholder.) The possession of shares is thus equated with equity in or ownership of a fraction of corporate assets in an amount corresponding to the number of shares held, whether by an individual, an investment firm, a pension fund, or some other body. On the neoliberal account, that possession in turn explains why shareholders are granted certain rights of control over any given corporation, including but not limited to the right to vote for directors, to inspect corporate records, to sue for wrongful acts committed by managerial personnel, and of course to receive dividends should a governing board elect to devote a share of profits to this end.

Why the Neoliberal Theory of the Corporation Is Pernicious and Ideological

As the nexus of contracts argument implies, the corporation belongs in liberalism's private sphere; and, as the shareholder primacy argument implies, the corporation is a form of capitalist property owned by those who inhabit the private realm that is the economy. The consequences wrought by this construction have been devastating, as many have explained far better than I can.[9] To cite but a few, the strategies adopted to secure the neoliberal corporation's exclusive purpose have included (1) maximal distribution of accumulated revenue in the form of stockholder dividends, thereby drawing resources away research and development; (2) corporate buybacks of shares, which has the effect of enriching the tiny minority that holds the vast majority of stock in the United States; (3) reductions in corporate tax rates, thereby hobbling governmental social welfare programs that draw funding from that revenue; (4) decimation of unions, which effectively forecloses the possibility of collective bargaining about wages and benefits; (5) outsourcing and offshoring corporate operations, thereby disempowering domestic workers who might otherwise demand better working conditions; and (6) termination of long-term employees in favor of independent contractors, which eliminates the requirement to contribute to medical insurance premiums and pensions.

Today, the United States is characterized by levels of economic inequality not seen since the Great Depression. The gulf that separates rich from poor and that renders most pawns of forces they can neither grasp nor control is in large part a consequence of the neoliberal corporation's commitment to the doctrine of shareholder primacy. In the early 1980s, major US corporations disbursed less than half their earnings to shareholders whereas between 2007 and 2016 that figure rose to 93 percent. David Ciepley is therefore quite right to contend that the credo of shareholder primacy has engendered a form of "cannibalism, with stockholders consuming the corporate body. It robs the future to pay off the present, and reflects a massive reallocation of corporate revenues, with much of what used to be shared with workers, or reinvested in the firm, now disgorged to stockholders, executives included."[10] When value extraction replaces value creation, the result is stagnating productivity combined with gross injustices that resist political remedy because the power exerted by neoliberal corporations renders them largely immune to democratic interventions. The ensuing frustrations provide fertile ground for fascist demagogues masquerading as US presidents as well as conspiratorial sects that cast about for villains to blame for their thwarted dreams.

For these reasons, the neoliberal representation of the corporation is pernicious, but it is also ideological insofar as it masks who gains and who loses from the machinations it sanctions.[11] To sustain its reading, the neoliberal must regard all action within the corporation as the fruit of contractual transactions among so many autonomous agents. This free market fundamentalism is evident, for example, when Arman Alchian and Harold Demsetz declare that the corporate firm is nothing but "a highly specialized surrogate market" characterized by "no power of fiat, no authority, no disciplinary action any different in the slightest degree from ordinary market contracting between any two people."[12] Easterbrook and Fischel draw the obvious (but erroneous) conclusion when they insist that "the contractual approach does not draw a sharp line between employees and contributors of capital" because, in the last analysis, each merely brings to the bargaining table a factor of production that may or may not generate a contractual relationship depending on the self-interested calculations of each.[13]

On the one hand, by presenting shareholders as owners of the corporation, this reading affirms the prerogatives of property that, on a capitalist construction, characterize the vertical relations between persons and their possessions. On the other hand, by presenting the corporation as a nexus of contracts generated by free agents engaged in market exchange, the neoliberal account erases the relations of power that define this hierar-chically ordered corporation. Obfuscation of the latter, to return to Eliza-beth Anderson's notion of "private government," is most apparent when neoliberalism's apologists insist that the relationship between employers and employees is not one of domination and subordination because each is equally free to exit their agreement at any time.

Given this account, neoliberal ideologues cannot acknowledge the background conditions of capitalist employment that are not the product of contractual negotiation but are not for that reason any less real. Unlike agreements that emerge from voluntary choices made by equals, these con-ditions invest in some forms of authority denied to others. These contracts, as I noted in chapter 1, typically incorporate a clause specifying the at-will character of employment, which means that some possess the authority to fire while others are defined by their vulnerability to termination. As I also noted, these contracts include but do not as a rule expressly enumerate the common law right of employers to modify the responsibilities of any given job as well as the legal obligation of employees to obey (or risk receipt of a pink slip). In short, the inegalitarian structures of power that define employment within capitalist corporations must be made to disappear if neoliberal fictions are to stand.

Another sort of occlusion appears in the neoliberal account of corporate governance. The issue of governance, on this reading, is a matter that con-cerns shareholders, boards of directors, and chief executive officers. Their relationship constitutes a problem because the members of each group are rational economic agents bent on securing their own advantage. How, then, to ensure that senior management will act in accordance with the interests of shareholders and the boards they select? The solution is to cre-ate a structure of incentives that will increase the likelihood (but never guarantee) that executives will manage the resources under their control in ways that maximize the dividends paid to shareholders. Examples in-clude the adoption of proxy access, which entitles shareholders to place rival candidates on board ballots; the separation of a corporation's chief ex-ecutive officer from the chair of its board, which enables the latter to better pursue the interests specific to shareholders; and, perhaps most important, the inclusion of stock options in chief executive officers' compensation pack-ages so that, like other shareholders, they too have an immediate stake in maximizing the sole end of the neoliberal corporation.

What vanishes from this narrative about corporate governance, of course, are those who do the productive work that generates profit, that is, those employees who are neither shareholders nor board members. Their absence is no surprise, however, because these employees can affirm no claim to ownership of corporate assets and, for that reason, are denied any right to participate in corporate governance. These hired hands are therefore so many subjects, but their status as such must be concealed if the neoliberal is to sustain a representation of the corporation as a creature of so many voluntary contracts. Only if that fable remains intact can the expropriation and exploitation accomplished by shareholders and senior executives be presented as a product of free exchange among equals. Paddy Ireland is therefore correct in concluding that the neoliberal account of the corporation is but one "part of a more general ideological project aimed at providing instrumental justifications for the private appropriation by shareholders of corporate surpluses which are the products of an increasingly *social* production process."[14] The neoliberal corporation, in short, is an oligarchy in which those whose consider themselves owners elect boards they consider their representatives, and those representatives in turn hire executive agents who rule over employees in accordance with contractual terms that mandate the terms of their subordination.

The destructive work accomplished by the neoliberal corporation, so conceived and justified, extends into domains we often consider extra-economic but in fact are parts of a more comprehensive capitalist political economy. So, for example, the project of capital accumulation can succeed only if the market's operational logic is permitted, indeed encouraged, to reconstruct as many spheres of collective action as possible (think, for example, of for-profit prisons, childcare centers, and universities); this is what neoliberals call "privatization." That reconstruction requires that any political or legal restrictions that might otherwise retard profit maximization be minimized if not eliminated (think, for example, of the Glass-Steagall Act, now repealed, which once separated retail from investment banking); this is what neoliberals label "deregulation." That in turn demands that the state's capacity to enact and fund policies based on values other than those dictated by capitalist markets (think, for example, of popular sovereignty) must be enfeebled; this is what neoliberals characterize as "starving the beast." In sum, if the pursuit of private gain is to realize its promise of economic abundance, the corporate incarnation of this quest must be emancipated from all forms of accountability other than those inherent within allegedly competitive markets; and their unfettered play is what Friedman calls "freedom."

Why the Neoliberal Theory of the Corporation Is Incoherent

The harms perpetrated by neoliberal capitalist corporations have been chronicled by many. Very few, however, have noted that the neoliberal representation is conceptually confused in the sense that it cannot acknowledge certain essential elements of the institutional form that is a corporation without undoing its own characterization. If the incorporated US academy is itself assuming neoliberal form, as I argue in part 4, then it too will harbor contradictions that vitiate its capacity to sustain the distinctive kinds of practice that merit designation as "education," whether in the form of studying, teaching, or learning.

Both cornerstones of the neoliberal theory of the corporation—its representation as a nexus of contracts and the doctrine of shareholder primacy—are specious. To see why this is so, let's begin with shareholder primacy and, specifically, neoliberalism's representation of shareholders as a corporation's "owners." On the neoliberal account, the corporation is conceptualized as a form of private property. As such, its owners must be entitled to the rights legally ascribed to all property owners within a capitalist economy. Setting aside laws that presuppose but then marginally qualify these rights (like the state's power of eminent domain), these include the exclusive right to choose how property will be used; the right to exclude others from access to or use of what is owned; and the right to alienate what one possesses, for example, by selling or renting it to someone else. To illustrate, ownership of my home as private property authorizes me to bar you from entry; to plant weeping willow trees in my backyard, no matter how much my neighbors object; to sell my house and the land on which it sits to the highest bidder; and so on. The denominator that is common to each of these rights is private property's status as a rivalrous good: only one user may possess legal title to it at any given moment in time and hence enjoy the enforceable rights that accompany this exclusive possession.

If this is what ownership is within a capitalist economy, then shareholders cannot be said to own the corporation. Unlike the possessions I own, corporate assets are legally possessed by a juridical person that neither you nor I will ever be. Because this "artificial" entity owns those assets, the corporation cannot itself be an object of the full panoply of capitalist property rights. We effectively acknowledge this truth when someone asks whether you or I, or we together, "own" the streets, sewers, and parks of an incorporated municipality. The correct answer is that no one does, for the creature of law that is this municipality owns these goods, and the same response obtains when we ask about the assets of private corporations. True, persons may hold shares in a for-profit company. But shares are financial instruments that are accompanied by certain limited governance and income rights but cannot be identified with the assets held by a corporation. Although shareholders may sell their shares on Wall Street, they cannot withdraw, borrow, or lend corporate assets, for these goods are not their alienable property. No matter how many shares of Apple stock I may hold, I cannot walk into one of its retail stores and, without paying, appropriate the latest iPhone as my own. Nor, for that matter, may its chief executive officer, Tim Cook.

For much the same reason, nor can shareholders assert ownership rights over the profits generated by Apple each quarter, and that is so even after this corporation's contractual obligations to others have been satisfied. How that residual is apportioned is not determined by its shareholders, as I could were I to sell my home and then choose to do as I please with whatever profit remains after I pay off my mortgage. Rather, decisions about the distribution of residual income are made by Apple's board of directors, who, if they choose, can dedicate the company's profits to other purposes (for example, to expand offshore production, to wine and dine legislators, or to invest in the Apple Support College Program). Payment made for these other ends reduces the income that would otherwise be available for disbursement in the form of dividends and so mocks the shareholders' conviction that they own a corporation and hence are entitled to its proceeds. In response, they may seek to secure the election of other board members with different priorities, but that should not be confused with affirming a legal title to a portion of a corporation's revenues equal to their investment.

To neglect these facts is to forget that one of the principal purposes of creating a corporation is to vest assets in a legal entity whose ownership of that capital shields shareholders from claims that can be directed against unincorporated individuals. Should a corporation be summoned to court in response to a civil suit, the doctrine of limited liability ensures that its individual shareholders will not be required to pay any damages that exceed the amount of their investment. So, too, should a corporation file for bankruptcy, its individual investors will be shielded from personal accountability for that firm's debts. This is so, once again, because it is the corporation that owns the assets it incorporates whereas the corporation itself cannot be owned by persons, singly or collectively, without destroying its very existence as a corporation. However counterintuitively, corporations are created to *foreclose* certain of the rights claims that individual owners of capitalist property are entitled to make about their private possessions.

A corporation, Lynn Stout suggests, is a sort of "time-machine" that is invested with the capacity to outlive its merely mortal investors and thereby enable its accumulated assets to remain amassed, at least in principle, forever.[15] Essential to this possibility is the legal doctrine known as "asset lock-in." This tenet states that shareholders, contrary to what I can do with my personal property, cannot unilaterally withdraw from the firm whatever capital they have invested. When I invest in a corporation, I become a stockholder who can of course seek a buyer for my shares on secondary markets. But that sale cannot be identified as a shift from me to you of what was once my share of corporate assets, for I never owned them in the first place. Were matters otherwise, a corporation would be functionally indistinguishable from a partnership whose members can withdraw their investments at will and at any time. But that of course is the possibility that precludes a corporation from securing the sempiternal status intimated by Stout's metaphor. Unlike an unincorporated partnership that will perish when its last partner expires, a corporation possesses the property of "perpetual succession," which means that it can acquire new members while, in the eyes of the law, remaining unchanged.

Because the legal fiction that is a corporation owns the capital invested within it, David Ciepley rightly labels incorporated assets a form of "socialized property."[16] Ironically, it is the socialization of corporate property and hence its immunity from private appropriation that protects individual shareholders from extractions that would otherwise eat into their personal gains. Milton Friedman and his acolytes notwithstanding, it is only because corporate property is *not* held as the private property of its so-called owners that shareholders who place bets on future revenue can reasonably expect to profit from their speculative investments. Absent property's socialization, that is, its effective ownership by no one, capitalism's corporate investors will find themselves at the mercy of self-regarding shareholders who, at any moment, may elect to withdraw the capital that is a necessary condition of a corporation's persistence through time.

But can such socialized property be generated by means of a nexus of contracts, as neoliberals would also have us believe? The answer is no, and that brings us to the second fundamental error of the neoliberal representation. Corporations are not reducible to a nexus of contracts; nor are they solely creatures of marketplace transactions; and nor are they entirely economic in nature. Corporations may enter contracts, but these artificial persons cannot be created by means of contractual agreements made by private parties. That is so because the rights, powers, and immunities that define corporations, including the right to contract, cannot exist absent antecedent existence of the specifically legal instruments that are the necessary condition of their possibility. So, too, only authorization by the state can constitute corporations as juridical entities that exist apart from any parties that engage in contractual transactions with them, whether internal (as in employment contracts) or external (as in independent contractor agreements).

When I first signed an employment contract with Whitman College, that contract was between me and the corporation so named. Should I elect to sue my employer for wrongful termination, I will sue not Whitman's provost (even though his signature appears on my contract), but its board of trustees in their corporate capacity. To discourage future miscarriages of justice, my colleagues may elect to form a union, and the collective bargaining agreement they endorse may be signed by Whitman's president or perhaps even its board chair. But each will do so not as natural persons, but in their capacity as officers of this nonprofit corporation and in its name. Indeed, because juridical personhood is a defining property of the corporate form per se, should Whitman College one day elect to become a for-profit purveyor of educational commodities, every claim made in this paragraph will remain true.

The neoliberal account cannot admit the independent reality of juridical personhood without undermining its economistic reduction of the corporation to a nexus of contracts among private parties. To acknowledge that reality is to concede that corporations are inherently political, and that is so in at least three ways. The first I have already identified: no matter how many private contracts may become intertwined within a nexus, these contractors cannot summon a corporation into being on their own. To note this is to go beyond claiming that corporations require the state, for example, to furnish the statutory forms that enable entities to file for corporate status or, once incorporated, to adjudicate and, if need be, punish violations of any contracts to which those corporations are a party. Rather, this is to say that corporations owe their very existence to the state. Even under general incorporation laws, the papers filed with a secretary of state do not simply register an antecedently existing corporation. To secure legal standing as a corporation requires the filing of an application crafted in conformity with a state's general provisions of corporate law; and any applicant retains provisional status until the forms filed have been duly certified by an officer of the state. However powerful a corporation may be, in the last analysis, whatever independence it enjoys attests to its status as a political dependent and whatever autonomy it exercises testifies to its heteronomous generation.

Second, whatever powers a corporation holds and exercises are and can only be granted to them by the state. This much Chief Justice John Marshall got right when, in the 1819 *Dartmouth* case I discuss in chapter 6, he wrote: "A corporation is an artificial being, invisible, intangible, and existing only in contemplation of law. Being the mere creature of law, it possesses only those properties which the charter of its creation confers upon it."[17] Those properties include a corporation's privileges and immunities but also its legal rights. Therefore, to claim that a corporation can assert rights *against* the state, as legal minds of a neoliberal disposition are wont to do, is to forget that any rights a corporation can claim are granted to this artificial being *by* its maker. This is not to deny that corporations can sometimes advance legal claims against governments. But it is to say that their rights are not "natural," if by this term we mean something akin to inherent in the very nature of corporations and so subject to the same constitutional protections guaranteed to you and me. That erroneous contention is the premise of several deeply problematic recent Supreme Court decisions, most notably *Citizens United* and *Hobby Lobby*, both of which held that corporations, as much as any person, enjoy the protections enumerated in the Bill of Rights of the US Constitution.[18] To maintain that view is to exempt corporations from any accountability to those who, by statutory means, have established the very conditions of their existence; and that of course is precisely what the neoliberal intends.

For my purposes, the most salient power granted to corporations is not the power to sue and be sued, to enter into contracts, to borrow money, to buy and sell property, and so forth, but the power to practice self-governance. Unlike unincorporated associations, corporations are granted considerable authority to govern themselves, specifically by enacting, imposing, and enforcing rules applicable to those subject to their jurisdiction. (Think, for example, of the bylaws of Texas Southern University or the ordinances of incorporated towns or, for that matter, the work rules that govern employment within any neoliberal corporation.) Unlike a voluntary association (such as an online canasta club), which lacks the authority to adopt rules that bind its members, corporations of all stripes can do so and hence, as Anderson insists, are properly regarded as so many "private governments." Their standing as governments explains why the college and university charters I examine in later chapters typically refer to these incorporated entities as "bodies politic," and that in turn explains why the eighteenth-century English jurist William Blackstone referred to corporate bylaws as "a sort of political reason to govern" these bodies.[19] This does not render corporations identical to the state whose creatures they remain and whose laws they must obey; but it does mean that, within these confines, they are granted the powers and hence the autonomy as well as the authority that are indispensable conditions of the capacity to rule their own affairs.

No matter how that authority is distributed, organized, and exercised, this represents yet another element of corporate identity that the neoliberal cannot acknowledge. To do so would be to refute the neoliberal characterization of the corporation as an authority-free zone constituted entirely by means of voluntary contracts. What that fiction misses, to repeat, is what Blackstone and Anderson understand: Corporations are consolidated instruments of governance, but the powers they exercise are derived from the states that the neoliberal locates squarely in the public sphere. A corporation, whether for-profit or nonprofit, is therefore a peculiar sort of hybrid that does not sit well on either side of liberalism's categorical divide between public and private. Rather, a corporation is what Ciepley calls a "franchise government. . . . It is privately organized, financed, and staffed, but the state creates it as a legal entity, prescribes its basic governance structure, and authorizes its management to control the property and personnel."[20]

Who, then, are the rulers of these corporate franchises? As we saw in Texas and Oklahoma, although the power of rule may be delegated to subordinate officers, in the last analysis a corporation's board of directors exercises this authority. Boards or something akin to them are required because a corporation, as a juridical person, has no will and cannot act on its own. On the neoliberal account, these boards are considered agents of corporate shareholders who, as we have seen, are themselves construed as owners; and the authority of directors to govern is held to follow from their election by these same shareholders.

This proposition seems reasonable enough to those of us who believe we live in a democracy, but it is nonetheless wrong. Once constituted, the authority of corporate boards is original. It is held by directors solely because they have been granted this authority by the charters, articles of incorporation, or notices of certification that prescribe the general forms of corporate governance. They do not rule because, like feudal lords, they own property or, like state legislators, because they have been selected by shareholders. Rather, directors rule because they hold offices within a legally constituted entity to which certain powers have been ceded by the state, which encompasses the power to determine whether shares will or will not be issued on the stock market. Contrary to neoliberal commonsense, therefore, if shareholders exist, that is because a board of directors has authorized their existence, not the other way around.

For this reason, boards are not legally obligated to do the bidding of shareholders (although directors may find it prudent to do so and shareholders may adopt reforms that make it hard for them to do otherwise). When persons invest capital in a corporation, they cede control over that corporation's assets to a board of directors that is legally independent of those investors. In exercising that control, at least in principle, boards employ their authority to do what they think best to advance the purpose for which a corporation was formed. Accordingly, and like the trustees of Texas Southern and Tulsa University, the directors of for-profit corporations are also fiduciaries whose primary duty is to manage well the assets with which they have been entrusted. Should directors choose to fulfill that duty by, for example, doubling the wages of all employees, shareholders may object on the ground that a board has violated its fiduciary duties, but they cannot claim that their authority has been usurped or, as we have seen, that their property rights have been contravened.[21]

Cracks in the Neoliberal Corporation

The last political dimension of the corporation I wish to note is implicit in the identity of directors as fiduciaries. I will say more about this matter later, but for now I merely want to pose a question whose answer at present is contested: What is the purpose of a corporation? On the neoliberal account, as Friedman declared, the answer to this question is unproblematic: the sole purpose of a corporation is to maximize shareholder value in the form of dividends.

But, of course, this is not true of all corporations. For example, the city of Walla Walla, Washington, where I now live, was incorporated in 1862. So formed, according to state law, the city holds the powers granted to all corporations, and these powers must be exercised not to advance the interests of any private parties, but "for the common benefit."[22] So, too, the seminary that later became a liberal arts college located in Walla Walla was granted its charter of incorporation in 1859 by the territorial government only because it pledged to advance a collective good: "the instruction of both sexes in literature, science, and art."[23] But, the neoliberal will be quick to remind us, this commitment to a distinctively public purpose is not true of capitalist enterprises, for they are formed to reap profit for their self-interested investors.

Yet perhaps this reminder seems obvious to us only because a historically specific form of corporation, one that now assumes neoliberal guise, has secured such a firm grip on our political imagination. In colonial and early America, charters of incorporation were issued to persons only because their work promised to secure specifically collective ends (for example, by building a canal or a road that would facilitate commerce, broadly construed). These acts of authorization empowered non-state agents, in their capacity as investors, to pursue public goods that the state either would not or could not accomplish on its own.

These hybrid entities were granted their corporate powers only on condition that they remain true to the substantive purposes specified in their charters. Should they fail to do so, the government to which they owe their existence (or any of a corporation's members) could initiate in court *ultra vires* or *quo warranto* proceedings. The former seeks an injunction to prevent a corporation's board of directors from employing its powers beyond the scope of the purpose for which they were granted. (This is essentially what the Concerned Faculty of Tulsa University was up to when it explored the possibility of seeking an injunction against TU's board from Oklahoma's attorney general.) The latter and more radical remedy aims to secure dissolution of a corporation on the ground that actions taken in its name are no longer consonant with or violate the end for which this artificial person was created.[24]

Today, while these legal options remain available in state statutory codes, they are not often employed. In part, this is to be explained by the widespread adoption, which accelerated throughout the nineteenth century, of general incorporation statutes.[25] Advocates of these statutes were chiefly republicans who sought to eliminate the favoritism displayed by state legislatures in choosing to grant corporate charters to this but not that petitioner. To bring such cronyism to a halt, states adopted statutes that enabled any group of persons to apply for and secure corporate status so long as its specified purpose was not illegal.

In one of US history's many ironies, this move to "democratize" the formation of corporations backfired because it encouraged multiplication of the for-profit businesses whose accumulated power would soon undermine the very foundations of democratic governance. *Quo warranto* and *ultra vires* actions slipped into desuetude because, as the idea of corporate purpose assumed the status of an empty formalism, it became far more difficult to sustain claims about a corporation's departure from or violation of its substantive ends. Thus was the terrain prepared for neoliberalism's eventual construction of the corporation as a creature of private contracts aimed exclusively at amassing profit for individual shareholders.

Although pushed into the shadows by this construction, the question of whether corporations are political in the sense that they should or must pledge to advance public purposes as a condition of their formation has never entirely disappeared. Indeed, today, this question is experiencing a revival that belies Hansmann and Kraakman's 2001 proclamation to the effect that in the absence of any viable alternative to the neoliberal account we now witness "the end of history for corporate law."

Some challenges to this death notice are emerging from improbable sources and, for that reason, should be taken with a skeptical grain of salt. Consider, for example, the title of a press release issued in 2019 by the Business Roundtable: "Business Roundtable Redefines the Purpose of the Corporation to Promote an Economy That Serves All Americans."[26] This appeal to "corporate social responsibility," however useful for public relations, is but a call for voluntary self-regulation and is unlikely to upset the predatory operation of neoliberal firms.

Of somewhat greater significance is the recent emergence of "public benefit corporations" that remain for-profit entities but loosen the rule of shareholder primacy by authorizing their directors to take into account the interests of other "stakeholders," including customers, employees, and even society as a whole.[27] If truth be told, however, the state laws providing for public benefit corporations offer little more than a permission slip that may be embraced by some companies (and has been by Plum Organics, Patagonia, and others), but any publicly traded corporation that takes this allowance too far will, in all likelihood, soon hear from its shareholders.

The question of whether all corporations, as a condition of their existence, must pledge to advance specifically public goods acquires sharper teeth in a bill introduced into the US Senate by Elizabeth Warren in 2018. The "Accountable Capitalism Act," which Warren represents as a frontal attack on the doctrine of shareholder primacy, would require corporations whose gross annual receipts exceed $1 billion to apply for federal charters as a condition of doing business. Unlike general incorporation statutes, these charters would be granted only on condition that an applicant expressly commit to securing "a general public benefit," which the bill defines as "a material positive impact on society resulting from the business and operations of a United State corporation when taken as a whole."[28] Assessment of a corporation's success in fulfilling that benefit would require that directors consider not just the dividends it pays to shareholders, but also its impact on employees, customers, the communities in which they operate, and the local and global environment. Should a corporation be granted a charter but harm these other stakeholders, the Office of United States Corporations would be authorized to revoke its charter, thereby withdrawing its powers and causing it to dissolve.

Were Milton Friedman to read the "Accountable Capitalism Act," no doubt he would insist that it relies on an antiquarian theory of the corporation that regards it as a creature of the state rather than as an economic by-product of voluntary contracts forged in capitalism's marketplace and dedicated to securing maximal gain for its investors. In truth, however, Senator Warren's bill reminds us of what Friedman and his students hope we forget: in multiple senses, the corporation is an essentially political being that ultimately derives its powers from the state, and ongoing exercise of those powers is conditional on realization of a purpose the people, via their elected representatives, have endorsed. The introduction of Warren's bill, in sum, signifies that the self-evident persuasiveness of the neoliberal corporation is now wobbling, and we should take that fact as an invitation to explore alternative corporate forms as well as their import for the constitution of the American academy.

I will return to the neoliberal construction of the corporation in part IV when I explain how America's colleges and universities are now adopting its misbegotten shape. For now, let me recap what this chapter has affirmed: When we think beyond neoliberalism's self-serving (mis)construction, we see that corporations (1) are not owned by shareholders but, instead, are entities that effectively socialize the assets invested within them; (2) are defined by independent juridical personhood and hence the capacity to exercise certain legal powers in their own name (albeit as exercised by their all-too-human agents); (3) are governed by boards whose members, even when selected by shareholders, derive their ultimate authority from the state; and (4) are additionally political insofar as they are granted powers of self-governance that are denied to unincorporated associations. A corporation's powers of self-rule, however, may be organized in autocratic or republican form, and that is the issue to which I now turn.

3
Corporate Types

Traitor to the Academy

"The man who first devised the present mode of governing colleges in this country has done us more injury than Benedict Arnold," declared Francis Wayland in 1829, just two years into his nearly three-decade career as president of Brown University.[1] My discussion of recent events at Texas Southern and the University of Tulsa in chapter 1 indicates why Wayland's reproach is on the mark. But it is wrong, as Wayland surely understood, to attribute invention of this misordered mode to the scheming of any single individual, and it would be equally wrong to suggest that this mode was devised ex nihilo. In fact, the form of rule to which we submit today is the congealed fruit of a complex history that could have turned out very differently and that involved protracted clashes among multiple parties, all seeking control of America's earliest colleges.

The governance disputes within America's first colleges, which I explore in part II, turned not on the question of whether they would be constituted in the form of corporations but, rather, on how rule would be structured within these incorporated entities. In grappling with that question, the founders of Harvard, William & Mary, Yale, Princeton, and other early colleges drew on an inheritance whose roots can be traced through Roman, canon, and especially medieval and early modern English law. Within that history, one finds a corporate type that is not but should be familiar to us, since its republican principles informed the constitution of governance within the first joint stock companies to set foot in America, the colonies that emerged from them, and in time the Republic itself. That the American academy is not constituted on this same model renders it an anomaly that requires a justification that, in my view, cannot be furnished.

In telling this story, I draw extensively on David Ciepley's excellent work on the history of corporations as well as their contemporary neoliberal incarnation. Within the European and more specifically the Anglo-American tradition, corporations have been differentiated into multiple kinds: civil, lay, ecclesiastical, sole, aggregate, eleemosynary, nonprofit, for-profit, public benefit, and others. From this diverse inheritance, Ciepley extracts two principal types, which he calls "member" and "property" corporations.[2] Most fundamentally, these types are distinguished by how they organize the powers of self-rule granted to them by the state. To highlight this difference, I will often (but not always) call the member corporation "republican" and the property corporation "autocratic."

Before turning to the origins, history, and distinguishing features of each, a quick word about how I regard these conceptual categories as well as what work I ask them to do in the remaining chapters of this book. Not unlike Weberian ideal types, these categories are heuristic devices whose job is to accentuate certain features of the constitution of rule within colleges and universities as well as the quarrels about how that rule was to be organized at three periods in American history. Roughly speaking, the first extends from 1650, when Harvard was granted its initial corporate charter, to 1819, when the US Supreme Court decided the *Dartmouth* case and so consolidated the autocratic college; the second encompasses the several decades on either side of the turn of the twentieth century, as the emergence of large research universities reopened the question of how the academy was to be governed; and the third covers the past half century, as the shift from industrial to neoliberal capitalism has once again invited us to reconsider the constitutional form best suited to the academy's ends. In none of these eras does one find an unadulterated articulation of either of the two corporate types that concern me, but, in all, this distinction enables us to see things we might otherwise miss.

Property versus Member Corporations

To compress into a few paragraphs a complex history that deserves better, the earliest antecedents of property and member corporations can be located in ancient Roman law. Primarily applicable to disposition of the estates of decedents, the embryonic roots of property corporations can be traced to the category of *jus rerum*, which denoted laws regulating the rights and powers of persons over things. When these things were regarded as a whole, the encompassing category of *universitas rerum* was often employed.

This category was later folded within medieval canon law as a solution to a problem encountered by the Catholic Church when, beginning in the eleventh century, it sought to safeguard the estates of monasteries, abbeys, and bishoprics from encroachments by lay rulers. By affording recognition for this property in corporate form, the Church transferred ownership from individual vicars, parsons, and bishops to a legal entity that, because unburdened by mortality, would outlive these finite beings. The corporation thereby enabled a separation of ownership (*dominium* in Latin), which is held by this legal artifact, from control (*jurisdictio*), which rested with rulers in their capacity as officeholders.

This model departs from earlier egalitarian representations of believers as members united within the body of Christ insofar as ultimate authority over any aggregation of assets afforded corporate form is vested in an office whose occupant rules monocratically. Why rule must assume the form of a hierarchy that culminates in a singular head is grounded in Catholic theology and specifically the conviction, perhaps best articulated by Thomas Aquinas, that the rule of one represents the best possible form of human association. Anticipating Princeton's 1970 governance committee, which contended that disorder is sure to reign absent the university's rule by a governing board granted final decision-making authority, Aquinas justified absolutism because it replicates governance by the one God who "is the Maker and Ruler of all":

> If human beings by nature live in association with many others, all of them need to have some power to govern them. For if there are many human beings, and they provide for their own individual interests, the people would split into different factions unless there were also to exist a power to provide for what belongs to the common good. Just so, even the body of a human being or any animal would disintegrate unless there were to exist a general regulative power in the body to strive for the common good of all the body's members. And Solomon, contemplating this, said in Prov. 11:14: "The people will be destroyed if there is no ruler."[3]

The divinely created universe, in short, cannot endure as a well-ordered whole absent perpetual superintendence by one God. So, too, the Church can remain united only because it is ruled by the papacy or, rather, the officeholder who is appointed by and acts in the name of that God.

What is true of the spiritual realm within medieval Europe is equally true of the worldly realms formally subject to the papacy and hence to God: no body politic can retain its corporate coherence absent a single head that mimics divine rule. On this monocratic model, those within a political order's jurisdiction are figured as subjects of executive power monopolized by a sovereign authority. Because these absolutist monarchs are themselves temporal agents of God, they are obligated to act as fiduciaries on behalf of the purposes that animate the divinely ordained corporate bodies they govern, but they are legally unaccountable to those over whom they rule. The principal obligation of subjects, therefore, is to obey orders issued by superiors, and that of course is a defining characteristic of any autocracy worthy of the name.

The property corporation, in sum, is a hierarchically ordered entity that transfers ownership of assets to a sempiternal creature of law ruled by persons whose offices exist apart from their individual occupants, whose authority is derived from a higher power, and whose relationship to others is ultimately one of command. When stripped of its theological baggage, however dimly, one can see in this model certain antecedents of what in time, much transmogrified, will become the secular capitalist corporation. There, Ciepley explains, "the authority of its board does not derive from the stockholders, but from the state. So we have a governance structure in which a set of offices (the board) is created by a higher authority and granted autocratic authority over the corporation's property and employees—just like a bishopric."[4] That this form also resembles the structure of governance at Texas Southern and the University of Tulsa suggests that the deepest roots of "corporatization" reside not in the academy's conquest by an alien institutional form, but in its adoption of a specific model of what a corporation is.

The second type of corporation discussed by Ciepley, the "member" corporation, also finds its roots in Roman law. Its origins can be traced to invention of the legal category of *municipia*, which provided a way to assimilate conquered communities into the emerging empire by means of charters that defined their residents as "citizens" who retained certain powers of collective self-governance, including the right to vote for local magistrates. Unlike property corporations designed to ensure the intergenerational continuity of *universitas rerum*—that is, of property—member corporations are *universitates personarum*, composed not of property but of persons. Justinian's

Digest tells us that these corporations are built "on the model of the state" (*ad exemplum rei publicae*) and the issues of their concern are *res publica*—that is, "public things" or, alternatively, the "people's affairs."[5]

Rule within these republican corporations, Ciepley explains, assumes this character: (1) members jointly determine the admission of new members (as well as their expulsion should the need arise); (2) in accordance with the Roman legal maxim *quod omnes tangit ab omnibus approbetur* (what touches all is to be approved by all), members establish rules for themselves by means of debate followed by voting; and (3) rule is exercised either immediately by members or by elected officers chosen by majority rule based in the principle of "one member, one vote" (as opposed to the "one share, one vote" rule that now prevails within publicly traded for-profit corporations).

Should responsibility for taking action on these matters be vested in representatives or other officers, their fiduciary duty is to govern the *res publica* of a corporation on behalf of its members. That may involve serving as a court for adjudicating internal disputes, structuring relations with other corporate entities, or administering the assets owned by a juridical entity that cannot be equated with any or all of its members. However, because members never relinquish their power of original jurisdiction, these agents are never appointed in perpetuity and so can always be recalled or removed. On this model, and at odds with the pejorative sense intended by contemporary academics, "corporatization" signifies not a violation of the principle of collective self-governance but, instead, a form of rule that exemplifies it.

What distinguishes these two types is not the way each organizes the ownership of property, for both vest assets within corporations that are legally distinguishable from natural persons, but, rather, how each organizes the power of rule. Unlike the republican member corporation, the constitution of the property corporation must have a head and hence is essentially rather than incidentally authoritarian. Because the capacity to govern is not shared among equals, following Aristotle, there can be no citizens within the property corporation, for the term *citizen* names those who rule and are ruled in turn. Nor, strictly speaking, can there be any members in a property corporation, for, within them, the power of rule is wielded not with colleagues but over subjects. Finally, within a property corporation, there can be no *res publica*, for the conduct of its collective business is the monopolistic preserve of an unchosen few. In sum, within the property corporation, the specifically political character of the member corporation is displaced by the antipolitical rationality of administration, as those who might otherwise share in the collective power of governance become underlings managed by external officeholders who rule from above rather than among their fellows.

Contra that classic neoliberal Margaret Thatcher, who famously declared that "society" is but an aggregation of individuals, to be a member of a corporation organized on republican principles is to be something other and more than a mere individual. To see the point, recall that the Latin verb *corporare* is sometimes translated "to embody" but is perhaps better rendered as "to form into a body." Consistent with this sense, prior to the mid-nineteenth century "incorporated entities were regularly conceptualized as their members *merged* into a legally distinct entity."[6] This understanding, Paddy Ireland has shown, was signified by frequent use of the pronoun *they* in speaking of these creatures of law. In time, as indicated by gradual displacement of *they* by *it*, the legal personhood of corporations was more neatly distinguished from that of the persons within their jurisdiction. Be that as it may, within member corporations, persons remain parts *of* this creature of law in a way that those subject *to* an autocratic property corporation can never be. Although constituted in the form of a legal person that cannot be equated with or reduced to any or all of its members, when they gather together to deliberate and decide its affairs, they *are* the corporation in corporeal form and their majoritarian decision-making *is* that corporation's will.

Coming to America

As Ciepley notes: "In the wake of the recovery of Justinian's *Digest* in 1135 and the Roman law of corporations in the eleventh century, Europe was gradually reorganized as a civilization of corporations—a dense web of monasteries, bishoprics, confraternities, universities, towns, communes, and guilds that governed the associational life of an energized Europe."[7] For reasons that need not detain me here, the property corporation gains limited traction in early modern England, although it does elsewhere in Europe (and, as I show in chapter 6, it appears in specifically capitalist guise in the opinion John Marshall pens in *Trustees of Dartmouth College v. Woodward*). Instead, the member corporation predominated in England, whether in the guild, the university, or the municipality; and it is this type that travels across the Atlantic and informs the constitution of colonial governments before the Revolution and, after 1776, their republican descendants.

The member corporation makes its initial appearance in America in the form of trading companies created to exploit the natural resources and, often in the name of Christian conversion, to conquer the Indigenous peoples of the "New World." Formation of these companies is novel because this represents an extension to commercial operations of corporate privileges that up until that time had largely been confined to churches, guilds, municipalities, and, as we will see in the next chapter, universities. To understand these new formations adequately, it is helpful to distinguish them from the unincorporated partnerships and joint stock companies that preceded them (although these distinctions would not be fully articulated and legally codified until the late nineteenth century).

Although this account is oversimplified, as a rule, partnerships were economic enterprises formed by a small group of persons who typically knew one another and were closely involved in a company's management. Joint stock companies differed insofar as they were formed by investors, often unknown to one another, who would pool their resources to generate an accumulated capital fund. Each investor would own a share of the company based on the amount of stock purchased; and, unlike partnerships, that equity could be transferred freely to another without securing the consent of a company's other investors. So long as these companies remained unincorporated, however, they had no legal identity apart from the contractual agreements that merged their resources.

What distinguished commercial corporations from unincorporated partnerships and joint stock companies was their status as creatures not of contract but of charter, whether issued by the Crown or, later, by Parliament. In the case of trading companies, these charters granted corporations privileges they would not otherwise have—for example, the right to possess property in its own name, limited liability on the part of investors for debts incurred, and often exclusive jurisdiction over a specified territory. These privileges would be conferred, however, only on condition that an enterprise seeking corporate status commit to realizing not just profit for its investors but also a benefit deemed public or, more cynically, a good that would advantage the state (for example, the opening of America to traders and, on their heels, the establishment of settler colonies).

The state thereby wedded what Bernard Mandeville in his *Fable of the Bees* called "private vices" to the achievement of public goods it could not accomplish on its own, whether because of a lack of financial resources, insufficient administrative capacity, or excessive risk. Unlike contemporary public benefit corporations, though, the obligation to accomplish these goods came equipped with teeth: should a corporation fail to accomplish the public good identified in its charter or, alternatively, exercise its powers for ends beyond the scope of that purpose, it could be disciplined or even dissolved by the state. To quote Ferdinand Maitland, the English jurist whose contemporary pupils include the Concerned Faculty of Tulsa and Elizabeth Warren, it is the state that has "breathe(d) the breath of a fictitious life" into this legal creature, and should that gift be withdrawn, it will become "no animated body but individualistic dust."[8]

The charters granted to these early commercial corporations afforded them the right to govern their own affairs; and it was the model of the member corporation that informed how that right was to be organized. To illustrate, consider the English East India Company. In 1600, this company was chartered by the Crown as "one body corporate and politick" with the end of advancing "our navigation and trade" (which is better characterized, I would argue, as "building an empire on the backs of conquered persons"). Much like self-governing municipalities, the company's original charter specified the company's constitution by (1) establishing certain offices, including a board of directors; (2) authorizing each of its shareholders to cast one vote to elect persons to fill these offices; (3) providing for the removal of any and all officers "at the pleasure of the said company, or the greater part of them, which shall be present, at any of their public assemblies"; and (4) entitling its board to adopt by majority rule binding "laws, constitutions, orders or ordinances . . . for the good government of the same company" as well as to dismiss, fine, inflict pain, and imprison those who violated them.[9]

Via these provisions, the English Crown ratified the constitution of the English East India Company as an entity that is to perform a public function but is not for that reason a mere agency of the state; for it enjoys considerable autonomy and hence immunity from state intervention in the exercise of powers that are inherently political in nature. That these powers were to be organized on republican principles was made abundantly clear by William Blackstone in the mid-eighteenth century. When several persons are consolidated within a corporation, "they and their successors are then considered as one person in law: as one person, they have one will, which is collected from the sense of the majority of the individuals: this one will may establish rules and orders for the regulation of the whole, which are a sort of municipal laws of this little republic."[10] Here we see the essential feature that distinguishes the member from the property corporation or, rather, the autocratic from the republican: this body is self-governing not merely in the sense that it enjoys considerable autonomy from subjection to those outside its jurisdiction, including the state as well as other corporate entities, but also in the sense that its members are this little republic's lawmakers rather than its servants.

Let us not romanticize these early trading corporations, however. While the principles of republicanism governed relations among their members, the unilateral jurisdiction they were granted over vast swaths of land in America and elsewhere included the authority to conquer their inhabitants and dispossess them of their homes. In 1823, when John Marshall grounded the so-called discovery doctrine in the US Constitution, the Supreme Court's chief justice merely provided a patina of legitimacy to facts on the ground that had been settled long before:

> The United States . . . have unequivocally acceded to that great and broad rule by which its civilized inhabitants now hold this country. They hold, and assert in themselves, the title by which it was acquired. They maintain, as all others have maintained, that discovery gave an exclusive right to extinguish the Indian title of occupancy either by purchase or by conquest. . . . The power now possessed by the government of the United States to grant lands, resided, while we were colonies, in the crown, or its grantees. The validity of the titles given by either has never been questioned in our courts.[11]

If the Piankeshaw tribe could not convey title to their lands to this case's plaintiff, Thomas Johnson, that is because the English Crown and later the new republic had preempted that possibility by extinguishing any legal claims grounded in occupancy alone. The state's exclusive right to determine disposition of these lands is in turn the unstated presupposition of the founding of America's earliest colleges, including William & Mary as well as Harvard, which I discuss in chapters 4 and 5, respectively. The constitution of each in corporate form is the foundation of their claim to considerable autonomy in governing their own affairs. Those affairs, we must never forget, included the wholesale subjection of those who were not their members but, instead, either hostile forces to be vanquished or infidels to be converted.

America, Inc.

When the English colonized America, they imported the principles and practices peculiar to member corporations. This inheritance informed not just the trading companies that exploited the continent's resources but also the colonies that emerged from those companies and, after independence, the states as well as the new nation that sprang from those colonies. Consider, for example, the charter granted by the Crown to the Massachusetts Bay Company in 1629. That document constituted this joint stock company in the form of a "body politic and corporate" and granted its members the right to "possess and enjoy" a demarcated "plantation" as well as its resources, including Indigenous "natives" who were to be "incited" to accept "the only true God and the savior of mankind." To govern this corporation, the charter authorized its members to elect annually (and, if necessary, to remove) a governor, a deputy governor, and eighteen "assistant magistrates" as well as to constitute an assembly empowered to make and enforce "laws and ordinances for the good and welfare" so long as they did not contradict the laws of the realm.[12]

It was this charter that John Winthrop inherited when in 1631 he was elected governor of this company, now named the Massachusetts Bay Colony. At the initial meeting of its assembly, he and seven others in attendance violated this writ's provisions by restricting the franchise to the assistant magistrates, and that in turn enabled Winthrop's reelection as governor for three more years. In 1634, delegations of freemen sent by the colony's several municipalities pressed to review the charter and, having done so, demanded their reenfranchisement. Winthrop acceded, and subsequent elections included all freemen and were conducted by secret ballot. Recognizing, however, that lawmaking would prove unwieldy if it required the attendance of all eligible to vote, as the charter formally mandated, a compromise was crafted that provided for each town to select and send two delegates to the general court as its representatives. Thus did a charter granted to a member corporation in the form of a self-governing company provide the foundation for a colonial government built on republican principles.

In 1691, the Massachusetts Bay Colony was formally rechartered as the Province of Massachusetts Bay. This new constitution retained much of the republican structure of its predecessor, although it provoked considerable controversy by providing for the governor and other senior officers to be appointed by the Crown.[13] This departure from the principles of a member corporation was effectively reversed a century later when in 1780 Massachusetts ratified its state constitution, thereby formally constituting itself as a commonwealth: "The body politic is formed by a voluntary association of individuals; it is a social compact by which the whole people covenants with each citizen and each citizen with the whole people that all shall be governed by certain laws for the common good." Equally important, that constitution explicitly banned the formation of corporations that exclusively serve private ends on the ground that such consolidations of power are only warranted if they advance distinctively public goods: "No man nor corporation or association of men have any other title to obtain advantages, or particular and exclusive privileges distinct from those of the community, than what rises from the consideration of services rendered to the public."[14]

The state constitutions of the new republic, explains Ciepley, drew much of their intelligibility from the late medieval model of the member corporation: "It is not widely appreciated how heavily popular sovereignty and the ruler contract lean on corporate theory for their plausibility. It is by virtue of their incorporation that the people have an original and inalienable jurisdiction, or sovereignty; that they have the legal capacity to contract or delegate as a unit; that majority consent, and not necessarily unanimity, can be sufficient to bind the whole; and that their contract with the ruler binds succeeding generations. . . . The modern concept of a sovereign people is a naturalized corporation."[15] Absent appreciation of this conceptual inheritance, we will not adequately grasp what John Locke intended when, in his *Second Treatise of Government*, he wrote: "When any number of men have *so consented to make one community or government,* they are thereby presently incorporated, and make *one body politic,* wherein the *majority* have a right to act and conclude the rest."[16] Locke's brief on behalf of popular sovereignty and rule grounded in the people's consent, in short, represents an extension to the nation of the principles that distinguished the member corporation from rival forms, including the autocratic property corporation.

This is not to say that the Commonwealth of Massachusetts is itself a corporation in the legal sense of the term, for the former is the sovereign authority that alone is empowered to confer juridical personhood on other incorporated bodies. Their structural homology, though, explains why, in the late nineteenth and early twentieth centuries, the terms designating a corporation's originating document (its "charter") and a state's founding instrument (its "constitution") were often employed interchangeably or as modifiers for each other. Thus, in "Federalist 49," James Madison refers to the fruit of the Framers' labors as the new nation's "constitutional charter" and to the governmental powers enumerated in that constitution as its "chartered authorities."[17] A quarter century later, John Marshall argued that ratification of the US Constitution was an act of incorporation and hence that the United States is itself a corporation: "The 'United States of America' is the true name of that grand corporation which the American people have formed, and the charter will, I trust, long remain in full force and vigour."[18] Another two decades later, extending these premises to their logical terminus, Francis Lieber's *Encyclopedia Americana* offered this: "All the American governments are corporations created by charters, viz. their constitutions. . . . The whole political system is made up of a concatenation of various corporations, political, civil, religious, social and economical," and the nation itself is "the great corporation, comprehending all others."[19]

In sum, although this sounds discordant to contemporary ears, early American commercial corporations assumed the form of constitutional republics, whereas colonies and indeed the new republic assumed the form of member corporations. What chiefly distinguishes the United States from its English and colonial antecedents is this: whereas the latter rooted ultimate governmental authority in the imperial "we," the exercise of state authority in the new nation was grounded in a republican body politic defined by its repudiation of monarchical absolutism.

How America's popular sovereign fashions the state that is to exercise this authority mirrors the means by which individual states, once their constitutions were ratified, created corporations. In both cases, a sovereign body (1) issues a constitution or charter that establishes a quasi-independent legal entity, whether that be a government or a nongovernmental corporation; (2) invests that entity with juridical personhood and so the rights, privileges, and immunities that attend this status (for example, to own property, to enter contracts, to sue and be sued, etc.); and (3) confers on that entity certain enumerated but ultimately revocable powers, including that of self-governance. Broadly construed, therefore, the body politic of the United States is a nested constellation of variations on the theme that is the republican member corporation.

Anomalous Autocracies

The American ideal of limited government, of the conviction that political power must always be checked by means of constitutional constraints, finds its roots in the history of British corporations and, more specifically, chartered member corporations. Those charters required that corporate powers always and only be confined to the purpose or purposes for which they were granted; that those who exercise these powers do so not by arbitrary decree but in their capacity as officeholders beholden to duties specified by law; and, finally, in wielding these powers, that these rulers are selected by and remain accountable to those they govern.

From this it follows that the appearance of autocratic property corporations within the United States is an anomaly that is prima facie illegitimate. Within the reified sphere we call the "economy," we may find it difficult to recognize the autocracies in our midst because, in certain respects, publicly traded for-profit firms appear akin to member corporations. We should not, however, be taken in by this ruse, as Ciepley makes clear:

> The annual stockholders' meeting is indeed the direct descendant of the member assembly of the regulated company. . . . But its principles of operation have been completely altered. A stockholder assembly is, within the limits of charter and statute, typically allowed to make and amend by-laws governing the procedures of shareholder meetings and board meetings. However, it does not operate on the principle of one-member-one-vote, but on the principle utterly alien to member corporations, of one-share-one-vote. The stockholders do not collectively control who becomes a stockholder, as shares are freely tradable. And most importantly, they do not elect a government over themselves as individuals, but a government over the employees of the firm, from whom value is extracted. This is no republic. For one group to appoint a government over another group is an imperial relationship.[20]

Within these corporations, especially in their contemporary neoliberal incarnation, the collective power that remains grounded in a body politic constituted as a member corporation is abstracted, reified, and imposed on those who are now that power's objects qua subjects; and it is this relationship of domination and subordination that, in time, we will come to know as "at-will" employment within corporations that inhabit capitalism's marketplace and hence are no longer understood as so many bodies politic.

By the same token, to anticipate the argument of part II, we may find it difficult to apprehend the autocratic nature of rule within America's nonprofit colleges and universities. There, with very few exceptions, the academic corporation *is* its governing board, and the trustees who occupy positions on that board are that corporation's sole members. But to confuse this with a republican member corporation is to ignore the fact that this is a monocratic body that rules over "employees" who, as objects of administration, are differentially distributed within the hierarchical structure I presented in chapter 1 as a pyramid of power. Unlike corporate members, these employees are guaranteed no right to take part in governing the academy's collective affairs and hence in the last analysis are but targets of commands issued by others. The autocratic American academy is, therefore, an antidemocratic alien that, absent more compelling justification than has been offered to date, deserves summary deportation.

II

Contesting the Constitution of College in Early America

4
William & Mary Dispossessed

What We Do Not Know

We academics know very little about the origins of the constitutional form that now prevails at US colleges and universities and even less about consolidation of their rule by external lay boards.[1] Reading the present into the past, we come to believe that this structure is somehow given in the nature of things and so uncontestable. Especially prior to the early nineteenth century, however, fundamental questions about how and by whom the American academy should be ruled were frequently disputed and vigorously so. Although these contests often emerged out of parochial disagreements about paltry matters, they were informed by diverse visions of what kind of corporation these colleges should become.

I begin part II with a brief account of the corporate constitution of the universities at Oxford and Cambridge, for these offered the models that most often informed debates in England's colonies. I then show how these debates played out at America's earliest two colleges: William & Mary, which can rightfully claim to be the first college planned for the colonies; and Harvard, which, with equal right, can claim to be the first college to operate (sometimes just barely so) in the colonies. My consideration of these colleges provides an appropriate backdrop for this part's final chapter, where I consider *Trustees of Dartmouth College v. Woodward*, which effectively brought to a close the colonial and Revolutionary-era contests about what sort of corporation the American academy was to be.

Before I begin, let me reiterate in slightly modified terms a caveat I registered in the preceding chapter. Drawing on the history recounted there, here, in part II, I speak of republican and autocratic corporations. Because these are heuristic devices, I do not mean to suggest that any of America's colonial college were fashioned as perfect articulations of either. To advance that claim would be to impose a conceptual straitjacket on a historical record whose messiness precludes that possibility. Nor do I mean to suggest that the conflicts at these colleges can be understood in terms of a tidy distinction between virtuous faculty members and villainous governing board members acting in cahoots with presidents and other senior administrators. Although tempting, were I to tell my tale in those terms I would read into the seventeenth century occupational categories that make sense to us today but were quite unsettled at the time. To steer clear of this anachronistic reading, it is better to figure these conflicts as so many struggles to determine how inherited understandings of the corporation imported chiefly from England should inform construction of an academy situated within a "New World" where they do not quite fit.

Cambridge across the Pond

In ancient Rome, those who spoke of corporations often employed the terms *collegium* and/or *universitatis*. At their most basic, the first of these terms denoted things that have been gathered together, and the second to any whole made up of its constituent parts. In time, both came to refer to any group of three or more persons who were collectively united in a common purpose and, once recognized by law, said to have a body (*corpus habere*) and so to be incorporated as a single entity.

This etymology is what Adam Smith recalls when, in *The Wealth of Nations*, he reminds us that in Rome all corporations, no matter what their purpose, were called "universities."[2] Only in medieval Europe did the *universitas scholarium*—that is, a formally constituted body of scholars— materialize as a specific species within this larger genus. As with bakers, blacksmiths, and tailors, these bodies emerged out of guilds of scholars and their apprentices who, as their numbers grew, sought more stable organization. The corporate articulation of this quest, the university, was construed not as a determinate place in space and certainly not as an employer but as an association of those seeking some measure of autonomy in the exercise of their craft. Toward that end, their members demanded a right to be free of interference in their internal affairs; and this capacity for self-governance was exercised, for example, by licensing those permitted to join as new apprentices, electing their own officers, and meeting in general assembly (*concilium generale*) to set rules binding on all.[3]

The colleges at Cambridge and Oxford, whose origins can be traced to the earliest European universities, especially the University of Paris (ca. 1150), adhered to this model and so are appropriately understood as member corporations constituted in the form of "little republics." Cambridge, for example, was founded in 1209 and chartered via a writ issued by King Henry III in 1231, although it was not until 1571 that the university was formally incorporated as a civil corporation and so invested with legal personhood and the powers that accompany this status.[4]

Each of the parties belonging to the corporation named "The Chancellor, Masters, and Scholars of the University of Cambridge" was regarded as a member *of* the artificial person that comprehended all. Because this unnatural person had no will of its own, it had no capacity to act. The conduct of rule, therefore, was exercised by those who had completed the apprenticeships that qualified them to teach and hence received their master's or doctoral degrees.[5] This sovereign "congregation," the "house of regents," was empowered to admit new fellows, to adopt statutes for their collective self-regulation, to regulate university property, and to elect its own officers. Among others, those officeholders included a chancellor as well as a proctor (literally, a representative) who enforced the university's bylaws, managed its everyday financial affairs, and arranged its schedule of lectures and disputations. Because these agents were selected by and hence removable by the congregation, their rule remained accountable to the corporation's members on behalf of whom they ruled.

Like other corporations, the right of Cambridge's members to rule over themselves was not without limit. Perhaps the most significant check on their authority was provided by what was called "visitatorial power." Provision for occasional intervention by those who are not members of any given corporation was justified, argued Blackstone, because disposition of the affairs of these creatures of law rests in the hands of human beings who, unlike corporations per se, are subject to all manner of frailties and foibles. Should there be allegations of financial improprieties, for example, a visitor might be designated by the Crown to inspect a corporation's records and, if these charges were proven, to remove officers in the name of ensuring fidelity to the mission specified in its charter. (It is effectively a form of visitatorial power that the Concerned Faculty of Tulsa appealed to when its members considered submission of their complaint to Oklahoma's attorney general.)

Given this check, it would be wrong to represent England's earliest universities as sovereign republics. Indeed, not long before the first colonial colleges in America were conceived, the Elizabethan statutes of 1570 compromised the capacity of Cambridge to rule itself by, among other things, prescribing the curriculum, circumscribing the powers of proctors, restricting the authority to interpret university statutes to certain specific officers, and imposing an expectation of celibacy on all fellows. What we can say is that these encroachments on Cambridge's autonomy compromised its identity as a member corporation and that those who resisted these encroachments sought to preserve the capacity for collective self-governance that is a defining feature of this corporate type. What we can also say is that this capacity and hence the university's autonomy—whether from state, church, or, in time, a capitalist economy—is a necessary condition of the possibility of sustaining a form of practice that, because distinct from others, deserves to be called "education" (as opposed, for example, to clerical or workforce training).

Oxford in Virginia?

Although a bit hyperbolic, Samuel Eliot Morison was not wrong when, in his history of Harvard, he wrote: "If we would know upon what model Harvard College was established, what were the ideals of her founders and the purposes of her first governors, we need seek no further than the University of Cambridge."[6] Much the same might be said of Oxford's influence on the founding of William & Mary. True, other models of corporate organization were available to those who cobbled together and disputed the early constitution of rule at America's inaugural colleges.[7] That said, between 1630 and 1646, about a hundred alumni from Cambridge and about a third that many from Oxford emigrated to colonial America and, once there, formed the nucleus of the faculties at Harvard as well as William & Mary. How did it come to pass, then, that the model of corporate self-governance exemplified by their English counterparts and in time embodied in the new nation's republican political institutions came to be supplanted by a form of rule antithetical to both?

Between 1606 and 1611, James I granted three charters to the joint stock venture named the "Virginia Company." Each more fully than the latter, these writs are informed by the logic of an English member corporation; and each in turn ceded to the company additional powers traditionally associated with political sovereignty. These charters thereby facilitated conversion of this merchant company into a political colony and, after the Revolution, a state organized on republican principles.

The first charter, issued on April 10, 1606, authorized the company to establish a "plantation" in lands that, prefiguring John Marshall's conclusion in *Johnson v. M'Intosh*, "are not now actually possessed by any Christian Prince or People." To this company the charter assigned exclusive commercial rights to any resources that might be extracted from these expropriated lands and, to make good on this right, the authority to "encounter, expulse, repeal, and resist" any who might challenge its monopoly over this territory and its fruits. About this plantation's governance the charter said little other than to specify, first, that the members of this company are to possess all of the "liberties, franchises, and immunities" customarily afforded to English citizens; second, that a council would be established in Virginia from among its members to "govern and order" its collective affairs; and, third, that an additional council would be created in England to ensure that this governance remain consonant with the Crown's "laws, ordinances, and instructions."[8]

Three years later, the second charter issued to the Company by the Crown formally "incorporated" this entity in the form of "one Body or Commonalty perpetual" and "by the Name of The Treasurer and Company of Adventurers and Planters of the City of London." To this body, the Crown granted several powers left undesignated in the first. These included (but were not limited to) the right to "make, ordain, and establish all Manner of Orders, Laws, Directions, Instructions, Forms and Ceremonies of Government and Magistracy"; to exercise "full and absolute Power and Authority to correct, punish, pardon, govern, and rule all such Subjects of Us, our Heires, and Successors"; and, finally, to admit new members as it sees fit but also to expel those found unfit. Conceding the difficulties occasioned by the need to coordinate the work of the two councils mandated by the company's initial charter, the 1609 version substituted a single body whose members, subject to the Crown's veto, were to be chosen by this corporation's members by majority rule; and to this council the charter granted the authority to "nominate and appoint" a "Governor or principal Officer," subject to the Crown's ultimate authority to reject any specific candidate.[9]

In 1611, the Crown issued its third charter, and this last document accentuated the expressly political character of the company's council and powers. Specifically, to ensure its "better government," this charter mandated that the corporation's council meet at least once a week "for the handling and ordering, and dispatching of all such casual and particular Occurrences, and accidental Matters, of less Consequence and Weight." For "Affairs of greater Weight and Importance," the charter required that assemblies open to all "members" be conducted four times a year. At these meetings, members were authorized to select and if need be remove officers of the council but also to "ordain and make such Laws and Ordinances, for the Good and Welfare of the Said Plantation, as to them from Time to Time, shall be thought requisite and meet," again with the proviso that these acts not be "contrary to the Laws and Statutes of this our Realm of England."[10]

Given the trajectory of these three charters, it is but a short step to 1621 when, in assembly, this incorporated body politic adopted an ordinance providing for adoption of a "Form of Government" consisting of a "Council of State" whose officers are selected by the corporation's members as well as a "General Assembly" whose members include the Council of State's officers but also representatives elected by majority rule from each "Town, Hundred, or other particular Plantation." Subject to the governor's veto, this assembly "shall have free Power to treat, consult, and conclude, as well of all emergent Occasions concerning the Publick Weal of the said Colony and every Part Thereof, as also to make, ordain, and enact such general Laws and Orders, for the Behoof of the said Colony, and the good Government thereof."[11] This member corporation was officially reconstituted as a Crown colony in 1624, and in time its political logic would furnish the ground for the republican state constitution adopted in 1776. What chiefly differentiated state from company and colony, of course, was its foundation in the principle of popular sovereignty and hence its rejection as illegitimate any pretenders to autocratic authority.

It is against this backdrop that we should consider the founding and early history of William & Mary and, specifically, its form of governance. It is this colonial college that comes closest to embodying the principles of republican member corporations (although, as we will see, its success in doing so was eventually undone). To tell this story is to show why the autocratic constitution of rule within American colleges and universities is not a foregone conclusion. But it is also to see how the academy's constitution as a republican corporation did not preclude its complicity in genocidal campaigns as well as the abomination that is slavery.

In 1617, Motoaka (also known as Pocahontas) was paraded through London and presented as an exemplar of what a properly educated savage could become—in other words, an English-speaking baptized Christian who took the name Rebecca. In response, a suitably impressed King James I initiated a fund-raising campaign for a college to be established in Virginia, patterned after its English counterparts and designed to propagate the Christian faith by force if necessary. One year later, the Virginia Company provided ten thousand acres of land seized from the Pamunkey people as a site for the college James had anticipated. James's dream took another step toward realization when, in 1619, the company's General Assembly petitioned the Crown to send "workmen of all sorts, for the erection of the university and college,"[12] most of whom were imported from England as indentured servants. The entire project was indefinitely deferred, however, when about a third of the white population, including the first deputy in charge of college lands, was killed during what came to be known as the Jamestown Massacre of 1622.

It was not until 1693 that William III and Mary II issued a royal charter (technically, "letters patent") founding a college in their name. In certain respects, the constitutional structure mandated by this charter was that of a member corporation patterned after English universities and specifically Oxford.[13] In other ways, though, this structure departed from the model of a self-governing community of scholars; and the net result was an unstable formation that for many years proved far better at inciting than resolving conflicts.

The 1693 charter opens with a recitation of the principal purposes of the college: to educate future ministers, to convert infidels, and to educate the colony's white youth "in good letters and manners." To realize these purposes, the charter authorized between eighteen and twenty "trustees," initially selected by the general assembly but thereafter to be self-perpetuating, "to make, found, erect and establish" the new college.

Although the trustees were not legally constituted as a corporation, the specific powers conferred on them by the charter were those routinely granted to such entities, including the legal title to possess land and derive revenue from it. However—and this is what renders William & Mary unique among colonial colleges—these powers were to be exercised by the trustees only until the college was "actually erected, founded and established." Once that was accomplished, the charter required that the trustees "give, grant, and transfer" the college's assets, as well as most of its governance responsibilities, to a "body politic and incorporate" to be "named the

President and masters, or professors of the college of William and Mary."[14] Once founded by its trustees, in short, William & Mary was to be reconstituted as a member corporation akin to Oxford or Cambridge.

The transfer of William & Mary from the trustees designated in the charter to its incorporated "professors" was not accomplished for more than three decades. In part this delay was caused by ongoing financial exigencies, but more fundamentally it can be explained by the interminable squabbles between the colony's governor and the college's first president, chiefly but not exclusively over the distribution of income derived from taxes on liquor and tobacco. Finally, on August 15, 1729, in return for a payment of ten shillings, the "longest livers" among the original trustees ceded to the corporation of professors the authority in perpetuity (1) to own and manage the college's properties, donations, and revenues, which included its "negro slaves," proceeds from a levy on exported tobacco cultivated by other enslaved persons and indentured servants, and funds extracted from pardoned pirates; (2) to appear in court "in all and every cause, complaint, and action," whether as plaintiff or as defendant; (3) to employ a seal that signifies that actions undertaken in the name of the college are enacted not by natural persons but by the legal person that is the corporation; (4) to act as a semi-autonomous entity insofar as the college's professors, one of whom is its president, are not to "be troubled, disquieted, molested or aggrieved . . . by us, our heirs, and successors, or any of our justices, escheators, sheriffs, or other bailiffs, or ministers, whatsoever"; and (5) in accordance with its status as a civil corporation dedicated to a public purpose, to elect one of their number or, alternatively, any one of the colony's "better sort of inhabitants" as a representative to Virginia's colonial assembly, thereby enabling the college to furnish (or withhold) its consent within a political body that itself assumed the shape of a member corporation.[15]

The 1693 charter, however, did not mandate that the trustees, now legally reconstituted as "visitors" (but not yet accorded an honorific capital *V* or reified as a "board"), cede to this corporation all of their governance capacities. Specifically, the visitors retained the power (1) to "elect and nominate" (i.e., to appoint) the president and professors; (2) to select the college's rector, who, in 1729, served as chair of the visitors (but also as the college's president); (3) to choose a nonresidential "chancellor," who served as the college's principal link to the Crown; and (4) to enact and enforce "rules, laws, statutes, orders and injunctions, for the good and wholesome government of the said college."[16] In short, rather than restrict the visitors to occasional interventions in response to serious abuses of power or departures from the college's mission, the 1693 charter authorized those who had relinquished ownership of its assets to select those who are to manage those goods. Still more problematically, having ceded control over the college's everyday affairs to its professors, including its president, the charter reserved to the visitors the right to make the rules according to which this corporation's members were to govern.

What we have here is a prescription for trouble. On the one hand, once the transfer was completed, "the president and masters" of William & Mary were constituted as a corporation in the form of a "little republic." Yet the charter awkwardly superimposed on this corporation visitors who were not themselves members of this commonwealth. The 1693 charter thus tears asunder the coherence of the member corporation by disaggregating certain of its political powers and assigning them to different parties. Because the nonresident visitors are endowed with legislative power as well as the power to appoint the college's officers, the corporation's members are effectively denied the prerogatives that render self-governance real. "As a consequence," write Hofstadter and Metzger, "the legal structure of the college was utterly anomalous: the faculty found itself formally empowered to exercise control of its business transactions, while the Visitors were legally left (through their control of the statutes) with broad and intrusive rights of intervention in academic matters."[17]

Neither the charter nor the transfer agreement specified how disputes arising out of this unstable combination of republican and autocratic corporate forms were to be resolved. Instead, the charter merely urged the corporation's members and the college's visitors, "as often as they shall think good," to "convocate" and, thus gathered, to "treat, confer, advise, and decree, concerning statutes, orders, and injunctions, for the said college."[18] This exhortation to play together nicely remained viable only so long as no matters that truly mattered emerged to test this constitution at odds with itself.

When Convocation Collapses

For several decades following the 1729 transfer, William & Mary's visitors did not often exercise the powers they legally held. As a result, the president and professors were left mostly undisturbed in governing the college's affairs; and that was exactly as intended by the two "longest livers" among the trustees who effected the transfer and, as part of its finalization, authored the college's first statutes in 1727.

In those statutes, with regard to the visitors, James Blair and Stephen Fouace wrote: "Let them maintain and support the ordinary authority of the president and masters in the administration of the daily government of the college, and let them refer all common domestic complaints to them: And not suffer themselves to be troubled, except in matters of great moment . . . or some other weighty business to be transacted." About the college's "daily government," the statutes stated: "Let the ordinary government of the college be in the president and the six masters, viz. the two professors of divinity; and the two professors of philosophy, and the master of the grammar school, and the master of the Indian school." Should a conflict arise among these professors, the statutes provided, it was to be brought to the president, who in turn was to seek resolution by a "meeting of the masters." Only if that meeting proved unable to resolve the matter at hand, and only if the issue were "of great weight and consequence," would it then be brought before the visitors for their "determination."[19]

Because ownership of and control over the college's material and financial assets were also vested in the corporation "named the President and masters, or professors of the college of William and Mary," its members exercised a capacity for self-governance akin to that enjoyed by their counterparts at Oxford and far greater than that commanded by their colleagues at any other colonial college. This state of affairs was not to last, though, as the visitors eventually began to exercise power in ways that violated the charter as well as the 1727 statutes penned by Blair and Fouace.[20]

The charter issued by King William and Queen Mary stated that the appointment of masters was within the purview of the visitors, but it left unclear whether this encompassed the power to dismiss, let alone whether dismissal must be for a formally adjudicated cause. Beginning in 1756, ostensibly provoked by the faculty's expulsion of two students from prominent families, the visitors took it upon themselves to resolve this ambiguity. They did so by dismissing three professors for their participation in the students' expulsion but also for drunkenness, irregular execution of duties, encouraging students to riot, and marrying in violation of college rules (although the record suggests that several of these allegations were trumped-up charges designed to retaliate against the insubordinate). When the accused refused to accept their termination or vacate the premises on the ground that the visitors lacked the authority to oust members of a duly constituted body politic, their opponents ordered the remaining two professors "to use all proper Methods for their Removal, by directing the Housekeeper not to supply them with any Provisions" and "the Servants not to obey their orders." This, too, failed to dislodge the recalcitrant, and so the visitors once again ordered the trio to depart. Should the professors remain defiant, the visitors added, they would resort to "Force & Violent Measures" to accomplish their end. Thus threatened, Graham, Jones, and Camm finally bowed to superior might. The visitors' victory proved Pyrrhic, however, as J. E. Morpurgo explains: "The carnage had been so great that the Visitors found themselves overlords of a College almost bereft of Professors, and, by their prodigality as firers, they had ruined most of their potential as hirers."[21]

Anticipating Texas Southern's board, less than a decade later, the visitors asserted their authority to appoint and terminate not only the president and professors but all other college officers as well. These purges were soon followed by still more intrusive efforts to rule the college's internal affairs by, for example, lowering admission standards to increase enrollment, selecting scholarship recipients, and prohibiting professors from holding outside employment. Most brazenly, in a statute adopted in 1763, the visitors affirmed their ultimate and complete control over the college, its officers, and its affairs.

To defend this unilateral decree, the visitors presented themselves as legal guardians of a trust established by the college's founders whose wishes they were specially obligated and equipped to honor. Without bothering to sugarcoat their wholesale expropriation of the corporation's powers, they declared:

> Experience hath shown that the pious and noble purposes intended by the founders and benefactors [of the college] will be frustrated without a due subordination of the president and masters or professors and the other officers employed therein to the visitors and governors upon which the well-being if not even the actual existence of the college depends: Therefore the visitors and governors henceforth have the control, superintendency and final determination of all orders made about the affairs of the college wherein the president and masters or professors usually direct, as well as in matters of greater moment, and let the visitors and governors or the major part of them at pleasure remove, displace and deprive the president and masters or professors, the ushers and other inferior officers in the college, and appoint another or others in their room and stead.[22]

On this account, the "professors" designated in the corporation's title are not governors of a college whose assets are owned by a commonwealth of which they are members. Rather, they are remunerated servants of those who assert exclusive qualification to ensure that the college remains faithful to the purposes of its now long-dead founders. Lest there be any doubt on this score, three years later the visitors adopted a second statute proclaiming that all powers exercised by the corporation's members are delegated to them by the visitors, and hence that these powers are not inalienable rights conferred by the 1693 charter but privileges that may be revoked at any time.

In an impassioned response, dated May 4, 1768, the president and masters of William & Mary presented to the visitors a "memorial for the better government of the college." This petition urged the visitors to draft a new statute that would "explain & settle in the most clear & explicit manner the just & proper authority of the visitors, as well as the rights, privileges, and powers of the said president and masters as deduced from the sense & spirit of the Charter." Of course, the petition conceded, that statute must acknowledge that the visitors are empowered by the charter to appoint the president and professors of William & Mary, but it should make equally clear that those appointed are not docile "servants of the visitors." To do so, this new bylaw must state unequivocally that, once appointed, the members of the body politic that is the corporation are "immediately invested" with all of the powers required to conduct the "ordinary government of the college . . . without further control from the visitors, who are to interfere in no respect whatever, but upon the grievance of a violation, or breach of some statutes made for that purpose."[23]

The professors' powers of rule, their memorial concluded, are not delegated but inherent in their status as members of the corporation and as such can neither be withdrawn nor checked by the visitors. To hold otherwise is to contravene the charter, and those who would do that are not the college's visitors but its usurpers. The corporation's memorial, however, elicited no significant concessions, and so the visitors' arrogation of its members' chartered powers prevailed. As these members were shorn of their right to participate in the exercise of power, what was once a body politic was depoliticized, and those who were once its "citizens" became subjects of rulers who now sit astride a corporation to which they do not belong.

John Bracken's Unhappy Suit

Before leaving Williamsburg, it is worth telling the story of John Bracken, who, shortly after the Revolution, challenged his dismissal from William & Mary. Bracken's story reveals much about the emerging constitution of the American academy as an autocracy, and especially its accomplishment through the mundane operation of protocapitalist employment practices.

As a member of the Virginia House of Delegates, in 1779, Thomas Jefferson drafted three bills aimed at fundamentally restructuring that state's educational system. The second of these bills, titled "A Bill for Amending the Constitution of the College of William and Mary," included provisions for reforming the college's curriculum and governance. These reforms cannot be accomplished by the visitors, Jefferson insisted, because they do not have the authority to modify the charter of which they are themselves the creatures. The state legislature, however, can do so because it effectively inherited the charter originally granted by the king and queen. For this reason, the college is "of right subject to public direction," and its founding charter may be "altered and amended, until such form be devised as will render the institution publicly advantageous, in proportion as it is publicly expensive."[24] Jefferson thereby construes William & Mary as a civil corporation that, like all others, is ultimately answerable to the citizens of Virginia.

Although Jefferson's bill was ultimately unsuccessful, in his role as one of William & Mary's visitors, he persuaded the board to adopt a new internal statute that abolished the grammar as well as the divinity schools and replaced them with schools in, among other things, natural philosophy, law, and medicine. As part of this reconsolidation, in 1779, the visitors terminated John Bracken, master of the now-defunct grammar school. Eight years later, Bracken filed a suit alleging that his dismissal had violated the college's charter and, on that ground, he sought from the state's general court a writ of mandamus restoring him to office. Three years later, in a one-sentence ruling, the Virginia Court of Appeals rejected Bracken's suit. Bowed but not beaten, nearly two decades later, Bracken filed a second suit seeking recovery of his salary and, on appeal, lost again.

What chiefly interests me about Bracken's case are the very different readings of William & Mary's governance offered by counsel for each side and their respective implications for our understanding of the relationship between the college and those who perform its work. Legal counsel for the visitors (who were now accorded the capitonym *Visitors* withheld in the charter and transfer agreements) was provided by none other than the future chief justice of the US Supreme Court John Marshall. Marshall's central argument, which is effectively a dress rehearsal for his opinion in *Dartmouth*, is that the court has no jurisdiction to act in this case. This argument turns on his rejection of any representation of the college, like that advanced by Jefferson, as a civil corporation subject to intervention by the state legislature in its capacity as the author, once removed, of William & Mary's charter. Instead, and fleshing out the argument intimated by the visitors' 1763 statute, Marshall insists that William & Mary is an "eleemosynary" corporation whose mission is to secure intergenerational fidelity to the wishes of its founders and initial donors. It is, in other words, a charity and should be governed by those who have been entrusted with that obligation—that is, the visitors in their capacity as the successors to William & Mary's original trustees.

If this is so, Marshall continues, the members of William & Mary's corporation have no rightful claim to participate in the college's governance. Rather, it is the trustees in their capacity as visitors who possess unilateral and exclusive authority to create anew or revise whatever "laws for the government of the college . . . as to them seem most fit and expedient."[25] The scope of this discretionary authority, Marshall continued, is not confined to statutes adopted following the 1729 transfer of authority from the visitors to the college's incorporated masters. Instead, it encompasses the very statutes prepared by Blair and Fouace two years earlier to specify how the corporation created by the transfer agreement is to be internally governed as well as how its relationship to the visitors is to be structured.

Absent incontrovertible evidence of a charter violation, Marshall added, courts should never second guess the better-informed judgment of the college's ultimate rulers, whether that apply to statutory or personnel matters; and that in turn renders virtually unreviewable any actions the visitors may take. In short, Marshall effectively represents the board of visitors as the sovereign interpreter of a charter that expressly required the college's original trustees to transfer ownership to the corporation but that he now reads as a mandate for that corporation's wholesale dispossession.

Applying these premises to Bracken's petition for reinstatement, Marshall argues that any position conferred on a professor is properly understood as a "voluntary gift" given by William & Mary's founding trustees and hence their successors. To this gift, the visitors may append any conditions "their will or caprice may dictate"; and once a professor chooses to accept this gift, "he accepts it subject to the conditions annexed by the donor." At William & Mary, one of these conditions is the visitors' right to abolish any position or terminate any appointment; and, when that decision is made, "the will of the Visitor is decisive" and hence beyond appeal. In sum, Bracken can claim no immunity from termination and no right to a hearing before or, for that matter, after his removal. That is so because in the final analysis Bracken is but an employee of those who, in firing him, have done no more than withdrawn a gift that was given with the proviso that it could be taken back at any time and for any reason or indeed for no reason whatsoever.[26] Although it will not be consolidated until late in the nineteenth century, Marshall thereby anticipates at-will employment doctrine as well as the authoritarian "private" government it subtends.

Before John Taylor, representing Bracken, can counter Marshall's arguments, he must first establish the court's jurisdiction over this matter; and, to do that, he must reject Marshall's representation of William & Mary as a "private corporation" and, specifically, an "eleemosynary institution." To do so, Taylor correctly notes that William & Mary was granted its charter by the Crown with the express understanding that it would advance the public good that is education; that it has received funds from the public treasury; and, finally, that the transfer agreement, once effected, authorized the corporation to elect a member to the state legislative assembly. From this it follows that William & Mary is, as Jefferson had maintained, a civil corporation whose principal obligations are not to the trustees or their heirs but to the Crown that chartered the college and, following the Revolution, to the people of Virginia. Hence, just as any citizen may sue the state, so too may Bracken sue its corporate creature.

Turning to the powers rightly exercised by the visitors, Taylor argues that they possess only those expressly conferred by the college's constitution, which, on his account, consists of the charter, the transfer agreement, and the 1727 statutes formulated to enact that agreement. True, those documents authorize the visitors to draft statutes for the college, but that power does not encompass the right to modify let alone violate the college's constitution since the visitors owe their own existence to that constitution and so cannot claim the right to amend their maker. Accordingly, because the transfer agreement as well as the 1727 statutes provided for a grammar school, the visitors exceeded their authority when they abolished that school and discharged its master.

Taylor's argument turns on a repudiation of Marshall's representation of the college as an autocratic regime predicated on incipient capitalist employment practices. Drawing on political categories familiar to his republican audience, he argues that the charter provides for governance of the college by three "collateral branches" (the trustees, the visitors, and the masters) and grants to each branch powers that in large measure are "separate and distinct." Yes, prior to enactment of the transfer, the "trustees" (who should not be identified with the visitors, since the latter were only called into being via effectuation of that transfer) were afforded "a bare and naked power" to fashion a college ex nihilo, as it were. But once the masters were "erected into a body politic and corporate," this corporation became a coequal participant in governance that derives its rightful powers "from the charter itself, and not from the trustees."[27]

The same, Taylor continues, is true of the visitors, for they too are a "subordinate body" within the more comprehensive constitutional order that is the college. To contend that any one member of that order has the authority to "destroy another creature of the same political regulation," as does Marshall, is to defend a doctrine that is "diametrically opposite to the fundamental maxims of our present and former government." At bottom, declares Taylor, Marshall's argument does no more than provide an aura of legitimacy to a regime that is "as completely a tyrannical government, as human cunning could have formed."[28]

If the visitors are permitted to rule by "fiat," as Marshall suggests they may, they will be in a position to "deprive the whole body politic, not only of their political existence, but, perhaps, of their natural existence, by reducing them to a state of beggary." (Here do note the telling use of the plural possessive *their* in speaking of the singular noun *body*.) But this the visitors cannot rightly do, for Bracken is not an employee of William & Mary, at least not in the sense presupposed by Marshall. Granted, the visitors are authorized to nominate persons to vacant faculty positions. But, that done, the professor does not become an abject subject of the college's ultimate rulers, construed by Marshall as autocratic employers. Rather, once the visitors have completed the task they are authorized to perform, professors become permanent "member[s] of the body corporate" that was anticipated in the charter, called into being via the transfer agreement, and whose governance powers were outlined in the 1727 statutes.[29]

"The president and masters," Taylor explains, are "a lay [as opposed to ecclesiastical] corporation, having rights, privileges and emoluments, of which they" cannot "be deprived; at least, without some form of trial." Once appointed, therefore, a professor becomes the holder of an office that, barring charges of sustained incompetence or serious misconduct adjudicated in a formal hearing, is granted to that master in perpetuity. To make this point, Taylor invokes a category that would have been readily comprehensible to his fellow students of the law but appears strange to us today. Specifically, Taylor argues that on appointment a professor comes into possession of a "freehold" or, as he sometimes puts it, "an estate for life."[30] In the common law of feudal and early modern England, although freeholds can assume diverse forms, all consist of ownership rights in a form of property, whether a holding in land, an office, or some other thing. Possession of such property has no finite duration, as would be the case were his a fixed-term contract, but it does require the ongoing performance of certain duties to or services on behalf of the party who grants these rights. As the holder of a freehold in the form of an office, Bracken is therefore required to fulfill the duties he assumed on appointment, but he can no more be stripped of this estate than he can be deprived of any other property without lawful cause.

That we find this construction of a faculty appointment unfamiliar does not make it false. Rather, our response testifies to the fact that Bracken's representation cannot be comprehended as a form of capitalist employment in which one commodity, labor power, is exchanged for another, that is, an hourly wage or for the more fortunate a salary. Bracken's claim appears perfectly sensible, however, when we situate it within the context of a republican member corporation.

Recall that creation of the entity "named the President and masters, or professors of the college of William and Mary" entailed transfer of the college's assets, including its tangible property as well as its offices, to its incorporated members who are now authorized to exercise control over those assets. Can the visitors now seize those assets, as they do when they abolish Bracken's position and so effectively terminate him? To see why that cannot be, Taylor offers this hypothetical: We know that the trustees of William & Mary prior to the act of transfer were authorized to receive donations on behalf of the college. But once legal ownership of those gifts is ceded to the corporation created by that transfer, can the visitors claim them as their own? To pose this question, Taylor avows, is to know its answer.

In short, in dismissing Bracken, the visitors have taken property to which they have no rightful title. This act of dispossession will appear justifiable only if one confuses the visitors with the corporation, thereby claiming for the former the powers of the latter; and that, Taylor tells us, is exactly what the visitors have in fact done: "The Visitors seem wholly to have mistaken their office. They seem to have considered themselves as the incorporated society."[31] Should this conflation be endorsed by the court, as Marshall commends, the president and masters of William & Mary will be divested of their collective right to govern the goods of which they are the corporate custodians and will instead become mere pawns of those whose claim to unilateral authority is without right.

Matters are still worse, however. By eliminating the position Bracken held, the visitors have defrauded a member of this civil corporation of his right to participate in electing that body's representative to the Virginia Assembly; and that is no more justifiable than is deprivation of any citizen's right to the franchise. Marshall can sanction annulment of this essential political freedom only because he mistakes William & Mary for a private charity, thereby denying its status as "a corporation for public government."[32] Doing so, he fails to grasp why the college's corporation is entitled to representation in that government. Equally important, he fails to understand why a college chartered by that government should itself be constituted in the form of a "little republic."

In the early history of William & Mary, we witness two insidious but complementary developments that make a mockery of the member corporation exemplified by Cambridge and Oxford at this time. First, we see the members of the incorporated entity denominated as "the President and masters, or professors of the college of William and Mary," deprived of the right to self-governance as they become subject to the will and whim of those who are not themselves members. Second, we see those who are in fact members of this body politic deprived of what once was their common wealth but has now been reconfigured as a trust to be managed by those who are so many outside agents. In sum, William & Mary is fast taking on the depoliticized trappings of an autocratic property corporation.

Dispossession's End

In 1906, the final nail was driven into the coffin of William & Mary's corporation of scholars. In that year, the board of visitors was *itself* constituted as a legally autonomous corporation. To eliminate the possibility of conflict with its predecessor, the Virginia legislature reappropriated the powers hitherto granted to "the corporate body designated 'the president and masters or professors of the College of William and Mary in Virginia'" and then reinvested those powers in this external lay board. Dropping the other shoe, control over the property once owned by the corporation was transferred to the board while its title was ceded to the state of Virginia. To furnish a veneer of consent to the state's expropriation of this incorporated creature, the final section of the 1906 act stipulated that its terms would not become effective "until and unless" the old as well as the new corporations endorsed this deal. Under a threat of imminent financial collapse and desperately needing an infusion of cash, ruler and ruled alike quickly did so.[33]

"Thus ended" what Hofstadter and Metzger labeled "the only sustained attempt by college teachers to reproduce in the colonies the English pattern of academic autonomy."[34] To declare this conclusion "inevitable," as Hofstadter and Metzger also do,[35] is to do a considerable injustice to John Bracken, John Taylor, and others at William & Mary who fought, albeit unsuccessfully, to preserve the college's corporate constitution as a self-governing commonwealth.

5

"The College of Tyrannus"

An Unseemly Beginning

"Indian enemies destroyed; internal enemies crushed; the Devil routed on both fronts—it was time to get on with the College."[1] With Anne Hutchison banished and the surviving Pequots soon to be enslaved or expelled, the Great and General Court of Massachusetts Bay, once the governing body of a joint stock enterprise but now a corporation in the form of a colony, set about founding an academy on a site once named Newtown but soon to be rechristened Cambridge. At its meeting on October 28, 1636, after granting £5 to a certain George Munnings for the accidental loss of his eye, the court voted to allocate £400 "toward a school or colledge [sic],"[2] with half of this sum to be disbursed in 1637 and the remainder to be paid on completion of the project.

One year later, presaging the bane of academic life, the court formed an ad hoc committee whose amorphous charge was "to take order for the college"[3]—that is, to begin to fashion the court's appropriation into what, at this time, was a school only in name (but also absent a proper name). This committee ought not to be confused with a governing board, for there was no college over which it might govern. Its first act, accordingly, was to appoint a "master" to whom the committee assigned the task of constructing a few buildings, including that master's own home, to manage any additional donations that might be given in support of this effort, and to make a first stab at the business of teaching.

Nathaniel Eaton's service in this capacity did not go well. Eaton, one student later lamented, was "fitter to have been an officer in the inquisition, or master of an house of correction, than an instructer [sic] of Christian youth."[4] On the cow pasture that in time would become a campus, most menial tasks were assigned to Samuel Hough, the first documented Black person to be enslaved in New England, and to Eaton's wife, who was later accused of serving students hasty pudding laced with goat dung. The work of instruction was chiefly performed by Eaton, who, persuaded that he should never "give over correcting till he had subdued the party to his will,"[5] routinely whipped his first nine charges. After cudgeling his own assistant for nearly two hours with the stout branch of a walnut tree, Eaton was taken to court, convicted, fined, and dismissed in late 1639. As he fled the colony, some gossips alleged, Eaton absconded with a good chunk of the funding disbursed by the General Court (although the historical record leaves unclear whether this sum was ever paid in whole or in part), and perhaps also a portion of the proceeds secured by sale of the estate left to the college by John Harvard in 1638. What Cotton Mather would later dub the "School of Tyrannus,"[6] but which was soon given a name that erased Eaton's brutality from Harvard's founding tale, promptly closed for the 1639–40 academic year.

After a year of what Samuel Eliot Morison called a "state of suspended animation,"[7] the General Court invited Henry Dunster to become "president" of this work in progress, and, in August 1640, he did so. Two years later, conceding that the makeshift committee it had created in 1637 was ill equipped to exercise ongoing superintendence of the college, the court invented a new body composed of the colonial governor and deputy governor as well as the magistrates of six townships and an equal number of ministers from area churches, all of whom were Cambridge University alumni or relatives of its graduates. Although this body was not legally constituted as a corporation, the court nonetheless conferred on it many of the powers possessed by those entities that were. Specifically, doing its business by majority rule, the "overseers" were granted "full power and authority to make and establish all such orders, statutes, and constitutions as they shall see necessary for the instituting, guiding, and furthering of the said college" and "to dispose, order and manage" all "gifts, legacies, bequeaths, revenues, land and donations" they might receive.[8] This body's authority was qualified, however, insofar as any of its decisions could be appealed to the General Court.

Just as the court's 1637 committee should not be confused with a governing board, nor should we read the future into the past by characterizing this "company of overseers" as an external lay board, at least as we understand them today. External lay boards govern incorporated entities, which Harvard would not become until 1650; and these corporations are granted powers of self-governance only because, legally speaking, they have some measure of autonomy from the state that creates them. Harvard's initial overseers, however, were appointed in their capacity *as* officeholders within churches, municipalities, and the colonial assembly, and their task was to rule the college on behalf of these bodies. In its earliest years, therefore, Harvard was effectively a dependent agency of the colony ruled by overseers principally accountable to political and religious notables.

This way of organizing Harvard's rule poses a puzzle. Hofstadter and Metzger correctly note that there is "no evidence that the founders of Harvard College at first intended to depart from" the "familiar and respected practices of academic government" that prevailed at Cambridge and Oxford.[9] Clearly, though, governance of an unincorporated entity by nonresident overseers who were not selected from among nor by those whom they rule does not conform to the model of the "little republic" that is the member corporation. Why, then, did the colonial government depart from this prototype?

In answering this question, which is the principal purpose of this chapter, I offer a complement to my partial history of William & Mary. As in Virginia, in Massachusetts we witness an appropriation of the American academy's corporate powers by elites keenly interested in securing control over an institution designed to cultivate their descendants for a world they were sure to inherit. As at William & Mary, that usurpation met with significant opposition predicated on a rival conception of the corporation and its governance. In laying out the now mostly forgotten arguments of those who challenged the consolidation of autocratic rule at Harvard, my purpose is to honor their efforts but also to provide ammunition, however musty, to those who might wish to reconsider the academy's corporate constitution today.

Harvard, Inc.

Even had the founders of Harvard wished to re-create Cambridge in Massachusetts, they could not have done so. The class of 1642, the first to graduate from Harvard, consisted of nine men awarded bachelor's degrees (a number that exceeded by two the annual average over the course of the next four decades). That degree certified their recipients' status as apprentices now eligible to pursue the higher degrees that, once received, would effectively render them peers of the masters and doctors who ruled Cambridge. But in Massachusetts no guild of scholars antedated Harvard's creation, and so few if any were formally qualified to assume the governance responsibilities of their English counterparts.

Instead, almost without exception, the "tutors" who taught at Harvard and other early colonial colleges were sources of inexpensive labor who regarded teaching as a short-term prelude to more prestigious clerical positions. These contingent instructors rarely stayed at Harvard for more than a few years and before 1720 never numbered more than three. Within this context, the model of a self-governing faculty ruling an autonomous university was fanciful at best. Invention of Harvard's overseers was therefore not an answer to the question of what constitutional form would best serve the educational needs of its students. Rather, it was an expedient of seventeenth-century colonial history invented by interested elites who jettisoned a model they considered undesirable and impossible under present circumstances (although the member corporation established at William & Mary suggests otherwise). Once installed, these "absentee proprietors" soon grew enamored of their "sweeping powers" and so, as Hofstadter and Metzger note, proved reluctant to cede them, "being, like other parents, unwilling to accept the fact of their own obsolescence."[10]

This, though, is not the end of the story, and that is so chiefly because idealized recollections of Cambridge and Oxford endured and informed the challenges to Harvard's constitution of rule that erupted episodically over the course of the next two hundred years. The first fruits of these conflicts were evident in Harvard's reconstitution in the form of a corporation just eight years after the power of the overseers was officially consolidated. The impetus to modify Harvard's constitutional form came from Dunster, who hoped that the college's incorporation would secure it some measure of institutional immunity from meddling overseers and the established political and clerical authorities they represented. The ex officio overseers, the president complained, were difficult to assemble in one place, ill qualified to exercise prudent judgment in selecting the college's instructors, and had little appreciation of its most urgent financial needs. No matter how inexpert, he surmised, Harvard's resident officers and tutors were almost certainly better equipped to govern than were those appointed to rule the college only because they happened to hold positions elsewhere.

On May 23, 1650, Dunster delivered to the General Court a proposed charter of incorporation for Harvard, and, one week later, it was approved by the assembly and signed by the governor. The charter provided that the corporation be named "the President and Fellows of Harvard College" and specified that its mission was to educate "the English and Indian youth of this country, in knowledge and godliness."[11] Its membership consisted of the president, the treasurer, and five "fellows" (which at this time included four resident instructors, and, shortly thereafter, a tutor as well). To this "body politic and corporate in law" was granted an amplified version of the powers that hitherto had been vested in the overseers. These included the power (1) to elect the corporation's members when seats come vacant; (2) to "make, from time to time, such orders and by-laws for the better ordering, and carrying on the work of the College, as they shall think fit"; (3) to "purchase and acquire to themselves" various forms of property, including but not limited to lands, donations, and estates; (4) to appoint and remove subordinate officers of the college; (5) to sue and be sued in any court within the colony's jurisdiction; and, finally, (6) to prepare and employ a seal that, when affixed to documents, certifies their official issuance by this immaterial entity.[12]

Were this the end of the matter, the governance of Harvard might have come to resemble that of Cambridge (leaving aside the not unimportant fact that membership in Harvard's corporation was restricted to five fellows rather than extended to all qualified faculty, as at William & Mary). Dunster knew, though, that he could not secure the charter's approval unless it provided some ongoing role for the overseers. The charter circumscribed their powers, however, which it ambiguously specified as follows: (1) to provide "counsel and consent" regarding the corporation's election of its members as well as its passage of college bylaws; and (2) to participate in joint meetings with the corporation regarding "great and difficult" matters on which its members could not agree.[13]

Whatever uncertainty may have lingered about the exact distribution of powers between the corporation and overseers was effectively resolved in 1657 when the General Court amended the charter as follows: "The Corporation shall have power from time to time to make such orders and by laws for the better ordering of the college, *as they shall see cause, without depending upon the consent of the overseers,*" provided that the overseers reserve the ultimate authority to review its actions.[14] This amendment anticipated that Harvard's board of overseers would generally defer to the corporation and, when it did engage, to do so only in response to actions already undertaken by the college's principal governors.

On these terms, arguably, the college was to possess a measure of autonomy that exceeded that of Cambridge and Oxford. As I explained in chapter 4, although infrequently exercised, as a matter of common law, Harvard's English counterparts were subject to intervention by visitors invested with sweeping authority to take any steps deemed necessary to ensure conformity to the designated mission of these colleges. In contrast, Harvard appears to be imagined by the 1650 charter, as amended in 1657, as a self-governing corporation subject not to the ultimate rule of a lay body external to or above it but, instead, to consultation with that body and in a few key areas to ratification (or veto) of actions already decided by that corporation's members.

The charter's constitution of Harvard on the model of a member corporation is additionally confirmed by the rules that governed conduct of the college's internal business: "For the better ordering of the government, . . . the President, and three more of the Fellows, shall and may, from time to time, upon due warning or notice given by the President to the rest, hold a meeting, for the debating and concluding" of affairs concerning the execution of its laws as well as disposition of its assets;[15] and, at these meetings, majority rule was to prevail. Indeed, even should a "great and difficult" issue arise that required a joint meeting of the corporation with the overseers, the role of the latter was confined to offering (or withholding) its consent to whatever "the major part" of the former shall conclude. On this account, the overseers' ought never supplant the college's governors but merely collaborate on an infrequent basis in ensuring Harvard's ongoing dedication to fulfillment of its public purpose.

"Charter Mongering"

The first two decades following the charter's adoption were relatively peaceful, perhaps because Harvard remained inconsequential and so not much worth fighting over. During the last quarter of the seventeenth century and the first decades of the eighteenth, however, the charter's terms became a vexed subject of contestation among the college's internal constituencies as well as external elites whose interests sometimes converged but often did not.[16]

Although tensions had been brewing for some time, struggle over the charter's language proved unavoidable when, in 1684, the English Court of Chancery revoked the Massachusetts Bay Colony charter on the ground that its governors had adopted laws at odds with the Navigation Acts and, more offensive still, had melted down coins to create its own currency, minus the king's image. This revocation had the perhaps unanticipated effect of nullifying the charter granted to Harvard by the now-defunct colony and, by implication, the incorporated body it had established in 1650. Now entirely exposed to the will of the Crown, Harvard's existential crisis was attenuated but not overcome when, in 1691, the Crown issued a new charter to what was now dubbed the province of Massachusetts Bay. While this document reaffirmed Harvard's legal title to its properties and revenues, it did not include a revamped charter for the college. Legally speaking, Harvard was thereby left standing as an unincorporated quasi owner of assets absent clear title to regulate their disposition (or, for that matter, to confer degrees on its students).

One year later, when not otherwise occupied with the trial and execution of accused witches in Salem, Harvard's president advanced a new charter to the General Court. The document proposed by Increase Mather effectively eliminated any possible conflict between the board of overseers and the corporation by eliminating the former and vesting all power in the latter, including the authority to select its own members and officers, to enact and enforce its own statutes, and to manage its own property. As with its 1650 predecessor, these provisions for autonomous self-governance sought to secure Harvard's relative immunity from political interference; and, for Mather, that was an essential condition of the college's continued control by orthodox Congregationalists. Mather was foiled in 1697, however, when the Crown disallowed the 1692 charter because it did not authorize the monarch, via an express grant of visitorial power, to intervene in Harvard's affairs.

With good reason, Morison has characterized the two decades following 1692 as the era of "charter-mongering,"[17] as version after version was proposed only to be neglected, rejected, or lost as a result of bureaucratic bungling in London. Harvard was finally able to resecure its corporate identity only because of a controversy precipitated by an accident. In 1707, Harvard's interim president, Samuel Willard, cut his finger while eating oysters, suffered a severe allergic reaction, and expired. The nomination of John Leverett, a liberal Congregationalist, to succeed Willard was bitterly opposed by those more conservative. Hoping to quell this conflict, the province's governor, Joseph Dudley, proposed a deal that pleased the progressives by confirming the appointment of Leverett but conciliated the traditionalists by reaffirming Harvard's first charter. Cleverly circumventing the problems posed by the Crown's assertion of veto power over any new charter, the General Court affirmed the dubious proposition that the 1650 charter had never been repealed or nullified and so remained in effect.[18]

Revolting Tutors

While the settlement crafted in 1707 partly tempered sectarian schisms within the colony, it did little to quiet emerging conflicts involving the corporation, the board of overseers, and disaffected tutors. This discord erupted openly in the early 1720s and then again in the mid-1820s. Both were rooted in partisan squabbles, but, as I will show in the next section, framed as principled battles over Harvard's corporate constitution, and especially how it would distribute power among multiple claimants within as well as without the college.

The protagonists of the 1720s conflict were animated, above all else, by dispossession of what they took to be their rightful seats on the corporation. A few years prior, three seats on the corporation came vacant, and several tutors anticipated their appointment. Instead, pressed by President Leverett, whose rule was trending autocratic, the corporation broke with the tradition of appointing senior tutors to the status of fellow and instead nominated three liberal Congregational ministers. Exacerbating their aggrievement, the corporation also adopted a three-year renewable term limit on faculty appointments, thereby ensuring that any future troublemakers could be removed in short order.

Especially vexed was one of Harvard's three tutors, Nicholas Sever, who had reluctantly accepted a position at the college in 1716 only because strained vocal cords rendered him unable to continue his duties as an ordained minister.[19] In 1718, Sever submitted a detailed protest to the corporation in which, among other things, he complained about his salary and workload; the college's failure to formally announce his appointment, which undermined his stature among students; and, finally, the president's denial of his right to discipline his charges when they failed to attend his lectures.

When Sever secured no satisfaction from the corporation, he sought allies among the other tutors; and, in 1720, Henry Flynt and Thomas Robie joined him in submitting a second memorial. Unlike the first, this document focused not on Leverett's disregard for the tutors' authority but on the corporation's appointment of persons who were not instructors to a majority of the five positions reserved by the 1650 charter for its "fellows." Sever's personal pique was thereby elevated into a collision over the college's constitution.

When the corporation ignored this second petition, now joined by the recently appointed William Welsteed, Sever appealed to the board of overseers, and in retaliation the corporation refused to renew his appointment as a tutor. Seeing an opportunity to oust at least one liberal Congregationalist from the corporation, the more orthodox board then voted to restore Sever to his position on the ground that it had never endorsed the term limit on tutorial appointments. To placate those hostile to Sever and his cohorts, the board then offered a compromise whose terms were outlined in a memorial submitted to the General Court. There the board proposed an enlargement of the corporation's size so that it could include resident as well as nonresident "fellows." This, though, had the effect of perturbing the tutors still more, since, arguably, it violated the 1650 charter by denying their claim to exclusive appointment as the corporation's fellows.

After several more rounds of memorials and a series of arcane political maneuvers that satisfied no one, a frustrated President Leverett crafted a new college charter that would have eliminated his opponents by abolishing the board of overseers entirely. Leverett, however, had no opportunity to submit this version for consideration because, in 1724, he died, thus removing Sever's principal opponent. One year later, Sever was at last appointed a fellow of the corporation, only to resign his position at the college in 1728. Controversy about how and by whom Harvard was to be governed was thereby ameliorated not because this issue was resolved but because its two most bitter antagonists, by different means, had left the scene.

For the remainder of the eighteenth century and into the next, governance conflicts at Harvard generally took shape as minor skirmishes that could be resolved without reigniting the bigger battles of the early 1720s. The distribution of power within the confines of this unsettled regime, though, did not remain static, for the controversy initiated by Sever had the unintended effect of rendering the board of overseers keenly interested in securing control over the college's affairs. Its accretion of power went mostly unchallenged, however, because it no longer sought to achieve its ends by seeking to reform or reinterpret Harvard's charter. Instead the board adopted a far less visible but more insidious strategy that might be called "dispossession by committee."

Between 1754 and 1768, the overseers appointed forty-four committees, many of which were initially constituted on an ad hoc basis but in time became standing enterprises that met and reported annually. By this means, the board asserted its prerogative over college affairs in ways never anticipated by the 1650 charter or its 1657 amendment. To cite but a few examples, these committees advanced to the board recommendations concerning the curriculum, including courses to be taught as well as methods of instruction; supervision of the college's financial affairs, principally by mandating annual examination of the treasurer's records; and personnel matters, chiefly by requiring that the board as well as the corporation examine all candidates for tutorial appointments and in time fellows nominated to serve on the corporation itself.

Emboldened by these successes, especially after national independence was declared, the board began to undo the fragile accommodation secured in the 1720s, and it did so by packing the corporation with political, economic, and ministerial elites drawn from outside the college. This effort culminated in 1806 when a resident instructor, Professor Eliphat Pearson, resigned from the corporation. His replacement by yet another nonresident, Theophilus Parsons, chief justice of the Massachusetts Supreme Court, completed the removal of resident instructors from the corporation, and it was this that provoked Harvard's tutors to assert their role in ruling the college once again.

In 1824, Henry Ware, nine other Harvard tutors, and a docent submitted a memorial declaring that the governance rights of the college's resident fellows had been "entirely wrested from them by the nonresident members of the Corporation" and then demanding that they be restored to the five positions reserved for its "academic fellows."[20] This memorial elicited no response from the corporation (which is perhaps unsurprising: if its members had endorsed the tutors' central argument, all would then have had to be ousted from their positions). Instead the corporation disclaimed jurisdiction over this matter and pitched the memorial to the overseers, who appointed yet another committee to look into this question and then adjourned.

Eight months later, in January 1825, the board heard the committee's report, which recommended against the memorialists, first on the ground that Harvard's resident instructors have no "exclusive right to be chosen members of the Corporation" and second on the ground that nonresidency does not disqualify persons from membership on that body. To no one's surprise, the board endorsed these two recommendations, thereby validating its own fait accompli. Henceforth, there could be little doubt that the corporation, like the board of overseers, would be dominated by outsiders and specifically by what Morison, in his 1936 history of Harvard, called "the solid men of Boston—lawyers, jurists, physicians, financiers, and an occasional statesmen, bishop, or man of letters."[21] If one discerns in this denouement the triumph of a prototype for external lay boards ruling in the service of dominant elites, that is as it should be.

The Tutors' Credo

Let us not romanticize Harvard's instructors by representing them as selfless heroes of a resistance movement, let alone as radical democrats, seeking to overthrow tyrants who would reduce them to servitude. Nor were the college's teachers political theorists who developed a sophisticated account of the constitutional form that will best secure the academy's "true" ends.

But nor will we do justice by Harvard's dissidents if we consider them mere malcontents, and we will not give them their due, let alone appreciate what we might learn from them, if we fail to articulate the affirmative vision that informed their critiques. To do so, my exposition here weaves together the memorials submitted by Nicholas Sever and his occasional coauthors in the 1720s as well as that advanced by Henry Ware and his ten colleagues in 1824. Although separated by a century, they offer a strikingly consistent case, first against the academy's rule by the progenitors of today's autocratic governing boards and second in favor of an academy built on the model of a republican member corporation, albeit one that is more attenuated than that achieved, if only for a while, at William & Mary.

In their several memorials, Harvard's in-house critics contended that the 1650 charter places the college's *"instruction, government, and financial administration"* in the "same hands, giving dignity and energy to each other."[22] The powers required to manage these collective affairs belong to the corporation, and the five positions reserved for that body's "fellows" can only rightly be filled by the college's resident instructors. Nonresidents, however, now occupy many and in later years all of these positions, and so the college suffers under a "foreign yoke" from which it "groan[s] to be delivered."[23] Thus misruled, they concluded, Harvard can no longer fulfill the mission for which it was first granted corporate status.

This conclusion is predicated on reasons of practice as well as principle. To begin with the former, because they have little familiarity with the everyday business of the college, nonresidential rulers cannot be expected to govern well, especially as their principal attentions are directed elsewhere: if a "clergyman," his "great pledge in life is to his church," and, if a lawyer, "to his character at the bar and on the bench."[24] To allow those otherwise preoccupied to superintend Harvard or for that matter any college is on its face nonsensical: "Every one would be struck with the absurdity of entrusting the concerns of a mercantile body, to those who were not merchants, or of an agricultural society, to those who were not agriculturists; and the absurdity would be greatly enhanced, if the gentlemen who received the trust were, at the same time, so separated from the establishment which it was there [sic] business to govern, as to render it impossible for them to acquire any practical knowledge of its concerns."[25] What, for example, should one expect when these interlopers convene but two or three times a year and, at one of those meetings, turn their attention to faculty compensation? "These favors are bestowed mostly, on persons which the Nonresidents had never saw or heard of in their lives before. So that in this business they shoot at random, if therefore they hit the mark it must be by chance."[26]

Should those whose principal business lies elsewhere reply by arguing that it is their very distance from the college that renders them disinterested and so impartial in determining its affairs, the memorialists will ask: "Whence this sovereign virtue of non-residence? What is there to secure gentlemen living in Boston, from the reach of the same suspicions, as would effect other men?" On what grounds, for example, should we exempt the college's nonresidential rulers "from the same suspicion of grasping themselves at the office within their reach, and with regard to those which are not, securing them for brothers, sons, cousins, and nephews?" Indeed, in virtue of "their station in society," which situates them squarely in the midst of "political controversy," is it not entirely probable that these elites will soon fall prey to the enticements of patronage and partisanship?[27]

Although peculiarly ill equipped to rule the college's affairs, Harvard's nonresidential rulers are also unusually well positioned to mask their incapacity. Among the public, "it is scarcely known out of a small circle, who are the governors of the college, according to the existing distribution of power," let alone what those powers are. If truth be told, even among the college's residents, it would require "some effort of memory . . . to state correctly the names" of its unrecognized governors.[28] The work done by those who ultimately control the college, performed behind closed doors, is thus shielded from public scrutiny and remains mysterious even to those who labor daily on the college's behalf.

Their shadowy status enables the college's autocrats to claim responsibility for successes that are not theirs but also to disclaim accountability when matters go poorly. Hence, when the incompetence of nonresident navigators "run[s] the ship ashore . . . and reform[s] the college to the ground," they are quick to "cast all the odium upon the residents." But when matters go well, they are equally quick to claim credit to which they are not entitled: "When the residents have labored in this vineyard, for other men to come and put their sickle into our harvest [not] of their sowing and which has cost themselves nothing, is neither just to the residents or themselves; for in so doing they ascribe less to the residents than is their due, and more to themselves than of right belongs to them."[29] The (mis)appropriation of credit for good deeds done by others, like the expropriation of tangible assets produced by others, may be less visible but remains a kind of theft.

Most fundamentally, nonresidential rule is misguided because it cannot help but "defeat the great end for which the College was founded": the "Learned and pious Education of Youth, their Instruction in Languages, Arts, and Sciences, and having their minds and manners formed aright." This end will be far better served if the college's governance is restored to those who best understand its affairs, especially those resident tutors who are (or, rather, should be) members of the college's corporation. To confine their responsibilities to imposing petty fines on disobedient youth is to invite students to assume an attitude of casual contempt toward those whose respect they must have. Should students find that instructors are not masters in their own home but rather mere servants doing the bidding of others, they will soon "grow slack and negligent in their studies," and "there will of course be a failure in their learning."[30]

To argue on behalf of the superior capacity of resident instructors to govern the college is not to think them blessed with a monopoly on virtue. Contradicting those who justify rule by nonresidents by holding them uniquely disinterested, it is precisely because Harvard's resident instructors are in fact very much interested that they should govern: "The resident instructers [sic] are persons, whose reputation, happiness, and even pecuniary interest are immediately dependent" on the college's welfare and "who are therefore bound by the strongest ties to promote its progress." Should the college be ill governed, no member of the board of overseers, "with the single exception of the President, who is a resident officer, will gain or lose either in interest or reputation to any considerable degree, most probably not at all."[31] But to strip from instructors the authority to make the laws by which they are governed, to select those by whom they are to be ruled, and to manage Harvard's assets is to harm the college by severing the bonds that wed duty to self-interest. Should the college's instructors be foolish enough to act in ways that compromise Harvard's well-being, concern for their own welfare will soon demonstrate how and where they have gone wrong.

This account of the unhappy effects engendered by nonresident rule is underwritten by a principled vision of the constitutional order specified in the 1650 charter as amended in 1657 and reaffirmed in 1707. Granted, the key contours of this model are sometimes obscured by the memorialists' boundless appetite for legalistic squabbling over the meaning of specific terms (for example, the word *fellow*). That vision is there, though, and it merits unearthing precisely because it discloses a path not taken and hence a possible starting point for critical inquiry today.

The touchstone for this vision is not the General Court's 1636 initial commitment of £400, which at best was merely a statement of legislative resolve. Nor is it the court's 1642 order creating a committee of magistrates and ministers authorized to superintend an entity that, because unincorporated, had no legal autonomy from the colonial government that created it. Instead, this vision's foundation is the charter that conferred on the college the status of a corporation, for it was this deed that invested Harvard with the powers of self-rule that render it something other than a mere appendage of the state.

Via the act of incorporation, the nature of every participant in the college's governance as well as their relations to one another were essentially reconstituted. Of course, prior to 1650, specific persons held certain positions within the college—for example, the president, treasurer, and tutors—and these officers were filled as needed by those authorized to act on behalf of the colonial government, that is, the overseers. But, in 1650, these officeholders became *members* of a self-governing corporation rather than *agents* exercising authority delegated to them by the overseers. Indeed, even the overseers who, until this time, had been mere ministers of the state now became immanent parts of a body politic that defines their purpose and role. The chartering of the college is therefore a performative act that, quite literally, calls into being that which it names the "President and Fellows of Harvard College" and, at the same time, folds the board of overseers within a constitutional order of which they too are creatures.

What, then, is the nature of the comprehensive corporation constituted by the charter? In issuing this document, the General Court ordered the following: "Henceforth that the said college, in Cambridge in Middlesex, in New England, shall be a Corporation, consisting of seven persons, to wit, a President, five Fellows, and a Treasurer or Bursar." In the eyes of the law, therefore, this "body politic and corporate" *is* the college: "The word, '*college*,'" one memorialist explained, "is here used in its primary sense, to denote a number of persons associated together for some common purpose. This college, these individuals, are by the charter constituted a Corporation."[32]

Within this college, these individuals no longer exist qua individuals but, instead, as constituents integrated within an entity that will endure long after each of them has died. When the corporation's members act, therefore, they do not do so as natural persons. Rather, they act as its essential organs: "The President and Fellows of Harvard college, *in their corporate capacity*, . . . shall have, hold, use, exercise and enjoy all the powers, authorities, rights, liberties, privileges, immunities and franchises" granted them by the General Court.[33] When the corporation's officers exercise these powers, strictly speaking, we ought not say that the college is governed *by* the corporation, for that presupposes the very bifurcation the act of incorporation denies. Rather, we should say that these officers act in the name *of* the incorporated college; and that is exactly what the Harvard seal, when affixed to any document, signifies.

What does this understanding of Harvard's corporation imply for the principal question at issue in the 1720s as well as the 1820s? What, more precisely, qualifies someone for election as a "fellow" of the corporation, and what disqualifies one from serving in this capacity? According to the charter, which specifies that the corporation is to number seven, the president and treasurer are among the members of the corporation but are not among its five "fellows." Frequently pointing to the example of Cambridge and sometimes Oxford, the memorialists therefore insist that the charter's reference to "fellows" intends only those persons who are *"resident at the College, and actually engaged there, in carrying on the duties of instruction or government, and receiving a stipend from its revenues."*[34] All three qualifications—residence, participation in instruction and government, and receipt of a stipend—are necessary, but it is residency that sits at the heart of the matter.

Harvard's incorporation, according to the charter, is a means to promote the "education of the English and Indian youth of this country," and its assets must be employed to advance this purpose, including "maintenance of the President and Fellows."[35] Prudence dictates, as we have already seen, that these officers be residents rather than outsiders. That the fellows must and can only be residents follows from the very terms of Harvard's incorporation: "If, as the charter says, the corporation *are* the college; wheresoever the corporation is, there, the college, is; and if the corporation is not at Cambridge, the college is not at Cambridge; and if the college is not at Cambridge, the charter is violated."[36] As we saw in John Bracken's suit against William & Mary's visitors, use of the plural *are* here is not a grammatical error but rather an acknowledgment of the fact that the corporation, although not reducible to an aggregate of its members, does not stand as an abstraction independent from or opposed to them.

By insisting on its spatial situatedness, Edward Everett does not mean to identify the college at Cambridge with, for example, its material infrastructure. Were he to do so, and were Harvard's campus to be demolished tomorrow, that would spell the end of the college's existence. But surely that cannot be. Just as any immaterial corporation can survive the expiration of all its current members, so too can the college persevere absent its physical incarnation in this form as opposed to that. That, though, does not mean that the college's location is immaterial, since, according to the charter, its emplacement here but not there is essential to this corporation's very identity. Those who are members of the incorporated body must therefore reside there as well. To hold otherwise—that is, to maintain that residence is an incidental criterion of membership—is to invite trespass by those who do not and by definition cannot belong to this incorporated body politic.

Expropriating Overseers

Because the charter of 1650 is Harvard's constitution, it cannot be altered by those who owe their very existence in the eyes of the law to its enactment. This framework may be revised by its author, that is, by the colonial government that issued the charter; and of course those who work within its confines may at any time petition that government for modifications of its terms. But the powers delegated by the charter to the college do not encompass that of remaking this constitution. Should anyone lay claim to authority that the charter does not expressly allocate to them, that must be declared an act of illegitimate usurpation.

These powers, for example, do not authorize the overseers to select and appoint persons to fill vacant seats on the corporation, let alone all of them, as they eventually do. When they do so, the overseers violate the charter, first by depriving the corporation of its powers of self-governance and second by stripping the corporation's fellows of property to which they are entitled. While I will treat these transgressions separately, in principle they should be considered together. To infringe on one is to jeopardize the other, for they are complementary elements of the "franchise" of special privileges granted to the corporation by the 1650 charter. Absent the power of self-governance, the corporation cannot regulate the assets without which it can only exist as an immaterial legal fiction. Absent legal ownership of and control over those assets, the corporation's right to self-governance lacks the material means that render this right real.

The first of these two charges is easily explained: By the charter, the corporation is invested with the power to govern the college. True, those who hold office within that body may delegate certain duties to subordinate officers, whether "steward, butler, handicraftsmen, and menial servants,"[37] but these entrustments are contingent and may be modified or withdrawn at any time. What the corporation cannot do is to divest itself or to allow others to deprive it of the governance powers specified in the charter, for that would be to dissolve the college's constitution and hence to abolish the college itself.

For example, the charter authorizes the corporation to "elect" its new members, subject to the overseers' "counsel and consent." Should the overseers withhold their affirmation, that does not void the corporation's selection, for the board is not authorized to rescind the corporation's actions. Rather, to refuse consent is to leave any given action incomplete and so requires that the corporation either plead its case again or advance the name of another. From this it follows that should the overseers pretend to select and seat someone on the corporation, that person is not and cannot be a de jure member and so cannot rightfully engage in exercising any of its powers.

The corporation's right to self-governance will also be contravened should any one of its members, including the president, be granted unauthorized powers over others. For example, in 1824, a committee of overseers recommended that the president be granted unfettered veto power over any and all actions taken by the corporation. This, too, must be rejected because it flouts the charter's express commitment to the principle of majority rule. To vest this "arbitrary and irresponsible" power in but one of the corporation's officers "is foreign from the whole spirit which breathes around us in our republican habits and institutions." Indeed, to allow this to occur is to transform the corporate body politic into "a little despotism" and, by extension, to regard all but one of its members as "idle day-laborers, who will not do their work faithfully without an overseer."[38]

The second charge leveled by Harvard's instructors against the overseers requires a bit more explanation. To be appointed a "fellow" within the corporation that is Harvard is to come to hold "a very valuable property, a very important vested right,"[39] or, as John Bracken put it at William & Mary, a "freehold." If we understand such an appointment on the model of capitalist employment relation, we will fail to grasp why Harvard's residents fought so tenaciously to preserve their exclusive title to these positions. In a capitalist economy, the phrase *wage labor* is shorthand for the contractual relationship between an employer and employee. The former purchases labor power from the latter in return for compensation, whether paid per piece, per hour, or, if more privileged, in the form of a salary. Because agreement to these contractual arrangements is said to be freely given and imposes no enduring obligations on either party, employers retain the right to fire their employees without cause and at any time and, correlatively, employees retain the right to seek a higher bidder for their labor.

That, however, is not how Harvard's resident fellows think of their appointment to offices within the incorporated body of which they thereby become members. To see why this is so, recall that Harvard's charter granted the corporation sole ownership and hence management rights over the college's assets. That document vests in the overseers no powers over these assets, although it does authorize the corporation to call joint meetings with the board about "great and difficult" issues when its members cannot come to agreement. At such meetings, the board may offer advice and even refuse to consent to the corporation's disposition of, for example, an estate bequeathed to the college. But should the overseers do so, that does not dictate what is to be done with any given asset. It merely leaves the matter open for additional debate, with the ultimate decision to be made by a majority of the corporation but only once it has secured the board's concurrence. Should the right to dispose of any college asset be affirmed by those who are not among the corporation's members, that must be counted an unjust forfeiture.

To illustrate why that is so, consider this episode: As far back as 1645, Harvard's fellows were taken to be the proprietors of what was known as "Fellows' Orchard," and their title to this small field was eventually confirmed via discovery of the original deed composed in Latin. For well over a century, this land was let by the fellows to tenants, and the rent they collectively received provided a modest increment to their annual stipends. Around the turn of the nineteenth century, the value of Cambridge real estate rose dramatically; and so, far from oblivious to this world's ways, the tutors decided to sell the orchard, invest the proceeds, and establish a permanent fund to augment their income as well as that of their successors. This plan was foiled by the overseers, who, by that time, had succeeded in packing the corporation with its appointees: "The tutors had been gradually excluded from the board of Fellows; the Corporation, *so called*, had forced itself into their place, and claimed to be the rightful Fellows; so that the power of the tutors to sell the land was denied."[40] What we see here is a telling instance of dispossession by means of charter misconstruction perpetrated by outsiders who cannot be members of this corporation because they are not residents, do not teach, and receive no compensation from the college.

To the fellows, what is true of this orchard is equally true of all assets vested in the corporation by the charter, including the offices they hold. This particular asset is considered "a very valuable property" because, once conferred, its possessor holds this position during good behavior and so cannot be removed except on impeachment for misconduct (for example, for "overt acts of intolerable mismanagement").[41] Occupancy of these positions is, in short, a "vested right," and so an officeholder cannot be denied it absent a show of cause as well as a hearing conducted by a body composed exclusively of those who are this corporation's members.

This anticapitalist understanding of officeholding grounds our contemporary understanding of tenure, so perhaps we should think twice before dismissing it as anachronistic. To summarily strip someone of this form of property, Harvard's memorialists contend, is an act of capricious privation. If, today, we do not regard termination absent a fair trial conclusively adjudicated by one's colleagues as an instance of larceny, that signifies not the error of the memorialists' argument but, rather, the tight grip on our imaginations of capitalist constructions of at-will employment as well as our inability to recall what it is to be a member incorporated within a self-governing body politic.

Capitalist constructions of wage labor are also likely to cause us to misconstrue the compensation Harvard's faculty members and other officers receive. That compensation takes the form of an annual "stipend." These stipends, to quote the charter, are furnished for the "maintenance" of those who render service to the college. Figured later in the charter as goods provided for the "use and behoof" of the corporation's members, the term

maintenance is not well understood on the model of quantitatively specified wages paid in return for the expenditure of a set amount of abstract
labor power, as measured by the number of hours worked or, in a piecework
economy, the number of units produced (or, for that matter, the number
of students graduated).

Rather, a stipend furnishes that which someone needs and, more precisely, that which enables someone to fulfill the responsibilities that
compose any given position. Unlike a wage, a stipend does not provide
remuneration for work already completed; rather, it enables ongoing performance of the duties one assumes on appointment. Think, for example,
of a minister or perhaps a soldier, both of whom are "maintained" so that they
can contribute on an ongoing basis to the goods that define the collective
enterprises of which they are members. While a stipend may assume the
form of a salary paid in the medium of money, its distinctive nature is better illustrated by the provision of a qualitative good such as housing. That
good is a condition that enables one to do one's work well rather than a
cash payment that is then employed to purchase commodities external to
one's job. As such, the term *stipend* coheres with a vocabulary that speaks of
fulfilling the obligations of a "vocation," thereby advancing an enterprise's
"mission." If this language now appears quaint, that is itself a revealing indicator of our difficulty in recalling the unique nature of corporations that
are anything but engines of capital accumulation.

Expropriation Codified

As Harvard's faculty grew, albeit incrementally, its members began to meet
apart from the corporation and, beginning in 1725, to keep an official record of their proceedings. Although an extraconstitutional body, during
the next few decades what came to be known as Harvard's "immediate
government" quietly assumed considerable responsibility for the college's
curricular as well as student conduct issues. This unrecognized body provided Harvard's instructors a modest counterweight to the overseers as
well as a measure of independence from the corporation, from which, as
we have seen, resident fellows were entirely excluded by the early nineteenth century.

One of the signatories to the 1824 memorial, Andrews Norton, gave a
voice to Harvard's immediate government when, one year later, he delivered an audacious speech before the overseers. In his extended oration,

Norton argued that the resident instructors of the college are its "proper representatives." Because they alone are "accountable for the state of the institution," they must be formally granted "all the powers . . . that accompany such responsibility," including the power to nominate all faculty members and to originate "all laws respecting its instruction and discipline" of students. In exercising these powers, the faculty should only be checked by the community's representatives, which Norton identified with the board of overseers but only because its membership included the governor and other state officials as well as several clergy and laypersons: "The resident instructers [sic], as immediate governors of a college, and the public, for which they labor, under whose direction they should be, and to which they should be responsible, are the only two parties properly concerned in the management of such an institution." Because no other body should intervene between the professors and the public, the "vexatious oversight" of the corporation must be attenuated or, better still, eliminated altogether.[42]

With this impolitic argument, Norton effectively conceded the resident instructors' inability to resecure control of the corporation. To compensate, he proposed a reassignment of its governance capacities to the entire faculty in its capacity as the college's "immediate government," with the overseers confined to the modest oversight functions specified in the 1650 charter. Without mentioning Norton by name, the board of overseers effectively rejected his proposal when, a few months later, it approved a new code of statutes for the college, which was quickly endorsed by the corporation as well.

This code sought to pacify Norton and his ilk by first throwing the faculty an apparent bone. Specifically, in section 12, the code formally acknowledged the independent existence of a body that it called "the Faculty of the University" but that was previously known as its "immediate government." This redesignation may sound inconsequential to contemporary ears, but it is not. Whereas "immediate government" figures instructors as indispensable participants in ruling the college's daily affairs, this new designation does no such thing. This is made emphatically clear in section 13, which reads in its entirety: "The Corporation and Overseers constitute the Government of the University."[43] The faculty are thereby denied any rightful claim to rule, as unaccountable others affirm a monopoly over that power's possession and exercise.

If the "Faculty of the University" is not an intrinsic part of Harvard's government, then what exactly is its place and role within the college? According to the new code, this body is assigned "the immediate care and government of the students" and, in discharging this duty, the responsibility "to hear, determine, and punish any offence" committed by its charges. The faculty is thus figured as a subordinate body to which certain quasi-parental duties are delegated by the "Government of the University." These responsibilities may be reconfigured or revoked at any time by those who, because they are exclusive governors of the college, can longer be held accountable by those to whom these disciplinary tasks have been assigned. The faculty, in other words, must now act within the confines of a constitutional order it no longer governs. No longer citizens of an incorporated body politic, they are now subjects in the guise of employees who, as such, must fulfill any duties that "have been, or may be, assigned to them by the Government."[44] Harvard's professors, to quote Norton, are thereby "degrade[d]" to the status of "mere ministerial officers" whose job, as is true of all such officers, is to execute with exactness the mandates of their superiors.[45] (Here, note the emerging opposition between the "administration" and the "faculty," which, on my account, we will come to consider misguided when the academy is eventually reconstituted as a republican member corporation.)

The 1825 code does not render these employees entirely voiceless (although, arguably, it aims to tame that voice by authorizing the faculty, for the first time, to conduct its business by "committee"). Specifically, the code states that the faculty shall meet periodically "to perform the duties incumbent on them; to communicate and compare their opinions and information respecting the conduct and character of the Students and the state of the University; and to consider and suggest such measures as may tend to its improvement." A later section, admittedly, gives the appearance of ceding greater power to the faculty by authorizing its members "to *propose* at all times to the Government, any laws or measure, which they find requisite or useful for the effectual exercise of their functions."[46] But the power to propose to another remains a far cry from the right to dispose of one's own collective affairs, and that capacity the faculty no longer possess.

According to this inversion of the constitution established in 1650, it is the board that initiates, the corporation (whose members the board has selected and installed) that concurs, and the faculty that may speak if it pleases but must finally obey. What this revolution portends for the scope of faculty authority is clarified when the board's 1825 code mandates modifications to Harvard's admission policies, divides the faculty into departments, and, although the faculty indicated its unequivocal opposition, specifies curricular changes that one day will morph into Charles Eliot's elective system. Granted, individual faculty members remain "authorized to make such occasional changes and substitutions in the ordinary course of study" as they see fit to "excite the Students to the most earnest and successful application."[47] But this is so much tinkering within the margins of an educational program dictated by those who are not members of a "little republic" but rulers of an autocracy.

At bottom, expulsion of Harvard's instructors from the corporate offices assigned them by the 1650 charter is predicated on their opponents' antidemocratic and arguably un-American animus toward the form of self-rule mandated by that founding document: "The resident tutors should never be able to make a major part [of the corporation], because we think it contrary to the light of nature, that any should have an overruling voice in making those laws, by which themselves must be governed."[48] Had a comparable usurpation occurred at Oxford or Cambridge, Ware and his colleagues predict, no doubt that would have "raise[d] a rebellion." That this has not occurred at Harvard testifies to "the *gradual manner*, in which the invasion of our charter has taken place," which has engendered "a forgetfulness and oblivion of our early traditions" and so in time our "acquiescence."[49] As these little acts of appropriation have accreted over time, "the entire control of the college has been carried from its walls and monopolized by the leading gentlemen of Boston."[50] If that is so, then its tutors are quite right to conclude that what is still called "Harvard" is no longer the college that once deserved this name.[51]

6
The Marshall Plan

When Webster Wept

"'It is, Sir, as I have said, a small college. And yet there are those who love it.' Here the feelings which he had thus far succeeded in keeping down, broke forth. His lips quivered; his firm cheek trembled with emotion; his eyes were filled with tears. 'When I see my Alma Mater surrounded, like Cesar [sic] in the senate house, by those who are reiterating stab upon stab, I would not for this right hand have her say to me, 'Et tu quoque, mi fili [And thou, too, my son].'"[1]

Refusing to skewer a college he likens to his mother in the guise of a Roman dictator, Daniel Webster closed his argument before the US Supreme Court in *Trustees of Dartmouth College v. Woodward* (1819). The opinion for the Court, written by John Marshall, who borrowed heavily from Webster, did much to bring to a halt the governance controversies that had roiled William & Mary as well as Harvard for the better part of two centuries. To do so, Marshall effaces questions of college governance, and he does that by denying the inherently political character of the academic corporation in favor of its construction as a charitable enterprise created by means of contract and organized in the form of a trust.

This representation does much to hasten the transformation of faculty members into employees rather than as members of an academic corporation entitled to participate in governing its affairs. In *Dartmouth*, although he only mentions instructors in passing, Marshall establishes a condition that is key to construction of their work in capitalist terms. Specifically, he defines the college as itself a form of private property that is rightfully, exclusively, and unilaterally managed by those figured as its owners. If the right to administer college assets is entirely vested in governing boards qua proprietors, others can lay claim to those resources only in the form of compensation for services rendered.

One might be tempted, therefore, to consider *Dartmouth* a pivotal moment in the academy's "corporatization." That gets matters wrong because, again, the question is not when the academy became a corporation but, rather, what kind of corporation it is to be. Deployment of this epithet is more apt, however, if its purpose is to call our attention to the reconstitution of American colleges as autocratic property corporations. This transmutation is obscured by the common representation of trustees in charters and elsewhere as sole "members" of the academic corporation. This term is mistaken, however, because there are and can be no "members" in the autocratic variant of the corporate form. Neither rulers nor ruled qualify for this designation because neither inhabits a republican body politic that may select leaders but has no place for monopolists of power defined by their unaccountability to those they govern.

More's Indian Charity School

While serving as pastor of a Congregational church in Connecticut, the charter of Dartmouth College explains, Eleazar Wheelock "clothed, maintained and educated a number of the children of the Indian natives, with a view to their carrying the Gospel, in their own language, and spreading the knowledge of the great Redeemer, among their savage tribes."[2] To improve the prospects of this school in the making, in 1754 Wheelock persuaded his neighbor, Joshua More, to purchase and then donate the land on which it sat. On completing this deal, More was appointed master of an enterprise that, in recognition of his bounty, now bore his name. Seeking to inspire confidence in other potential benefactors, one year later, Wheelock, More, and several other locals established a legal trust to manage the charity's assets, including several recently purchased enslaved persons. These plans were scuttled, however, when More died, the trust was dissolved, and More's widow regranted the land to Wheelock.

For the next eleven years, hoping to put the school on a secure legal foundation and so persuade others to open their purse strings, Wheelock sought a charter from the colonial assembly. These efforts came to naught, and so, in 1768, Wheelock dispatched a fellow pastor, Nathaniel Whittaker, and Samson Occom, a converted Mohegan and More School alumnus, to England and Scotland on a fund-raising campaign. Thanks chiefly to Occom's inspired preaching, their efforts proved far more successful than anticipated. As gifts accumulated, several wary donors asked how they could be certain that funds given to Whittaker, who had been granted power of attorney by Wheelock, would in fact be used to support the school. To assuage these worries, nine English gentlemen, headed by William Legge, the earl of Dartmouth, were designated trustees of these funds, and a second group, composed of local ministers, was appointed to manage the school's affairs in the colonies.

When Whittaker and Occom returned to America, Occom learned that Wheelock had betrayed him: first, by failing to make good on his promise to safeguard Occom's wife and seven children from destitution; second, by relocating the school from Lebanon, Connecticut, to Hanover, New Hampshire; and third, by declaring his intent to exclude Indigenous students. "I am very Jealous," wrote Occom, "that instead of Your Seminary Becoming alma [nourishing] Mater, She will be too alba [white] mater to Suckle the Tawnees, for She is already adorned up too much like the Popish Virgin Mary."[3] Occom's complaints were ignored, as Wheelock turned his attention to securing "a legal incorporation in order to the safety and well-being of said seminary, and its being capable of the tenure and disposal of lands and bequests for the use of the same."[4] That accomplished, Wheelock understood, this legal form would reconstitute the school as a body politic in possession of powers it could not exercise so long as it remained but a trust.

Dartmouth, Inc.

In 1769, on behalf of King George III, the colonial governor of New Hampshire issued a charter for a college now named after one of its English trustees. The prototype for the document drafted by Wheelock was the 1745 charter issued to America's third colonial college and his own alma mater, Yale. By prescribing a single board to which all powers of governance and rights of ownership were assigned,[5] Yale's charter departed from that of William & Mary, which provided for a corporation of masters but also a board of visitors, as well as that of Harvard, which provided for a corporation of fellows but also a board of overseers. So constituted, write Hofstadter and Metzger, the founding of Yale "marks a momentous break in the origins of American academic government, the dividing line between the dual system of the first two charters and the single board that was to be the almost universal pattern ever afterwards."[6]

Very much aware of Harvard's internal conflicts and eager to prevent a repeat of its lapse into liberal Congregationalism, the orthodox framers of Dartmouth's charter mimicked their Connecticut neighbors by providing for a unitary board composed of Wheelock and eleven other persons drawn from the province's government and ministry: "The trustees of said college may be and shall be one body corporate and politic, in deed, action and name, and shall be called, named and distinguished by the name of the Trustees of Dartmouth College."[7] By establishing a monocratic source of rule, Dartmouth's charter preempted someone like Nicholas Sever from appealing to a second governing body to contest his exclusion from the corporation of which, on his account, he was rightfully a member. By appointing only laypersons to that board (with the exception of Wheelock, whom the charter designated as the college's first president), Dartmouth's constitution also precluded irksome instructors, like John Bracken at William & Mary, from suing to reclaim an office within a corporation from which, on his account, he could only rightfully be removed by his fellow members.

In the eyes of the law, then, Dartmouth College *is* its corporation, and this corporation *is* its board of trustees. Like its predecessors, the 1769 charter granted to Dartmouth's board the usual panoply of "privileges, advantages, liberties, and immunities" that define all corporations: the power to "plea and be impleaded" in courts of law; to "possess and enjoy" forms of property, including "tenements, hereditaments, jurisdictions and franchises"; to "nominate and appoint" the college's tutors and professors; to grant degrees to its students; "to make and establish such ordinances, orders and laws, as may tend to the good and wholesome government of the said college"; and to devise a seal whose employment bears witness to the authoritative actions of this sempiternal juridical person, as these are enacted by its mortal agents.[8]

In the exercise of these powers, Dartmouth's board is not subject to review by the functional equivalent of Harvard's overseers or William & Mary's visitors, and so we might conclude that it is altogether unbound. After all, its members alone determine the corporation's composition, so it is a self-perpetuating elite; its members alone are authorized to manage this corporation's property, so it is a monopolist; and, finally, its members alone possesses the power to rule, so it is an autocrat. Of course, that board may delegate some measure of what the charter calls the college's "immediate care" to a president, senior administrators, and even to professors. But no matter how much power Dartmouth's trustees elect to cede, that does not render these others anything but subordinates whose opportunity to take part in governance depends, in the last analysis, on the ongoing acquiescence of the board.

But is the Board of Trustees of Dartmouth College truly sovereign, as this representation appears to suggest? Not exactly. The board is at least formally checked by the charter's requirement that its powers be exercised in pursuit of the end for which they were granted: "We" [the royal "we"] "will, ordain, grant and constitute that there be a college erected in our said province of New Hampshire by the name of Dartmouth College, for the education and instruction of youth of the Indian tribes in this land in reading, writing, and all parts of learning which shall appear necessary and expedient for civilizing and Christianizing children of pagans, as well as in all liberal arts and sciences, and also of English youth and any others."[9] The board's character as a fiduciary of this purpose leaves open the possibility, as the Concerned Faculty of Tulsa understood, that someone could seek a writ or some other court order aimed at compelling the board to do what its state-issued charter says it must.

Equally important, the board is not without check because it can take no action that contravenes the sovereign laws of the land. But this leaves another and still more basic question unanswered: Can the corporation's political creator, whether the Crown, the provincial governor acting in the monarch's name, or, in time, the New Hampshire legislature, amend Dartmouth's founding document and thus remake the college's constitution? Or is that charter, once conferred, beyond modification by its creator absent the concurrence of its creature? To affirm this last claim would be to issue Dartmouth's governing board a remarkable grant of authority as well as autonomy from the sovereign people's legislative agent. Whether the board can in fact sustain this bold claim is, in the last analysis, the question that is resolved in *Woodward v. Trustees of Dartmouth College*.

Standoff at Hanover

On August 26, 1816, two opposed boards of trustees convened on the Dartmouth campus, each claiming rightful standing as the college's corporate representative. To thwart their rivals, eight members of the board constituted in accordance with the terms of the 1769 charter gathered in Dartmouth's library, locking the door behind them. Undeterred, the second board, constituted in accordance with revisions to the charter adopted by the New Hampshire legislature in 1816 (more on this enactment later), met in the office of the college treasurer, William H. Woodward.

Unable to muster a quorum, the board renamed the Trustees of Dartmouth University by the 1816 act returned to the legislature and pushed for passage of one bill that reduced to nine the number of persons required to do business and then another that provided for imposition of a $500 fine each time any officer took action under the authority of the older board—in other words, the Trustees of Dartmouth College. In response, the targets of these acts, now dubbed the "Octagon," asserted their "corporate rights" and declared that they would not obey the 1816 act. To justify their refusal, the gang of eight claimed that the legislature had exceeded its legitimate powers and hence that this issue must now be adjudicated by the courts.

The Octagon's suit was directed specifically against Woodward because he had cleverly hidden away the college's charter, seal, financial accounts, and other essential records. When his opponents demanded that these goods be returned, Woodward refused, and hence, in an act of suspect legality, the older board removed him from office. Not to be outdone, supporters of the newer university board devoted the better part of a weekend to vandalizing the locks that had thwarted them earlier. Dartmouth's existence as a legal entity was now very much up for grabs, for each of two boards affirmed exclusive title to personate this juridical creature.

In August 1817, the college and the university, each commanding the allegiance of different student bodies, scheduled simultaneous commencement exercises. When a group of about sixty persons armed with clubs and canes occupied the building where this ceremony was customarily held, representatives of the university, although fortified with rocks, concluded that prudence was the better part of valor and so relocated to another building. Three months later, a second altercation occurred as the university's supporters wielded an ax to force their way into the libraries of two student literary societies. More violence was averted only when, met by about 150 students and friends of the college, the perpetrators were "persuaded" to leave without the books they had come to secure.

The Autocratic Academy within a Political Republic

How, we might wonder, did matters at Hanover come to such an awkward stalemate? Like every other governance controversy discussed in this book, the dispute at Dartmouth and, in this instance, the constitutional question it eventually spawns has tangled roots that are personal as well as political, petty as well as principled. I cannot do justice to these roots here.[10] They require some mention, however, because any account of *Dartmouth* that conceals this case's grubbier dimensions, as students of constitutional law typically do and Dartmouth's self-congratulatory website does even better,[11] occludes this case's embeddedness in partisan struggles over status, privilege, and, of key importance here, the question of how the power of rule is to be distributed within the corporate academy. To sanitize these disputes is to lose sight of the larger question posed by *Dartmouth*: How are we to think about the situation of an academy that organizes this power autocratically within a body politic committed to the principles of republicanism?

Dartmouth finds it earliest origins in a conflict between the college's president and its trustees, one that eventually exceeded the capacity of both to control its course. When Eleazar Wheelock died on April 24, 1779, his twenty-five-year-old son, John, was appointed president. John, it appears, did not lack self-esteem: "I am convinced," a contemporary suggested, "that this great man's erudition has bounds, but *he* is of a different opinion."[12] Inheriting his father's autocratic disposition, John soon clashed with the board over multiple matters, including the president's rightful role in selecting new trustees. These animosities spilled into public view when in 1804 John Smith, who had served for several decades as professor of classics as well as minister of Hanover's College Church, expressed his hope that the newly appointed Phillips Professor of Divinity, Roswell Shurtleff, would take over his ministerial duties. The church's congregation, "having endured Smith's monumental dullness for years, heartily concurred."[13] Wheelock, however, refused to permit Smith, a Presbyterian, to offload his pastoral duties, which irked several of Dartmouth's Congregationalist trustees who were eager to see him go. When the two sides proved unable to reach a compromise, Wheelock's associates began to meet in the college chapel, while Shurtleff's followers holed up in Hanover's meetinghouse.

With their breach now entangled in sectarian controversy, the trustees took additional steps to constrain the power of a president they had never much cared for by removing his disciplinary prerogatives and, soon after, his title to participate in recitations of the senior class. Sure that the trustees would not cease their harassment until they succeeded in ousting him, Wheelock enlisted the aid of his longtime friend Elijah Parish. Doing the president's bidding, Parish anonymously published an eighty-eight-page attack on the trustees that was in fact penned by Wheelock and given the innocuous title *Sketches of the History of Dartmouth College, 1770–1815.*

With this document's appearance, an internecine feud was reconfigured as a controversy about Dartmouth's corporate constitution and, more particularly, about how and by whom this body politic was to be governed. *Sketches* contended that the trustees' "tyrannical" aim was to secure absolute control over the college by stripping Wheelock of all power, thereby violating the charter and specifically the provision that vests "the care of education and government of the students in the president":[14] "Each member" (of the board of trustees), *Sketches* alleged, "has the spirit of a despot, and united they form the accumulated despotism of the *corps.*" Their oppressive designs, "formed in secret," are now checked only by the integrity of Dartmouth's beleaguered president who, if he sometimes appears irksome, has good reason to do so: "We [recall that "we" is Wheelock himself] believe he possesses too much elevation of mind to be delighted with animosities and contentions, that quagmire of vermin. If firmly to retain the religion of his fathers, consecrated by divine revelation; if to retain principles sanctioned by the experience of ages; to be inviolably attached to the original establishment and design of the seminary, may be called contention, then he is contentious." In closing, *Sketches* called for a concentrated show of public support in favor of Dartmouth's current president. Absent that, he will not long prove able to ward off the nefarious designs of "strangers" who know not "the springs and wheels of the Institution" and who too often "inhale their conceptions of plans, and measures, from visionary or interested informers."[15]

Charged with violating the college charter, fostering a schism in a local church, perverting college funds, colluding against the president in electing hostile trustees, and undermining the education of its students, the trustees responded with a pamphlet of their own: *A Vindication of the Official Conduct of the Trustees of Dartmouth College.* Characterizing *Sketches* as an "inconsistent, incorrect, contradictory, confused and unintelligible mixture of fact, reasoning and invective," *Vindication* insisted that it was not the trustees but Wheelock who harbored despotic aims: "Dr. Wheelock claims the right to exercise the supreme Legislative, Executive, and Judicial powers of the whole Corporation," which, were this consolidation to be fully accomplished, would render the trustees superfluous. Indeed, *Vindication* ominously speculated, the president's clandestine ambition is to secure control of Dartmouth's assets so that he can "make the College his heir; but upon the condition that the Institution, its authorities and funds, should pass, like a West-India plantation with the slaves and cattle upon it, to his actual heirs and descendants."[16]

In what he called a "sequel" to *Sketches*, Wheelock responded to *Vindication* by warning that Dartmouth's cabalistic board may soon ally itself with other oligarchical interests that "have an interest of their own separate from the common good."[17] Should that occur, there is little reason to doubt that Dartmouth's trustees will soon employ their reinforced power to "*affect the political independence of the peoples, and move* the springs of their government."[18] The very constitution of New Hampshire as a republic, in short, is now jeopardized by a corporation whose members, aided by other wannabe despots, hope to seize powers never conceded by Dartmouth's charter or by the state's citizens. Should this come to pass, the only entity that might be able to muster sufficient clout to challenge this usurpation is "that body, which is armed with all of the power of the former sovereign [i.e., the Crown]—the *legislature of the state*, established and authorized by the Constitution to secure the rights of the citizens."[19]

Wheelock's plea for political intervention into Dartmouth's affairs was taken up when in 1816 the Republicans rousted the Federalists by gaining control of New Hampshire's state government. Adopting this cause as his own, the new governor, William Plumer, reiterated Wheelock's fear that the college, dominated by its trustees, might soon be captured by interlocking elites more interested in using the college for selfish ends than advancing higher education's true purposes. The current trustees must therefore be defeated. Still more fundamentally, Dartmouth's rule by a self-perpetuating board must be denied, for this vestige of monarchical absolutism is "hostile to the spirit and genius of a free government": "The American demands a college without an oligarchy, an oligarchy without a despot."[20]

Dartmouth's charter must therefore be revised, Plumer concluded in his inaugural address. The autocratic rule sanctioned by that charter is antithetical to the principles for which the Revolution was fought, and in support of this position, Plumer was quick to cite William & Mary's best-known alumnus, Thomas Jefferson:

The idea that institutions established for the use of the nation cannot be touched nor modified, even to make them answer their end, because of rights gratuitously supposed in those employed to manage them in trust for the public, may perhaps be a salutary provision against the abuses of a monarch, but is most absurd against the nation itself. Yet our lawyers and priests generally inculcate this doctrine, and suppose the preceding generations held the earth more freely than we do; had a right to impose laws on us, unalterable by ourselves, and that we, in like manner, can make laws and impose burdens on future generations, which they will have no right to alter; in fine, that the earth belongs to the dead and not to the living.[21]

On Jefferson's account, certain privileged gentry have a material stake in rendering the autocratic constitution of the American academy untouchable. To do so, they deny to today's republican citizens the authority to unmake a form of rule that their forebears, too much infatuated with England's monarchy, established to secure their own power. To camouflage this purpose, they dress up their defense, first, by identifying their partial interests with the public good and, second, by claiming that any frontal challenge to these autocrats is sure to endanger everyone's inalienable rights. These pretensions must be unmasked if the American academy is serve as a homologous helpmate to a free political order rather than as its antithetical contradiction.

Heeding Jefferson's exhortation, in June 1816 the New Hampshire legislature passed and the governor signed into law a bill that reaffirmed the general powers of incorporation granted to the trustees by the 1769 charter but also amended that document by renaming the Trustees of Dartmouth College the Trustees of Dartmouth University; increasing this body's number from twelve to twenty-one (but without removing the current trustees); adding a board of overseers vested with the power to confirm, disapprove, or veto actions taken by the trustees; appointing to this new board as ex officio members the governor and lieutenant governor as well as the president of the state senate and the speaker of the house; authorizing the governor's council to fill vacancies on the board of overseers and appoint new trustees; and, finally, providing for the nomination of all professors by the trustees but subject to final approval by the newly created board of overseers.[22] It is this law that the Trustees of Dartmouth College refused to obey and that in turn set the stage for recasting this essentially political quarrel as a depoliticized dispute about the import of Article I, Section 10, of the US Constitution for a charter now (mis)read as a contract and a body politic now (mis)construed as a trust.

The State Presents Its Case

The constitutional question at issue in *Dartmouth* is framed as follows: Did the New Hampshire legislature violate the US Constitution when, via its 1816 act, it modified the terms of the college's 1769 charter? That question cannot be answered absent determination of the kind of corporation created by the charter; and the answer to that question in turn will specify the college's correct constitution of rule.

Both parties to *Dartmouth* inherit from English common law a typology of corporations codified by William Blackstone in his *Commentaries*. For present purposes, most pertinent is the distinction he draws between ecclesiastical and lay corporations (devoted, respectively, to spiritual and temporal matters) and, as illustrated by John Bracken's case at William & Mary, the latter's subdivision into civil and eleemosynary bodies. Examples of civil corporations include municipalities, like the City of London, but also those enterprises, like the Massachusetts Bay Company, that aim to harness private interest to the accomplishment of public goods. Eleemosynary corporations, by contrast, are charitable enterprises whose purpose, Blackstone tells us, is "perpetual distribution of the free alms, or bounty, of the founder of them to such persons as he has directed," and whose most frequently cited examples "are all hospitals for the maintenance of the poor, sick, and impotent."[23]

To explain why the state of New Hampshire considers Dartmouth a lay corporation of the specifically civil sort, its counsel begins by making several points that on the face of it appear beyond challenge. What the charter of 1769 created was a corporation. That corporation was summoned into being when a sovereign—in this instance, King George III—created an artificial person and conferred on this immaterial being a bundle of powers so that it could better achieve its designated purposes. Although certain of these purposes implicate religion (saving the souls of heathens, for example), that does not render Dartmouth an ecclesiastical corporation, for it is not a church. Rather, achievement of this denominational end is "for the benefit of said Province,"[24] and only because the college pursues this broader civic purpose has the state granted it the authority to award recognized degrees. To say this is not to deny that Eleazar Wheelock and his supporters are rightly denominated the "founders" of Dartmouth College. But their deeds should not be confused with the constitution of Dartmouth as an incorporated entity. After all, it is only in virtue of its status as a disembodied creature of law that the college can endure long after Wheelock and its donors have expired.

The sovereign's issuance of Dartmouth's charter was not the fulfillment of an obligation or the satisfaction of a request (although petitions to the Crown often did in fact antecede the granting of corporate status), but something more akin to the giving of a gift: "And we do further, of our special grace, certain knowledge and mere motion, for us, our heirs and successors, will, give, grant and appoint that the said trustees and their successors shall forever hereafter be, in deed, act and name, a body corporate and politic."[25] Common in proclamations issued by the Crown, the phrase "special grace, certain knowledge and mere motion" indicates that this action is taken by a sovereign who freely and knowingly bestows on a subject a bounty that was neither required nor earned and so could have been withheld. In this instance, the Crown's grant takes the form of a "franchise," which Blackstone defines as "a royal privilege, or branch of the king's prerogative, subsisting in the hands of a subject,"[26] or, in this case, the college.

When the legal trust established by Wheelock in 1768 to ensure safekeeping of the donations secured by Whittaker and Occam was reconstituted in the form of a corporation, the sovereign's authority over this franchise did not disappear, but it was significantly attenuated. Once the charter is conferred, the Trustees of Dartmouth College is now in possession of certain powers that can be affirmed against state encroachment. But unlike the inalienable "natural" rights of persons, as canonized, for example, in Jefferson's "Declaration of Independence," these capacities and liberties do not exist prior to or independent of that state and so are not absolute.

To illustrate, this corporation's right to enact and enforce bylaws applicable to all within its jurisdiction is a power conferred on it by the state via the charter. The delegation of this power does not create a principal-agent relationship—that is, one that renders the latter nothing but an instrument for accomplishing the will of the former. Instead, the college qua corporation is granted considerable discretionary authority to determine how best to accomplish its public purpose, and that autonomy is encapsulated in its right to exercise self-rule. The incorporated college, therefore, is not entirely autonomous, but neither is it a mere administrative unit of the state. Dartmouth is a legal dependent insofar as it is ultimately a creature of the state, but at the same time it is operationally independent of that state in its possession and exercise of the powers that constitute it as a corporation.

The Revolution did not modify this corporation's legal status, attorneys for New Hampshire proceed, but only transferred authority over it to the nation's sovereign people, acting through their elected representatives. Nor did the Revolution alter the purpose for which these powers were granted, which remains that of securing the distinctly public good that is education. Nor, finally, did the Revolution undo the status of Dartmouth's trustees as well as the college's other personnel as servants of this public good (although, again, this is not to say that they are to be identified, for example, with tax collectors, municipal clerks, or other persons who are legally required to execute with exactitude the mandates of the formal political bodies that employ them).

What this representation implies for the principal question at issue in *Dartmouth* is summed up by an attorney for the state of New Hampshire: Dartmouth's charter "is not a contract of a private nature concerning property or other private interest." Rather, it is "a grant of a publick nature, for publick purposes," and, for this reason, it is "liable to be revoked or modified by the supreme power of the state."[27] No one questions the legislature's ultimate authority to alter the laws of incorporated municipalities or otherwise preempt their powers as a state's collective good requires. Nor does anyone contest the state's authority to infringe on private interests when compelling public interests are at stake (think, for example, of the power of eminent domain). Why, then, should the state's prerogative be otherwise in the case of a corporation whose powers are held in trust for the people of New Hampshire? In sum, the corporation named "Trustees of Dartmouth College" was created not "for the accommodation of the incumbents but for the benefit of the community" and so must "yield to such changes as the legislature deem that the publick good requires."[28]

On this account, argues the chief justice of the New Hampshire Superior Court, Dartmouth's board members are not lords ruling over a petty fiefdom by unilateral fiat but, rather, guardians of a public commission: "The education of the rising generation is a matter of highest public concern and is worthy of the best attention of every legislature. But make the trustees independent and they will ultimately forget that their office is a public trust—will at length consider these institutions as their own—will overlook the great purposes for which their powers were originally given, and will exercise them only to gratify their own private views and wishes, or to promote the narrow purposes of a sect or a party."[29] Again, this is not to render the college a mere branch of government, for that would eliminate the autonomy it acquires once incorporated and which it must enjoy if those who retain this independence are to determine how best to accomplish the college's public purpose. However, this is to remind us that in the last analysis the college's powers remain accountable to those who established this corporate body politic as an integral part of the larger republic to which it belongs.

Were someone to deny that the New Hampshire legislature has the authority to amend the college's charter absent approval by Dartmouth's trustees, the state's attorneys conclude, that would indicate a misunderstanding of the source and nature of corporate authority. To hold that a corporation can block modification of its charter by refusing its assent is to "make[s] the deputy superior to his principal," to "raise[s] the servant above his master."[30] Dartmouth's incorporated trustees, in short, must not be considered a private sovereign vested with the capacity to thwart those who conceded the very powers this body now exercises.

So, too, were someone to deny the authority of the state to modify the charter on the grounds that this somehow violates the private rights of current board members, that would misconstrue what it is to be a trustee of a civil corporation. Via the charter of 1769, Dartmouth's governing board "was clothed with various powers, capacities, and franchises, all of which were to be exercised for the benefit of the publick, but not one of them for the advantage of its own members, or of any individuals whatever."[31] Do individual trustees have any particular interest in or reap greater rewards from the education of New Hampshire's residents than do the state's other citizens? They do not, and hence they can claim no specifically personal wrong should the legislature reduce the efficacy of each by, for example, increasing the size of Dartmouth's board from twelve to twenty-one.

To think otherwise is to regard the office held by a trustee as so much private property for which judicial redress is available should its proprietor's rights be violated. But, in their capacity as fiduciaries of a public trust, the trustees own none of the college's assets, including the offices they now hold. It is not they but the impersonal entity named "Trustees of Dartmouth College" that is their rightful and sole owner: "The old members had not personally any such title that could be taken from them; and the new members have personally acquired none," for the "title remains unaltered in the corporation."[32]

John Marshall Responds

Following a state superior court ruling in favor of the New Hampshire legislature, the Trustees of Dartmouth College appealed to the US Supreme Court, where this ruling was reversed by a vote of five to one. Writing on behalf of the majority, Chief Justice John Marshall argued that the 1769 charter is a contract; that this contract's inviolability is guaranteed by the US Constitution; and, therefore, that the state of New Hampshire violated the highest law of the land when it amended Dartmouth's founding document.

How does Marshall arrive at these conclusions, each of which requires that he overlook, deny, or misrepresent essential features of the institutional form that is a corporation? To answer this question is to see how the Court's ruling and Marshall's opinion contribute to the constitution of the American academy as an autocratic corporation whose consolidation I sketched in the preceding two chapters but that is now fortified by a capitalist understanding of private property and the prerogatives of ownership. *Dartmouth* thereby does essential work in paving the way for the contemporary academy's assumption of neoliberal form as it comes to be defined, first and foremost, by its contribution to capital accumulation, which is what I discuss in part 4.

What, according to Marshall, is the nature of the charter issued by the Crown in 1769 and effectively reissued by New Hampshire when, on achieving statehood, it became that charter's new authorizing agent? Foreshadowing the neoliberal construction of the corporation as a nexus of binding agreements, Marshall argues that via this charter New Hampshire and Dartmouth entered a "transaction" whose form is that of a legally binding "contract."[33] As I explained in chapter 2, however, this reading betrays a fundamental confusion. Incorporation by the state is not a bargain between two natural persons who, in pursuit of separate advantage, freely enter a pact whereby each acquires a legally enforceable right to that which the other has promised. Instead, contracts are made between two parties who, in the eyes of the law, *already* exist as subjects capable of entering into such agreements. In this instance, however, the charter is the legal device through which one of those two parties is created via an exercise of the state's prerogative power. To characterize Dartmouth's charter as a contract is, in other words, to presuppose that the incorporated college already exists as what it will become only once that charter is issued.

Marshall, however, must either ignore or deny that this is so. Indeed, in a preemptive strike aimed at forestalling all contradiction, Marshall avows that his representation of Dartmouth's charter as a contract is beyond debate: "It can require no argument to prove that the circumstances of the case constitute a contract. . . . This is plainly a contract to which the donors, and the Crown (to whose rights and obligations New Hampshire succeeds) were the original parties." On this representation, had the Trustees of

Dartmouth College consented to New Hampshire's modification of this contract's terms, the plaintiffs would have no cause to complain. They do in fact have cause, according to Marshall, because the state unilaterally altered the charter, understood now as contract, and in doing that essentially remade the college itself: "It is reorganized, and reorganized in a manner as to convert a literary institution, moulded according to the will of its founders, and placed under the control of private literary men, into a machine entirely subservient to the will of government."[34] Should the defendants prevail, in short, the college will in fact become merely an administrative arm of the state.

This unhappy result is foreclosed, Marshall contends, when the charter is rightly understood as a legally enforceable agreement that guarantees to the Trustees of Dartmouth College certain rights that are immunized against trespass, including and perhaps especially that perpetrated by the people's representatives. To authorize government to engage in such transgression is to forget, counsel for the plaintiffs insists, that "the security of private rights is the only valuable and important advantage, which a free government has over a despotick [sic] one."[35] Were the New Hampshire legislature allowed to modify Dartmouth's charter, that would sanction violation of the rights of the college at the hands of the state, and to permit that would be to jeopardize the principal distinction between the new American republic and its monarchical predecessor.

Why, though, is the charter the sort of contract that is protected by the US Constitution, and specifically Article I, Section 10, which denies individual states the authority to impair the "obligation of contracts"? That the Constitution guarantees the inviolability of private contracts was generally accepted at this time. Extension of this guarantee to the relationship between a state and the corporations it charters, whether a college, a commercial enterprise, or a church, was anything but beyond debate,[36] as the defendants' counterarguments make clear. To contest these arguments, Marshall does not contend that the Constitution protects all contracts against state impairment (hence, for example, state governments may unilaterally modify their civil laws governing divorce). Instead, he claims that the Contract Clause was specifically designed to protect the inviolable right to property against legislative infringement.

How, then, are the property rights of Dartmouth College's board violated by New Hampshire's 1816 act? To answer that, we must see how Marshall's conflation of a charter with a contract becomes entangled with his equally mistaken characterization of the college's charter as the very different legal instrument that is a trust.[37] Toward the start of his opinion, Marshall presents the charter's creature in terms that would have been altogether agreeable to Blackstone and that obtain regardless of whether we consider their civil or eleemosynary variants: "A corporation," Marshall writes, "is an artificial being, invisible, intangible, and existing only in contemplation of law. Being the mere creature of law, it possesses only those properties which the charter of its creation confers upon it either expressly or as incidental to its very existence." So, too, Marshall concedes the precapitalist representation of corporations as bodies that are granted their powers by the state only because they are committed to a "benefit to the public" rather than the self-regarding advantage of private parties.[38] By the end of his opinion, however, Marshall has come to characterize "the body corporate" as a legal instrument whose purpose is that of "representing the donors for the purpose of executing the trust."[39]

To what trust does Marshall refer and, as a preface to answering that question, what exactly is a trust? Created in the form of a private contract but in accordance with terms specified in law and enforceable by the state, a trust is a three-party relationship in which one party, the trustor (or "settlor"), transfers the bundle of rights that compose ownership of property (which may take the form of an estate, land, money, or any other asset) to a second party, the trustee, on behalf of a third party, the beneficiary (or equitable owner). Certified by a deed of trust, legal ownership of entrusted assets by the trustee is thereby separated from equitable ownership by the beneficiary. The former, however, remains bound to the latter by a fiduciary relationship that entails an obligation to manage the property transferred by the trustor in ways that ultimately serve the trust's beneficiary.

A trust and a corporation are distinct legal instruments. Creation of a trust, for example, does not call into being a body politic on which the state confers certain specific powers, including but not limited to the power to govern by establishing rules enforceable on those subject to the jurisdiction of any given corporation. A trust generates no body politic because its object is neither to structure the internal governance of a multimember association nor to facilitate the accomplishment of a uniquely public purpose but, instead, to manage private property and specifically to regulate its use through time. To serve as a trustee in this latter sense is, therefore, not identical to that anticipated by King George III when, in 1769, he declared that "the trustees of said college may and shall be one body corporate and politic, in deed, action and name, and shall be called, named and distinguished by the name of the Trustees of Dartmouth."[40]

Interpreting the charter as a document that creates a trust enables Marshall to represent the Trustees of Dartmouth College not as a legal entity whose officers derive their authority from the state's act of incorporation but as heirs obligated to do the bidding of the college's founder, Eleazar Wheelock, as well as the benefactors who supported his cause. Marshall, in other words, presents Dartmouth's earliest donors as something akin to settlors who invested their funds in a trust managed by the college's original "trustees." Via the charter, on his account, these trustees were then reconstituted as something akin to trustees with benefits and, specifically, the powers that accompany their legal constitution as a governing board.

Strictly speaking, on this account, the purpose of Dartmouth's incorporation is not to ensure the college's fidelity to the educational mission stated in its charter but to ensure the college's fidelity to the will of its benefactors. Yes, it is true that these benefactors hoped to promote the end of education. But the trustees are obligated to remain faithful to that purpose not because the state affirmed this end in the college's charter but because this is what its founders wished and for which they made their donations. As one attorney for the plaintiffs stated, in their corporate capacity, the trustees "merely take[s] and hold[s], in an artificial capacity, what they [Dartmouth's founder and original donors] before held, as natural persons, and to the same uses."[41] Or, as Daniel Webster put it, Dartmouth's acquisition of corporate status "is only done to perpetuate the trust in a more convenient manner. . . . The very object sought in obtaining such charter, and in giving property to such a corporation, is to make and keep it private property, and to clothe it with all the security and inviolability of private property."[42] Or, finally, as Marshall says of the college's benefactors, the "corporation is the assignee of their rights, stands in their place, and distributes their bounty as they would themselves have distributed it had they been immortal."[43] Dartmouth's trustees, in sum, are merely the incorporated agents who do the bidding of their unincorporated predecessors.

Marshall's reading of Dartmouth as a trust constituted as an eleemosynary corporation enables him to avoid figuring the college as a "civil" corporation, as the defendants had contended. Were Marshall to concede that point, he would then have to consider its trustees and perhaps also its faculty and staff as officers of a body politic whose powers, including that of self-governance, have been granted to it by the state. That in turn would open the door for governmental intervention in its affairs, including modification of its charter. To ward off this conclusion, Marshall resorts to asking questions that misrepresent the matter at hand: "Are the Trustees and professors public officers invested with any portion of political power pertaining in any degree in the administration of civil government, and performing duties which flow from the sovereign authority?"[44] To this question, he must answer no, since the office of trustee cannot be equated with, say, that of a mayor or any other state official. But this way of framing the matter is a red herring, for it distracts attention from the public purposes for which corporations such as Dartmouth are chartered but without thereby becoming so many administrative branches of government.

In sum, to sustain the Court's ruling, Marshall must effectively discredit his own initial representation of Dartmouth as an incorporated body politic that derives its existence from and owes its powers to the state-issued charter that affirmed the college's obligation to fulfill the distinctively public purpose that is education. Instead, Marshall presents the college as the product of a contractual agreement with the state that assumes the form of a trust created by its founders and benefactors for the purpose of ensuring that their property be forever employed in accordance with their original designation. With this misconstruction in place, he can then conclude that the Trustees of Dartmouth University must now return the college's property to the Trustees of Dartmouth College, including the financial records that track its disposition over time. To do otherwise would be to countenance the violation by one party of a contractual agreement both knowingly and voluntarily entered, and that of course would be to sanction what can only be described as an act of theft.

The violation perpetrated by the state of New Hampshire concerns not just these material artifacts, Marshall contends, but also injury done to the corporation itself. This harm was committed when the state enlarged the number of trustees and created a new body, the board of overseers. Marshall is coy about whether he believes that individual trustees can affirm a property right in their offices and hence represent the legislature's modification of the college's constitution as an act of confiscation. Marshall need not go there because, on his account, the corporation qua corporation can claim harm to a beneficial interest that is itself susceptible to judicial remedy: "The body corporate, as possessing the whole legal and equitable interest and completely representing the donors for the purpose of executing the trust, has rights which are protected by the Constitution."[45] If this be so, to return to Webster's peroration, the 1816 statute enacted by the New Hampshire legislature was an act not of law but of "violence" against an incorporated entity that can be injured even though, when stabbed, it does not bleed.[46]

Capitalizing on Autocracy

How should we think about Dartmouth College after *Dartmouth* in terms of the distinction between member and property corporations elaborated in chapter 3? Dartmouth is clearly not a member corporation, but nor is it unequivocally a property corporation, at least not as this legal fiction was anticipated in Roman and later realized in canon law. Instead, Dartmouth after *Dartmouth* is an odd hybrid: it is a property corporation whose board is constituted as a self-governing member corporation that rules autocratically over those who are not this corporation's members but its subjects.

A member corporation, recall, is a "little republic" whose members engage (or are entitled to engage) in the collective self-governance that is but one of several privileges granted to corporations of this sort. A paradigmatic example is the medieval European university, including but not limited to Cambridge and Oxford. The members of these bodies politic set binding rules for themselves and hold ultimate jurisdiction over the property owned by this corporation. Officers elected to regulate its quotidian affairs are not separate from but remain incorporated members to whom the entire body politic delegates specific responsibilities that can be modified or revoked at any time, just as officeholders themselves can be removed as the corporation's members see fit.

As we have seen, colonial America's most adequate academic incarnation of the member corporation can be found at William & Mary, where all professors, following execution of the 1729 transfer agreement, acquired the legal status of members of a self-governing college, whereas the role of its visitors, at least in its earliest years, was deferential and consultative. A more attenuated example of a member corporation was called into being by Harvard's 1650 charter, which restricted membership in the college's self-governing corporation to its president, treasurer, and five fellows, and, as at William & Mary, considerably circumscribed the capacity of overseers to intervene in its affairs.

At Dartmouth, something akin to a member corporation can be identified in its board of trustees who, by majority rule, are authorized to establish the bylaws that are to regulate its own internal affairs. But the "members" of this body are not members of a self-governing college but only of its governing board; and to this body and this body alone does the 1769 charter grant the powers, privileges, and immunities that define its legal status as a corporation, including the power to rule that college. A college so constituted is, therefore, an incorporated autocracy in which the participation of anyone but trustees in collective governance is not a right but a contingent concession of power—a gift, if you will—that can always be modified or recalled. The form of collective self-governance that defines a member corporation vanishes as the board's monopolization of the power of rule, which encompasses "the exclusive power to manage the funds, to choose the officers, and to regulate the corporate concerns according to their own discretion,"[47] usurps its place.

Is Dartmouth College therefore a property corporation? The answer is yes, but with a pernicious twist. As we saw in chapter 3, a property corporation is constituted via an incorporation of property. Furthermore, it is this abstract artificial person rather than any natural person or persons that is the legal owner of this property, and it is managed but never owned by this corporation's officers. The Trustees of Dartmouth College, however, is not its property incorporated but an incorporation of the college's rulers. Because Marshall misconstrues that corporation on the model of a legal trust, he represents these trustees not as officers who manage incorporated property but as that property's owners. *Dartmouth* thus imports into Dartmouth the autocratic governance structure that defines a property corporation but effectively erases any distinction between the body that owns this property and the officers who manage it.

How exactly is the character of rule transformed when Dartmouth is construed as a form of property and the board as its owners? The common law conception of property that prevailed in the late eighteenth and early nineteenth centuries is given apt articulation by Blackstone in his 1765 *Commentaries*. Therein Blackstone represents the right to property as an absolute dominion over things: it is the "sole and despotic dominion which one man claims and exercises over the external things of the world, in total exclusion of the right of any other individual in the universe."[48] With this definition in place, Blackstone then draws distinctions among the types of things that can be owned as property by noting that some are movable (such as crops), whereas others are immovable (such as land); and he further divides the latter into "corporeal hereditaments" that are tangible (such as a building) and "incorporeal hereditaments" (such as a political office) that are not. Over all forms, however, owners are sovereigns of the sort Blackstone calls "despots."[49]

Though not fully emancipated from preliberal understandings, *Dartmouth* essentially endorses Blackstone's representation of the prerogatives of private ownership, but with an important qualification: Because

Dartmouth is an eleemosynary corporation, its board is obligated by law to employ the college's property on behalf of the charitable ends specified in the 1769 charter, and hence its individual members cannot enrich themselves by employing that property for personal gain. In and of itself, though, this does not alter the fact that governing boards are now conceived as owners of the resources entrusted to them and, with this one caveat, are exclusively authorized to determine their disposition. In their capacity as property owners, moreover, governing boards are vested not just with the affirmative right to manage resources as they see fit but also to deny access to anyone who would trespass on that right. (To see the point, have another look at the sign at the beginning of chapter 9.) In *Dartmouth*, this right to exclude encompasses state actors, including those who represent the sovereign people. But it also extends to those who are subject to the jurisdiction of governing boards, including those who within a different corporate form we would call "members" but within this form we must call "employees." So designated, employees are subjects whose subordination is no longer considered political in nature because they are no longer deemed members of a corporation constituted on republican principles.

The Dispossessed

In *Dartmouth*, Marshall is almost entirely silent on the status of Dartmouth's employees. This is perhaps not surprising given that those who do compensated work for the college are not readily categorized in the terms of his analysis. They cannot be considered members of Dartmouth's corporation, for that standing is reserved to the college's trustees. But nor can they be this trust's beneficiaries, for, strictly speaking, that beneficiary is the mission for which donors contribute to the college qua trust (although, in a derivative sense, students fulfill this role insofar as they benefit from fulfillment of that mission).

How, then, should we figure Dartmouth's employees? In his concurring opinion, Justice Story provides only the slimmest of answers: the Trustees of Dartmouth College "shall have authority to appoint and remove the professors, tutors and other officers of the College, and to pay them . . . out of the corporate funds."[50] While this tells us very little about the particulars of the employer-employee relationship, the argument advanced in *Dartmouth* does much to pave the way for what, by the end of the nineteenth century, will come to be known as the "at-will employment doctrine."

When Marshall confuses Dartmouth's charter with a trust, he erroneously identifies the college's trustees as the effective owners of its incorporated property. If all others are by definition excluded from that property's possession, as affirmation of a sovereign "right" to specifically private property entails, then those who derive their livelihood from the college must be those who sell what the college does not own—that is, their labor power—in return for a wage. That this is so is made clear when Webster, in his oral argument, declares that faculty are not "members of the corporation; but they are appointed by the trustees, are removeable only by them, and have fixed salaries payable out of the general funds of the college."[51] Those who do compensated work for the college, in short, are neither members nor owners but, instead, something more akin to independent contractors whose defining link to the college consists of the cash nexus.

Representation of workers as employees whose sale of labor power to employers is mediated by a contract between two free and equal parties is a contingent historical accomplishment. It cannot come to prevail until earlier feudal characterizations of the relationship between superior and inferior are enfeebled or suppressed altogether. To see the point, recall John Bracken once again. In his suit against William & Mary, Bracken represented his position as a "freehold" or, as his counsel put it, "an estate for life." On this account, Bracken is the occupant of an office, Grammar School Master and Professor of Humanity, that is a form of incorporeal property; and he is entitled to retain that property so long as he performs the duties incumbent on its holder. Consequently, Bracken cannot be removed from his post via an act of discretionary authority, for that would constitute an unlawful deprivation of that which is rightfully his. To say this is not to render Bracken entirely immune to termination. But it is to say that he can only be removed for cause (i.e., on the ground that he has failed to fulfill the obligations of the office that is his); and it is to say that he cannot be ousted absent a hearing that adheres to the norms of due process and that is conducted by his peers. If these are missing, his dismissal will be an arbitrary act of force akin to that in which despots specialize.

As I mentioned in chapter 4, in *Bracken*, we see the medieval roots of the doctrine of academic tenure, a practice that was initially deployed to secure freeholds, whether in land or office, from encroachments by church or Crown. This representation of the office held by the subset of employees we call "faculty members" is not entirely absent from the juridical world Marshall and his ilk inhabit.[52] But it is losing its intelligibility as employment relations are disembedded from the web of feudal and ecclesiastical entanglements that once thwarted emergence of "the economy" as a de-politicized and autonomous sphere of activity ruled by the marketplace's self-regulating laws of supply and demand. On this new account, represen-tation of the academy as a body politic collectively governed by its incorpo-rated members gives way to representations of the academic corporation as but one more site where the conduct of compensated work is ruled by the harsh imperatives of capitalist labor markets.

True, traces of precapitalist understandings remain embedded here and there in American labor law (and, indeed, to call instructional employees "faculty *members*" is itself one such anachronism). Where these archaicisms linger, however, they chiefly benefit employers and hence, within the con-text of the academy, governing boards. For example, courts have held that employment contracts entail a tacit but generalized obligation on the part of employees to obey their employers unless an order is patently illegal or unethical. This requirement of deference ultimately derives from the feu-dal relationship between lord and serf and, specifically, its asymmetrical distinction between those entitled to command and those required to do as they are told. Employees, therefore, have a generalized duty of loyalty to their employers. However, aside from those that are expressly mandated by law (for example, to provide a workplace free from recognized safety hazards), employers have no corresponding fiduciary responsibilities to those they employ.

The lopsided distribution of power inherent within any autocratically organized property corporation, whether academic or otherwise, is thereby reinforced by a medieval relic that on the face of it is out of place within an economy that presupposes the equality of its formally free agents. This, recall, is the point Elizabeth Anderson makes when she argues that author-itarian forms of domination, what she calls "private government," remain at the heart of what appears to be so many uncoerced exchanges between those who hire and those who are hired. The political character of this rule is denied, however, when *Dartmouth* refashions the corporation on the model of a charitable trust whose purpose is to manage bequests on behalf of the dead. Doing so, Marshall disenfranchises and dispossesses the living who, on a different conception, might stand as "citizens" entitled to govern the corporations of which they are members but not owners.

In *Dartmouth*, the bone of contention is what Marshall misconstrues as a contract between the state of New Hampshire and the Trustees of Dartmouth College. Here, though, we are considering a contract between the trustees and employees, the terms of which are enforceable by the state of New Hampshire. This college is not a "little republic" constituted as a corporate franchise enfolded within a more comprehensive republic, but an autocratic private government guaranteed considerable immunity from state intervention by the Contract Clause of the US Constitution. More like a gated community than an ivory tower, *Dartmouth* does much to shield the college from political control while, at the same time, concentrating the power of trustees over their subordinates. By construing that power's objects as so many free economic agents, the specifically political character of this domination is obscured and in fact categorically denied.

Quis Custodiet Ipsos Custodes?

I close this chapter by returning to a question I raised earlier: What limits, if any, constrain governing boards, as these are represented in *Dartmouth*, within the autocratic academy? *Dartmouth* provides the foundation for a form of power, exercised by the academy's governing boards, that is best characterized as specifically "dictatorial." In *Special Report: COVID-19 and Academic Governance*, recall, the AAUP expressed its concern that rule by the sort of dictate it calls "unilateral fiat," if left unchallenged and unchecked, may become the new normal. The AAUP attributes escalation of this mode of power to the pandemic and in particular the opportunities this crisis afforded for "emergency" decrees that flouted established norms and processes, including those expressly incorporated within faculty handbooks. In fact, however, the possibility of this sort of rule has lurked within the constitutional structure of US higher education since *Dartmouth*, and the pandemic has merely laid this truth bare.

To see why this is so, remember the pyramid I drew in chapter 1 to illustrate the hierarchical character of rule within American colleges and universities. What that diagram failed to indicate was how the governing boards who sit at this pyramid's apex are decoupled from those subject to their authority. From the vantage point of a republican member corporation, to redeploy the words of John Bracken's attorney, the academy's trustees have mistakenly come to consider "themselves as the incorporated society," whereas those subject to their jurisdiction are excluded appendages. To capture this misconstruction, we would have to redraw governing boards as so many severed heads that rule but are not organs of the academic body politic. Confronted by this new depiction, we would then be right to ask: Who or what in the last analysis ensures that these heads remain accountable to the academy's purpose, whether mandated by charter, statute, or constitutional provision, and on behalf of which trustees have been granted the powers they wield?

At Harvard as well as William & Mary, this question was answered by authorizing a body other than the incorporated trustees, whether called "visitors" or "overseers," to intervene should their governors, to quote Blackstone, "deviate from the end of their institution."[53] With respect to civil corporations, Blackstone argues, the state always retains this authority because it is the author of the charter by which they are founded. However, when Blackstone turns to eleemosynary corporations, he distinguishes between the Crown (or, later, Parliament), who is their legal founder (*fundatio incipiens*), and their benefactors, who, as the source of the assets that are a prerequisite of these corporation's persistence through time, are founders in a second sense (*fundatio perficiens*); and it is to this latter group that Blackstone awards the right of visitation.

What does *Dartmouth* do with this conceptual inheritance? In his concurring opinion, Justice Story insists that the Trustees of Dartmouth College, as with all corporations, must be "subject to the controlling authority of its legal visitor, who, unless restrained by the terms of the charter, may amend and repeal its statutes, remove its officers, correct abuses, and generally superintend the management of the trusts."[54] In whose hands, then, is this power to reside?

From *Dartmouth*, we have learned that the college is not a civil corporation; that neither the people nor their legislative representatives can impinge on its contractual rights; and hence that its visitors cannot be located in the state. Instead, Webster maintained in oral argument, the answer to this question is inherent within the charter's status as a legal trust fashioned to ensure that private property gifted to the college remains true to the will of its donors:

> The right of visitation arises from the property. It grows out of the endowment. The founder may, if he please, part with it, at the time when he establishes the charity, and may vest it in others. Therefore, if he chooses that governours, trustees or overseers should be appointed in the charter, he may cause it to be done, *and his power of visitation will be transferred to them.* . . . This is a private right, which they can assert in all legal modes, and in which they have the same protection of the law as in all other rights.[55]

Webster makes two points here: (1) the authority of Dartmouth's visitors ultimately derives from the college's founders and specifically their right to dictate the future disposition of the property they have bequeathed; and (2) this authority has been granted by the college's donors to its trustees in their capacity as the incorporated keepers of the founders' trust. From the postulates announced by Story and Webster, Marshall derives this conclusion: "Where Trustees or Governors are incorporated to manage the charity, the visitatorial power is deemed to belong to them in their corporate character."[56]

By means of this legerdemain, Webster, Story, and Marshall conspire to conflate the distinction between visitors and trustees. Under these circumstances, it is fatuous to claim that governing boards are obligated to uphold the college's mission, whereas visitors are bound to ensure that the powers granted to trustees are exercised in accordance with Dartmouth's charter. True, Dartmouth's visitors are not thereby freed from all constraint: "As managers of the property and revenues of the corporation, they [the trustees] were amenable to the jurisdiction of the judicial tribunals of the State; but as visitors, their discretion was limited only by the charter, and liable to no supervision or control, at least unless it was fraudulently misapplied."[57] In other words, Dartmouth's governing board in its visitorial incarnation stands as the charter's unbound interpreter unless there is evidence of criminal conduct (embezzlement, for example) on the part of one or more of its members. Should an allegation of that sort be made, charges adjudicated in court (but never the legislature) are appropriate. Absent an indictment, however, common law dictates that courts should defer to the discretionary judgment of trustees qua visitors.[58]

What cannot be adjudicated, therefore, is the question of whether a governing board has employed its duly authorized powers in ways that are at odds with a college's mission as specified in its charter. After all, there is no one but the governing board to whom this question might be addressed, and, in any given instance, that board has effectively preempted this query via whatever action it has already taken. Rule by self-justifying and hence unchallengeable fiat, therefore, is not an aberration but a possibility inherent within the college's constitution as a trust whose trustees are at one and the same time visitors whose sole task is to ensure the security of its founders' property rights in perpetuity.

Dartmouth perfects the autocracy that Harvard's overseers and William & Mary's visitors could only dream of. The AAUP is misguided, accordingly, when it worries that we may now be slipping into Humpty Dumpty's dystopia, "where what is broken cannot be mended and words can have any meaning that anyone wishes to attribute to them."[59] Within the academic regime imagined by *Dartmouth*, it is not "anyone" but rather a very specific body that possesses the unaccountable power to determine what this college's charter means and hence what is to count as fulfilling its educational mission. In this respect, Lewis Carroll got matters exactly right:

> "When *I* use a word," Humpty Dumpty said in rather a scornful tone, "it means just what I choose it to mean—neither more nor less."
>
> "The question is," said Alice, "whether you *can* make words mean so many different things."
>
> "The question is," said Humpty Dumpty, "which is to be master— that's all."[60]

III

A Bet Gone Bad

7
Psychasthenia Universitatis (or The Malady of the Academy)

Swatting a Gadfly

After several abortive attempts, in 1917 Columbia University's board of trustees finally succeeded in terminating James McKeen Cattell. During his quarter century at Columbia, Cattell did much to earn his reputation as "the most prominent academic gadfly of his time."[1] To cite but a few examples, Cattell routinely branded Columbia's president, Nicholas Butler, the embodiment of "academic autocracy"; he denounced the faculty pension program created by the Carnegie Foundation as a ploy designed to induce malcontents to retire before their time; and in 1913 he published a study showing that an overwhelming majority of faculty members favored a wholesale reconstitution of the American academy on republican principles (more on this later).

It was Cattell's extramural activities, though, that ultimately led to his dismissal. In March 1917, Columbia's board of trustees announced an inquiry aimed at ascertaining whether any faculty members were teaching doctrines that "tend to encourage a spirit of disloyalty to the government of the United States, or the principles upon which it is founded."[2] Two months later, Columbia's acquiescent president suspended the exercise of academic freedom for the duration of World War I. To justify this preemptive strike, Butler argued that debate about the wisdom of US participation in this conflict was permissible but only until a declaration of war was adopted by Congress: "What had been tolerated before becomes intolerable now. What had been wrongheadedness was now sedition. What had been folly was now treason."[3] Cattell responded, as was his wont, by circulating a memo calling for the president's home to be converted into a club where faculty might gather to cultivate loyalty to the war's cause.

Not long after, on Columbia University letterhead stationery, Cattell mailed to three members of Congress a letter urging them to vote against a bill that would authorize the deployment of US conscripts on European battlefields. One recipient soon informed Cattell's employer that he was "sowing the seeds of sedition and treason with the sanction of the institution."[4] Ignoring a faculty committee's recommendation that he be allowed to depart gracefully, the board fired Cattell and released to the press a statement falsely claiming that Columbia's professoriate as a whole had endorsed his dismissal.

The "Professors' Literature of Protest"

Cattell was the most irascible participant in a broader movement of academics who, during the final two decades of the nineteenth century and the first two of the twentieth, called for a radical rethinking of rule within US colleges and universities. The names of some contributors to what one dubbed the "professors' literature of protest" remain known to us today;[5] think, for example, of Upton Sinclair (*The Goose-Step: A Study of American Education*) and Thorstein Veblen (*The Higher Learning in America: A Memorandum on the Conduct of Universities by Business Men*). Most, though, are now forgotten: J. E. Kirkpatrick, James Munroe, Jacob Gould Schurman, John Jay Chapman, John Stevenson, J. E. Creighton, George Stratton, George Ladd, Stewart Paton, and Joseph Jastrow, to name but a few. Often at odds with their employers and sometimes their own colleagues, contributors to this literature deserve better, and giving them their due is a subordinate but not unimportant aim of this chapter.

More important for my purposes, the "professors' literature of protest" offered early expression to the critique of the academy that, today, most often goes under the banner of "corporatization." In certain ways, though, their version of this critique is superior to that offered by their heirs. Consider, for example, contemporary analyses that represent "corporatization" as an insidious process whereby so many capitalist miscreants overpower the ivory tower and sully the pristine affair that is "higher education." The "professors' literature of protest" offers a corrective to these self-vindicating tales of villains and victims by explaining that the academy's autocratic rule engenders a systematically deranged whole within which the uncorrupted can no longer be found. The constitution of the academic body politic is diseased from top to bottom, and that is what this chapter's diagnostic title is meant to suggest.

The "professors' literature of protest" is additionally noteworthy because its contributors deployed expressly political categories drawn from republican, social contract, and democratic theory to characterize the academy's current constitution and imagine alternatives to it. This, too, distinguishes their critique from contemporary accounts that are typically predicated on appeals to the apolitical ideal of professionalism, as I explain more fully in the next chapter. If faculty participation in governance is now in disrepair, so this story goes, that is because the scholarly profession has been deprofessionalized in recent decades, and that, once again, is to be explained by the sinister forces of "corporatization." Cattell and his kin offer a similar argument insofar as they insist that the academy must not be run on the model of a capitalist enterprise. But, unlike most today, they also understood that the sense of the term *corporation* is not exhausted by its for-profit variant. The "professors' literature of protest" therefore called not for the corporation's expulsion from the academy's Eden but, instead, for a democratic reincorporation of colleges and universities; and that is the principal reason their work deserves attention here.

Dartmouth's Vicious Circle

The argument advanced within the "professors' literature of protest" cannot be understood absent some appreciation of how *Dartmouth* enabled a remaking of the American corporate landscape beyond the confines of the academy. The ruling in *Dartmouth* did so by preparing the terrain on which the corporate formation that defines a modern capitalist political economy would eventually emerge. It did so by encouraging the displacement over the course of the nineteenth century of business enterprises understood as civil corporations serving public purposes by a form of autocratic property corporation anticipated but never fully imagined by Marshall in *Dartmouth*.

This displacement did not occur without a fight. *Dartmouth*'s invocation of the Constitution's Contract Clause did much to immunize corporations from legislative intrusions that could be figured as violations of charters construed as contracts. In response, those inspired by Jacksonian republicanism often pressed for and secured inclusion within the charters of new corporations provisions that reserved to the authorizing states the right to alter, repeal, or renew these founding documents. So, too, many legislatures adopted statutes that restricted the duration of corporate charters, limited the extent of their capitalization, and imposed term limits on board members.[6] None of these measures were construed as infringements on the rights of private property rights, and all reflected widespread anxiety, especially in antebellum America, about corporate power and its capacity, if left unchecked, to compromise the constitution of a well-ordered republic and sap the civic virtue necessary to its preservation.

These measures, however, proved ill equipped to counter the broader import of *Dartmouth*'s construction of Dartmouth as a device created by contract to better secure the founders' rights of private property against encroachment, and especially intrusions initiated by legislatures. Throughout the nineteenth century, this representation was extended to the joint stock trading corporations that, in an earlier era, had been chartered by governments to harness self-interest in the service of public ends. However ironically, this reconceptualization achieved its consummate expression in the general incorporation statutes that were adopted by many states, mostly during the second half of the century. As I noted in chapter 2, although these statutes were originally intended as a republican safeguard against the state's preferential granting of charters to those it favored, in time they enabled business enterprises to secure the powers and privileges of corporate status absent specification of any end other than profit maximization.

Thus was the modern US capitalist corporation abstracted from the sociopolitical contexts within which it had once been embedded. That emancipation in turn is a necessary condition of emergence of the "economy," now imagined as a freestanding sphere governed by its own laws, located squarely within liberalism's private sphere, and thereby immunized against virtually all forms of political regulation. Inversion of older understandings of the relationship between state and corporation was effectively announced when, in 1886, the Supreme Court decided *Santa Clara County v. Southern Pacific Railroad Company.* Justice John Marshall Harlan's opinion for a unanimous court clearly implied that the equal protection guarantees provided by the Fourteenth Amendment apply not just to persons but to for-profit enterprises as well. If that is so, then it would appear that a primary if not overriding purpose of the liberal state is not to promote the ends of the people but to protect the rights of *Dartmouth's* privatized offspring against exercises of popular sovereignty. The age of the rapacious business corporation, soon to be associated with the likes of John D. Rockefeller, Andrew Carnegie, and Cornelius Vanderbilt, thereby declared its ascendancy over earlier corporate formations.

What I have said thus far about *Dartmouth's* legacy is not new. Less often noted, however, are the internal transformations of the for-profit corporation that occurred during the nineteenth century. To appreciate what the "professors' literature of protest" found objectionable about reconstruction of the academy on this model, a few words must be said about that metamorphosis as well.

In chapter 3, I explained that early modern English trading companies were constituted as member corporations in the form of "little republics" and that in time these bodies morphed into the colonies that, following the Revolution, became states. Although not universally so, the member corporation remained the model for many American businesses well into the nineteenth century. Consider, for example, the Pennsylvania Railroad, which was chartered by the state legislature in 1847. To forestall the accumulation of executive power in the hands of a few, that charter rendered the railroad's board of directors electable by the company's shareholders for one-year terms, and this representative body was authorized in turn to select a president from among its members. At its annual meetings, by majority rule, the company's members were granted plenary power to make, alter, or repeal any policies, regulations, or bylaws adopted by the board. Moreover, if a petition was signed by not less than 10 percent of the corporation's members, the president was then required to convene a special assembly to consider specific grievances arising from the board's conduct of the company's collective affairs.[7]

The members of business companies constituted in this fashion were figured metaphorically on the model of citizens exercising suffrage rights within an egalitarian political community. This analogy offers a striking contrast to what is familiar to us today. Rather than apportioning votes in accordance with the number of shares owned by any given investor, as is now almost always so, these corporations granted to each and every member a single vote in all decision-making.[8] Here shareholders were construed not as owners of diverse amounts of capital that secured them differential control rights but as corporate republicans entitled to equal shares in the right to rule a body politic in the form of a business company. By the end of the nineteenth century, however, practices of this sort had largely disappeared as the interests of major investors within large industrial corporations prevailed, and property-based inequalities superseded the principle of equal corporate citizenship.[9]

The shift from corporate democracy to financial plutocracy was accompanied by a transformation in the nature of shares themselves. In earlier joint stock companies, shares were chiefly understood as equitable interests in the material assets that, once incorporated, were now owned by these creatures of law. The emergence of an established stock market, replacing the individual brokers that had previously managed interinvestor trades, effectively enabled shares to be abstracted from their ground in the tangible assets of any given company. Shares, that is, became fungible financial instruments whose value was determined not primarily through reference to the worth of a company's productive capital but through reference to the dividends they were expected to accrue in the future. Thus does Blackstone's right to exercise absolute dominion over property in the form of corporeal and incorporeal hereditaments become a right to dividends from profits not yet realized.

This reconfiguration of what it means to hold shares in a company effectively reconstituted those who were once members of a corporation but who were now becoming passive investors in corporations that exist apart from these speculators. These reified entities in turn came to be figured not as so many egalitarian bodies politic endowed with the powers essential to the practice of collective self-governance. Rather, they became privatized economic entities whose exclusive purpose is to maximize efficiency in the service of maximal productivity and whose value is measured solely by the profit these commodities reap. That profit is then unequally distributed in the form of dividends proportional to stock ownership, thereby enabling the wealthy to acquire still more shares and hence to secure still greater sway within the corporations they are now coming to think they own. From here it is but a short distance to the ideological neoliberal construction of the corporation I critiqued in chapter 2.

The irony of *Dartmouth*, therefore, is this: consolidation of the academy in the form of an autocratic property corporation, most perfectly articulated in *Dartmouth*, antedated and in effect provided the template for an analogous transformation of the American business corporation. The unhappy logic of "corporatization" finds its source not in the sphere of capitalist economic production but in a court ruling regarding the academy that is so often viewed as corporatization's prey. The academy's "victory" in *Dartmouth* spawns the capitalist creatures that in time will remake America's colleges and universities in their own image.

The Academy's Cooke Book

Throughout the first three-quarters of the nineteenth century, college governance was usually monopolized by strong presidents appointed by governing boards absent any input from instructors, let alone noninstructional staff. At best, the professoriate's aspirations to rule were "directed toward convincing the trustees to delegate to the faculty power over education and discipline; toward developing as it were, a limited faculty imperium within a trustee imperio."[10] At worst, "the system of control by a nonresident board . . . evolved into an instrument of academic government that was officious, meddlesome, and often tyrannical."[11] Under these circumstances, there could be little doubt that the academy assumed autocratic form because that rule was personified in the figure of a president who answered chiefly if not exclusively to the academy's absentee proprietors.

The turn of the twentieth century, however, witnessed a steady replacement of older elites on governing boards by representatives of what Thomas Carlyle in 1843 had dubbed "captains of industry." To illustrate, consider the following: Between 1861 and 1929, at private colleges and universities, the percentage of clergy on external lay boards dropped from about 41 to 9 percent; the percentage of "businessmen" increased from 19 to 51 percent; and, finally, when lawyers are included in this latter category, their cumulative total rose to just shy of 66 percent. During these same years, much the same pattern was apparent at public colleges and universities, as the representation of clergy nearly disappeared; officers of corporate enterprises grew from a fifth to nearly half; and, again, when lawyers are thrown in, their cumulative total rose from 43 to 67 percent.[12]

In part, this recomposition of governing boards is what vexes contributors to the "professors' literature of protest." Many, though, understood that there is more afoot here than meets the eye. In chapter 3, I pointed to certain structural homologies between England's early trading companies, America's colonies, and in time the new nation's states, all of which were informed by the egalitarian logic of the member corporation. So, too, does a structural likeness inform the constitution of newly ascendant for-profit industrial enterprises, the land grant universities fashioned in accordance with the initial Morrill Act in 1862, and, even more so, the public and private research universities that followed the founding of Johns Hopkins University in 1876.[13] Here, though, the logic that comes to rule is the instrumental rationality that is indispensable to the cause of capital accumulation and whose adoption justifies and indeed requires unprecedented forms of authoritarian rule.

As processes of industrial production were reorganized to achieve maximum efficiency (think of the assembly line), a comparable form of reason emerged within the academy. When the Carnegie Foundation embarked on its project to reform higher education, its president, Henry Pritchett, turned to the inventor of industrial time and motion studies, Francis Taylor, for guidance. Taylor in turn commissioned an ambitious young mechanical engineer, Morris Cooke, to conduct an inquiry that was published in 1910 under the title *Academic and Industrial Efficiency*.

The aim of Cooke's book was to articulate a calculus that would enable the productivity of educational institutions to be measured in much the same way industrial enterprises reorganized in accordance with Taylor's studies were assessed. The primary impediment to doing so, Cooke acknowledged, was the absence within higher education of a metric comparable to the profit-and-loss statements that enabled capitalist corporations to determine the success or failure of specific modifications aimed at perfecting the efficiency of operations and hence enhancing net gain. A surrogate, however, could be found in the unit of measurement Cooke called the "student-hour" (what we now call the "credit hour"), which he defined as "one hour of lectures, of laboratory work, or recitation room work, for a single pupil."[14] If this is considered higher education's principal output, Cooke argued, the next task is to calculate the cost of each of its inputs, including, for example, faculty labor and the academy's material infrastructure. Once these standardized inputs and outputs are entered on the academic balance sheet, it will then become possible to determine the cost-effectiveness of individual faculty members, courses, fields, departments, and, indeed, entire universities when ranked against one another.

If this calculus is to operate with precision, obstacles to its smooth application must be eliminated. For example, the antiquated representation of faculty work as a calling must be jettisoned in favor of its construction as so much mental labor that differs from its manual counterpart only insofar as it is conducted by heads rather than hands. So, too, the push on the part of faculty to institutionalize tenure, especially at emerging research universities, must be nipped in the bud, for that practice merely permits the inefficient to compromise the provision of cost-effective education. Just as an industrial economy must enable employers to respond nimbly to changes in market demand by issuing only at-will employment contracts, faculty contracts must be short-term, and decisions to retain or terminate must be made exclusively through reference to individual productivity. Each professor, moreover, must be disabused of the quaint notion "that the lectures he gives and his pedagogical mechanisms are his own property."[15] Instead, as is true of capitalist assets more generally, all intellectual property must be owned by the university, and its trustees and senior administrators must be granted an exclusive right to determine its most effective distribution, including its reallocation whenever courses, majors, departments, and specific teachers are no longer considered worthy of purchase by education's consumers.

Finally, faculty must be stripped of all governance roles in the academy, for any time committed to these tasks will detract from the specialized expertise that is required for efficient manufacture of the "student-hours" that are higher education's sole products. Like the for-profit corporation, therefore, the university must also be organized as a hierarchy in which a few rule and all others execute orders issued by superiors euphemized as "administrators." What Cooke commends, in short, is the academy constituted in the form of a property corporation but now subsumed beneath the rationality of capitalism. What we find in the "professors' literature of protest" is this mutation's most insightful critique.

Psychasthenia Universitatis:
Its Symptoms, Etiology, and Cure

A 2020 essay published in the *Chronicle of Higher Education* claims that Thorstein Veblen "was the first sociologist of academe to notice the enormous and pernicious power wielded by university trustees from the business world."[16] This is wrong. In 1918, when Veblen finally got around to publishing *The Higher Learning in America*, he was quick to acknowledge that his work relied on that of a previous generation of scholars. Partial to polemics, Veblen pressed his predecessors' arguments to conclusions many were reticent to embrace, but it was they who provided the ammunition necessary to his more radical deductions.

Early in *The Higher Learning in America*, Veblen tells us that the work that furnished the essential "ground and material" for his argument was James McKeen Cattell's *University Control*, published in 1913.[17] This consummate expression of the "professors' literature of protest" is an odd volume. Part I consists of a proposal for a reconfiguration of the academy's corporate form that Cattell had originally published in 1906 but had then expanded into a two-part article that appeared in 1912. Part III reproduces ten articles written between 1902 and 1912 by academics sympathetic to the cause, including one by Cattell himself. Part II, the book's ungainly midsection, consists of 299 unattributed letters submitted by "leading men of science" responding to Cattell's proposal,[18] which he had circulated in 1911. Of the nearly 300 responses, by Cattell's count, 185 embraced his scheme; another 68 endorsed the principle of greater faculty authority but expressed reservations about specific elements of his plan; and a mere 46 rejected his proposal and so effectively defended the existing regime.[19]

Cattell's sympathizers do not speak with one voice; nor do they offer a sophisticated theoretical account of the academy's current plight; and nor, finally, do they frame their arguments through reference to the distinction between property and member corporations (although their arguments are easily read in these terms). What *University Control*'s contributors do provide are the raw materials that can be assembled, as I do here, into a coherent analysis of what ails the academy as well as a prescription for its remedy. Within this critique, we hear echoes of the complaints registered by Harvard's fellows as well as William & Mary's professors in their battles with overseers and visitors, respectively. But we also hear, and sometimes uncannily so, anticipations of the academy's assumption of neoliberal form a century later as well as that academy's critique, especially when framed in the discourse of "corporatization."

Metaphorically extending to the academy a neurological disorder first identified around the turn of the twentieth century, the proper name for the disease that afflicts the academic body politic is "psychasthenia universitatis."[20] This is a malady that leaves no one untouched, for it a disorder whose symptoms appear from head to toe: "A system that does not leave room for freedom affects injuriously the ruler as well as the ruled."[21] Palliative measures may ease these symptoms, of which the three explored below are the most significant, but such half steps will not address their underlying causes. To accomplish that requires a reconfiguration of the mutually constitutive relations among this body's members, and that in turn demands a fundamental reconstruction of the academy's corporate form.

Psychasthenia Universitatis's Primary Symptom: The Trustee qua Philistine

"The disease which is endemic in the university is subordination of the teacher to the academic machine, a kind of hookworm disease which leaves the entire institution anemic."[22] Atop this machine sits the external lay governing board. This entity finds no counterpart in medieval European universities, including Oxford and Cambridge, that were constituted as "free guilds of men professionally interested in the higher learning, with power to determine their own membership, elect their own officers, administer their own property."[23]

The autocratic constitution of America's earliest colleges in the Northeast was born, instead, of the "old theocracy of New England."[24] To fashion youth fit "for service in church or commonwealth," their founders "placed over them men of notable authority."[25] The externality of these authorities to the colleges they rule is perhaps a relic of pre-Revolutionary British policy, whereby "a small corporation, or 'company,' often resident in distant England, controlled its colony through a single local governor."[26] If this be so, then today's governing boards merely replicate the role of the absent company, and the presidents they appoint are but local agents of colonial domination. It is this genealogy that explains why in the United States "university government has assumed a form that we might have expected to see in a land accustomed to kings. European universities have a constitution that might have come from some American political theorist; American universities are as though founded and fostered in the bourne of aristocracy."[27]

Whether the result of an "accident of history or a bungle of the law makers," at bottom this constitution is an autocracy run by "absentee and quasi-hereditary" overlords or, more pointedly, "philistine outsiders."[28] Their rule betrays the ideal of a self-governing body politic that animated the Revolutionary War and, since that time, has informed struggles to realize the promise of American democracy. Perhaps, one might argue, such rule was appropriate to the colonial college, where instructors stood in loco parentis and when "the care of youth so tender in their years may easily have suggested patriarchal forms—forms that, we know, rise readily to monarchical."[29] It is ill suited, however, to "a people so jealous of private rights, so patient of the inconveniences of weak and scattered powers and changing persons in political government, lest the individual should be oppressed."[30] That this form persists today signifies nothing more than "thoughtless piety" toward an antiquarian relic that has no rightful place in the present.[31]

"The swaddling clothes of the semi-theological college" must therefore now be shed.[32] After all, "advancing democracy has burned its bridges behind it. No one believes that a city should be owned by a small self-perpetuating board of trustees who would appoint a dictator to run it. . . . Why should a university be conducted that way?"[33] Indeed, to maintain that "the citizenry of the nation as a whole is capable of self-government, while the citizenry of the universities of the nation are not capable of self-government," is nothing short of "monstrous."[34]

As the foundation of the American economy has shifted from agriculture to industry, as powerful corporations have consolidated their control over its business, the symptoms occasioned by this anachronism have gone from bad to worse. Today "the extraordinary legal power given to college trustees has gradually passed from the hands of the clergy into those of trustees" who are "chosen in view of their fitness to manage the financial affairs, very rarely with reference to their familiarity with educational matters."[35] No matter how much these rulers may protest otherwise, the members of this secular priesthood are far from independent. Like their ministerial predecessors, they too answer to a higher power: "the dead and living hands of donors demanding that their gifts be safeguarded by stable and substantially irremovable trustees."[36] Kin to the trustees who are their agents, these benefactors are themselves most often men of business who, to quote Upton Sinclair, are drawn from the "House of Morgan" and whose highest hope for their respective universities is that their production of students and scholars will become "an industry as thoroughly established, as completely systematized and standardized as the production of automobiles or sausages."[37]

As what Sinclair calls a system of "interlocking directorates" weds the "headquarters of our plutocratic empire" to "the headquarters of our plutocratic education,"[38] the sense of the term *trust*, as hitherto employed in discussions of the American academy, undergoes yet another mutation. Harvard's 1650 charter envisioned the college's trust as a grant of state power issued on condition that its governors advance educational ends that are public because they are said to benefit all, ruler as well as ruled.

The trust modeled by Dartmouth's board, as conceptualized in *Dartmouth*, is a specific type of legal instrument whereby private donors entrust their funds to a body whose foremost obligation is to ensure fidelity to the purposes specified by those benefactors as well as any others who may give in future years. As we move into the twentieth century, however, Sinclair employs the term *trust* to gesture toward the corporate conglomerates that are the targets of the 1890 Sherman Antitrust Act and that are now coming to enmesh the academic corporations that are their (too) eager partners.

On this construction, the academy's claim to existence ever more turns on its capacity to generate assets that may be exploited in the interest of capital accumulation. If this capacity is to flourish, as Cooke had argued, the rationality of the factory, the bank, and the department store must be extended to the academy. Convinced that the "academic nervous system finds its solar plexus in the purse," governing boards now treasure "results that can readily be measured" as well as "things that can be expressed in statistics" and, still more problematically, worship that "most meaningless" but also "most dangerous" of deities: the god of efficiency.[39] Regarding efficiency as an end unto itself, as captains of industry are prone to do, trustees soon forget that "there are efficient fools and knaves and meddlers and weather-vanes and apologists and dissemblers."[40] Because the university's interlopers do not understand that "even so directly a utilitarian thing as a signpost is efficient only when you know where you want to go and where not," they cannot see why the appeal to efficiency "should never be permitted to appear in educational discussions without a chaperone."[41] Because that guide is now absent, "we stand in jeopardy every hour of becoming mechanized degree-factories."[42]

At its most benign, when trustees discover that intellectual matters resist reduction to the techniques of for-profit bookkeeping, they grow disinterested and "drift into the belief that their trust is discharged by attendance upon stated meetings."[43] Too often, though, they pursue simulacra of capitalist enterprises, for example, by "bidding for students" to increase their "share of the annual freshman crop" or placing university "investments in real estate—in buildings, plants, and inventories of trade catalogues—to be pointed at with pride so long as one is blessed with an easy conscience."[44] Confusing education's end with consumer satisfaction, governing boards fetishize their university's "rating in the educational Bradstreet,"[45] and so the quest for prestige displaces the enhancement of academic quality. "Advertising looms large," not surprisingly, as an ever greater share of institutional resources is devoted to enticing students "towards the local Athenopolis and away from the rival one."[46]

Recognizing that the market's demand for educational commodities is forever fickle, trustees demand demonstrations of the academy's "power of rapid adjustment to a changing situation, the power to strike while the iron is hot."[47] Desperate to demarcate themselves from their competitors, trustees "rush forth at every cry of 'Lo, here!' or 'Lo, there!'"[48] as they embrace the latest disruptive innovations dangled before their eager eyes. Counterintuitively, however, the very desire for a distinctive brand generates not differentiation but standardization. As is true in capitalist marketplaces, no competitor can afford to forgo any fad that proves advantageous to another, and so all become drearily alike.

To obscure regress to this sorry mean, ever-greater sums must be devoted to "high-cost stage properties and press-agents, public song and dance, expensive banquets, speech-making and processions." While these displays are aimed partly at increasing applicant flows, more fundamentally, they are designed to interest "that more select body of substantial citizens who have the disposal of accumulated wealth" and from whom the academy "hopes to draw contributions to its endowment." The predictable upshot is "a genial endeavor to keep step with the moribund captains of industry and the relics of the wealthy dead."[49]

Psychasthenia Universitatis's Secondary Symptom: The President qua Potentate

"Psychasthenia universitatis" may originate in the untethered head of the academy's body politic, but its symptoms soon extend to its appendages. Its effects, for example, are readily apparent in those whom Veblen, modifying Carlyle's epithet, designated the university's "captains of erudition."[50] Today, Veblen insists, those appointed as the academy's chief executive officers "are selected primarily with a view to give the direction of academic policy and administration more of a businesslike character."[51] Yes, it remains true that presidents are most often plucked from the ranks of the faculty and officially belong to that body. But as these lieutenants lose the sensibilities appropriate to an academic community and acquire those of bosses standing athwart a burgeoning bureaucratic apparatus, it becomes ever more difficult to recognize "in the glorified presidential butterfly the humble professorial worm."[52]

So remade, the president is the most public figure of those affiliated with the university but also the most vilified: "So often uncritically the recipient of praise as the visible embodiment of the source from whom all blessings flow, he is as naturally chosen as the one on whom all curses fall."[53] Petitioned by flatterers within the academy's walls but obliged to play sycophant before those without, the demands of the presidency place its occupants in an impossible situation: "The president of a college or university is the great reconciler of irreconcilabilities; he is the chemist who mixes oil and water, the high priest who makes peace between God and Mammon, the circusrider who stands on two horses going in opposite directions; and all these things not by choice but ex-officio and of inescapable necessity."[54]

Caught between professors who call on the president to plow ever more resources into salaries and trustees who ask that their appointee engage only in cost-effective management of the academy's assets, this beleaguered figure cannot satisfy both simultaneously and so becomes the "most variegated prevaricator that has yet appeared in the civilized world."[55] To keep up appearances, college and university presidents must present what in fact are so many "expedients of decorative real-estate, spectacular pageantry, bureaucratic magnificence, elusive statistics, vocational training, genteel solemnities and sweatshop instruction" as examples of "unwavering devotion to the pursuit of knowledge."[56] Because this pretense is so strained, presidents often resort to a desperate ploy designed to satisfy their diverse audiences: they exhaust themselves in frenetic activity that, if this stratagem works, persuades everyone that they care about nothing so much as fulfillment of the academy's noble end.

No matter how crooked these contradictory demands may render the president's soul, as the academy's public personification, this character must "act as though he were a statue of himself erected by public subscription."[57] When this pretender confuses that monument with his self, as often occurs, the president comes to "regard common-sense as agreement with him, common loyalty as subservience to him, respect for the opinion of mankind as deference to that small portion of mankind which has money to give."[58]

In sum, the unelected president appointed by an unrepresentative board is "an anachronism in this modern age, and an anomaly in a democratic country."[59] If the power wielded by this relic corrupts its holder even more than it abases its subjects, maybe we should "regard the music and the ribbons, the pomp and the paraphernalia, of the inauguration ceremonies as consecrating a victim for a free-will sacrifice than as raising a deified monarch to a sort of imperial throne."[60] Perhaps, therefore, "the only type of man safely to be entrusted with the prerogatives of the presidency is one whose principles would require him to decline the office."[61]

Psychasthenia Universitatis's Tertiary Symptom: The Professor qua Subject

Subject to officious trustees who meddle in curricular matters they know nothing about and executive agents who must pretend to know everything, the professoriate displays its own unique symptoms of psychasthenia universitatis. If faculty members conform to the trustees' caricature of them as quarrelsome bumblers who know little of the world's ways, that is "not the excuse for but largely the *result* of" the academy's autocratic formation and "the depressed atmosphere which it breeds."[62] This collective malaise invariably emerges within "all bodies long deprived of their constitutional rights."[63] When this malady surfaces within the academic body specifically, it cannot help but subvert that body's proper end; for in time this distemper must drain the academy of the intellectual vitality that is its lifeblood.

If faculty so often prove resentful, that is because they have good reason to believe that governing board members have little respect for the work they do. Because, for example, trustees view scholarship as a "luxury carried on by professors as a pleasant relaxation from the ordinary drudgery of routine duties,"[64] they are ill equipped to appreciate its status as knowledge's wellspring. Should governing boards value this work, they will do so only insofar as it measurably contributes to the pseudo-currency that is institutional prestige, for research is but an expense to be recorded in the collegiate equivalent of profit-and-loss ledgers. We should not be surprised, therefore, when these calculations drive the academy toward the "truly dismal combination" of "high-priced imperious management'" and "low-priced docile labor."[65]

The faculty's everyday subjection to the executives appointed by these boards engenders still more troubling symptoms. Knowing that this "modern Caesar" exercises "the powers of academic life and death" over instructors who serve at the president's pleasure, too often the university comes to be populated by "a few sycophants and a crowd of mediocrities," neither of whom dares to question whatever a president may mandate.[66] Such obedience ought not to be confused with loyalty, because the president is "a ruler responsible to no one whom he governs"[67] and so has but limited claim to the allegiance of these academic subjects. True, this legitimacy deficit can sometimes be mitigated via the alchemy whereby "academic service" is transmuted "into dollars by an esoteric procedure" whose "specious" character is hidden by "waving" the "magic wand of 'merit.'"[68] When acquiescence is purchased by a mess of pottage, however, what presidents take for loyalty will vanish as soon as these seductions are no longer forthcoming.

Debased by the conditions of their occupation, most faculties divide into two principal groups. Members of the first think of themselves as mere hired hands, and those in the second consider themselves victims of a "tyranny" that deprives them "of their just rights. In both cases alike the result is unfortunate, and one that loudly calls for remedy. A man who regards himself as merely an employee is not likely to give to the university more than his theory demands, while a man who lives with a constant sense of grievance, knowing that there is no court before which he can claim redress, can not reasonably be expected to be greatly in love with his profession."[69] The disaffected thus "become incompetent or nihilistic or restless according to temperament. If disposed to act under a sense of personal injury, they become militant; if organized with the prospect of control, they become insurgent; if academic, they apparently become dormant."[70] What all share, though, is a penchant for assigning blame elsewhere when matters go awry: a constitutional form that animates a politics of petty resentment and petulant rebellion cannot do other than invite faculty "to place the responsibility anywhere but on themselves."[71]

If this faculty appears a poor candidate to engage in institutional governance, that is because its members are now excluded from rule: "It has been said that university faculties are poor legislative bodies; if true, this would not be surprising, so long as their deliberations are confined to discussing questions such as whether they shall wear gowns at commencement, the decision being with the trustees."[72] We must never forget, however, that this "confirmed incompetence has been gathered under the overshadowing presence of a surreptitiously and irresponsibly autocratic executive, vested with power of use and abuse, and served by a corps of adroit parliamentarians and lobbyists, ever at hand to divert the faculty's action from any measure that might promise to have a substantial effect."[73]

The principal power delegated to the faculty is the power to talk without end, not the power to regulate the conditions of their collective work. The professoriate's logorrhea explains the spectacles of demoralization known as faculty meetings, which are defined by their "hesitant, dispirited, nibbling, myopic, lame and wearisome discussions that are a trial to spirit and flesh": "It is nothing short of absurd to withdraw from faculty discussion all the real educational issues, and expect a company of scholarly men to grow enthusiastic over the privilege of wearily debating how a sophomoric attempt to vault over or climb around the regulations shall be thwarted, or whether the mandolin club both played and behaved so badly upon its last venture that its leading strings should profitably be shortened."[74] We may romanticize faculty meetings as deliberative arenas where reason reigns. But what that reason considers is much ado about very little, and so what these gatherings most often accomplish is the faculty's self-stultification.

The pacifying effects generated by these palavers are compounded by "the many committees-for-the-sifting-of-sawdust into which . . . the well-administered university is organized. These committees being, in effect if not in intention, designed chiefly to keep the faculty talking while the bureaucratic machine goes on its way under the guidance of the executive and his personal counsellors and lieutenants." The capacity of these little groups to quell discontent is perfected when faculty meetings are themselves devoted chiefly to considering the reports issued by these same committees. A faculty so occupied "no longer requires[s] a vigilant personal surveillance from the side of the executive."[75] Overt exercises of power are superfluous when the tedious yoke of busy-ness reigns.

Paradoxically, what renders the professor peculiarly unable to use "his reason and his pen as actively as he ought in protecting himself, in pushing his interests, and in enlightening the community about educational abuses" is his own inflated self-conception:

> The professor in America seems to think that self-respect requires silence and discretion on his part. He is too great to descend into the arena. He thinks that by nursing this gigantic reverence for the idea of professordom, such reverence will, somehow, be extended all over society, till the professor becomes a creature of power, of public notoriety, of independent reputation as he is in Germany. In the meantime, the professor is trampled upon, his interests are ignored, he is overworked and underpaid, he is of small social consequence, he is kept at menial employments, and the leisure to do good work is denied him.[76]

Because fastidious professors believe that collective struggle to secure their rightful place in the university contradicts their status as members of the "mystic guild" that is a profession, they render themselves "helpless as all-around fighters."[77] Instead, their discontent takes the form of ad hoc petitions and sporadic protests that are readily dismissed not only by presidents and boards but also by those faculty members who deem such conduct unseemly. Absent a fundamental reconstitution of the academy, it appears, we are ill-advised to look to this organ of the university's body politic to remedy the malady that is psychasthenia universitatis.

When Psychasthenia Universitatis Proves Terminal

While the academy's autocratic constitution is the underlying cause of psychasthenia universitatis, according to contributors to the "professors' literature of protest," its etiology assumes a quite specific form within a capitalist industrial economy. That form was intimated when Henry Pritchett, the Carnegie Foundation president who retained Morris Cooke, offered this rhetorical question as the title of a 1905 essay: "Shall the University Become a Business Corporation?"[78] Insofar as the academy is transformed on the model of what Cattell labeled the "department store system,"[79] it loses its character as a distinct institutional formation defined by its own unique purposes and practices. So divested, this is an academy that no longer warrants a name that distinguishes it from what Pritchett would have it become.

While Cattell and his fellow contributors to *University Control* proved keen observers of this disease's symptoms, it was Veblen who provided the most prescient account of its governing rationality as well as this reason's incompatibility with that of the academy. Although a sad commentary on the present, we urgently need to be reminded, Veblen insists, that the academy is first and foremost the institutionalized incarnation of a free association of scholars. The key feature that distinguishes the academy from other associational forms, he explains, is its commitment "to no ulterior end" and no "consideration of expediency beyond its own work."[80] If the academy is to preserve this identity, it must be insulated from forces that betray not some melancholy ideal that exists only as an object of fantasy, but its character as a historically specific institutional formation that, if assimilated to others, will no longer remain worth saving.

Veblen was quick to acknowledge that business practices have a legitimate place within the academy when it is a matter of addressing its "fiscal affairs and the office-work incident to the care of its material equipment." These practices prove perverse, however, when the instrumental logic that informs them is conflated with the academy's ends, as capitalism's theoreticians in the guise of administrators so often do. The academy's chief financial officers, for example, privilege short-term measurable gains over "those intangible, immaterial uses for which the university is established." Because these "uses have no physical, tangible residue in the way of durable goods, such as will justify the expenditure in terms of vendible property acquired," to erudition's captains, these fruits of the academy necessarily appear "prima facie imbecile."[81] Quite literally, these goods are nothing but nonsense when assessed in the reductionist terms furnished by the form of reason in which these officers specialize.

Wholesale adoption of the logic of capitalist accumulation renders the academy end-less, for the end of accumulation is but more accumulation. Or, more precisely, a capitalist political economy is a regime in which all productive work is subordinated to the self-expansion of capital and hence to the imperatives of profit maximization. As the values of "authoritative control, standardization, gradation, accountancy, classification, credits and penalties" permeate the academy, nothing can "stand scrutiny as a final term to this traffic in ways and means."[82] The academy is thus corporatized not in the sense that it is conquered by business tycoons but in the sense that its reason becomes indistinguishable from that of capitalist enterprises.

Accomplishment of the capitalist academy's end without end is best secured when the university is subject to monocratic rule organized hierarchically: "The government of a competitive university is necessarily of an autocratic character, whatever plausible forms of collective action and advisement it may be found expedient to observe."[83] Just as a capitalist enterprise must expand if it is to survive in a competitive marketplace, so too must the capitalist academy capture new markets or die. That end requires multiplication of the administrative officers necessary to generate new revenue streams, and that in turn requires the bureaucratization illustrated by any standard organization chart. In time, Veblen predicts, this army of administrators will itself become a means whose sole end is its own self-reproduction. That end will be fully realized when there is "so much administration that there will be nothing to administer."[84] On that day, the academy will finally collapse into the nihilism that defines the logic of bureaucratically organized capital accumulation.

That this end is near, Veblen warns, is indicated by the proliferation of "Schools of Commerce," for "commercial management" stands to today's ruling class "in a relation analogous to that in which theology and homiletics stood to the ruling interest in earlier times when the salvation of men's souls was the prime object of solicitude." So, too, "businesslike fitness" (or what we now call "entrepreneurialism") is coming to "count progressively for more in appointments and promotions," so it is no surprise that faculty members are themselves now acquiring "a disturbing interest in commercial ventures" that introduce the profit motive where it does not belong. So, too, among students we witness "an increasing habitual inclination . . . to value all academic work in terms of livelihood or of earning capacity" and thus to fixate on education's return on investment.[85] Whether trustee, president, professor, or student, all come to embrace a form of reason that strips the academy of its character as a distinctively academic enterprise; for, after all, in a capitalist political economy, "what is good for business is felt to be serviceable for the common good; and no closer scrutiny is commonly given to that matter."[86]

Toward the close of *The Higher Learning*, Veblen asserts that governing boards and their executive appointees are deeply implicated in reproduction of capitalism's structural inequalities and hence that a necessary but partial first step toward fulfilling democracy's promise must be "abolition of the academic executive and of the governing board. Anything short of this heroic remedy is bound to fail, because the evils sought to be remedied are inherent in these organs, and intrinsic to their functioning." If we are now unlikely to entertain this possibility, that is because the academy's rulers fetishize order for order's sake and present themselves as the sole source of the discipline necessary to its accomplishment. Absent its autocratic constitution, we are now unfortunately persuaded, the academy will "incontinently fall to pieces."[87]

Properly understood, this conviction is but one more symptom of psychasthenia universitatis, for the academy's abject subjects have now come to believe that they are no longer capable of governing themselves. If this conclusion signifies that the malady of the academy is in fact terminal, Veblen conjectured, perhaps our task today is not to ask how colleges and universities might be restored to good health but, rather, how they might be "relieved" of "work which they are no longer fit to take care of." If "academic establishments, old and new, are no longer competent to take the direction of affairs in this domain," maybe we should now turn our attention to fashioning "retreats or shelters for the prosecution of scientific and scholarly inquiry in some sort of academic quarantine."[88] When the academy's disease becomes endemic, its health requires a cure that neither a mask nor even a vaccine can provide.

The Road to Recovery

"We appear at present to be between the Scylla of presidential autocracy and the Charybdis of faculty and trustee incompetence," wrote Cattell. "The more incompetent the faculties become, the greater is the need for executive authority, and the greater the autocracy of the president, the more incompetent do the faculty become."[89] As faculty respond to the incentive structures built into capitalism's construction of their work, they assume the character of rational economic actors interested in securing as much gain for as little work as possible. Of necessity, their rulers then deploy multiple forms of control and surveillance to curtail the indiscipline of their subjects. Learning that they are considered untrustworthy, these subjects become still more recalcitrant, and that of course requires intensification of the disciplinary techniques needed to keep them in line. As this circle turns vicious, a culture of mutual suspicion and recrimination replaces any sense of joint commitment to a common endeavor.

To interrupt this cycle, Cattell proffers a vision of an academy that might one day become a "democracy of scholars serving the larger democracy of which it is a part."[90] The first step toward imagining this university is to disabuse governing boards of an illusion they very much cherish: "More and more have they strengthened in themselves the delusion that *they* are the college or university."[91] This conceit turns on a confusion of what the academy is with its current configuration as a property corporation of the sort ratified by *Dartmouth*; and that is an academy whose autocratic rulers can affirm no claim to legitimacy because, in the last analysis, "real authority only exists in so far as it is shared by others."[92]

The rival vision Cattell advances draws inspiration from the self-governing scholarly republics found at Oxford and Cambridge as well as the medieval academies in Paris and Bologna. But Cattell and his respondents afford these models a distinctively American complexion. Indeed, because "the spirit of a university can only spring from a free soil,"[93] the United States is peculiarly well suited to perfect what these earlier universities could accomplish only in part, given their situation within feudal economies and monarchical regimes. The affirmative project of the "professors' literature of protest," then, is neither one of recovering a lost idyll nor one of aping European idols but, instead, a matter of articulating a constitutional form that is appropriate to the educational promise peculiar to America.

In offering an account of Cattell's proposal, which is not much more than a sketch, I do not mean to endorse all of its particulars (although nor do I mean to reject any out of hand). Instead, I read his proposal as a summons to reconstitute the academy on the model of a member corporation (although he does not call it such). Interpreted through this lens, these particulars offer several frontal challenges to the twentieth-century capitalist corporation, as sketched earlier in this chapter, and hence of the academy's reformation in its image.

Cattell begins by calling for the creation of "a corporation consisting of the professors and other officers of the university, the alumni who maintain their interest in the institution, and members of the community who ally themselves with it."[94] Should the size of the educational corporation be expanded to include all "those who are most actively interested in the work of the university," Cattell explains, the elitist cabals we now call "governing boards" will be denied their hubristic self-conception and replaced by bodies better positioned to hold "the university in trust for all the people."[95] Thus enlarged, this corporation effectively counters the "privatization" inherent in *Dartmouth*'s representation of the academy as a device for extending the rights of specific property owners through time. To "publicize" the academy in this sense is not, though, to render it a pawn of "the people," as Marshall predicted would be the case. Constituted as a corporation, the academy is invested with powers that ensure its considerable autonomy but never the capacity to declare itself entirely independent of the republican body politic to which it belongs.

The members of this reconstituted corporation, Cattell continues, are to elect trustees whose duty is to take "care of the [academy's] property and the representation of the common sense of the corporation and of the community in university policy."[96] This "taking care" is not to be confused with exercising the rights of private ownership, as *Dartmouth* does when it misconstrues Dartmouth's charter as a trust. Instead, such caretaking is better understood on the model of stewardship of goods that are owned by a corporation of which trustees too are members. Because these trustees are selected by and so remain accountable to this corporation's members, the academy's assets are far less likely to be twisted to private purposes masquerading as instantiations of a common good.

When the power to govern remains thus grounded in this corporation's members, disposition of its incorporated capital remains subordinated to the democratic decision-making of this body politic. Adherence to the principle of "one member, one vote" thus entails the repoliticization of property that, within the academy constituted as Marshall would have it, operates as a depoliticized agent of domination. In the autocratic academy, the governing board's dissociation from the body it rules finds its perfect complement in a form of property, best illustrated by the stock market's free-floating shares, that is equally disembedded from the substantive work of education. Just as the member corporation reincorporates the governing boards that now stand apart and above, so too does this corporation reappropriate the collective property that has been expropriated and is now monopolized by those same boards.

This anticapitalist corporate model demands that we reject the "absolutely specious" distinction conventionally drawn between, on the one hand, the university's financial concerns, which are managed by the university's trustees and senior administrators, and, on the other, its curricular affairs, whose supervision is now contingently delegated to the faculty. Instead, within the academy qua member corporation, the academy's capital assets hold value only because and insofar as they contribute to education's ends. The question, for example, of whether "to build a large stadium for athletic contests . . . depends upon the place to be assigned to athletics in the educational scheme,"[97] and no other consideration may be permitted to displace or supplant this criterion. This decision must therefore be placed in the hands of all members of this body politic rather than any partial segment claiming exclusive or final authority.

Adoption of this standard will mean little if the faculty's role is confined to mere consultation, for that effectively denies their standing as corporate members on equal footing with all others. To illustrate how this principle might be institutionalized, an anonymous contributor to *University Control* reported that at Stanford each proposal of major import for the university, ranging from the capital to the curricular, is brought to an advisory board of faculty members prior to trustee consideration. If substantial opposition emerges within this board, the proposal is withdrawn. Exercise of this prior veto power thereby ensures that no matter of substance of any sort "will be taken up by the board of trustees at its own initiative."[98] So, too, this provision substantially increases the likelihood that the language of efficiency, which is the hollow vernacular of capital abstracted from human needs, will remain subordinate to debate about the qualitative ends of education as well as how best to accomplish them.

The primary organizational units of this republican academy, Cattell recommends, are to be departments whose financial and educational autonomy, in accordance with the American principle of federalism, shall be respected to the maximum extent possible. To nurture virtues akin to those fostered by democratic townships, each department "should be large enough to meet for deliberation and to represent diverse points of view, but small enough for each to understand the whole and to feel responsible for it."[99] Each department's members, moreover, are to elect their own chair as well as an executive committee, but these officers will stand not as mini-autocrats but as servants of the constituencies to which they owe their positions.

Lest these departments forget that they are organs of a more encompassing body politic, each is to select representatives to "a senate which should legislate for the university as a whole and be a body coordinate with the trustees."[100] Neither senate nor trustees, therefore, will monopolize the monocratic authority that enables governing boards within the academy as presently constituted to dictate the terms of collective governance. Instead, their joint agreement is a prerequisite of all statutes adopted and all actions taken in the name of a corporation neither unilaterally rules. Whereas the current regime has the effect of foregrounding the interests that divide faculty and trustees, to require that they concur is to highlight "the duties and responsibilities that belong to all in virtue of their membership in the common corporate life of the university."[101]

To further secure power's decentralization, these departments will retain the authority to nominate their own members: "The requisites of a true profession are that its members shall authoritatively represent, advance and control its own interests, as well as the qualifications for membership."[102] To check the faculty's penchant for parochial self-reproduction, these nominations will be forwarded to an advisory board that includes members of the department in question as well as related departments within the university but also several experts in the relevant discipline from other institutions. Final selection will be made by the university senate subject to veto by the trustees, thereby enabling those elected representatives to recall the interests of the corporation as a whole but absent the power to choose and then impose their own preferred candidates.

Once appointed, faculty members shall hold their positions "for life, except in the case of impeachment after trial" conducted by their peers.[103] This commitment to collegial adjudication presupposes a constitution of the faculty in the form of what one contributor to *University Control* labeled an "isocracy,"[104] for each of its members is granted equal power to judge every other member's competence. When joined to tenure, this due process provision does do much to undo capitalist employment relations as well as the authoritarian proclivities they encourage on the part of those now invested with the discretionary power to hire and fire. Unlike those reduced to the status of employees, the members of the academic body politic imagined by Cattell are reinvested with the political character that vanishes when colleges and universities are figured as in *Dartmouth*— that is, as apolitical property corporations. That repoliticization is inherent within the academy's constitution as a corporation vested with the power of collective self-governance, but only when that power is distributed and organized democratically rather than autocratically.

Equally important, the remuneration received by these scholars is not a capitalist wage but, rather, that which enables them to do their work well: "The fundamental assumption that the relation involved between a professor and his university is similar to that between employee and employer," wrote an early contributor to the "professors' literature of protest," "cannot be admitted for an instant. . . . The business policy of a university must not be that of the commercial market in which the employer who succeeds in securing a given article or labor at the lowest cost may expect to reap the benefit of his shrewdness, but it should be to supply each holder of a university living with the equipment—professional, personal, and social—which shall develop to the maximum the capacity of the individual to serve his university and his fellow-men."[105] Tenure and peer review are thereby complemented by a form of remuneration that construes scholars as contributors to the academy's larger cause rather than as economically rational agents whose interests are antagonistic to employers seeking the biggest bang for the smallest buck.

Considered as a whole, Cattell's proposal for a reincorporated academy expresses a quintessentially American distrust of power concentrated in any single location and, toward that end, denies to any one actor the capacity to rule by imposition. This denial applies as fully to faculty as it does to president and trustees: "Experts and intellectuals are not, as a rule, to be trusted to act for the common good in preference to their personal interest. The professors of an endowed university can not be given the ultimate control."[106] As in a well-ordered republic, the operation of an interlocking system of checks and balances is an indispensable condition of the academy's constitution as what one of Cattell's respondents envisioned as a "free commonwealth."[107] That commonwealth, suggested a contrarian Cattell, will be characterized by "as much flexibility and as complete anarchy throughout the university as is consistent with unity and order" (where "anarchy" is understood not as a condition of chaos but as any departure from vigorous engagement in the practice of democratic self-governance).[108]

Two Cheers for the "Professors' Literature of Protest"

As I noted at the beginning of this chapter, what is perhaps most bracing about *University Control* is its employment of explicitly political categories to challenge the turn-of-the-century university and imagine alternatives to its corporate constitution (for example, "autocracy," "self-governance," "rights," "republicanism," and "democracy").[109] What vitiates the analysis offered within the "professors' literature of protest" is its contributors' failure to appreciate the more expansive import of Cattell's exhortation that the academy become a "democracy of scholars serving the larger democracy of which it is a part." Cattell's colleagues focus their attention almost entirely on the academy's internal structures of rule and their reformation and hence, with very few exceptions, do not ask whether the very possibility of reforming those structures entails a corresponding reconstitution of the "larger democracy of which it is a part."

To their credit, Cattell and Veblen do exactly that. For example, in a 1912 essay titled "A Program of Radical Democracy," Cattell argues in favor of (1) providing free health care to all; (2) extending full economic, political, and legal rights to women; (3) guaranteeing to all the civil liberties that are the guarantors of political freedom; (4) adopting progressive income, inheritance, real estate, luxury goods, and corporate taxes; (5) reforming the court system so as to eliminate the immunities presently enjoyed by the wealthy; (6) eliminating the private debt that now enriches only the "kleptocratic classes"; (7) adopting maximum labor hour and minimum wage laws; (8) funding public education for all; (9) decreasing the power of the federal government, and especially that of the presidency by reducing this officeholder to the status of an "executive officer of Congress"; (10) converting the army into a "corps for engineering work and other improvements"; (11) furnishing old-age and disability pensions as well as subsidies for childcare; (12) offering state subsidies for labor-saving technological inventions with the aim of reducing by three-quarters the work each must now do; and (13) transferring ownership of the "tools of production" to those who labor, with any surplus returning to those who generated it: "The industrial slavery which has resulted from the passing from individual production to group production can be abolished only by group ownership. The group might be the community, but when possible it should be those who work in the factory, cultivate the farm, sail the ship, etc."[110]

Although he does not expressly draw this connection, with these proposals Cattell effectively suggests that achievement of a "democracy of scholars" entails not just a reincorporation of the academy but also a reconstitution of the capitalist political economy within which it is embedded. Absent that regime's transformation, there is little reason to believe that the academy can be much more than a device for reproducing existing forms of class domination and silencing those who denounce its role in doing so. "It will avail little to speculate on remedial corrections for this state of academic affairs so long as the institutional ground of this perversion remains intact," and that ground, Veblen tells us, "is the current system of private ownership."[111]

8
"Shared Governance" as Placebo

"Take Me Back to Tulsa"

In July 2020, two faculty members employed by the University of Tulsa offered an autopsy of the controversy provoked by the board's adoption of "True Commitment" (see chapter 1). In a piece titled "How to Resist a Corporate Takeover of Your College," Jeffrey Hockett and Jacob Howland urged colleagues at other colleges and universities not to "repeat our mistake." Faculty members elsewhere, they explained, must "take preemptive action" aimed at "avoiding much of the damage our university has suffered." These strategies include, among others, forming a chapter of the American Association of University Professors and articulating "a meaningful conception of shared governance, one in which faculty members have a substantial say in the selection of upper administrators and the determination of all matters affecting teaching and learning."[1]

But what if appeals to the form of empowerment called "shared governance" actually ratify the faculty's disempowerment? And what if the foremost champion of shared governance, the AAUP, has done more to reinforce than to challenge the autocratic constitution of rule within American colleges and universities? What if, in short, the strategies offered by Hockett and Howland do not furnish a prescription for combating "a corporate takeover of your college" but instead are an intrinsic part of the problem Hockett and Howland call on them to solve?

This chapter explains why each of these questions should be answered in the affirmative. In doing so, I do not mean to discount the valuable work of an organization of which I am a member, especially in defending the cause of academic freedom. But I do urge us to turn a critical eye toward the AAUP's defense of shared governance and, more particularly, its representation of the professoriate's claim to participate in ruling the academy as a prerogative that turns on its status as a specifically modern profession. This characterization, which is coeval with and indeed constitutive of the AAUP, represented a choice but also a wager. It was a choice insofar as alternative conceptions of the professoriate were available at the time; and it was a wager insofar as the outcome of this choice was far from certain. The history of shared governance is the story of this ill-fated gamble.

The Political Economy of Modern Professionalism

Because past is prologue to present, it is worth noting that the roots of modern professionalism can be traced back to medieval European guilds. Between about 1150 and 1400, guilds became one of the principal ways of organizing work that assumed the form of skilled crafts, as practiced by metalsmiths, bakers, leatherworkers, weavers, and others. The purpose of these associations was to secure a monopoly over the skills their members mastered as well as the products they made and, by doing that, to control the market for both. By regulating the conditions of entry, guilds limited the supply of labor that could practice any given craft; by regulating the tools and techniques of those admitted, they controlled their collective working conditions; and by regulating the production of goods, they effectively fixed their prices. To reinforce these powers, guilds often sought charters, issued in the form of letters patent and typically granted in return for payment of taxes, that recognized their status as incorporated societies.

To call a guild a "universitas," as was not uncommon, was to include it within the broader category of member corporations. Forming the associational prototype for the earliest universities, including those at Bologna, Oxford, and Paris, these guilds were self-governing associations whose form of rule was distinct from that exercised by princes, feudal lords, and ecclesiastical authorities over their respective subjects. The powers of self-governance practiced by guilds, academic or otherwise, included the right not just to control who was or was not admitted to their societies but also to select members of their governing assemblies and to codify the rules that were to regulate their internal conduct as well as the sanctions to be imposed on those who violated them.

Presaging the fate of modern professions, what eventually destroyed craft guilds was the insinuation of merchant capitalism within their operations. As craft differentiation proliferated and competition among guilds increased, their members found it necessary to turn to those who specialized in trade, whether wholesale or retail, to secure the raw materials necessary to their practice and to extend the scope of the markets where their goods might be sold. In time, to oversimplify a complicated history, these merchants developed their own guilds, which eventually overwhelmed their craft counterparts, chiefly by securing ownership of the means of artisanal production. That in turn generated a transformation in the governance structures of craft guilds, as those who were once their junior members, whether apprentices or journeymen, were now hired by merchant owners as wage workers. Decomposition of work organized in the form of craft guilds, in short, was a key precondition of what in time would become industrial production organized on capitalist principles.

Specifically modern professions display significant traces of these member corporations but should not be equated with medieval guilds, for they emerge within and in response to a very different political economy.[2] To furnish an adequate account of this new regime of accumulation, which I can only hint at here, would require a chronicle of the displacement of an agricultural by an industrializing economy; the transformation of small entrepreneurs and independent farmers into an urban working class composed of dispossessed wage earners; the escalating importance of technological innovation to an economy geared to mass production; the correlative invention of scientific management as a field of inquiry tasked with ensuring the cost-effective integration of human labor power with forms of fixed capital; and so forth. Together, these disruptions opened new occupational opportunities for those seeking to capitalize on the decline of merchant capitalism.

This new form of capitalism required kinds of knowledge that were not and could not be provided by the medieval craft guilds, whose tacit know-how was fully embedded in skilled practice and transmitted from one generation to the next chiefly by means of apprenticeships. Nor could this knowledge be furnished by the humanistic curriculum that had defined American colleges since the seventeenth century; that was afforded its most famous defense in the Yale Report of 1828;[3] and that principally aimed at cultivating the character as well as the mental discipline of educated elites. Whereas the so-called classical curriculum privileged the study of ancient Greek and Latin texts situated within a Judeo-Christian architectonic, the imperatives of industrial capitalism required forms of expert knowledge that were abstracted from the skilled practice of artisanal crafts, that could be systematized as formal disciplines, and that were grounded in the rising natural sciences and eventually the social sciences as well.

Neither the small-scale technical institutes nor the modest agricultural and mechanical colleges of the nineteenth century were able to satisfy the demand for such expertise. The newly invented research universities of America, however, were quick to do so.[4] Beginning with the formation of Johns Hopkins in 1876 and collectively organized via the American Association of Universities in 1900, in prestige and resources this new sort of academic corporation rapidly superseded the small sectarian undergraduate colleges that dotted the American landscape in the nineteenth century. Drawing their inspiration principally from German models and funded either by state appropriations (think land grant universities) and/or by wealthy philanthropists (think Leland Stanford, John Rockefeller, and Cornelius Vanderbilt), these are the institutions that so vexed contributors to the "professors' literature of protest" and elicited their call to reconstruct the academy on the model of a self-governing republic.

The triumph of the research university is attributable in large measure to its success in forming alliances with the emerging occupations that provided the expertise required by industrial capitalism and that claimed an identity as professions in order to distinguish their work from that of robber barons but also wage laborers. In his history of US higher education, looking backward, Roger Geiger notes that "professional education, with the partial exception of theology, grew progressively estranged from the college during most of the nineteenth century and similarly distanced from the frontiers of knowledge."[5] One of the major victories of the new American university was its reversal of this trajectory. This was accomplished by securing jurisdiction over bodies of specialized knowledge that can only be acquired through extended formal training in academic disciplines and that, once attained, warrant conferring the credentials required for authorized occupational practice. Graduate programs thereby joined within a single institution the inquiry that generates the forms of knowledge required by ascendant professions as well as the authority to train and certify those who make a living from that knowledge's employment.

The faculty of the American research university thus became what we might call the "uber-profession," and it did so by establishing itself as the exclusive gatekeeper authorized to determine who may be certified as masters of the specialized forms of knowledge that yield the privileges of professional occupation outside the academy. The professoriate of the ascendant university thereby joined forces with, for example, the elite cohort of attorneys who in the late nineteenth century sought to disqualify the law offices that provided apprenticeships in civil law to those with no postsecondary education. So, too, did many proprietary teaching hospitals affiliate with research universities to discredit nineteenth-century spiritualists, railway surgeons, and others who competed for business in ministering to the body's woes. No amount of empirical experience, insisted the university's champions, could qualify one to practice law or medicine. Only credentialed mastery of bodies of esoteric knowledge distinguishes quacks from true professionals, whether these be snake oil salesmen as opposed to licensed physicians or unscrupulous pettifoggers as opposed to certified lawyers.

Steven Brint neatly defines modern professions "as those occupations exercising the capacity to create exclusive shelters in the labor market through the monopolization of advanced degrees and other credentials related to higher education that are required for the attainment of the social and economic opportunities of authorized practice."[6] Like the formation of medieval craft guilds, professionalization is a process whereby certain occupations create but also seek to control a market not for tangible commodities but, instead, for the certified expertise they monopolize. By adopting credential requirements that only universities could provide and in some instances by persuading the state to impose licensing requirements only it could mandate, modern professions regulate the supply of their labor by denying entry to those without the necessary qualifications. By claiming exclusive authority to set the standards of competent professional practice, they secure considerable autonomy from those who do not possess this esoteric knowledge and so are unable to judge the adequacy of its occupational application. By denying that their practice can be reduced to a prescribed set of routinized tasks of the sort that defines, for example, work on an assembly line, modern professionals affirm their discretionary authority to do their jobs as they see fit instead of merely obeying orders issued by employers or giving consumers what they think they want. Through these means, the modern professions fashion what Brint calls "labor shelters," and what these shelters provide is some measure of independence from and protection against the mundane forms of workplace control that define the relations between capitalists and workers or, in the case of bureaucracies, managers and subordinates.

These bastions of qualified autonomy were fortified via creation of national professional associations: for example, doctors founded the American Medical Association in 1847, and attorneys founded the American Bar Association in 1878. According to the terms of their constitutions, these are self-governing associations that control their own membership, elect their own representatives, create their own bylaws, and establish standards of occupational practice that can be invoked when necessary to censure, suspend, expel, or place on probation those who fail to meet them.[7] In short, these associations are member corporations that are distinguished from their medieval precursors not by how they structure governance but by their affiliates' standing as distinctly modern professionals.

The Mythology of Modern Professionalism

Because modern professions claim workplace perquisites denied to others, they remain forever subject to challenge and so require a mythology that will help immunize them from attack. For example, because their status is predicated on certified claims to cognitive expertise and hence an expectation of deference on the part of those who need their knowledge but are ignorant of it, professions find themselves vulnerable within market economies grounded in the conviction that the consumer is always right. So, too, because the goods proffered by the professions may sometimes be unrecognized, unvalued, or even rejected by their beneficiaries, they are jeopardized within democracies grounded in the conviction that individuals are ultimately the best judges of their own interests. Perhaps most important, because the professions impede the otherwise unfettered operation of capitalist labor markets, they are forever liable to attacks initiated by those whose class interests will be advanced by eliminating these occupational harbors.

To keep these threats at bay, modern professions require a credo that will legitimate the authority that is a necessary condition of their relative autonomy. That doctrine's essential elements are nicely captured by Larry Gerber who in *The Rise and Decline of Faculty Governance* characterizes professionalism as the deployment of "expertise in a disinterested way to achieve the common good."[8] The authority of modern professions thus turns on two idealizations. First, their practice is grounded in the form of disinterested reason that is modern science; and, second, their occupations are not jobs but vocations. Braided together, these elements enable modern professionals to affirm that their work is categorically distinct from the inexpert but also from the labor of those engaged in the self-interested pursuits that define commercial enterprises, and that is so regardless of whether one is a boss or a hired hand.

Prior to the twentieth century, as illustrated by medieval guilds, the term *expert* was employed in vernacular reference to anyone whose skill was rooted in extensive empirical experience within any given domain. What distinguishes the specifically modern expert is the grounding of skilled practice not in the accumulation of experience but, instead, in the bodies of abstract reason we now call "science." What exactly counted as modern science around the turn of the twentieth century was, admittedly, defined more by what it was not than by what it was. For example, whether taking shape as the disciplines that gradually emancipated themselves from the once-comprehensive category of "natural philosophy" or those that emerged from "history" and "political economy" as the several social sciences, inquiry claiming this mantle was distinguished from the deductive moral and metaphysical systems that were quickly losing their cachet. Moreover, incessant invocation of the "experimental method" made clear that modern scientific rationality was something other than inductively generated taxonomic classifications of observed phenomena. Beyond that, what affirmatively counted as modern science was less clear; and, arguably, this term did little more than gesture toward forms of inquiry that distinguished themselves from their inferior predecessors by employing protopositivist terms such as *objective, neutral, disinterested,* and *facts.* Whatever its exact sense, the partisans of modern science harbored few doubts about the superiority of its epistemological authority to all previous pretenders to the status of knowledge.

The second ingredient of this ideal, which cannot be supplied by the first alone, concerns the character of professional occupations as vocations. This preindustrial construction of work, as Max Weber taught us, can be traced back to the Calvinist extension of the clerical idea of a "calling" to earthly occupations understood as the fulfillment of one's spiritual obligations in this world. Once secularized, this idea provides the foundation for the characterization of modern professional labor as the performance of a service on behalf of others.

An orientation to useful service, however, is insufficient to differentiate modern professionals from others who also serve, whether they be merchants who supply goods to customers or politicians who furnish benefits to constituents. What raises professional work above these less noble forms of work is its conduct on behalf of ends, like those advanced by its ministerial precursors, that transcend purposes considered mundane. These are the inherently valuable ends—for example, health and education—that are universal or "common," to employ Gerber's term, because they are held to promote the true interests of all and so are not specific to any given class or party. The emergent professions, in sum, seek to secure a monopoly of control over certain occupational markets as well as the materials benefits that ensue, but then transmute these advantages into affirmations of authority by invoking the pre- and indeed anticapitalist precepts signified by phrases such as *the common good* or *the public interest*. A claim to specifically scientific expertise, folded within a characterization of work as a vocation, thus provides the bedrock for the professions' declaration of their special authority and dignity.

The Road Taken (and Others That Might Have Been)

Everything I have said thus far about modern professions in general can be said of the professionalizing professoriate in particular. Prior to the turn of the twentieth century, except at a few elite institutions, most college teachers were poorly compensated, often itinerant, routinely harassed by unruly students, and subject to the authoritarian rule of chief executives appointed by absentee trustees. Making matters worse, it was during the second half of the nineteenth century that the unforgiving doctrine of "employment at will" was consecrated in law and extended to professors. To cite but one example, when Scott Nearing was dismissed from the University of Pennsylvania because of his socialist and antimilitarist commitments, its governing board invoked *Dartmouth* as the basis for its claim that "the present equipment and endowment of the University are indeed the property of the trustees, to be administered as they see fit," and for this reason "the relation of a University professor to the trustees" is "the same as that of a day laborer to his employers." Nearing's dismissal was thereby rendered beyond the law's purview because those who "own" the academy have no ongoing obligations to those they hire other than to pay them;

and, for that reason, employers can dismiss faculty members "whenever the interests of the college required."[9]

Transformation of these unorganized and disempowered teachers into a profession in the making was signaled by, among other things, the growing presumption that graduate training and, more often than not, receipt of a doctoral degree is required for instructional appointments, thereby affirming the professoriate's hegemony over the academic profession itself; the expectation that academic employment will assume the form of a full-time salaried career characterized by upward mobility through ranks on the basis of merit; the anticipation that research in addition to teaching will be an essential element of that career; the invention of disciplinary associations, such as the Modern Language Association (1883), the American Physical Society (1899), and the American Political Science Association (1903), to promote that scholarship; and, of course, eventual formation of a national association claiming to represent the academic profession's members as one.

Mimicking a strategy employed by the legal and medical professions, an unrepresentative group of elite faculty members drawn mostly from East Coast research universities founded the American Association of University Professors in 1915. Formation of the AAUP is often represented as an act that gave voice to an already professionalized profession. Better, though, to think of this as a performative act that actively participated in creating a transinstitutional profession whose authority turns on the mythology of vocational expertise. This self-representation in turn furnished the foundation for asserting certain workplace prerogatives, including tenure, academic freedom, and participation in institutional governance, that cannot be claimed by those whose work fails to qualify as professional. Indeed, these perquisites are peculiar to the academic profession insofar as they are not claimed by other professionals, for example, doctors, lawyers, and civil engineers.

The AAUP's choice to represent the professoriate as a specifically modern profession may appear self-evident today. It is important to recall, however, that this collective identity was not preordained but, instead, was one possible identity among several that might have been chosen. For example, the AAUP would have become a very different organization had it, following the lead of the "professors' literature of protest," insisted that the academy be reconstituted as a republican body politic and its members as that body's "citizens." This, as we saw in the last chapter, was very much a live option; and in fact its loudest exponent, James McKeen Cattell, was the first to propose formation of national association of higher education faculty.[10]

Had Cattell's vision prevailed, the AAUP almost certainly would have done what it did not: mount a vigorous challenge to the academy's autocratic constitution in the name of equal rights to participate in "university control." That something akin to this was more than a mere theoretical possibility is indicated by the now mostly forgotten struggles of the Populist movement to press for wholesale reconstruction of the American academy, especially within the land grant universities founded during the last third of the nineteenth century on land whose expropriation from Indigenous peoples was effectively consummated via their establishment.[11]

Populist voices within the academy, including Christian Balzac Hoffman, Thomas Elmer Will, E. V. Forell, and others, joined their condemnation of corporate capitalism to a broader appeal on behalf of the university's democratization. To do so, they extended their denunciation of economic and political aristocracies to elitist universities that sought monopolistic control over the production and dissemination of knowledge. Contending that democracy could flourish only if "equal knowledge" became the "common property of all classes,"[12] in Kansas, North Carolina, Nebraska, and elsewhere the academy's Populists forged strategic alliances with the Farmers' Alliance, the Knights of Labor, and the Grange to secure partial and in at least one instance complete control over the governing boards of several public universities. Besides calling for the academy's emancipation from plutocratic control, these coalitions also demanded universal access to higher education, full funding of public universities by state governments, formulation of a curriculum that rejects the invidious distinction between work of the head and that done by hand, transformation of universities into cooperative ventures insulated from a market economy, and protection of scholarly inquiry from perversion by moneyed oligarchs bent on extinguishing academic freedom.

So, too, the AAUP could have identified itself with the labor movement then emerging among American teachers. Indeed, in 1919, Cattell wrote: "When the present writer first proposed the establishment of such an association his plans were more directly in the form of a union. It might now be desirable for the more radical academic teachers to form a national union affiliated with the American Federation of Labor."[13] Thinking Cattell correct, the AAUP's first president, John Dewey, was also an officeholder within the American Federation of Teachers, founded in 1916.

Denying that his membership in the latter was incompatible with his status in the former, Dewey argued that the AAUP could not fulfill its mission absent a strong union prepared to use its collective clout to advance the economic interests of faculty: "There is need for a working, aggressive organization that represents all of the interests that teachers have in common, and which, in representing them, represents also the protection of the children and the youth in the schools against all of the outside interests, economic and political and others that would exploit the schools for their own ends, and in doing so, reduce the teaching body to a condition of intellectual vassalage."[14]

Dewey's position, however, was not embraced by the AAUP. In his 1919 presidential address, Arthur Lovejoy insisted that the situation of the professoriate is essentially different "from that of the wage-earner bargaining with the private capitalist over the division of the profits of industry."[15] Were the AAUP to represent itself as a trade union, Lovejoy went on, that would jeopardize its identity as a profession constituted as an expert vocation committed to a good that is shared by all. Should the professoriate prove partisan, Lovejoy concluded, its claim to authority will vanish.

Rejecting these rival paths, the AAUP staked its existence on the professional ideal and hence the invidious distinctions that are essential to that identity. Whether explained by the seductions of Progressive ideology, a status-based aversion to identification as common laborers, and/or intimidation by the Red Scare's ideologues, the AAUP opted for a reformist project that sought to ameliorate the lot of faculty members but left unchallenged the academy's received constitutional frame. Accepting as unalterable what Dewey called the "inherently absurd" and creaky "machinery" of academic governance inherited from "colonial days and provincial habits,"[16] the AAUP jettisoned the goal of securing "university control" in favor of a far less threatening commitment to "shared governance." This choice, which Clyde Barrow has aptly called an "accommodationist strategy,"[17] involved accepting final control over colleges and universities by governing boards increasingly dominated by representatives of corporate capitalism but then seeking limited concessions from those ill prepared to appreciate the distinctive work of the academy.

The history of what comes to be known as "shared governance" is the story of a struggle to negotiate the dilemma confronted by those who are employees but whose status as vocational experts demands that they not be treated as such. That history is a tale of the AAUP's ultimately bootless attempt to figure out how to locate and preserve the horizontal relations of authority that define member corporations within the confines of property corporations predicated on a vertical construction of rule. In the last analysis, this tale is a tragedy whose professorial protagonist required an effective labor market shelter as a condition of its survival but whose professional self-identity rendered it ill equipped to defend that shelter against its enemies.

The Holy Trinity

Representation of professional work as the enactment of a vocational duty to employ nonpartisan expertise on behalf of universal ends justifies its practitioners' partial exemption from the full force of capitalism's prosaic disciplinary mechanisms. In the case of the professoriate, these exemptions compose the AAUP's holy trinity: academic freedom, tenure, and shared governance. These prerogatives are essentially interdependent insofar as each is the condition of the others' possibility. Absent tenure, argued the AAUP's foundational "1915 Declaration of Principles on Academic Freedom and Tenure" (hereafter the "Declaration"), faculty will not possess the job security they must have if they are to exercise academic freedom. Absent academic freedom, faculty will fear reprisal should they take issue with employers outfitted as senior administrators, and that will chill if not silence the contributions to institutional governance they alone are qualified to make. Absent participation in shared governance, faculty will be unable to safeguard the mission of colleges and universities from those who, within as well as without, find academic freedom and tenure unfamiliar if not indefensible.[18] The AAUP's bet, placed at its inception and still in effect today, is that the professoriate's identify as a profession can protect this trio of prerogatives from an economic formation bent on weakening and in time removing all impediments to capital accumulation. This gamble, as we shall see, was ill-advised from the get-go and has now proven a wholesale bust.

As is true of all modern professions, the AAUP argues that what qualifies the professoriate for this status is, first, its mastery of forms of cognitively based expertise that can only be acquired through "prolonged and specialized technical training"; and, second, its employment of this expertise "exempt from any pecuniary motive" in the service of ends that transcend all parochial interests. What renders "the academic calling" the most precious of all professions is its unique commitment to secure the "progress in scientific knowledge" that is "essential to civilization."[19] The academy, on this Enlightenment construction, provides a home for inquiry that presses beyond the boundaries of received wisdom and, by doing that, enables all to overcome the fetters that otherwise block humanity's emancipation from a retrograde past now congealed as the present.

When the professoriate disrupts conventional truths, backlash is sure to follow, whether from a public whose opinions are discomfited by the unfamiliar and/or from those whose power and privilege turn on maintenance of the status quo. Therefore, the "Declaration" contends, faculty members must possess the freedom that enables them "to perform honestly and according to their own consciences the distinctive and important function which the nature of the profession lays upon them."[20] Whether in the classroom or in the conduct of scholarly inquiry, the doctrine of academic freedom affirms the professoriate's collective right to be exempt from unwarranted interference by those who, when it comes to such matters, do not know what they are talking about.

The AAUP's endorsement of codified tenure policies is justified in the "Declaration" because they protect academic freedom, and they do so by ensuring qualified immunity from the terms of at-will employment within a capitalist economy. That shield is secured not by challenging capitalism's construction of work as the sale of labor for a wage and hence as a contractual relationship between employer and employees but, rather, by tweaking its terms. Specifically, the AAUP argues that termination of an employee by an employer must be preceded by a hearing before one's peers and predicated on demonstrated inability or failure to fulfill the responsibilities incumbent on professionals. Whereas the adequate cause provision tempers the arbitrariness inherent in at-will employment, the requirement of due process stipulates that colleagues rather than employers should determine whether their peers have violated professional standards.

To defend these departures from capitalist employment practices, the AAUP insists that professorial work is something other than and indeed superior to the work done by those who are in fact only employees. The work of the professor must not be regarded as "a purely private employment, resting on a contract between the employing authority and the teacher."[21] To illustrate why that is so, the AAUP likens professors to judges who are appointed by politicians but who hold office "during good behavior." Professors, then, are not ordinary laborers hired in accordance with specific terms of employment; instead, they are more like commissioned officers of associations dedicated to goods that serve all. Unlike workers who are legally obligated to obey whatever orders employers issue, professors qua professionals cannot and must not be expected to do as they are told. To act as a professional is, by definition, to exercise discretionary judgment in determining how best to achieve the ends that define any occupation constituted as an expert vocation. Indeed, were a professor to do only what an employer commands, that would constitute a betrayal of the professional ideal.

From this, it follows that the obligations of professors extend far beyond the colleges and universities that pay them: "For, once appointed, the scholar has professional functions to perform in which the appointing authorities have neither competency nor moral right to intervene. The responsibility of the university teacher is primarily to the public itself, and to the judgment of his own profession; and while, with respect to certain external conditions of his vocation, he accepts a responsibility to the authorities of the institution in which he serves, in the essentials of his professional activity his duty is to the wider public to which the institution itself is morally amenable."[22] In other words, even though the expertise of a professionalized professoriate is sold as a commodity in a capitalist labor market, the contractual terms that govern this employment do not exhaust the academic's responsibilities qua professional. The more comprehensive and compelling duties of professors are owed to ends that transcend the walls of any specific college or university, and so their fulfillment must not be circumscribed by anyone within their perimeter.

To affirm this, the AAUP acknowledges, is not to deny that the professional academic is legally obligated to perform the tasks outlined in a contract specifying the terms of employment. Nor is it to claim that faculty members are protected from discipline for incompetence, refusal, or failure to satisfy these terms. After all, the "Declaration" concedes, governing boards and the executive agents to whom they delegate certain responsibilities are "the ultimate repositories of power" within the academy; and hence, in the last analysis, those at the apex of this autocracy retain the legal authority to dismiss any employee with or without cause. So, too, the AAUP admits that governing boards retain the ultimate legal right "to determine the measure of academic freedom which is to be realized" within any given college or university;[23] and, for that reason, it is not clear what if any remedy is available should this freedom be attenuated or even abolished, thereby rendering accomplishment of the academy's mission impossible.

Lacking any legal foundation for its claim that governing boards should not treat faculty members as mere employees, the AAUP can only rely on exhortation grounded in the professional ideal. To supplement this exhortation, the "Declaration" seeks to rethink not just what it is to be a professor but also what it is to be a governing board member. If it is true that trustees have "no moral right to bind the reason or the conscience of any professor,"[24] that is because, properly understood, they are not simply employers but also guardians of the collective good that is education. Just as appointment as a professor should "be regarded as a quasi-public official employment," so too those who assume office as trustees should "act not as private employers or from private motives but as public trustees."[25] As fiduciaries of a unique common good, governing board members are therefore obligated to uphold the conditions essential to that good's accomplishment and so should refrain from exercising the autocratic powers they never relinquish.

The "Declaration," however, gives us little reason to expect that trustees will in fact exercise such self-restraint and plenty of reason to think this improbable at best. As one would anticipate, the "Declaration" demands that colleges and universities be organized "in such a way as to make impossible any exercise of pressure upon professorial opinions and utterances by governing boards of laymen." Yet it also acknowledges that the practice of scholarly inquiry will often engender views that "point toward extensive social innovations, or call in question the moral legitimacy or social expediency of economic conditions or commercial practices in which large vested interests are involved."[26] Fulfillment of the scholars' vocation, therefore, cannot help but provoke attempts to rein in those whose work displeases the powers that be.

Within private institutions, calls to do so will most often emerge from "benefactors, as well as most of the parents who send their children to privately endowed institutions" and who "belong to the more prosperous and therefore usually to the more conservative classes." These demands are likely to find a receptive audience among governing boards because they too are "made up of men who through their standing and ability are personally interested in great private enterprises."[27] Indeed, as we saw in chapter 6, the acquiescence of boards to benefactors within the US academy is not a contingent feature to be remedied by educating trustees about their "true" obligations. Rather, this subordination is structurally baked into private colleges by *Dartmouth*'s construction of academic charters as trusts and hence governing board members as trustees whose principal legal obligation is to ensure that the will of founders and donors be observed in perpetuity.

Within public institutions, the "menace to academic freedom" is still more pronounced because scholarly inquiry will often give rise to conclusions that "differ from the views entertained by the authorities" on whom "the university is dependent for funds." This peril is compounded in democratic orders because the work of government officers and especially elected representatives demands responsiveness to the shifting tides of public opinion. "The tendency of modern democracy," after all, "is for men to think alike, to feel alike, and to speak alike," and so "any departure from the conventional standards is apt to be regarded with suspicion." The "tyranny of public opinion," a form of despotism that draws strength from the doctrine of popular sovereignty, does not bode well for an institution whose purpose, among others, is "to help make public opinion more self-critical and more circumspect, to check the more hasty and unconsidered impulses of popular feeling."[28]

In short, in public as well as private institutions, "the points of possible conflict" between governing boards and a professionalized professoriate are "numberless," and the academy's ability to stand as an "inviolable refuge" for free inquiry will remain forever fragile. To secure its independence from those in positions of power as well as from those who are not, the AAUP must persuade not merely governing boards and presidents but also the public more generally to guarantee to the professoriate certain occupational privileges that are alien to most employers and denied to the vast majority of employees. Indeed, these employers and employees alike must agree not only to refrain from treading where they do not belong but also to defer to the esoteric expertise of those who challenge their most cherished beliefs as well as the order from which the powerful now derive considerable profit. This is a tall order for any honorific ideal, and the AAUP has given us every reason to suspect that the mythology of modern professionalism is not up to the task.

How the AAUP Shrank Shared Governance

The final element of the AAUP's holy trinity is the gospel of shared governance, and its scripture goes something like this: If academics can rightfully claim to share in institutional governance, that is because they are professionals. As specialists in forms of esoteric knowledge their rulers lack, their participation is necessary to the "academic calling" and hence the mission of higher education. For example, the conduct of peer review in assessing candidates for promotion or in determining whether utterances are protected by the doctrine of academic freedom constitute forms of collective self-regulation that professors are entitled to because they possess expertise others do not. This same argument obtains when faculty members claim primary if not exclusive authority over the curriculum on the grounds that they know better than do students, administrators, or politicians what best advances the cause of education. This rationale loses some of its force but not all plausibility when faculty lay claim to a governance role in other institutional domains that have a direct bearing on the academic program—for example, the formulation of annual operating budgets. The possibility of additionally extending this principle ends, however, when we arrive at matters for which the faculty's claim to specialized expertise is specious—for example, in the assignment of on-campus parking spots. Here faculty members may grouse, but their complaints can lay no claim to authority.

The AAUP formalized its attention to governance matters in 1916 when, one year after the "Declaration" was issued, it created Committee T on the Place and Function of Faculties in University Government and Administration. How this body framed its initial report signals the abiding influence of the overtly political categories that informed the "professors' literature of protest." The presence of these categories indicates in turn that the apolitical mythology of professionalism has not yet become so much conventional crust, although that will happen soon enough.

The opening section of Committee T's report, issued in 1920 and written by J. A. Leighton, posits two "extreme types of university organization—the autocratic and bureaucratic," on the one hand, and "the democratic," on the other. The first is fundamentally flawed for all the reasons advanced by Cattell and his fellow contributors to *University Control*: "The worst situations," Leighton explains, "arise when successful men of affairs, who constitute a preponderating proportion of the membership of boards of trustees, having a slight acquaintance with educational problems, labor under the illusion that they are educational experts and proceed to interfere in the internal conduct of the universities."[29] The autocratic academy, in short, is an institutionalized contradiction in terms because it places ultimate power in the hands of those who fail to grasp the end for which that power was first granted and is now wielded.

The democratic type is also flawed, but for different reasons. On this model, as Leighton presents it, the faculty would control all educational policies, select its own members as well as the president and other senior administrators, and determine the annual operating budgets of colleges and universities. The task of trustees on this construction "would be simply to hold and administer, in accordance with the wishes of the faculty, the property and income of the university." On this definition, board members would not be rulers but more akin to dismissible bankers entrusted with the funds of those who in the last analysis may always take their business elsewhere.

The problems that accompany this model, Leighton tells us, are these: "The lack of concentration of authority and responsibility would conduce to inefficiency; there would be a lack of initiative and leadership; personalities and politics would play too large a part in university government and administration; members of the faculty would spend too much of their time in the details of administrative and executive work, to the great neglect of their main duties as teachers and investigators."[30] The faculty's incapacity to assume the reins of collective self-governance, on this account, is not a consequence of their contraction of psychasthenia universitatis but, instead, is inherent within any scholarly enterprise that is organized democratically. Like its autocratic counterpart, this academy is also self-defeating, for its constitution of rule undermines the end for which it was founded.

Having framed his constitutional inquiry through reference to these defective bookends, Leighton offers a compromise that aims to incorporate the virtues of both without importing the vices of either: "The only solution lies in joint responsibility and control, with the distribution of emphasis on responsibility and control varying with the particular aspect of the whole matter of the conduct of university affairs which may be uppermost in a given situation." In their capacity as custodians of the academy's capital, for example, trustees should have "the principal and final control" over issues of "property and income," but the faculty should be "represented and heard on the matter." When it comes to "the determination and carrying out of educational policies, however, the members of the faculty are the experts, and should usually have the principal voice in the decision."[31]

What qualifies as an "educational policy" Committee T defines quite expansively. Extending far beyond curricular matters, this category encompasses setting standards for admission, specifying the student-faculty ratio, appointing faculty members, nominating deans and presidents, determining workload, selecting department chairs, promoting research, and apportioning funds between human and fixed capital. Should there be disagreement between faculty and trustees about whether this or that issue in fact counts as a matter of educational policy, Leighton insists, this question should be decided by "conference between trustees and faculty representatives and only after opportunity has been given for the faculty to consider and decide its views upon the matter."[32]

This last provision does not deny trustees any role in academic affairs, for they retain the "right to take the initiative in matters of educational policy." Their initiative, however, should never be more than a matter of "recommending for consideration by the faculty such changes thereof as they deem desirable." So that they may plead their case, trustees "should be invited to be present and to speak, without vote, in all university faculty meetings called to discuss general educational policies." But in considering any trustee recommendations, the faculty must retain its rightful role as "the legislative body for all matters concerning the educational policy of the university" and therefore never be denied its "right of consent." True, in strict legal terms, governing boards never relinquish their "voice in the final determination of its educational policies." But that voice should never be allowed to displace or replace the faculty's authority to conclude substantive questions about the academic program, broadly construed: "Except in financial matters, the trustees should not exercise directly the final power over educational policies and interests which, at the present time, they legally possess."[33]

It is against this backdrop that we should read the now canonical 1966 "Statement on Governance of Colleges and Universities" (hereafter the "Statement"). Prepared in consultation with the American Council on Education (ACE) and the Association of Governing Boards of Universities and Colleges (AGB), the "Statement" was "recognized" by ACE and the AGB as "a significant step forward in the clarification of the respective roles of governing boards, faculties, and administrations" but never formally endorsed by either.[34] Only the AAUP did so, and since its official adoption by the association's members in 1967, this document has become "the standard institutional reference for desirable academic governance policy."[35]

The 1966 "Statement" opens by indicating the circumstances that explain the urgent need for its composition: "The academic institution, public or private, often has become less autonomous; buildings, research, and student tuition are supported by funds over which the college or university exercises a diminishing control. Legislative and executive governmental authorities, at all levels, play a part in the making of important decisions in academic policy." Its independence threatened by powerful forces seeking to distort its mission, the academy's key constituencies must now sublimate their differences so that, in coalition, they can fend off enemies that imperil all.

The question that animated composition of the 1920 report was how best to distribute and organize "the respective powers and duties of boards of trustees, faculties, and administrative officers,"[36] and its answer was framed through reference to two possible models for the academy: the autocratic and the democratic. Tellingly, the 1966 "Statement" fails to fashion its analysis through reference to these or, for that matter, any other political models. This document thereby demonstrates that representation of the academy as a body politic whose organs are not employers and employees but members afforded equal rights to participate in its collective governance has now lost whatever power it once held to challenge the academy's constitution in the form of a property corporation. It is no surprise, therefore, that the "Statement" simply presents as a given and without comment the status of governing boards as "the final institutional authority."[37] Doing so, the AAUP occludes this fact's status as a contingent artifact whose consolidation required defeat of those who once dared to dispute the academy's autocratic constitution. Rather than contesting the academy's current distribution of power, the AAUP quietly capitulates.

With this fait accompli in place, the 1966 "Statement" advances two broad principles to guide colleges and universities in deciding issues that, because they implicate several constituencies, should not unilaterally be resolved by any one and so require "joint planning and effort: (1) important areas of action involve at one time or another the initiating capacity and decision-making participation of all the institutional components, and (2) differences in the weight of each voice, from one point to the next, should be determined by reference to the responsibility of each component for the particular matter at hand."[38] At first blush, these principles do not differ materially from those advanced in the 1920 report. A closer look, however, makes clear that the 1966 "Statement" represents a significant retreat from its 1920 counterpart and so should be read not as a source of faculty empowerment but as a surrender.

As already noted, the 1920 report acknowledged that the American academy is "autocratic in legal structure," whereas the 1966 "Statement" is replete with innocuous appeals to "communication," "consultation," and "participation" among the parties to "shared governance," thereby obscuring the power differentials that dictate who rules and who does not. The penchant for accommodation latent within this depoliticized pablum is equally apparent when, without comment, the "Statement" presents the self-perpetuating character of many governing boards as another incontestable given. The 1920 report, by way of contrast, made clear its opposition to rule by insular elites when it declared that a "board of trustees should never be a wholly self-perpetuating body, nor should trustees ever be elected for life."[39]

When the "Statement" turns its attention from governing boards to presidents, it lends the AAUP's imprimatur to precisely the sorts of actions that vexed the contributors to *University Control* and worried Committee T. Magnanimously portrayed as the incarnation of "institutional leadership," the "president has a special obligation to innovate and initiate" and, anticipating Tulsa's trustees, "must at times, with or without support, infuse new life into a department." Indeed, anticipating the regents of Texas Southern, presidents must be prepared to "solve problems of obsolescence" by exercising their authority to dismiss employees so long as their discharge observes the niceties of due process.[40] So much, then, for the 1920 report's representation of the faculty as a "legislature" that should control all educational policies, including personnel matters, and whose "right to consent" must never be abridged.

Whereas the 1920 report grounded the right to nominate deans in the professoriate, its 1966 counterpart assigns this responsibility to the president, who need only solicit advice from "the appropriate faculty." So, too, whereas the 1920 report defined the phrase *educational policies* in capacious terms and insisted that disputes over this term's scope should be resolved by conferences of faculty and trustees, the 1966 "Statement" significantly narrows this category's reach: "The faculty has primary responsibility for such fundamental areas as curriculum, subject matter and methods of instruction, research, faculty status, and those aspects of student life which relate to the educational process." Even in these matters, moreover, the "Statement" acknowledges the right of governing boards or their executive agents to exercise "the power of review or final decision," whereas the 1920 report aimed to confine these would-be autocrats to a merely consultative role.

Granted, the "Statement" insists that the power of trustees and presidents to override faculty conclusions in educational matters should be limited to "exceptional cases." But this is the exception that proves the rule and does nothing to challenge the underlying principle of trustee sovereignty. Perhaps not surprisingly, when the "Statement" asks how this power might be checked, it can do no more than exhort trustees to "undertake appropriate self-limitation."[41] We should recall, though, that the 1915 "Declaration" explained quite clearly why the exercise of such restraint is improbable at best, and hence why this is so much wishful thinking.

The 1966 "Statement," therefore, is not so much a battle cry to be invoked whenever the faculty's governance claims are jeopardized but, rather, an amplification of the accommodationist strategy adopted by the AAUP at its inception.[42] Abandoning the specifically political critique offered in *University Control*, conceding much that the 1920 report challenged, the AAUP in 1966 ensures that faculty affirmations of power will assume domesticated forms that can be disingenuously embraced by the academy's rulers even as they prove ever more disposed to do what they will. In short, the paradoxical conclusion to *COVID-19 and Academic Governance*, which appeals to the university's autocrats to save the cause of "shared governance," is but an articulation of the contradictions inherent within the 1996 "Statement."

The Professional Professoriate Undone

Failure of the doctrine of shared governance testifies to the broader failure of the project of academic professionalism. That project is predicated on a tenuous article of faith: constitution of the academic workforce in the form of a profession will enable it to sustain a labor market shelter that can immunize its members from the conditions that define most work in a capitalist economy. The fallacy of this credo is demonstrated by the sad situation of the contemporary US academic workforce. Here I cite but a sliver of the evidence that might be advanced to show why characterizations of the professoriate as a profession are today more fiction than fact.[43]

Although often overlooked, the AAUP's mission includes promotion of "the economic security of faculty, academic professionals, graduate students, post-doctoral fellows, and all those engaged in teaching and research in higher education."[44] This commitment to promote the professoriate's collective self-interest is awkward when juxtaposed to the AAUP's affirmation of this profession's status as a vocation, that profession's dedication to selfless ends that are specific to none and so good for all, and the AAUP's refusal, until late in its history, to embrace unions on the ground that their working-class members pursue partisan advantage. Be that as it may, since its inception the AAUP has always aimed at securing a middle-class position for faculty members, one that is distinguishable from blue-collar workers at one end and captains of industry at the other.

This class project has now come a cropper. Perhaps the most telling indicator of this debacle is the present status of tenure. Over the course of the past half century, the ratio of contingent appointments to those eligible for tenure has essentially flipped. In the late 1960s, about three-quarters of academic positions were tenure track, and the remaining quarter were contingent. Today those figures are nearly reversed; and, even more noteworthy, about half of all academic appointments in the United States are now not merely contingent but also part time.[45] This striking turnabout has been accomplished not primarily by the elimination of tenure-track positions (although the pandemic has provided cover for governing boards to do exactly that), but by their replacement by as well as the addition of new contingent positions. Hence, although the overall number of academic appointments has increased considerably over the course of the past half century, less than a quarter have been to full-time tenured or tenure-track positions. If it is true that by 2040 only 10 percent of academic appointments will be to tenure-eligible positions, as one study has predicted,[46] the history of tenure may come to appear a short-lived aberration from the general rule of at-will employment.

What are the employment conditions of the part-time contingent positions that now constitute a majority of all faculty appointments? As a rule, these adjuncts are employed on short-term contracts; few are eligible to apply for professional development funding or promotion to a higher rank; most receive meager compensation, averaging about $3,500 per course; many are itinerant in the sense that they teach on multiple campuses to secure something approximating full-time employment; fewer than half are eligible for employer-provided medical insurance; and, according to a recent study conducted by the American Federation of Teachers, approximately 80 percent sometimes struggle to cover basic household expenses.[47]

For these instructors, academic labor is not one element within a professional identity that exceeds the logic of capitalist employment, let alone a "career," but instead an exploitable just-in-time commodity that satisfies the desires of those fickle consumers we call "students." Higher education's army of adjuncts is now very much a part of what Guy Standing first dubbed "the precariat," and its members are located within what Adrianna Kezar and her colleagues have labeled "the gig academy."[48] If we consider receipt of postsecondary credentials sufficient to warrant use of this term, I suppose we may choose to call this workforce "professional." If truth be told, however, the terms of contingent employment cannot and do not furnish the autonomy that, according to the AAUP, identifies professionals. Nor can these terms secure for these instructors a labor market shelter that furnishes a haven from the relations of domination and subordination inherent within a capitalist economy.

The middle-class aspirations of the professional professoriate are additionally compromised by significant class stratification within the academic labor force itself; and, arguably, this sort of inequality renders impossible a profession's very existence. The achievement of specifically academic professionalism requires creation of a lateral space occupied by peers who, although not necessarily of equal intellectual acumen or accomplishment, can credibly call one another "colleagues." The specific form of equality implied by this term is an indispensable premise of the practice of peer review as manifest, for example, in assessment of one another's qualifications for reappointment and, for the fortunate few, tenure and/or promotion. This practice becomes a sham, however, when some have the luxury to devote considerable time to teaching and scholarship while most are treated unfairly when measured by the standards appropriate to the professoriate's diminishing elite.

More fundamentally, the assumption of coequal status undergirds the conviction that higher education's instructors qualify as members of a single profession and so share interests that override any that might otherwise divide them. Today, however, the existence of this horizontal space is subverted by structural inequalities that mock any pretensions to common identity. The academic workforce is now segmented into a privileged aristocracy and what might euphemistically be called an "underprivileged" majority but is better characterized as "the exploited." In a 2014 report issued by Democratic staff members of the US House Committee on Education and the Workforce, this polarization was represented as follows:

> The post-secondary academic workforce has undergone a remarkable change over the last several decades. The tenure-track college professor with a stable salary, firmly grounded in the middle or upper-middle class, is becoming rare. Taking her place is the contingent faculty: nontenure-track teachers, such as part-time adjuncts or graduate instructors, with no job security from one semester to the next, working at a piece rate with few or no benefits across multiple workplaces, and far too often struggling to make ends meet. . . . Their story is another example of the

shrinking middle class and another point in the widening gap between rich and poor.[49]

What this committee describes is the academic workforce's bifurcation into, on the one hand, a diminishing minority whose members are compensated well, enjoy the security of tenure and academic freedom, participate in shared governance, receive institutional support for research, and are afforded significant prestige as well as the deference that accompanies it; and, on the other hand, everyone else.[50]

This division undercuts any semblance of a shared professional identity but also actively pits members of the instructional labor force against one another. "Many tenured faculty," writes Joseph Schwartz, "believing that resources are scarce, worry that improvement in the conditions of other campus workers, including non-tenured faculty, might mean less reward for the tenured class—or, at least, higher teaching loads."[51] These conflicts between those who have and those who do not become still more troubling when we recall that a majority of "the tenured class" consists of older white men, whereas women and persons of color make up an ever greater percentage of the class of contingents.[52] For this reason, to insist that all faculty share a status as professionals, as does the AAUP in its "One Faculty" campaign,[53] is to undermine our capacity to recognize the profound inequalities as well as the inequities that pervade the professoriate, thereby replicating the egregious economic, political, and status disparities that pervade a neoliberal political economy more generally.

The Rise and Decline of Faculty Governance?

The title of Larry Gerber's recent book, rendered here in the form of a question, does not in and of itself explain why the practice of shared governance rose and fell as he alleges that it has. To do that, Gerber argues thus: the cause of shared governance rose steadily throughout the first three-quarters of the twentieth century as the professoriate became "professionalized," reaching its zenith during the Cold War era, and then began its rapid decline as the faculty was "deprofessionalized." The cause of deprofessionalization Gerber explains by invoking the unhelpful epithet *corporatization*. To wit: "In recent years the greatest threat to the practice of shared governance has come from those administrators, governing board members, and public officials who seek to corporatize American higher education," and essential to that enterprise is the move to "deprofessionalize the professoriate."[54] From this follows what is now a pedestrian prescription: what ails shared governance can be remedied by repudiating the academy's corporatization, which in turn will restore the professoriate's status as a profession capable of reclaiming its rightful role in governance.

Gerber's title, which suggests an analysis in the shape of a parabola, suffers from at least three problems. First, the AAUP's periodic surveys of the state of shared governance indicate that its history has been far more erratic and far less successful than Gerber implies. The appendix to the 1920 report written by Committee T, for example, provided the results of an inquiry into "the actual status of faculties in university government." That report closed on an optimistic but qualified note: "Our information indicates a growing tendency in the better class of institutions to accord to the faculty official participation in the selection of its own members, in the nomination of deans and president, and in the preparation of the budget, as well as in the determination of educational policies." But that appendix also conceded that these advances have been confined to a few elite universities and that at most colleges and universities the faculty's role in governance remained circumscribed and uncertain, especially when based, as was usually the case, on uncodified informal understandings: "Without the legal form to protect it, the substance is liable to vanish with a change in the administration."[55]

About two decades later, the AAUP conducted a second survey, and it too provided little reason to believe that the association's bet on professionalism was bearing much fruit. This report's author, George Sabine, noted that progress toward implementing the reforms commended in the 1920 report "has not been as rapid as could be desired," that most advances still "display a tendency to rest upon indefinite arrangements for consultation and participation," and, finally, that the informality of these arrangements "give color to the presumption that consultation is an act of administrative grace."[56] Indeed, Gerber himself admits that faculty participation in institutional governance between the First and Second World Wars was "uneven" at best: "The idea that faculty should exercise primary responsibility for most aspects of academic decision making did not gain as widespread acceptance in practice in this period as did the principle of academic freedom and the recognition of tenure as a means of protecting that freedom."[57]

Much greater headway, Gerber argues, was made during the first few decades following World War II; indeed, by the 1960s "the general principle of shared governance had become a widely accepted norm in higher educa-tion."[58] Even so, an AAUP report based on a survey conducted in 1969–70 concluded that the transformation of principle into practice remained "a far cry from the ideals envisaged by the 1966 Statement on Government."[59] For the most part, this report concluded, faculty control was restricted to curricular matters and only seldom extended to the selection of presidents and deans, involvement in the formulation of budgets, and/or participa-tion in institutional planning. If that is so, what we witness here is not ac-tive engagement in the everyday exercise of power but, instead, occasional influence within confines whose key parameters have been set by others.

The uneven and partial institutionalization of shared governance throughout the twentieth century poses a second problem for Gerber's argument. That argument presupposes that the professoriate did in fact at some moment in time achieve the status of a proper profession. That, though, is a questionable proposition. To qualify as a specifically modern profession, in principle, any given occupational sector must (1) secure ex-clusive control over who is and is not qualified to engage in its practice; (2) restrict occupational entry to those who have earned degrees that certify competence in that profession's formalized body of specialized knowledge; (3) ensure that the production of professional providers does not exceed the market's demand for its services; (4) maintain control over formula-tion of the standards by which professional practice is evaluated; (5) form effective transinstitutional associations that enable practitioners to defend their collective interests; and (6) obtain from the state an effective guar-antee that it will respect these prerequisites of a profession and hence its autonomy.[60]

If these are the markers that define what a profession is, there are a host of reasons for concluding that the professoriate never achieved this status, and that in turn explains the relative ease with which the academic labor force has been thoroughly debilitated in recent decades. For example, the professoriate has never secured an alliance with the state that requires all practitioners to be licensed, as is true, for example, of lawyers, doctors, and barbers. Nor has the professoriate proven able to enforce requirements regarding the credentials—for example, receipt of a doctoral degree from an accredited institution—that certify one as eligible for instructional employment by a college or university. Nor has the professoriate demon-strated a capacity to prevent the emergence of or, alternatively, to shut down competitors such as for-profit enterprises and in-house corporate "universities." Nor can the professoriate's principal professional association, the AAUP, do more than investigate and, if warranted, sanction institutions that violate the tenets of shared governance or censure those that compromise tenure and/or academic freedom. Nor, especially in recent years, has the professoriate proven able to keep at bay state legislators who appear ever more keen on specifying the conditions of academic employment and interfering in faculty work. Nor, and perhaps most important, has the professoriate done what must be done to ensure that the supply of professorial labor not exceed demand, which is the sine qua non of any effective labor market shelter.

If the academic workforce has never adequately secured the structural conditions essential to its viability of a profession, the invocation of "deprofessionalization" as an explanation for its current plight presupposes a past that never was; and that brings me to the third shortcoming of Gerber's argument. Gerber's appeal to the categories of "corporatization" and "professionalization" are too abstract to do the work he asks of them. Because these categories are not adequately grounded in an understanding of the shifting dynamics of American capitalism over time, especially as they pertain to the demand for faculty labor, they cannot adequately explain "the rise and decline of faculty governance."

It is not by chance that the AAUP's initial push for what eventually comes to be known as "shared governance" coincided with the shift from an agrarian to an industrial economy and, specifically, that economy's need for new forms of specialized occupational expertise. The newly created land grant and research universities capitalized on this demand by securing an effective monopoly over the provision and credentialing of this expertise. Translating that power into a claim to elite status, the AAUP employed this collective self-representation as the foundation for affirming certain workplace prerogatives, including tenure, shared governance, and academic freedom, that were unavailable to the vast majority of ordinary laborers. The "1915 Declaration of Principles on Academic Freedom and Academic Tenure" is this market shelter's manifesto.

Nor is it accidental that the next effective push for faculty empowerment coincided with postsecondary education's major expansion during the Cold War era. Like its predecessor, this expansion responded to a transformation in the nature of US capitalism and, in this instance, displacement of the laissez-faire industrial order that so vexed the "professors' literature of protest" by its state-managed counterpart. Here too we see a rapid increase in the demand for new forms of specialized expertise as the authority of professional knowledge insinuated itself within, to cite but a few examples, the managerial and accounting practices of corporate capitalism, the initiatives undertaken to ensure the workforce's health and hence its productivity, and the so-called industrial-military complex as the United States sought to secure its hegemony around the globe.

The state's deep implication in this re-formation of American capitalism was apparent in the enormous increases in federal funding provided for Cold War research and developments projects, the 1944 GI Bill and later the Higher Education Act of 1965, and, finally, the creation of a burgeoning network of community colleges. As was true at the turn of the twentieth century, the consequences included a significant shortage of qualified faculty labor and hence an increase in the value of this commodity. The AAUP thereby found itself well positioned to press once again for the faculty's empowerment under the banner of professionalism. If the cause of shared governance reached its acme during the Cold War, this was not because the Association of Governing Boards experienced an epiphany about "the desirability of recognizing a significant role for faculty in institutional governance,"[61] as Gerber maintains. Rather, that success was accomplished because academic labor was in short supply and hence its bearers were able to extract concessions, including grants of power, they could not claim during less prosperous times.

Understood in these terms, the ascendancy of the professional professoriate during these decades can be read as a manifestation of the broader Keynesian bargain struck after World War II between capital and labor. In a nutshell, Keynes's macroeconomic theory responded to the Great Depression by arguing in favor of increased government expenditures to reduce unemployment, thereby stimulating aggregate demand, and, via active manipulation of fiscal and monetary policies, to mitigate capitalism's inability to stabilize itself. So, too, workers were effectively promised a rising standard of living, more or less full employment, protection of collective bargaining rights, and provision of welfare state benefits that partly shielded them from the hazards inherent within a capitalist economy's routine operation. In return, labor tacitly agreed to accept the basic parameters of this economy, including the rights of private property and the construction of labor as a commodity to be sold in a competitive marketplace.

Higher education faculty in the United States participated in this same bargain, but with the additional benefits conferred by a labor market shelter that, however attenuated, enabled its members to affirm certain prerogatives of professionalism. In return, with few exceptions, the professoriate of the Cold War era effectively agreed not to mount any fundamental challenges to the constitution of the academy as an autocratic property corporation. Articulating the principles that are to govern the distribution of power between governing boards and presidents, on the one hand, and faculty, on the other, the 1966 "Statement on Government of Colleges and Universities" codified the terms of this truce.

Gerber is no doubt correct to argue that the faculty's role in academic governance has declined since the Cold War ended. Little is accomplished, however, when that regression is explained by invoking the terms *corporatization* and *deprofessionalization*. These abstractions cannot be other than empty signifiers unless they are located within the context of American capitalism's first major post–World War II crisis, which was precipitated by, among other things, the oil embargo that began in 1973. For present purposes, suffice it to say that this crisis assumed a form that mainstream economists thought impossible: slow economic growth, high rates of inflation, and declining rates of profit—that is, what came to be dubbed "stagflation."

Neoliberalism is an imprecise but handy label for grouping together the interrelated strategies that first emerged around the time of Ronald Reagan's election to the presidency and that were designed to remedy this crisis of capital accumulation. Although many others might be cited, one cluster of tactics aimed at decreasing the cost of labor by, for example, busting unions, adopting right to work laws, outsourcing tasks to "independent contractors," moving production to offshore sites, cutting back on pension plans, and removing government regulations designed to ensure workplace safety. Together, these strategies increased profits by attenuating the power of labor to hold on to the gains secured by the Keynesian compromise.

It is within this broad context, I suggest, that we consider the staggering displacement of tenure-track positions by contingent appointments, beginning in the 1970s and continuing apace today. Just as politicians have come under considerable pressure to reduce or terminate the redistributive strategies that defined the liberal welfare state, so too have the academy's autocrats come to feel the need to vitiate or eliminate practices that have now become too "expensive." Much like occupational safety regulations, tenure but also shared governance and academic freedom come to be considered unaffordable luxuries that compromise higher education's ability to respond to the shifting dictates of globalized capitalism. Just as that order's profitability turns on marginalization of democratic interventions that might otherwise slow the rapid circulation of capital and/or retard the mobile reallocation of labor, so too must the academic equivalents of these practices be undone. At bottom, this is what is intended by those who proclaim that the academy's very survival now turns on its ability to respond "nimbly" and "flexibly" to the mercurial demands of the "new" economy.

The project of capital accumulation, Marx contended, requires that its beneficiaries periodically destroy their own creations. Today that project demands decimation of the unique form of professionalism that emerged around the turn of the twentieth century in response to the imperatives of an industrializing economy. The harshness of today's reality is not always recognized, in part because some colleges and universities retain some opportunities for some faculty to participate in institutional governance. The precariousness of these practices, though, is precisely what COVID-19 has exposed, as rule by what the AAUP calls "administrative fiat" is normalized in the land of Humpty Dumpty.[62]

IV

When Autocrats Meet Their Makers

FIGURE 9.1 Sign on the perimeter of
the University of California at Berkeley
(from zunguzungu, "Breaking Trust")

9
Outsourcing Self-Governance

From Corporation to Contract

Were John Marshall one day to happen upon this sign on the perimeter of the University of California at Berkeley (fig. 9.1), I suspect he would find it to his liking. Consonant with his argument in *Dartmouth*, this message in metal presents the academy as a form of property that entitles its owner to assert specific rights regarding its disposition and, in this instance, the prerogative to exclude anyone that owner opts to keep out. This owner is identified in turn as the Regents of the University of California, which the state constitution identifies as a corporation. That corporation, the constitution also tells us, "shall be vested with the legal title and the management and disposition of the property of the university,"[1] and that is the foundation for this sign's mandate.

When corporations are constituted, academic or otherwise, they are endowed with certain powers that enable them to pursue more effectively the purpose or purposes for which they are created. One of those powers, implicit in this sign, is the power to regulate assets owned by any given corporation. Another is the power of self-governance, that is, the capacity of a corporation to regulate its own affairs by enacting and enforcing what are now typically called "bylaws" but were once more commonly known as "statutes." Should these key powers be forfeited, seized, or allowed to erode over time, a corporation may persist in name, but it will lose key conditions of its (relative) independence. Should that occur, a corporation's capacity to accomplish the end or ends enumerated in its founding document, whether that be a charter, articles of incorporation, enabling statute, or constitutional provision, will be compromised and perhaps in time forgotten altogether.

Such is the not yet fully realized fate of the contemporary US academy, as I show in chapters 9 and 10. To defend this claim, here I offer three examples, each of which illustrates a different means by which the academy is now becoming incorporated within a neoliberal capitalist political economy: (1) the absorption of education within the enterprise of workforce training; (2) the transformation of scholarship's fruits into profitable commodities; and (3) the emergence of what are euphemistically called "public-private partnerships" but in fact signal the academy's reformation as an instrument of capital investment.

In each case, but most transparently in the third, the consequence for the academy is ironic as well as self-destructive. The power to regulate a corporation's assets, for example, encompasses the power to enter into contractual relationships with employees but also with entities that are "external" in the sense that they are not under a corporation's immediate jurisdiction (as its employees are). The constitution of the academy as a corporation is a necessary precondition of its capacity to enter into the contracts that embed it within a capitalist political economy. The terms of these contracts, however, can and often do undermine the academic corporation's capacity to govern its own affairs, thereby eroding one of the other key powers that define a corporation as a corporation. As this latter capacity deteriorates, the academy's ability to safeguard distinct forms of institutionalized practice worthy of the name "higher education" is squandered as well. Whereas Veblen feared that the cause of education would one day be absorbed within a bureaucratized university that comes to regard efficient administration as an end unto itself, in this chapter, we see how education becomes a means that has no end other than reproduction of capital and the conditions necessary to its amassment.

Why Our Familiar Taxonomy of Higher Education Will No Longer Do

For perfectly understandable reasons, those of us who work within "higher education" are deeply invested in believing that this category bears some independent signification and hence that what happens in colleges and universities is something other and indeed more than a key contributor to the upkeep of a distinctively capitalist political economy. That conviction is sustained, at least in part, by our conventional taxonomy of higher education, which might be diagrammed as follows:

	PUBLIC	PRIVATE
NONPROFIT	Montana University System	Princeton University
FOR-PROFIT	Oxymoron U.	University of Phoenix

Here, colleges and universities are distinguished on two dimensions: (1) public versus private; and (2) nonprofit versus for-profit. On this scheme, the distinctions between public and private colleges and universities, as well as that between for-profit and nonprofit, are binary insofar as no institution can at one and the same time be public *and* private or, alternatively, for-profit *and* nonprofit. Any given college, however, can be private as well as nonprofit, public as well as nonprofit, or private as well as for-profit. No college, though, can be public as well as for-profit, and that is why this cell can only be occupied by Oxymoron U.

Occupants of the cell where "for-profit" and "private" meet include the diploma and/or certificate mills, like the University of Phoenix, that are first and foremost sources of profit for their investors, and unabashedly so. All other colleges and universities can be located either where "private" and "nonprofit" meet (Princeton) or where "public" and "nonprofit" join (Montana State). When compared to the likes of Phoenix, Princeton and Montana are more respectable because they devote their resources not to the cause of shareholder aggrandizement but to the unique public good we call "education," and that is why the Internal Revenue Service grants them tax-exempt status.

Precisely because it is so familiar, this categorization scheme blunts our capacity to see how the academy's incorporation within a specifically neoliberal capitalist political economy has confounded the lines that divide each cell from the others. Accordingly, if we are to understand what sort of academic enterprise emerges from this confusion of categories, we must first pry this scheme loose from the crust of convention. That is not difficult to do once we recognize that what this diagram presents as a given is in fact a contingent artifact whose roots can be identified in *Dartmouth* and whose cells would have made little sense to those who came before.

The colleges of colonial America could not be and were not neatly categorized as either public or private. This follows from the understanding of corporations that prevailed at the time, which I elaborated in chapter 3. Unlike neoliberalism's representation of the corporation as an entirely private endeavor that emerges out of the capitalist marketplace and is exclusively dedicated to profit maximization, the colonists thought of corporations as creatures of the state that, although dependent in this sense, were granted considerable operational autonomy. That independence is made real via the several powers granted to corporations, including but not limited to the right to engage in self-governance, manage its assets, and stand as a juridical person capable of entering contracts.

When the Crown conceded some measure of its power to these franchises, recall, it did so on condition that these creatures advance collective purposes that the state would or could not achieve as effectively on its own. In some cases (for example, canal or turnpike building), the members of a corporation might derive personal profit from accomplishment of its designated end whereas in others (for example, Harvard as well as William & Mary) they could not do so. This, though, did not render one of these corporations private and the other public, and to think otherwise is to read into them a distinction that had not yet been unambiguously articulated. Should we therefore consider these corporate entities public-private partnerships? That hypothesis is equally ill conceived, for it too presupposes a conceptual bifurcation between public and private that will not be consolidated within the United States until well into the nineteenth century.

As evidence, recall Harvard in its early centuries. We may be tempted to consider this college "private." But if we do so, how shall we make sense of the fact that the 1780 Massachusetts Constitution, consistent with the General Court's order of 1642, provided that Harvard's board of overseers include not just ministers but also the governor and other officers of the commonwealth? Or recall the suit John Bracken filed against William & Mary following his dismissal in 1787. If this too is a "private" institution, how are we to understand Bracken's contention that he had been deprived of his right to political representation because he could no longer participate in the college's selection of a member of the Virginia Assembly? If these facts seem peculiar today, that merely confirms my point.

Gordon Wood has argued that the incipient seeds of a sharp demarcation between public and private can be traced to the republicanism of the American Revolution, and especially its affirmation of the primacy of civic goods over all self-regarding ends, and hence the need to secure the former against corruption by the latter.[2] That may be so. But after the Revolution, as popular sovereignty came to be regarded by wealthy elites as a threat to their vested interests, the distinction between public and private was carved out and sharpened, chiefly by Federalists seeking to erect judicial barriers against legislative encroachment on the rights of private property as well as the contracts that secured those rights.

It is against this backdrop that we should understand *Dartmouth*, and it is this decision that paves the way for the taxonomy of higher education we find too obvious today. At its founding, Dartmouth College could not be neatly shoehorned into a box labeled "private" or another labeled "public." Yet that, in effect, is precisely what Marshall does when he represents Dartmouth as an eleemosynary corporation and its board as a body obligated to perpetuate the legal trust established by its founder and benefactors. To render this trust's terms immune to modification by representatives of the public, as we saw in chapter 6, Marshall figures the college as so much private property and its charter as a contract whose inviolability by the New Hampshire legislature is guaranteed by the US Constitution.

The effect of this construction is not just to "privatize" Dartmouth but also and in the very act of doing so to "publicize" the state by doing what the colonists never did, that is, to categorically differentiate and oppose each to the other. As a logical matter, the terms *public* and *private* are coconstitutive insofar as invocation of either is intelligible only in virtue of its tacit reference to the other. In *Dartmouth,* however, Marshall and still more so Justice Story in his concurring opinion begin to fashion this conceptual bundle into two neatly bounded and mutually exclusive spheres; and that in turn provides the foundation for our categorical distinction between "private" colleges founded and principally funded by their benefactors and "public" colleges founded and principally funded by state governments.

Dartmouth's distinction between public and private institutions of higher education is an articulation of modern liberal political theory. That doctrine presupposes the partitioning of politics and economy into two categorically distinct domains. Figured as a realm governed by its own self-regulating laws, the economy is said to be populated by so many self-interested subjects whose freedom turns on this realm's abstraction from the social relations in which it was once embedded. The economy's reification is in turn an essential condition of the modern liberal state's depiction as an enterprise whose job, among others, is to enact and enforce the rules that govern this economy's operation (for example, the laws that enable individuals to contract with one another). It can serve in this capacity only because it is separate from that economy and hence capable of acting as a neutral arbiter who makes the rules that govern capitalist competition but, as a condition of its own legitimacy, claims to favor the victory of none.

What distinguishes the specifically *neo*liberal imaginary is its representation of the market not as a distinct sphere but as an organizational principle that should govern *all* forms of collective action. According to the logic of neoliberalism, the state is not figured exclusively as the source of the law and order that a regime of private property requires. Rather, the state is considered an agent whose task, again among others, is to universalize competition among self-interested agents by extending market rationality to every sphere of collective life. "Privatization" on this account is a means of reconstituting formally noneconomic domains of conduct in accordance with the principles and practices of a property-based market economy; and that, of course, is a necessary condition of the inherently endless project of capital accumulation.

Contrary to Marshall's classical liberalism, within a neoliberal order, "state" and "economy" become not two separate spheres but integrated articulations of a capitalist political economy that comprehends both. What is true of state and economy is equally true of higher education, as it too becomes an articulation of this same regime. To bemoan this fate by mourning the academy's loss of independence, as those who lament its "corporatization" do, is to forget that the achievement of what we call "autonomy" is always an *effect* engendered by historically specific constellations of political, economic, cultural, and other forms of power. What is happening to America's colleges and universities today is not the ivory tower's conquest *by* the for-profit economy but, instead, a neoliberal reconfiguration *of* the coconstitutive relations that incorporate and hence condition the form higher education is now assuming. Therefore, should we persist in thinking about contemporary higher education in the terms furnished by my four-cell diagram, we are sure to misread what our categories cannot register.

The Neoliberal Academy, Montana Style

In the last chapter, we saw how the academy's neoliberalization has been accomplished in part via decimation of the academic "profession," as tenure-eligible faculty have been replaced by sources of labor that can be quickly hired and summarily fired in response to whatever the market is said to demand and budgets are said to permit. In the remainder of this chapter, I amplify this argument by identifying several ways in which the neoliberal academy is now becoming a vital if not indispensable contributor to the project of capital accumulation. While this argument has been made by others, to the best of my knowledge, it has not been framed through reference to the academy's constitution as a corporation. Doing so enables us to perceive things we might otherwise miss and opens up avenues of criticism that would otherwise remain closed.

Let's begin with a university, which, according to our familiar categorization scheme, belongs in the box where "public" and "nonprofit" intersect. In 1889, the US Congress approved and President Grover Cleveland signed into law the Omnibus Statehood Bill. Among other things, that act provided for the legal residents of the Territory of Montana (that is, free white males over the age of twenty-one) to be admitted to the Union after adopting and ratifying a state constitution. In its declaration of rights, the constitution adopted later that year affirmed that "the people of the State have the sole and exclusive right of governing themselves," that "all political power is vested in and derived from the people," and that any government this people forms may be altered or abolished "whenever they may deem it necessary to their safety and happiness, provided such change be not repugnant to the Constitution of the United States."[3] In sum, drawing on categories whose roots can be traced to the model of the republican member corporation, as modified by social contract theory, the people hereby incorporate themselves within a self-governing body politic whose officers derive whatever authority they exercise from that body's makers.

The 1889 constitution authorized the state government to establish institutions "as the public good may require," including but not limited to "educational, reformatory and penal institutions, and those for the benefit of the insane, blind, deaf and mute." Article XI, which is devoted specifically to education, mandated formation of a free public school system and authorized the legislature to create a state university. Control over both was vested in a state board of education whose members were to be confirmed by the state legislature and whose powers and duties were to "be prescribed and regulated by law."[4]

Montana's 1889 constitution also provided that any and all funds allocated to this university "shall remain forever inviolate and sacred to the purpose for which they were dedicated."[5] That purpose was specified by the state legislature in 1893 when it chartered the University of Montana: "The object of the University of Montana shall be to provide the best and most efficient manner of imparting to young men and women, on equal terms, a liberal education and thorough knowledge of the different branches of literature, science and the arts."[6] To secure this end, the legislature granted to the board of education the basic powers that define corporations, including the authority to enact bylaws for the university's governance, to select a president, to enter into contracts, to sue and be sued, and to "control" all "books, records, buildings, grounds, and all other property of the University."[7] However, because these powers were granted by the legislature rather than embedded in the state constitution, they remained modifiable by that body, and to that extent the university's autonomy was restricted.

In 1972, the people of Montana ratified a new state constitution. This version retained the requirement that moneys given to support higher education, no matter what their source, remain "forever inviolate and sacred to the purpose for which they were dedicated" but modified its designation of that purpose: "It is the goal of the people to establish a system of education which will develop the full educational potential of each person."[8] To better secure this broad end, the 1972 constitution provided for a new governing body, the board of regents of higher education, which it distinguished from the board of public education specified in its 1889 predecessor.

Although this new body was granted "full power, responsibility, and authority to supervise, coordinate, manage and control the Montana University System,"[9] it was not formally constituted as a corporation. However, because this board's grant of plenary authority was now separately specified and embedded within the constitution itself, the system's board of regents was granted far more autonomy than had been the case when its powers were subject to legislative prescription and modification. That autonomy in turn was represented as a necessary condition of the board's capacity to accomplish, absent infringement by the legislature or any other agent, the unique public good that is higher education.

The board of regents' foremost fiduciary responsibility, accordingly, is to fulfill the purpose for which the people of Montana have granted this body its powers. This purpose is categorically distinct from private interests, as the constitution makes clear when it authorizes the legislature to exempt from taxation "institutions of *purely* public charity, hospitals and places of burial not used or held for private or corporate profit, places for actual religious worship, and property used *exclusively* for educational purposes."[10] The system's mission statement also specifies that the standards to be employed in determining whether these purposes have in fact been fulfilled are unique to and hence distinct from those appropriate to non-educational institutions, whether economic, religious, or otherwise: "We will hold *academic quality to be the prime attribute of our institutions*, allocating human, physical, and financial resources appropriate to our educational mission."[11]

Neither of these documents makes unequivocally clear just what qualifies as "higher education," whether that assumes the form of a "thorough knowledge of the different branches of literature, science and the arts," to quote the 1889 Montana constitution, or one that "will develop the full educational potential of each person," to quote its 1972 replacement. That said, these passages clearly presuppose the existence of a good that cannot be collapsed into or equated with those that are private and, more specifically, those that aim at "corporate profit." Because that is so, as I explain below, there is good reason to conclude that the board of regents has now violated its constitutionally prescribed fiduciary duty and should be held accountable for this transgression. The board has done so by conflating any meaningful distinction between "education" and "workforce training," thereby rendering Montana's public institutions of higher education servants of purposes other than their own, and specifically those of a capitalist economy's for-profit sector.

In 2018, according to a *Hechinger Report*, Montana's governor, Steve Bullock, lamented what he called the "disconnect . . . between state government, the business community, and higher education." Because the Montana system relies "on outdated federal government data about employer needs," it continues to offer "majors whose graduates can't get work" and fails to create "new courses in subjects for which businesses have immediate openings." To overcome the compartmentalization of these sectors, the *Report* tells us, Montana has set about fashioning a collaborative entity that will link the Department and Labor Industry, the State Workforce Innovation Board, and its public university system. This new body's purpose will be to collect information continuously from employers and, thus informed, to "determine on an institution-by-institution basis what [academic and vocational] programs should be added, expanded or eliminated by [Montana's] universities and colleges."[12]

To spread Montana's good news, in his capacity as chair of the National Governors Association, Bullock later convened a series of workshops subsidized by, among others, Amazon, Google, Microsoft, the Lumina Foundation, and the Strada Education Network. These sessions culminated in publication of *A Governor's Action Guide to Achieving Good Jobs for All Americans*. To ensure that America's workers receive "real-time information" about "in-demand occupations," this guide calls on states to develop information analytic platforms that will "integrate data on skills needs, educational attainment and labor market outcomes."[13] These networked conduits will then enable states to steer students toward the programs and hence the occupations that will furnish the highest rate of return on their individual investments.

To borrow a term from Gary Hall, the model commended in the National Governors Association report signals higher education's "uberfication."[14] Private enterprises are customers in the market for trained human capital; the state is akin to Uber's digital platform that aggregates these needs and then directs individual colleges and universities to satisfy them; faculty members, especially those hired on a contingent basis, are akin to the independent contractors that are Uber's drivers; and students are those transported from the netherworld of the unskilled or inadequately skilled to that of the gainfully employed.

The success of this project requires evisceration of any meaningful distinction between education and skills training as, to invoke once again a term I introduced in this book's prologue, each becomes a moment within the more comprehensive enterprise that is "eduployment."[15] But this project's accomplishment also calls for creating the sort of self who will no longer find this neologism the least bit odd. That, however, is a self that cannot in fact be a self because there exists no stable or enduring referent that would warrant our use of this descriptor. Because the pace of technological innovation is now so fast, the National Governors Association informs us, it is difficult to know exactly what skills will be required by employers in the future. Hence colleges and universities must imbue in their pupils not just "specialized technical expertise" but also, and still more important, "the ability to adapt to change."[16] In virtue of their expertise, we may still label these adepts "professionals," but the sense of this term is one that cannot be squared with the commitment to a vocation that was essential to the mythology of the AAUP. For these neoliberal pseudo-selves, the idea of a "career" dedicated to a calling must collapse into an endless sequence of contingent jobs, each of which requires that these pliable subjects once again undertake their own refashioning at the behest of others.

Once this "soft" dispositional skill is mastered, employees will recognize that acquisition of whatever skills are in demand today no longer requires earning additional degrees, for that method takes too much time and money. Instead, the commitment of these malleable bits of human capital to programs of "lifelong learning" will be marked by their avid participation in "a digital badging system" that "systematically record(s) an individual's continuous learning and the skills acquired in formal and informal settings." These badges, which are for sale online at a fraction of the cost of courses taught in residence, will bear labels such as "adaptability," "resilience," "digital fluency," "entrepreneurial mindset," and the like. Representing as a choice what in fact signifies capitulation to what Marx called the labor market's "dull compulsion," the National Governors Association cheerfully reports that ever "more Americans appear to be turning to alternative work arrangements, which include independent contractors, on-call workers and 'gig' workers."[17] What Kezar and her colleagues call the "gig academy" is thereby seamlessly integrated within a neoliberal political economy defined by labor's precarity.

Should "public" colleges and universities resist adaptation to the imperatives of this endless churn, state governments should be quick to wield their carrots as barely veiled sticks: "Governors can assess whether their postsecondary institutions are effectively teaching in-demand skills by shifting funding to these institutions based on completion-of-degree programs and student labor market outcomes rather than on enrollment numbers."[18] Students, on this account, are not sovereign consumers in higher education's mall of America. Rather, they are subjects who come to want what their employers need, as that need is expressed via the states' decision to fund this but not that "academic" program.

What Bullock and his ilk imagine is a dystopia within which what we now call "higher education" is nothing but an endogenous element within a capitalist economy's infrastructure, much like the interstate highway system or the digital highway system that is the internet. Higher education's task is not to grease the quick movement of goods from here to there but to facilitate the cost-effective fashioning of human labor into the form of a commodity whose capacity to generate surplus value is greater than it would otherwise be. When this dream is fully realized, at any given moment in time, the market for higher education's credentials will generate just the right number of laborers with just the right skills; for that is the condition of what Bullock and friends will celebrate as "economic growth" but others might consider an amplification of labor's exploitation.

Where eduployment reigns, institutions of higher education may still stand as semidistinct institutional formations, but no longer will they cultivate forms of practice that are distinguishable from whatever goes on within the corporate "universities" created by Boeing, Apple, Motorola, Walt Disney, Google, J. P. Morgan, and so on. Here we will no longer be able to say what separates "higher education" from "labor force reproduction," and we will not much care whether one calls its vehicles "human capital training centers" or "colleges." Yes, a tweedy few may still ask, to quote the title of a recent essay in *Forbes*: "Is it a school or a workplace?" But we will know that the only sensible response to this question is that provided by this article's author: "An education disconnected from work-integrated projects and experiences and a job absent continual learning and up-skilling are both suddenly and horribly insufficient. The vision of the future is one where we will all have a difficult time discerning the difference between an educational institution and a place of work. Learning and working will become synonymous."[19]

The irony here is acute: granted considerable autonomy by Montana's 1972 constitution so that they could better accomplish higher education's special purpose, the academy's rulers now effectively cede the independence delegated to them by this state's popular sovereign. On Bullock's account, Montana's board of regents should be praised not because it has used its power well but because it has enabled that power's purposes to be dictated by the demands of capital accumulation. Standing our conventional categories on their head, the public good that justifies the tax-exempt status of Montana's institutions of higher education is the service they now provide to the private sector. The board has thereby violated the end that alone justifies the powers conferred on it and, in doing that, has forfeited its title to rule.

In what cell of our received taxonomy should we now locate Montana's state-funded institutions of higher education? To the extent that their curricula are heteronomously specified by private corporate employers, we cannot consider them enterprises that advance a uniquely public good. But nor can we view them as the antithesis of these enterprises—that is, as for-profit corporations defined by a boundless appetite to make ever more. Better, I propose, to think of Montana's state colleges and universities as the publicly funded entities to which the needs of the for-profit sector are now outsourced at nominal cost to itself. The expense of this "education" is borne by the students of Montana who pay tuition, thereby providing the for-profit sector an indirect subsidy; by the state government that appropriates annual funding, thereby shifting this fiscal burden onto taxpayers; and, finally, by students and taxpayers alike insofar as the constitution exempts the Montana University System from taxation.

The Neoliberal Academy, New Jersey Style

If the Montana University System troubles our categorical distinction between public and private institutions of higher education, my second example does the same with respect to the distinction between nonprofit and for-profit. Leaving aside for-profits, colleges and universities in the United States are categorized by the Internal Revenue Service as tax-exempt charitable organizations. To qualify for that status, they must be organized and operated exclusively for one or more exempt purposes. One of those purposes is education, and hence nonprofit colleges and universities are exempted from federal income tax but also state and local property taxes and sometimes sales tax as well.

In early America, this exemption was typically justified on the ground that colleges perform work that would otherwise need to be undertaken at public expense by government agencies and, for that reason, are entitled to what is in effect a subsidy for the accomplishment of a collective good. Today, although the point remains much the same, we are more likely to say that these institutions are entitled to tax-exempt status because that enables them to dedicate the entirety of the revenue they generate, minus operating expenses (salaries, building and equipment maintenance, the costs of conducting capital campaigns, etc.), to fulfillment of the public purpose they serve. From this, to quote the Internal Revenue Service, it follows that none of the revenue generated by nonprofit colleges and universities "may inure to any private shareholder or individual."[20]

What, then, is the public purpose advanced by the private nonprofit corporation that is Princeton University, thereby justifying its tax-exempt status? What would eventually be renamed Princeton University was chartered in 1746 by the governor of the province of New Jersey, acting on behalf of the Crown, as the College of New Jersey. That charter was issued for the purpose of promoting "the education of youth in the learned languages and in the liberal arts and sciences." To better enable this end's achievement, the charter established a "body politic and corporate" named "Trustees of the College of New Jersey,"[21] and to this entity it granted the powers that define corporations generally.

Establishment of this tight linkage between purpose, powers, and corporate identity is of more than antiquarian interest because, as the website for the Office of the President of Princeton University informs us, "the powers and allocations of responsibilities of the Board derive from, and are set forth in, Princeton's original charter of 1746."[22] The university's entitlement to tax-exempt status is therefore conditional on the fidelity of its governing board to the end for which this body politic was initially and remains empowered today. Therefore, if it can be shown that the board no longer dedicates its revenue exclusively to the public good designated in its charter or, alternatively, if it can be shown that Princeton's trustees now employ its assets in ways that further private interests, their authority will wobble and this corporation's entitlement to tax-exempt status will totter.

In 2015, the Borough of Princeton announced the results of its recent property tax revaluation. The new assessment increased by 21 percent the tax burden on those whose property had been valued in the bottom quintile but decreased by 13 percent the bill for those in the top quintile. Several months later, a complaint was filed in state tax court by four fixed-income retirees against the borough but also against Princeton University's board of trustees in their capacity as "the fiduciaries who supervise the University and have ultimate control for its corporate management."[23] The plaintiff's attorney, Bruce Afran, explained the university's inclusion as a defendant as follows: "The university is not paying its fair share of taxes and thus homeowners in the borough are shouldering a larger burden than they ought to be."[24] Indeed, by his estimate, local residents are now effectively required to pay 20 to 30 percent more in property taxes than they would if Princeton were to contribute what it should.

To set matters right, Afran contended, the university should be denied its nonprofit status and its property tax exemption should be revoked. To justify this claim, the plaintiffs pointed to several buildings that the university owns and from which it derives considerable revenue but that do not support its educational purpose and, for that reason, should be subject to taxation by the borough to the tune of about $40 million per year. Within these buildings, the 2015 complaint maintained, Princeton "engages in profit-seeking conduct through its patent, copyright and trademark licensing businesses, sells the use of its scientific and engineering facilities to outside commercial entities, maintains an Industrial Associates program and other programs in which it makes available its facilities to commercial use, operates venture capital businesses, operates retail businesses, operates a commercial real estate business and a residential real estate rental business, operates a profit-seeking hedge fund operation and other profit-based investment operations, operates a[n] office and hotel development business, private mortgage banking, commercial television, among other activities."[25]

In response, and quite predictably, a spokesperson for Princeton reaffirmed the university's unequivocal location within the taxonomic cell where nonprofit and private intersect: "New Jersey's Constitution and decades of state policy establish that nonprofit educational institutions serve public purposes and are entitled to property tax exemption so they can devote their resources to their educational and research missions."[26] The university, in short, cannot be charged with a neglect of its duties, financial or otherwise, because its raison d'être is to fulfill a unique collective good that the state has christened and society cannot do without.

The arguments of the plaintiffs, though, cannot be so readily dismissed. To show why that is so, of the many offenses listed in the suit, consider the licensing agreements the university has entered into with major for-profit corporations. Between 2005 and 2012, the complaint alleged, Princeton reaped $524 million from its agreements with Aculon to develop nanotech surface modification technologies, Etaphase to build integrated solar circuits, Orthobond to manufacture implantable prostheses, Tag Optics to produce tunable acoustic gradient index lenses, and Vorbeck Materials to create electronic smart cards, to name just a few.

By far the most lucrative of these deals is that between Princeton and the pharmaceutical giant Eli Lilly. As the owner of a patent for a lung cancer drug developed by a faculty member, in 2004, the nonprofit corporation that is Princeton entered a contract with the for-profit corporation that is Eli Lilly. That exclusive licensing agreement authorizes Lilly to market this pharmaceutical, Alimta, so long as it remains patented by Princeton. Via its global sales, Lilly generated $2.6 billion in revenue during 2012 alone, and a portion of the $150 million in royalties paid to Princeton was disbursed to faculty members, while the remainder was dedicated to construction of a new chemistry facility.

By means of this contractual arrangement, the complaint alleged, the fruits of research conducted within facilities exempt from taxation come under "the private ownership and control of the faculty for their private commercial gain."[27] That Princeton does not merely tolerate but in fact actively encourages shenanigans of this sort became evident when, in 2014, all science departments received a memo announcing the university's commitment to advance "the development of nascent technologies emanating from university labs into commercial development and, ultimately, the global marketplace."[28] Given this commitment, opined the president and CEO of the Association of Independent Colleges and Universities in New Jersey, one cannot help but wonder "whether Princeton researchers receiving royalties from their research are the equivalent of stockholders receiving dividends."[29] If so, perhaps these scholars should be considered not members of a professional faculty contributing to the public good but, rather, private investors within a university whose own financial well-being depends in no inconsiderable part on the profit margins of Eli Lilly.

No one was much surprised when Princeton responded to this suit by throwing up one roadblock after another, thereby driving up the cost to its plaintiffs. Among others, Princeton's attorneys sought partial summary judgment to avoid a trial; requested a change of venue to make it more convenient for university officials and attorneys to participate in the hearings; argued that the residents lacked standing to sue; and, finally, claimed that the plaintiffs should bear the burden of proving their case because the assessor's determination of Princeton's tax-exempt status should be presumed valid. Never suffering from a shortage of gall, Princeton's attorneys justified these strategies on the ground that the real victims of this uncivil suit are not the borough's residents but the university's faculty and students: "The university feels strongly that the resources necessary to litigate such a case should not be diverted from our central mission of teaching and research."[30]

Not long after a judge rejected the university's claim that the plaintiffs should bear the burden of proof in this case, twenty-three residents from Princeton's predominantly Black Witherspoon-Jackson neighborhood joined the ongoing suit. Several of these new complainants had inherited their homes from parents and grandparents who, in the 1930s, had been displaced from the downtown area so that the borough could build the upscale commercial square that is named after one of the university's most generous donors, Edgar Palmer, heir to the New Jersey Zinc fortune. These residents, noted Afran, "have been particularly hard hit with very high property tax increases due to the fact that some homes have been gentrified,"[31] and today these descendants of the dislocated once again face the prospect of removal by moneyed white elites.

Three days before this case was scheduled to go to trial, Princeton settled out of court. That agreement provided for $18 million to be paid to several parties. Specifically, Princeton agreed to make a voluntary $3.48 million payment-in-lieu-of-taxes to the borough in 2021 and 2022; a fund was established to provide college scholarships to Princeton high school students; and, finally, $10 million was placed into a fund to provide temporary tax relief to eligible local homeowners. Implementing this last provision, a university that owns more than one thousand acres of prime real estate whose value in 2016 was assessed at nearly $2 billion cut checks of about $2,000 for each of roughly seven hundred homeowners. Thus, Afran concluded, did a university whose endowment was recently valued at $37.7 billion "buy peace by paying a pittance" to Princeton's poorest residents while simultaneously preserving the tax-exempt status that shifts much of the burden of funding city services onto those same residents.[32]

What are we to make of this tale? My purpose here is not to assess the legal merits of the claims made by either plaintiff or defendant. Instead, as a complement to my account of Montana's collapse of education into workforce training, I mean to ask what happens when the fruits of scholarly research are converted by law's alchemy into the assets we call "intellectual property" and then sold as commodities within transnational capitalist marketplaces.[33] These products, whose exchange is contractually mediated and backed by the power of the state, thereby become something very different from the vocational expertise extolled by the AAUP in its 1915 paean to the professional ideal. What the AAUP there called "knowledge," which is essentially defined by its availability to all, is hereby reconstituted as a form of private property that confers on its owner the legal rights of alienability, including the right to sell this product as well as to invest revenue generated by that sale in new speculative ventures. Work that was once evaluated through reference to its claim to truth is now assessed not by its qualitative contribution to Princeton's purpose but by its quantitative value as measured in dollars. The substantive purpose for which the university was first incorporated is thereby sublimated into forms of practice that become ever harder to distinguish from profit-making and what, in some cases, we might even call "profiteering."

What I have said thus far will be familiar to anyone who, having read the work of Gary Rhoades, Sheila Slaughter, Larry Leslie, and others, is conversant with the concept of "academic capitalism."[34] This phenomenon takes on a new cast, however, when we ask not how academic capitalism signifies the university's "corporatization," as many would have it, but rather a reconfiguration of the powers that are constitutive of a corporation. How, we might wonder, does the property corporation established in *Dartmouth* mutate as it becomes embedded within the forms of capital accumulation that distinguish a specifically neoliberal political economy?

To answer this question, let's look more carefully at Princeton's contractual arrangement with Eli Lilly. Via this agreement, an asset owned by Princeton's legal persona is diverted from the purpose designated in the 1746 charter and employed instead to generate gain not just for the university but also the shareholders of Lilly as well as the faculty members to whom Princeton funnels a portion of the income it reaps. This may not render Princeton a for-profit corporation per se. But it does mean that the university is now ensnared within the dynamics and so subject to the imperatives of neoliberal capitalism. As Montana's regents did by other means, Princeton's trustees thereby cede some measure of their autonomy, which in turn compromises their capacity to accomplish the qualitative end for which this corporation was created and with which they were entrusted.

To determine whether an educational institution is excessively entangled with a for-profit corporation, the Internal Revenue Service asks whether the former "is severely impaired" in its ability to separate itself from the latter.[35] In that light, consider this statement from the 2008 annual report Eli Lilly filed with the Securities and Exchange Commission (SEC): this contract "is not subject to termination by Princeton for any reason other than a material breach by Lilly of the royalty obligations."[36] Princeton's board thus employs one of the powers conferred on it by the 1746 charter—specifically, the power to contract—to bind itself irreversibly to a for-profit corporation that, according to neoliberal legal theory, must aim first and foremost to maximize the dividends paid to its shareholders.

The university thereby yokes itself to a corporation whose interest in accumulating capital in the form of profit positions it as the antagonist of a nonprofit whose own interest, as Princeton's financial managers surely understand, is to wrest from Lilly as much of that revenue as possible. At the same time, however, Lilly and Princeton share a stake in ensuring the former's exclusive right to market Alimta for the duration of the latter's patent: "If competitors introduce new products or delivery systems with therapeutic or cost advantages," warned Lilly in its 2008 SEC filing, "our products can be subject to progressive price reductions, decreased volume of sales or both."[37] Blocking competitors from gaining any market share is, therefore, the condition of Lilly's capacity to extract as much profit as possible from its global sales and hence the revenue Princeton derives from those sales. This symbiotic relationship explains why in 2010 Princeton and Lilly joined forces by filing suit against three pharmaceutical rivals who hoped to develop a generic and much far less expensive version of this drug.[38] The basis for declaring one of these corporations tax-exempt but not the other is far from obvious when, at the expense of those who are prescribed Alimta, they jointly conspire to insulate their investment from capitalist competition in order to increase the spoils they then divide.[39]

Princeton's contract with Lilly has the additional effect of rearticulating the role of the state in relation to the university. When Princeton's charter was first granted, the Crown retained the authority to assume the role of a "visitor" and in that capacity to investigate and, if need be, to intervene should questions arise about this corporation's fidelity to its designated purpose. That possibility has now faded if not vanished altogether as the state has assumed the role not just of a funder but also a facilitator of technology transfer within a neoliberal political economy. The state's adoption of this role was first announced by passage of the 1980 Bayh-Dole Act, which was expressly designed "to promote collaboration between commercial concerns and nonprofit organizations, including universities."[40] By means of this act and later laws, the state effectively encourages the wedding of Princeton to Lilly, provides for the patent and licensing statutes that structure this marriage of convenience, and, should this prove necessary, deters or punishes anyone who conspires to violate their vows to each other. This, then, is not a state that cedes some measure of its power to a corporation so that this legal artifact can better accomplish the public purpose that warranted conferral of its charter. Rather, this is a state that seeks to maximize the productivity of neoliberal capitalism by fostering the commercialization of research's fruits and enabling "nonprofit" colleges and universities to claim a share of the payoff.

This process achieves what is perhaps its consummate articulation when universities license patents to faculty-founded startups in exchange for equity. "Equity," explains Brian Pusser and his colleagues, "gives universities options or financial claims on companies' future income; second, equity deals align interests of the university and the firm with regard to rapid commercialization of technology; [and] third, equity signals interested investors about the worth of the technology."[41] Here equity in the form of stock ownership transforms governing boards bound by contract *to* for-profit enterprises into capital investors *within* for-profit enterprises. The academy thus becomes an investor in its own investments, and so the distinction between governing board members as trustees and trustees as shareholders effectively disappears. Whatever we may choose to call it, this corporation can find no happy home in any of the four cells provided by our conventional taxonomy of colleges and universities.

The Neoliberal Academy, Indiana Style

We might consider Montana and Princeton "hybrids" insofar as, like a centaur, we can still discern the "public" and "private" as well as "for-profit" and "nonprofit" elements intertwined within each. That designation will not do, however, when it comes to making sense of my final example: Purdue University Global. Were we to attempt to squeeze Purdue Global into one of the four cells furnished by our received taxonomy, it would appear that only the box where "for-profit" and "public" intersect will do. But we also know that any institution located there must be an oxymoron. To make sense of Purdue Global, therefore, we must see how it altogether escapes the categories provided by this classification system; and it does that by subordinating the academy's corporate powers to the provisions of a contract designed to secure ends antithetical to that of education.[42]

Let us begin once again at the beginning. In 1862, Congress adopted the Morrill Act, which provided federal grants of already expropriated land to states for the purpose of financing the establishment of colleges whose "leading object shall be, *without excluding other scientific and classical studies, and including military tactics, to teach such branches of learning as are related to agriculture and the mechanic arts.*"[43] To enable the state of Indiana to claim this benefit, in 1865, the legislature "created a body corporate under the name of The Trustees of the Indiana Agricultural College."[44] This body politic was rechristened "Trustees of Purdue University" in 1869 when the state accepted John Purdue's donation of $150,000 as well as one hundred acres of land, with the proviso that the university be named in his honor. The statute that sealed this deal guaranteed Purdue a seat on this public university's board, thereby realizing with a vengeance *Dartmouth*'s construction of the university as a trust beholden to its benefactors.

A century and a half later, following six months of secret negotiations, the governing board of this public nonprofit university entered into an unprecedented agreement with Kaplan Higher Education that, for a time, was all the buzz in the *Chronicle of Higher Education*, *Inside Higher Education*, and the like. Kaplan Higher Education is but one branch of Kaplan Inc., which, among many other things, provides training for aspiring corporate professionals, invests in major campus capital projects, and operates business schools in

Australia, Malaysia, Singapore, and elsewhere. Kaplan Inc. in turn is a subsidiary of Graham Holdings Company, which, in addition to its foray into the business of education, traffics around the globe in television broadcasting, auto sales, online magazines, home health and hospice care, cybersecurity training, the manufacture of screw jacks, and much more.[45]

I will say more about the particulars of the 2018 agreement between Purdue and Kaplan later, but for now this will suffice: As outlined in a "Contribution and Transfer Agreement," for the sum of one dollar, Kaplan transferred to Purdue's board of trustees certain assets, including but not limited to student enrollment contracts, the curricula for its online courses, the property leases for its campuses, and the personnel records of its employees. A second document, the "Transition and Operations Support Agreement," provides for Kaplan to furnish certain services to a new corporate entity, Purdue Global University, over the course of a thirty-year contract. Those services include but are not limited to marketing, student advising, test preparation, facilities and property management, human resources, technology support, admission support services, financial aid, and international student recruitment.

Via what Wall Street investors call a "distribution waterfall," the "Transition and Operations Support Agreement" also indicates how revenue generated by student purchases of Purdue Global's online courses is to be apportioned among its several parties. To oversimplify a bit, Purdue Global's operating expenses are to be covered first, and during each of the initial five years of this agreement, the university is to receive an additional $10 million payment. When this period expires, as a second priority, Purdue Global's operating expenses will be covered, as will those of Kaplan, but the latter will also receive a fee equal to 12.5 percent of the university's annual income. Should any funds remain following this distribution, that surplus will go to Purdue Global.

Why would Purdue and Kaplan enter this arrangement? The university's stated purpose is to extend Purdue's land grant mission by enabling adults already in the workforce "to develop essential academic and professional skills with the support and flexibility they need to achieve their career goals."[46] Kaplan, of course, was quick to present itself as a high-minded partner in achieving this public good. This banal characterization, however, leaves much unsaid about the motives of each.

Between 2007 and the signing of its contract with Purdue, Kaplan had been cited in at least a dozen suits for exploitative practices. To name a few, Kaplan was subject to allegations of wrongful termination, sexual harassment, falsification of documents, violation of California wages and hours laws that apply to contingent faculty, and the use of high-pressure tactics to persuade prospective students to sign enrollment contracts before they had an opportunity to speak with financial aid counselors about whether they could in fact afford to pay for their courses. Compounding its ill repute, in 2009 a US Senate committee investigation determined that Kaplan routinely spent more money on marketing than it did on teaching students (which may help explain its six-year graduation rate of 7 percent). Having earned its reputation as a "predatory bottom feeder,"[47] to quote an officer of the American Association of State Colleges and Universities, we must assume that Kaplan entered its agreement with Purdue to make money for its investors but also to rehabilitate its unsavory brand.

To understand why Purdue University entered this deal, we need to locate it within the broader context that is the fiscal predicament of contemporary higher education in the United States. The nature of this pickle, which affects all but the wealthiest colleges and universities (think Princeton), is indicative of a larger tension within all capitalist political economies. The relationship between state and economy will always prove vexed because the latter requires the former to perform certain tasks it cannot accomplish on its own. To cite a few examples, think of the Federal Reserve's control over the supply of money and its regulation of fiscal policies more generally, the adoption of the laws that govern contracts and provide for the formation of corporations, and the maintenance of police agencies to protect private property in the name of "law and order." Champions of the free market may bad-mouth the state, but that should never fool us into thinking that they desire its abolition.

In large part, the state funds the work a capitalist economy requires of it by means of tax revenues extracted from individuals and for-profit corporations. Taxes paid by the latter eat into their profits, however, so for-profit corporations seek to reduce their tax liability by, for example, accelerating depreciation, providing stock options to employees, creating foreign subsidiaries, and of course lobbying for tax rate reductions. This systemic tax evasion assumes an especially aggressive form within for-profit corporations that are specifically neoliberal, for their fixation on short-term shareholder gain renders them still less inclined to fund the long-term projects they urgently need. The story of neoliberalism, then, is but one more chapter in capitalism's ongoing unwillingness to shore up and, indeed, its perverse drive to underfund and so debilitate the noneconomic conditions necessary to its own success.

The severity of this tension will ebb and flow, especially but not exclusively in response to rising or falling rates of profit within the private sector. It's no surprise, then, that a protracted era of austerity was one of the principal legacies of the Great Recession of 2007–9, nor that this austerity's effects remain apparent in the reduction of state support for two- and four-year public colleges and universities since that time. After adjusting for inflation, as of 2018, the cumulative amount allocated to these institutions is at least $7 billion less than it was in 2008; and, on average, the percentage of college and university annual operating budgets funded by state appropriations has fallen by half (from about 60 to 30 percent). To cover this shortfall, among other means, public colleges and universities have increased their tuition fees by an average of 37 percent, and that in turn has had the effect of privatizing the cost of an education, which is now funded in large part by debt assumed by students and/or their families.

The revenue streams required to sustain nonprofit colleges and universities, whether public or private, are additionally compromised as their monopoly over the sale of education erodes. When captains of erudition declare that their respective institutions must now capture a larger share of the higher education market, their rivals include not just other nonprofits but also for-profit competitors like the University of Phoenix. Equally if not more worrisome are online providers that offer not degrees but certificates, credentials, and badges that signify the acquisition of specific workplace skills.[48] Still more market competition is generated by workforce retraining programs provided in-house by for-profit corporations, including but hardly limited to Facebook, Disney, McDonald's, and Motorola Universities.

In sum, like for-profit firms under conditions of competitive capitalism, nonprofit colleges and universities now find themselves jockeying for scarce financial resources, confronting a host of new providers of their products, and encountering a shrinking customer base.[49] These are the conditions that account for proliferation of what have come to be known as "public-private partnerships," and perhaps it is beneath this umbrella that we should locate Purdue Global.[50] This innocuous label, however, poses more questions than it answers: Does emergence of these "partnerships" signify collapse of the distinction between public and private, and, if so, does that involve a return to a pre-*Dartmouth* era that did not know classical liberalism's version of this distinction? Or does the hyphen in this tag suggest hybrids that blend but do not entirely erase the distinction between public and private, and, if so, what is retained and what is shed of each? Or are these sui generis fruits of a neoliberal political economy that cannot be understood well through recourse to our familiar oppositions between public and private, nonprofit and for-profit?

Robert Shireman has suggested that Purdue's copulation with Kaplan has given birth to what "really is a different animal."[51] One way to mischaracterize this animal is to think of it on the model of a simple vendor contract. If this characterization were apt, we would think of Kaplan as the independent firm to which Purdue, for a fee, outsources the specific services enumerated in the "Contribution and Transfer Agreement," much as colleges do when they contract with Sodexo to feed their students or Blackboard to manage their online course platforms. But if that is so, how are we to explain the fact that Purdue bought, for the sum of one dollar, multiple assets from Kaplan, including its fifteen campuses, thereby indicating that this is something other than a mere sale of specific services? Should we therefore conclude that their marriage involves nothing more than the purchase by Purdue of certain assets once owned by Kaplan? Were that the case, completion of this agreement would transfer certain bundles of property rights from one party to another, leaving Kaplan with none of the contractual claims that, as we will see in a moment, it is entitled to make on Purdue Global's revenues for the duration of this contract. Perhaps, then, we should think of this arrangement as a merger. But the assets of Kaplan and Purdue are not combined within and owned by a new corporate entity, thereby eliminating the claim of each to independent legal existence, so that can't be quite right either.

In the eyes of the law, the relationship between Purdue and Kaplan takes shape as a joint operating agreement. This deal assumes the form of a contract between two enterprises, one a public nonprofit and the other a private for-profit, each of which agrees to contribute certain resources to a project they are to accomplish together but not as one. Kaplan and Purdue must in consequence address issues of differential power and control that would not arise were either to own or otherwise legally subsume the other.

The key to understanding how these issues are resolved is found in the relationship between, on the one hand, the corporation that is Purdue Global and, on the other, the contract that structures the joint operating agreement between Purdue University and Kaplan Inc. We must therefore begin by asking what sort of corporation Purdue Global is, and that is a more convoluted matter than one might anticipate. At first blush, Purdue Global's articles of incorporation appear to locate this entity within the same category as Purdue University, that is, a nonprofit public institution that advances a public good and therefore is eligible to apply for tax-exempt status: "The purposes for which the Corporation is formed are exclusively charitable, scientific, and educational," and to advance these purposes Purdue Global "will offer instructional or educational services and programs" that extend Purdue University's "land-grant and public service missions." Also like Purdue University, Purdue Global's articles of corporation specify that it is to be ruled by a board of trustees whose powers encompass the authority "to promulgate and adopt all rules, regulations, policies or procedures that, in the discretion of the Board, are required or proper to conduct and manage the University and to establish its internal governance processes." So, too, Purdue Global's board is granted the authority "to make and from time to time to alter or amend the Bylaws of the Corporation,"[52] thus conferring on it the power to remake the rules by which its own rules are made. On the face of it, then, Purdue Global appears to be an instance of a class of corporations we now know well: an autocracy whose rulers, once appointed by parties who are not its members, are vested with plenary power to manage its affairs, whether concerning persons or property.

Appearances can be misleading, however. According to Indiana law, Purdue Global is not a "state educational institution" but an "affiliate" of such an institution. As amended in anticipation of Purdue Global's founding, Indiana's statutory code authorizes a college or university designated as an affiliate "to provide instructional or educational services or training in Indiana using onsite, online, or any combination of these or other instructional modalities," but only on condition that it remains "controlled by a state educational institution" (in this case, Purdue University).[53] Here, then, we appear to have two separate corporations, each with its own governing board, but with a peculiar twist insofar as one, although ruler of its own affairs, is legally subordinated to the other.

Purdue University's control of Purdue Global is neither direct nor immediate, as would be the case were this new corporation a mere administrative subunit, branch campus, or subsidiary of Purdue. Rather, the corporate body named "Trustees of Purdue University" exercises its control "by virtue of its authority to elect" the members of Purdue Global's board of directors. But in conducting this election—and here matters take an especially intriguing turn—Purdue University's trustees act not in their capacity as that corporation's governing body but, instead, in their capacity as the "one member" of the corporation that is Purdue Global.[54]

According to Purdue Global's bylaws, at each of its annual meetings, the membership of the corporation that is Purdue Global is to convene "for the purpose of electing directors and conducting such other business as may properly come before the Member." Because these directors are in fact selected by Purdue Global's membership, they may also be "removed, with or without cause, at a meeting of the Member called for that purpose."[55] In short, and as is true of member corporations generally, Purdue Global's directors are selected by and must remain accountable to the membership of this incorporated entity.

This, however, is so much legal legerdemain. In its corporate capacity, Purdue Global has but a single member; and, absent the plurality that is its necessary condition, this corporation is not and cannot be constituted as a "little republic." Rather, what we see here is the American descendant of a sixteenth-century English jurisprudential invention, the "corporation sole," that first emerged in ecclesiastical law and was later adopted by the Crown for its own ends. That purpose was to explain how the English monarchy can retain legal dominion over the realm, itself construed as so much property, during the period that follows one monarch's death but precedes a successor's appointment.

The corporation sole solves this problem by designating the office of the monarch as a corporation and the current occupant of that office as its only member, thus enabling the Crown's claim to dominion to remain intact during an interregnum. This solution, on the one hand, indicates the tenacity of the hold exercised by the member corporation on English law. On the other hand, as Frederic Maitland noted in 1901, this solution also strains this category beyond credulity; and so it is with good reason that Maitland called the "corporation sole" a "curious freak of English law" that obscures the monarch's true status as "the head of a complex and highly organized 'corporation aggregate of many.'"[56]

As heir to this jurisprudential oddity, Purdue Global is a curious freak as well. Although it appears to be a self-governing member corporation, in fact this corporation's sole member is identical to that of the corporate body politic that exercises full control over Purdue University but also, according to state law, Purdue Global in its capacity as an affiliate. The subordination of the latter to the former is rendered still more perfect because Purdue University's governing board, when acting as Purdue Global's sole member, is authorized to "designate the slate of individuals to be elected by the Member to serve as directors on the Board of the Corporation" (in this instance, the corporation that is Purdue Global). Who, then, is eligible to stand as a candidate for Purdue Global's board? Well, according to its bylaws, no fewer than five of its six directors "shall be designated from among the membership of the Board of Trustees of the Member."[57] Hence, with the exception of the one "educational consultant" on Purdue Global's board, its membership is drawn exclusively from Purdue University's own board. Quite unlike its English monarchical counterpart, therefore, the member corporation that is Purdue Global's board is not merely curious but also self-abnegating, for those who sit on its board do so only because they have been appointed by the governor to sit on another.

In the last analysis, then, is the governing board of Purdue Global a ruler or a subject, autonomous or heteronomous? When framed in these binary terms, this question cannot be answered unequivocally. The correct answer will always depend on the specific context within which this question is posed. Viewed from within, the governing board of Purdue Global is authorized to manage "the business and affairs of the Corporation, including without limitation the conduct and administration of the University."[58] Viewed from without, this same incorporated body is but a subset of Purdue University's governing board, and hence Purdue Global's capacity for self-governance is merely apparent. Werner Heisenberg's uncertainty principle, so it seems, is alive and well in West Lafayette, Indiana.

The dual identity of Purdue Global's governing board is essential to assessing the relationship between it and the contractual agreement crafted by the lawyers retained by Purdue University and Kaplan. If that contract subverts the purposes and vitiates the powers designated in Purdue Global's articles of incorporation, as it does, then Purdue University's governing board must be compromised as well since it, after all, is Purdue Global's sole member. That subversion takes two forms, which I will distinguish for analytic purposes although they overlap in practice: (1) direct checks on the governance capacity of Purdue Global; and (2) financial incentives and possible penalties that qualify Purdue Global's powers by more insidious means.[59]

According to its articles of incorporation and bylaws, as already noted, Purdue Global's board of directors is formally granted broad authority to rule its affairs. On a cursory reading, the contractual documents that specify the terms of the joint operating agreement between Kaplan and Purdue Global echo this affirmation by, for example, proclaiming that the latter's board "shall have ultimate approval (including veto power) and decision-making authority with respect to all functions" of this new university.[60]

It's hard not to greet this affirmation with some skepticism, however, when we learn that Purdue Global is required by the "Transition and Operations Support Agreement" to create a so-called Advisory Committee consisting of two representatives designated by Purdue and another two by Kaplan. Acting as the formal governing board's ever-present shadow, this body is to generate "strategies" and "objectives" regarding Purdue Global's annual budget, marketing plans, tuition fees, admissions standards, creation or discontinuation of academic programs, and other matters. Should there be disagreements within this committee, its members are required to "seek consensus,"[61] thus equipping each member with something akin to veto power over its recommendations. True, all proposals generated by this body must be brought to Purdue Global's board for final approval. But this requirement is little more than a fig leaf insofar as the "Transition and Operations Support Agreement" also expressly states that the specific level of services to be provided by Kaplan each year will be determined "in connection with the development of, and conditioned upon the adoption of, a *mutually approved*" budget.[62] Representatives of Kaplan's profit-seeking shareholders are thereby included as coequal participants in this most fundamental decision-making arena. That cannot be openly conceded, though, without undermining Purdue Global's official status as a tax-exempt university governed by a board whose directors are obligated to extend the public service mission of Purdue University.

To gussy up this arrangement by calling it a "public-private partnership" is to do no more than provide a patina of respectability to an enterprise that is neither public nor private but, instead, neoliberal. Purdue Global's specifically neoliberal character becomes still more apparent when we consider the financial carrots and sticks embedded within Purdue's contract with Kaplan. The Higher Learning Commission, which gave Purdue Global its stamp of approval in 2018, requires that any institution seeking accreditation must demonstrate, first, that the "governing board preserves its independence from undue influence on the part of donors, elected officials, ownership interests or other external parties"; and, second, that its educational mission "take primacy over other purposes, such as generating financial returns for investors, contributing to a related or parent organization, or supporting external interests."[63]

Given that Purdue University's interest in maximizing tuition revenue from its affiliate is inseparable from Kaplan's interest in maximizing profit, it is not immediately clear why the commission blessed their deal by accrediting Purdue Global. For but one example of these overlapping interests, consider this: if Purdue Global achieves "cost efficiencies in its operation" in any given fiscal year,[64] as calculated by means of a complex formula that measures the actual cost of accomplishing any given line item against the amount budgeted for this purpose, the university is entitled to 20 percent of the savings. This contractual provision thereby incentivizes conduct that, for example, will decrease Purdue Global's per student expenditure on educational costs and, by this means, will increase the "profit" it extracts from each tuition dollar spent by its students.

Similar incentive structures cannot help but animate those on the Kaplan side of Purdue Global because its purpose, consistent with the doctrine of shareholder primacy, is to maximize the dividends paid to investors in Graham Holdings. Nothing in this deal renders Kaplan any less likely to develop marketing programs aimed at increasing enrollment and hence class size as much as possible, hiding from prospective students the full cost of their investment in education, and encouraging the assumption of debt to pay for that expense. There is, in short, no reason to think that the predatory practices that confirmed Kaplan's reputation as a "bottom feeder" will end merely because those practices are prettified via its association with a land grant university.

From Purdue Global's vantage point, even more consequential than these carrots are the sticks held by Kaplan. For example, should Purdue Global exit this agreement after the first six years of their contract but before its thirty-year term concludes, the university must pay Kaplan an "early termination fee" of 1.25 times its total revenues from the preceding year.[65] Because this is a penalty that almost certainly cannot be borne by an institution that is ineligible for state funding and so relies exclusively on tuition for its revenue, extrication from this contract is a nonviable option (mis)represented as a real choice.

Consider also the provision, dubbed the "ransom clause" by Robert Shireman,[66] that cautions Purdue Global's governing board against adopting any program or policy that will have a "significant adverse impact" on the university's revenues and hence on Kaplan's share of the proceeds. The "Transition and Operations Support Agreement" defines "a significant adverse impact" as "the effect or omission that Contributor [Kaplan] believes, in good faith has, or is likely to have, the effect of decreasing either or both of the then-current and/or future Revenues by $5 million or more."[67] The areas subject to this clause include admissions standards, program offerings, tuition, and deviations from outreach and admissions targets.

Given this provision, if Purdue Global's board were to reduce the cost of tuition in an effort to make good on its promise "to provide greater access to affordable, high-quality education,"[68] and if that move had the effect of cutting total revenues by $5 million or more, Kaplan would be entitled to seek restitution from the university. Alternatively, if Purdue Global were to raise its admissions standards, and if that had the effect of reducing the university's enrollment and hence tuition revenue by more than $5 million, that too would enable Kaplan to claim its pound of flesh. In either case, actions that may be justified on educational grounds will be foregone because their adoption would entail paying a sizable penalty to Shylock and his fellow investors.

So, in the final analysis, what is this thing that goes by the name "Purdue Global"? Were I Robert Shireman, I would answer by labeling Purdue Global a "for-profit" enterprise that "masquerades" as a "nonprofit" college.[69] On this reading, should we peek beneath Purdue Global's ideological cloak, we will find a capitalist enterprise designed to extract maximum surplus value by exploiting its customers and underpaying its employees on behalf of voracious shareholders. But this characterization, which effectively equates Purdue Global with the University of Phoenix and its ilk, fails to capture just how this odd academic duck eludes capture within any of the cells furnished by our familiar taxonomic scheme.

That Purdue Global cannot be classified in these terms may render it an aberration, but it is also a revelation because it consolidates under one roof many of the principal features that define the neoliberal academy. Specifically, Purdue Global folds together (1) a disempowered faculty whose instructors without exception are contingent employees; (2) an unvarnished assimilation of "education" to workforce training, as we see in Montana; and (3) a form of academic capitalism that is exemplified not by the transformation of scholarship's specific fruits into marketable commodities, as Princeton does when it licenses Alimta, but instead by conversion of the university itself into a key contributor to the project of capital accumulation.

How exactly does Purdue Global accomplish this last task? At Purdue Global, we witness the academy's "decorporatization," which, contra the critics of "corporatization," is a cause not for celebration but for consternation. As traditionally understood, when a corporation is founded, the state grants to this legal person certain powers it would not otherwise possess. One of those powers is the legal capacity to enter into binding contractual agreements with others. The corporation's antecedent existence as a creature of law is, therefore, the necessary condition of its capacity to exercise that specific power.

What distinguishes the neoliberal representation of corporations, as we saw in chapter 2, is its contention that they are called into being not by means of charter, statute, or constitutional provision but by means of multiple market exchanges among so many private parties, all of which assume contractual form. At most, on this account, the corporation is the node where these agreements intersect, and hence any powers the corporation exercises must either be expressly stated or implicit within the contracts by which it is constituted and of which it is made. The corporation's claim to stand as an autonomous legal person, according to the neoliberal, is therefore a fiction we can do without.

Purdue Global's articles of incorporation confer on its board of directors "the power and authority" to "govern" the university and, specifically, "to perform all lawful acts necessary and expedient to put and keep the University in operation."[70] We already know, though, that Purdue Global's capacity to rule its own affairs is essentially a sham because, as a matter of state law, it is an "affiliate" controlled by Purdue University and because its sole member is also its master. For this reason alone, we might well conclude that Purdue Global's board is an ersatz corporation, for it has been gutted of the powers that might otherwise render it something other than an administrative agent doing the bidding of others.

But that is hardly the end of the matter, for we also know that the substantive terms of the contractual agreements between Purdue University and Kaplan Higher Education qualify Purdue Global's capacity to govern in ways we would never identify were we only to read its articles of incorporation and bylaws. Indeed, given these constraints, we might want to ask whether the corporate constitution of Purdue Global is anything other or more than a legal formalization of the contract between Purdue University and Kaplan. To the extent that this is so, Purdue Global signals the incorporated academy's dissolution into the nexus of contracts by which it is constituted. Here neoliberalism's ideological account of the for-profit corporation, fashioned as a justification for the doctrine of shareholder primacy, assumes the form of an accredited fact. But it does so with the twist that Purdue Global's status as a nonprofit entity entitles it to apply for and secure tax-exempt status and so scam the public it claims to serve.

This is not to suggest that Purdue Global is a mere pawn of Kaplan, as Shireman would have it. Recall that Purdue University and Kaplan are partners in a joint operating agreement whose obligations to each other are specified contractually. Neither, therefore, is legally subsumed beneath the other. This renders their relationship a bit like that of early European trading companies whose unincorporated partners entered into contractual agreements that pooled their resources to fund expeditions and specified how their accumulated spoils would eventually be divided, at which time their partnership would be dissolved. What distinguished later incorporated trading companies from these short-term partnerships was the transfer of assets contributed by individual parties to the legal person that was a corporation created by means of a charter issued by the state, and it was upon this artificial being that the state conferred the powers constitutive of corporations. The corporation's effective socialization of hitherto private property protected it from those who might otherwise seek to reclaim or poach these cumulated assets; and its powers, including that of self-governance, secured that corporation considerable autonomy against those who might otherwise compromise its independence.

Setting aside Purdue Global, without exception, the founding documents of the colleges and universities we have examined thus far include a provision affirming the right of the corporations they constitute to "hold," that is, to own their assets and hence to determine their disposition. (This, recall, is the premise of the sign that appears at the beginning of this chapter.) Yet it is precisely this affirmation of corporate ownership rights over the university's cumulative assets that is absent from Purdue Global's articles of incorporation and bylaws. True, the contractual agreements between Purdue University and Kaplan prescribe penalties aimed at discouraging, for example, Purdue from exiting its agreement with Kaplan prior to its termination. But that departure is not prohibited, as would be the case were either exclusive owner of the assets governed by their joint operating agreement. In short, at Purdue Global what would otherwise be corporate ownership rights are contractually dispersed, and that is what entitles Kaplan's investors to claim a portion of the revenue this university accrues.

The revenue generated by Purdue Global is now shared with a class of rentiers interested not in furthering the mission for which this university is formally incorporated but in extracting as much surplus value from it as is possible. When contract trumps corporation, as happens here, the fiduciary responsibilities of Purdue Global's governing board (and hence of Purdue University's board as well, since the former is but a subset of the latter) are at best divided and at worst displaced by its legally enforceable obligations to Kaplan. When such effacement occurs, the practice of "education" becomes something akin to a residual claimant whose interests take a back seat to contractual obligations and shareholder stakes that are not merely different from but at odds with the mission formally specified as this corporation's raison d'être.

Toward a New (and Improved) Taxonomy of Colleges and Universities

The Carnegie Classification of Institutions of Higher Education, as up-dated in 2018, divides institutions of higher education in the United States into doctoral universities, master's colleges and universities, baccalaureate colleges, associate's colleges, special focus institutions, and tribal colleges, and each of these categories in turn is additionally subdivided to account for differences internal to each.[71] This typological scheme presupposes the taxonomy represented by my four-cell diagram and thus is no more ad-equate than it is. Based on the examples discussed in this chapter, what might prove a more adequate classification scheme?

I propose that we classify US colleges and universities through refer-ence to the specific nature of their respective contributions to a neoliberal political economy. On this scheme, rather than an entity whose identity is determined by what we imagine goes on behind its walls, we will think of the academy as a porously bounded agent situated within the fluid field of relations that is a neoliberal political economy. Unlike the diverse de-nominational colleges of the nineteenth century, none today stand outside this political economy, and therefore none are innocent of participation in reproduction of the forms of capital accumulation that define it.

To illustrate, although this oversimplifies matters, we might say that community colleges specialize in training the workforce demanded by a neoliberal political economy; research universities specialize in fashioning the stuff of cognitive capitalism; and liberal arts colleges, especially those bedecked in ivy, specialize in producing the elites who will inherit the earth. The task of governing boards, according to this typology, is not to ensure fulfillment of ends that can be distinguished as specifically educational but to structure any given college or university's mode of implication within late capitalism. This does not mean that the corporate powers granted to boards evaporate, but it does mean that they are chiefly employed to orga-nize the terms of the academy's heteronomy.

In this topsy-turvy world, the academy's contribution to the public good is equated with the work it does in facilitating the accumulation of wealth, whether through technology transfer, through workforce train-ing, or by breeding the next generation of Wall Street financiers. On this account, the universities that we may still anachronistically designate as "public" are in fact vehicles through which revenue extracted by the state in the form of tax dollars is funneled in support of "economic growth." The so-called "private" sector consists of those colleges and universities that accomplish this same end but rely more heavily on donations and, for the fortunate few, endowment revenue to supplement tuition.

Setting aside the investment opportunity that is higher education's for-profit sector, which does openly what these other types do surreptitiously, what these "public" and "private" institutions share is not their commitment to a distinguishable good called "education" but their tax-exempt status. That status is a means by which the state shifts the cost of training human and inventing cognitive capital away from those who derive the greatest profit from its expropriation and commodification. The neoliberal academy thus becomes an accomplice to a political economy bent on extracting maximal profit from students in the form of tuition, citizens in the form of taxation, and wage workers in the form of surplus value.

If our new classification scheme is to be complete, we will also need to indicate how each type, besides facilitating capital accumulation, produces and reproduces the structural inequalities that define this regime. To do that, our post-Carnegie typology will need to reflect the ever-widening gap between, on the one hand, the 120 colleges and universities that hold about three-fourths of higher education's total endowment funds and, on the other, the nearly four thousand institutions that hold what remains. Into one bucket, accordingly, we will place those colleges and universities that reject most of their applicants; that cater to economic, cultural, and political elites, especially but not exclusively those who are white; that can afford to add a dash of diversity to this demographic makeup via need-based financial aid; and that are sufficiently well endowed to offer the luxury good that is a residential liberal arts education geared toward a four-year degree. Into a much larger category we will then place the colleges and universities that chiefly serve working-class and poor students, especially from Black and Brown communities; that turn away hardly anyone; that offer courses, often online, purchased off-the-shelf from providers like Pearson; that rely heavily on tuition to fund their operating budgets and so spend much less per student; and, finally, that collapse education into the acquisition of workforce skills as marked by receipt of stackable credentials and little badges.

10

"Humpty Dumpty Sat on a Wall . . ."

A Swindle in Michigan

"Religion, morality and knowledge being necessary to good government and the happiness of mankind," Michigan's constitution affirms, "schools and the means of education shall forever be encouraged."[1] Michigan State University (MSU), founded in 1855 and redesignated as a land grant university in 1863, is one of several public institutions of higher education designed to accomplish this purpose: "to provide a liberal and practical education for the agricultural and industrial classes and all others, to prepare them for the various pursuits and professions of life."[2] Thus do the people of Michigan obligate MSU to provide an accessible education to the state's residents, especially members of the working classes, and to do so on behalf of a good its citizens have declared essential to their collective well-being, political and otherwise.

With this pledge in mind, consider these findings from a study of Michigan State published by the Roosevelt Institute in 2018: (1) between 2001 and 2015, the amount of MSU's long-term debt increased by 210 percent, and its interest payments rose from $7.351 million to $49.73 million; (2) by 2015, paying to adjust its debt structure, MSU had spent over $130 million in fees on the complex financial derivatives known as "interest rate swaps"; and

(3) in 2016–17 alone, for every dollar MSU spent on scholarships and fellowships, it paid thirty-two cents to hedge fund managers.[3]

When these costs are combined, the study estimates, the amount paid by Michigan State to banks and financiers totals nearly half a billion dollars, which, in 2018, would have covered the full cost of one year's attendance at MSU for over twenty thousand in-state students. Instead, between 2007–8 and 2017–18, the average debt load of MSU graduates rose by 56 percent, the largest increase at any public university in the state, and now exceeds $31,000 per student.[4] Given this evidence, it's hard not to conclude that MSU has forfeited its public trust and, today, participates in a massive scheme to redistribute income from those who can least afford it to those who least need it.

Whom shall we hold accountable for this swindle? According to the state constitution, the power to decide how best to accomplish Michigan State's mission rests with the "body corporate" that is its board of trustees: "This historic responsibility the Board of Trustees accepts, and to this obligation the Trustees pledge themselves, separately and collectively, and the material and human resources over which they have been given direction."[5] The buck, in short, stops with MSU's governing board. Accordingly, if that board has misused the university's resources, its members should be relieved of the authority granted by the state on behalf of the people.

Our rush to judgment may prove a bit less hasty, however, should we learn that those legally in charge are not in fact in control. In chapter 9's examination of Montana, Princeton, and Purdue Global, I suggested that the ruling capacity formally invested in their respective governing boards is compromised by the academy's situation within a neoliberal political economy. None of these examples, though, does justice to my primary concern in this chapter: the academy's implication within the circuits of accumulation that distinguish neoliberal capitalism from earlier forms and that are collectively labeled "financialization."

As I will illustrate by returning now and then to Michigan State, the academy's financialization renders its governing boards titular authorities who, ever more so, are but capital accumulation's functionaries. Exercising their powers in ways that effectuate this transformation, these autocrats are agents of their own dispossession, and that we may wish to celebrate. Less happily, their simultaneous perfection of the academy's conversion into a specifically neoliberal corporation anticipates the expiration of higher education as a differentiable practice, and that is anything but an end to commend.

The Logic of Neoliberal Capitalism
(or This Way Madness Lies)

As Marx explained and history demonstrates, capitalism is a structure of domination that turns on the power of some to extract and claim ownership of value created by others. Its continuity over time is marked by the relentless pursuit of capital accumulation. That pursuit is evident in capitalism's brutal conquest of new sources of raw materials for industrial production as well as new markets for its commodities (think colonialism and imperialism); its ceaseless invention of more efficient technologies to produce the goods marketed and sold as commodities (think of the assembly line and, more recently, robotics and artificial intelligence); its drive to reduce the cost of human labor (think of chattel slavery and the offshoring of production to sites where wages are low); and its hostility toward anything that hinders the rapid circulation of capital around the globe (think, once again, of the evisceration in 1999 of the Glass-Steagall Act that had separated investment from retail banking or the rollback in 2018 of the consumer protections codified in the Dodd-Frank Act).

The history of capitalism is a story of the crisis-driven displacement of earlier regimes of capital accumulation by newer forms. What distinguishes neoliberal capitalism from earlier variants (for example, merchant and industrial capitalism) is its turn to specific forms of financial capital as a principal source of surplus value. This turn has its own history, which, roughly speaking, can be traced to the economic downswing that began in the 1970s and that was first signaled by a sharp increase in the price of crude oil. Dubbed "stagflation," this crisis was defined by the co-occurrence of high unemployment and high inflation rates; and this unexpected combination, which could not be explained adequately by Keynesian economic theory, was accompanied by slow economic growth and declining rates of profit.

The political response to this disruption of capital accumulation can be dated to the selection of Margaret Thatcher as the United Kingdom's prime minister in 1979 and Ronald Reagan's election as president of the United States the following year. It was during their administrations that finance capital was largely deregulated, thus enabling money to flow more easily across borders, financial institutions to charge higher interest rates on loans, and new investment opportunities, such as equity and hedge funds, to gain a foothold in capital markets.

The expansion of financialized capitalism since that time, write Robin Greenwood and David Scharfstein, "is apparent whether one measures the financial sector by its share of GDP, by the quantity of financial assets, by employment, or by average wages."[6] Major sources of this increase, they continue, encompass the interest derived from securitized debt, including residential mortgages, consumer credit, and student loans, but also fees collected by the firms that manage mutual, hedge, private equity, venture capital, and other investment funds. Considered cumulatively, by one estimate, the share of profits funneled to the US financial sector had risen to nearly 40 percent by the mid-2000s.[7]

This "solution" to the problem posed by diminished profits succeeded in its own terms but did little to overcome sluggish economic growth and stagnant wages. This of course is what one would expect as investment capital shifts away from corporations that make and sell goods and toward, for example, the more lucrative consolidated financial services firms that go by the name of Goldman Sachs, J. P. Morgan Chase, Berkshire Hathaway, and the Bank of America. Joined to a single-minded preoccupation with short-term gain, that shift has led to a reduction in the deployment of profit for research and development, technology upgrading, worker upskilling, and other investments in productivity. Capitalism's financialization, in short, has done much to encourage ascension of the neoliberal corporation that I analyzed in chapter 2 and that is afforded its ideological apologia in the doctrine of shareholder primacy.

In large part, what enables financialized capitalism to amass its profit and hence its power is a novel extension of the logic of commodification in the form of the "derivatives" that proliferated toward the end of the twentieth century. Whether named "forwards," "futures," "options," or "swaps," at bottom all are financial contracts that derive their value from an underlying asset or group of assets, including but not limited to stocks, bonds, currencies, commodities, and interest rates. These become sources of renewed capital accumulation when relatively illiquid assets—for example, loans on bank balance sheets—are pooled together, divided and recombined, and then sold, resold, and sold yet again on secondary markets such as the New York Stock Exchange. Unlike primary markets—where capital is amassed as a means to some end other than itself, as when a firm borrows to expand plant capacity—capital in the form of securitized derivatives is employed to speculate on anticipated changes in prices, interest rates, and the like within capital markets themselves.

Here, as Marx explained, capital becomes "fictitious" not because it is unreal but because it now assumes "the form of credit, shares, debt speculation and various forms of paper money, above and beyond what can be realized in the form of commodities."[8] The profit reaped by derivatives within a neoliberal political economy, in other words, is not the same as that generated by the sale of more familiar goods, such as a refrigerator, which can be calculated by subtracting the cumulative expenses involved in their production and marketing from the total revenue generated by their sale. Nor can neoliberal profit be equated with that derived from a conventional mortgage issued by a bank to a buyer, for that amount remains rooted in an appraisal, for example, of a house.

Nor, although we might be inclined to think otherwise, can the capital accumulated by the circulation of derivatives be identified with the bankrolling of capitalists in previous eras, whether via the extension of credit or the sale of stock. Among Europe's early modern merchants, the provision of credit served as a means to the end of facilitating commerce; and, among modern robber barons, the issuance of stock served as a means to the end of building enormous enterprises like railroads. Although the ultimate goal of each was profit, in both cases invested capital remained functionally related to and embedded within the practices of producing and exchanging tangible goods and services, and its value was measured by its success in fostering these ends. Within financialized capitalism, however, the pursuit of profit is abstracted from the realm of use value and so becomes a self-contained universe in which capital, now itself commodified, is deployed for the sole purpose of amassing more of itself.

John Maynard Keynes identified a related feature of financialized capitalism's peculiar identity when he likened it to a casino. Here the project of capital accumulation assumes the form of an always precarious venture characterized by the placement of bets in a hyperextended game of chance. This game's volatility is inherent in its very nature; for financialized value is grounded not in durable assets but in others' shifting perception of a derivative's likelihood of increasing its worth from one moment to the next. Volatility, therefore, is always shadowed by vulnerability (and that of course explains the invention of credit default swaps, which are nothing but derivatives that commodify the risk assumed by holders of collateralized debt obligations).

What the metaphor of the casino intimates but does not quite capture is the way financialized capitalism generates a historically specific form of madness. As capital becomes radically detached from any ground in the so-called real economy, its accumulation becomes a self-referential means without end. Finance capitalism's annihilation of the distinction between means and ends is a function of the *essentially* speculative nature of its assets. Their value is based not in profit earned yesterday or today but in a prediction about the potential of those assets to generate profit tomorrow. In neoliberal capitalism, in other words, past and present dissolve into a future that is but a way station to yet another speculative investment, which is but a way station to yet another speculative investment, and so on ad infinitum. The shrewdness of these investments will of course be assessed by their current financial return. But that return must immediately be invested once again, for capital that remains at rest cannot accumulate and hence is nothing but so much capital in potentia. Because this chase has no end other than its own appreciation at a future date that will never arrive in the present, because this perpetual motion machine has nowhere to go, it is necessarily nihilistic and in that sense mad.

No matter how speculative and abstract the logic of financialized capitalism may be, as Marx also explained, capital remains a social relation by which some extract value from others, which then takes shape as so much power. Hence, when the casino goes bankrupt, the consequences are calamitous, especially for those least able to absorb loss, and that is what we witnessed during the Great Recession that began in 2007. That collapse was caused chiefly by the securitization of subprime mortgages issued by voracious speculators to hapless borrowers who in time discovered that they could no longer make their monthly payments. When this house of cards collapsed, the stock market lost approximately 50 percent of its value, unemployment rose from 4.9 to more than 10 percent, and American households lost at least $16 trillion in net worth. What the Great Recession did not do, though, was temper the obscene concentration of aggregate national wealth in an ever smaller number of hands, which continues apace today.[9] Pace Keynes, a neoliberal capitalist economy is not so much a casino where blind luck determines one's fate as a rigged lottery whose operation systematically enriches and empowers a plutocratic elite.

Humpty Dumpty in Hock

How does consolidation of a neoliberal political economy, rooted in these new mechanisms of capital accumulation, make itself known within US colleges and universities? The academy's ever-deeper implication in financialized capitalism assumes multiple forms.[10] In this section and the next I focus on debt; and, more briefly in the section that follows, I turn to the academy's investments in this economy (although, as we will see, the distinction between the two collapses when debt itself assumes the form of an investment). By these means, the academy's rulers become embedded within worlds not of their own making and so become more creature than creator.

When we think of debt in relation to higher education, most often we think of that accumulated by students, and there is good reason why we do so. After adjusting for inflation, over the course of neoliberalism's history—that is, during the past four decades or so—the cost of tuition has risen by more than 350 percent.[11] As state funding of higher education has declined, students and their families have turned to debt to bridge the gap. Indeed, as of this writing, the cumulative value of outstanding student debt stands at about $1.7 trillion, which exceeds the amount of credit card debt and is surpassed only by home mortgages. This total is spread across 45 million students and/or their families and averages about $37,000 per debtor (although, as one would expect, this amount is differentially distributed by race and class, with persons of color and those with little means assuming the greatest burden).

Less often discussed but more important for my purposes is the accumulation of debt by colleges and universities themselves.[12] This was not always so: Between 1948 and 1972, direct federal government expenditure fueled a major expansion of higher education via the 1944 GI Bill, the Higher Education Act of 1965, and, in 1972, creation of the grant aid program that would become Pell Grants. Because these funds were supplemented by ample state appropriations, tuition remained relatively low, and for the most part neither institutions nor students found it necessary to take on much debt.

Today, however, debt is an essential ingredient in the financing of colleges and universities, chiefly but not exclusively in the form of bonds issued to fund major capital improvements. By 2018, 74 percent of four- and two-year institutions, public as well as private, held some form of interest-bearing debt for a cumulative total of $294 billion.[13] That debt is now assumed, the *Wall Street Journal* tells us, by "schools with top-notch credit ratings, including Brown University and the University of Michigan, as well as lower-rated schools like Linfield University in McMinnville, Ore., and Alvernia University in Reading, Pa."[14] This of course means that the burden of repayment has been democratized as well; and, today, on average, 9 percent of annual college and university operating budgets goes toward servicing debt.

Because the payment of principal and interest is covered in large part by tuition, as noted earlier, the American academy now plays a key role in transferring wealth extracted from students and their families to banks and investment firms that profit from their indebtedness. No mention of this redistributive effect was made, however, when Michigan State's board of trustees, following its December 2021 meeting, excitedly announced approval of a $500 million bond "to advance excellence and impact." "This opportunity," one trustee crowed, will "improve MSU's financial stability and exists because the financial markets respect the innovative direction of our president."[15] Here the accumulation of substantial debt, once considered a form of dependence and a source of shame, becomes a cause for celebration that heralds MSU's commitment to those empty signifiers, "excellence" and "impact," as these are promoted by the university's latest champion of perpetual motion toward some unspecified but surely splendid future.

What Pat O'Keefe also did not mention is that Michigan State's financial situation requires "stabilization" in part because, just three years prior, its board had agreed to a settlement with the 332 confirmed victims of the sexual abuse committed by Larry Nassar over the course of two decades while serving as an assistant professor and team physician. Nor did O'Keefe note that in anticipation of the Nassar settlement two major rating agencies had downgraded MSU's credit score, thereby increasing the cost of its debt and so undermining the university's financial security. ("We expect operating performance to thin over the short-term," Moody's Investor Service had explained with characteristic opacity, "with ongoing legal costs and university investment into enhanced risk management and governance issues increasing costs.")[16] Nor did O'Keefe note that payment of these damages required the board to take on $500 million in debt, which was the equivalent of more than a third of its 2017–18 general fund, or that this debt's annual service cost was estimated to be about $35 million per year.[17] Nor, finally, did O'Keefe note that repayment of Michigan State's debt is secured by a lien on the university's annual operating revenue, approximately two-thirds of which has been furnished in recent years by student tuition and auxiliary fees.

These points need not be made, let alone justified by a board member who also happens to be the chief executive officer of a major financial consulting firm, because in all probability no one is likely to raise much of a fuss. That is so in part because the burden of repaying Michigan State's debt will be spread across thousands of short-term consumers who, barring the occasional tuition freeze, will be asked each year to pay just a bit more, and that increase will itself be subsidized by student debt whose repayment will be stretched out over many more years. Indeed, what is true of MSU's students in hock is true of the university itself: repayment of the bonds approved in December 2021 will extend over the course of a century, and its annual cost will be a mere $15 million, which, O'Keefe was quick to note, is but a drop in the bucket that is a $3 billion annual operating budget. The repercussions of today's announcement will become invisible tomorrow as its costs are buried within MSU's abstruse annual financial reports.

There is every reason, as O'Keefe also predicted, to expect that the bonds approved in 2021 will sell as briskly as did those that funded the Nassar settlement. Reassuring financiers who had fretted about Michigan State's ongoing creditworthiness, those bonds had attracted many more potential buyers than were actually required, and that, announced MSU's delighted treasurer and vice president for finance, testifies to "investor confidence in our institution's financial strength."[18] However tarnished MSU's reputation may now be, that public relations hit had no appreciable effect on those captains of neoliberal capitalism who were quick to seize an opportunity to profit from Nassar's criminal conduct and its fiscal fallout.

Shortly after Michigan State's board announced the Nassar settlement, the university adopted multiple cost-cutting measures, including an across-the-board cut to all departmental budgets.[19] The academic program and hence MSU's students must also apparently pay for the sins of Larry Nassar as the obligation to repay debt supplanted that of providing "a liberal and practical education for the agricultural and industrial classes and all others." The COVID-19 pandemic proved a blessing in disguise, therefore, because it enabled MSU's board and president to cite it, rather than the cost of servicing debt, as the principal cause of the budgetary crisis that also now required cuts to employee wages and retirement benefits.[20] This quest to reduce the cost of labor, ideally to zero, achieved its most perfect articulation when, in October 2021, MSU's senior vice president for residential and hospitality services pleaded with faculty and staff members to work in its dining halls as uncompensated volunteers.[21]

Humpty Dumpty: Meet John Moody

What are the implications of institutional debt specifically and the academy's financialization more generally for the governance of colleges and universities in the United States? One obvious way to answer this question is to point to the increasing presence of persons hailing from for-profit financial corporations on governing boards. Earlier I indicated that in the late nineteenth century, ministers on academic governing boards were displaced by industrialization's elites as the latter came to dominate a new regime of capital accumulation as well as the universities within them. So too, today, corporate tycoons are being replaced by those who represent the interests of finance capital. One study, for example, found that the percentage of financiers on the boards of twenty-two top private universities increased from 17 to 35 percent between 1989 and 2014.[22] A second found that, during these same years, the percentage of financial elites holding leadership positions on the boards of liberal arts colleges and private research universities rose from 28 to 44 percent at the former and from 26 to 56 percent at the latter.[23] That this trend is more pronounced at private colleges and universities whose boards are self-perpetuating does not mean that financiers are absent from their public counterparts. Rather, their boards now rely heavily on advisory committees dominated by financiers who effectively make key investment decisions, thereby sidestepping whatever accountability might otherwise accompany the trustees' selection by state officials or, in the case of Michigan, their election by its voters.

These changes in board composition, important though they are, pale in comparison to the significance of financialization's effects on the academy's autonomy. Achievement of autonomy is a matter not of securing a well-bounded place against unwelcome trespassers but of ensuring the academy's capacity to govern its own affairs absent interference by or subservience to others. Autonomy so construed is the sine qua non of the academy's exercise of all other powers granted to it, including the power to fashion the bylaws that specify the terms according to which this capacity shall itself be exercised. The foremost fiduciary duty of governing boards, therefore, is not to ensure the academy's ongoing financial viability, as their members so often seem to believe today, for solvency is but a means to the academy's distinctive ends. If this relationship is inverted, the conduct of higher education will become a mere footnote to the business of the academy.

Today institutional debt is a principal means by which this inversion is accomplished. When debt becomes a primary driver of capital accumulation, as it does within neoliberal orders, it calls into being a regime of power that differs from earlier political economies. This debt's asymmetrical discipline is not wielded directly via ownership of another (as is the case in chattel slavery). Nor is this power exercised via naked expropriation (as the English Enclosure Acts did by abolishing peasant usufructuary rights, thereby converting the feudal commons into so much private property).

Nor is financialized debt's power akin to that incorporated within capitalist at-will employment contracts, which presuppose what the Enclosure Acts accomplished: that is, labor power's expropriation and reduction to the status of a marketable commodity.

The power of specifically neoliberal debt is more insidious. Like the student in hock, the neoliberal academy qua debtor is situated within a complex network of power that is populated by bankers, brokers, and securities dealers. The exercise of power within this matrix often remains beneath the radar of public scrutiny and so is difficult to locate, let alone contest. When, for example, Michigan State or any other college or university takes on debt by issuing municipal bonds, it enters into a binding agreement called a "debt covenant." These agreements specify the legally enforceable conditions that accompany debt's issuance, and those conditions quietly constrain the debtor's freedom of action for the duration of the repayment period.

To illustrate, bonds issued in 2021 by the University of Colorado require the university to charge students tuition and fees at a rate that will be high enough to fund its annual operating budget but also to cover its debt service and make regular deposits into a reserve account.[24] So, too, the debt agreement signed by the agency that oversees capital projects for the nine regional state universities of Massachusetts "provide[s] for an intercept of legislative appropriations to the state colleges, if the Authority otherwise lacks sufficient funds to pay debt service in full and on time."[25] In the first case, a university is effectively required to do what is almost certain to harm students and their families (in this instance, raise tuition), whereas in the second a cluster of universities is threatened with confiscation of state funding should it fail to prioritize the interests of creditors over the cause of education.

As these examples indicate, debt covenants typically stipulate that a university must use its general fund first to pay its creditors, followed by everyone else: "Only after money has been set aside for the banks," Eleni Schirmer explains, "does a university begin to pay its workers, distribute financial aid to students, or grant sick time and health insurance to employees."[26] That which is owed to rentiers thereby takes precedence over any and all obligations to those who perform the academy's productive work, whether they be teachers, researchers, administrators, or the mostly invisible army of low-paid staff members without whom no one could accomplish much of anything. Education thus becomes something akin to a dependent variable as essential budgetary decisions are effectively dictated by what Schirmer and her coauthors call the academy's "shadow governors."[27]

Of the many spectral figures that haunt the neoliberal academy, credit rating agencies represent one of the more powerful. These enterprises derive their profit by generating predictions about the credit risk posed by specific colleges or universities or, as Moody's puts it, any given institution's "probability of default and loss upon an event of default."[28] Assessing the likelihood that colleges and universities will or will not do right by their creditors, present as well as future, Moody's and its ilk now operate one of the more consequential levers by which the academy's autonomy is compromised and hence its capacity to govern its own affairs is constrained.

Within the nonprofit higher education sector, Moody's tells us, the rating of any given college or university is based on six factors: (1) scale; (2) market profile; (3) operating performance; (4) financial resources and liquidity; (5) leverage and coverage; and (6) financial policy. Each factor is assigned a specific weight (for example, market profile = 20 percent), and, once each is measured, all are aggregated into an overall rating of creditworthiness, ranging from Aaa (exceptional) to Ca (extremely weak). When Moody's locates a college or university toward the top of this scale, that does much to ensure the availability of plentiful credit at relatively low interest rates. Should, however, Moody's relegate a college or university to this scale's nether end, that tells potential investors that this is not a smart place to park their surplus capital.

For my purposes, the details of Moody's methodology and its application to specific institutions are not important. What is significant is this methodology's representation of the sort of institution that is most creditworthy. The confidence of financial speculators, Moody's tells us, should be highest when a college or university has (1) diverse and reliable sources of revenue, whether from donors, endowment revenue, and, in the case of public universities, state governments; (2) the latitude to raise the price of tuition more or less free from restriction, governmental or otherwise; (3) a supraregional "brand" that attracts customers from all parts, domestic as well as foreign; (4) a demonstrated ability to address developments, especially but not exclusively demographic, that may reduce enrollment and hence net tuition revenue; (5) a capacity to respond deftly to emerging "competitor strategies," "periods of financial stress, where revenue may be subject to volatility and declines," and unexpected events such as "M&A, asset sales, spin-offs, litigation, pandemics or significant cyber-crime events"; (6) sufficient liquidity to repay currently outstanding debt, principal as well as interest; (7) a record of securing that debt by pledging forfeitable assets, including but not limited to annual operating revenue; and (8) a strong governing board as well as effective senior managers who, when they think it necessary, can quickly and decisively reduce the cost of a college or university's "human capital," whether through staff reductions and/or by cutting "compensation costs."[29]

None of these desiderata say anything directly about the quality of the education provided by a college or university and on behalf of which it is afforded the privileges of incorporation. Indeed, certain of Moody's criteria push institutions to make decisions on the basis of considerations that are at odds with those we might think appropriate to educational institutions. Consider, for example, Moody's praise of those colleges and universities marked by an "extremely close alignment of academic programs to market and consumer demand."[30] Predicated on the assumption that the consumer is sovereign, this imperative jettisons the quaint notion that students are those who do not know what they need and, by means of an education, may come to learn what they should want. On Moody's account, instead, the academy must become a market-driven vendor that specializes in just-in-time production of whatever fluctuating "educational" commodities are demanded by the ignorant; and that in turn is an essential condition of maximizing returns for those who invest in college debt.

For much the same reason, the academy tacitly commended by Moody's will, ideally, employ a workforce whose members can be hired and fired at will, are always eager to undergo reskilling to meet consumer preference, and possess no independent organizational capacity and so no ability to counter their reassignment or disposal. "Some public universities," Moody's warns, "have a highly unionized faculty and staff and are restricted in their ability to make swift labor expense reductions. Shared governance between faculty and administration, where sometimes competing interest are represented, also presents impediments to rapid change."[31] Only when these barriers are undone will governing boards and their executors prove able to do what must be done if a college or university is to attract the steady stream of investors required in an era of perpetual austerity, whether real or fabricated. Moody's, in short, encourages consolidation of the academy's constitution as an autocratic corporation in specifically neoliberal form.

Moody's accomplishes this end not by command or coercion but by playing on institutional hopes and, still more so, fears about possible downgrades to its credit rating and hence its ability to secure the debt it can no longer do without. Schirmer explains: "What the rating agencies deem important, universities must do. The firms prize branding strength, so universities pour money into marketing campaigns and targeted brand research. The agencies value a school's ability to unilaterally raise tuition, so public universities scramble to seek such authority from state legislatures. . . . Rating agency algorithms also consider a university's ability to control labor costs, in terms of both employee unions and faculty tenure. The more unionized and publicly regulated a university, the weaker its credit rating."[32] Each of the actions noted here—marketing higher education as a commodity, shifting the burden of generating revenue to individual consumers, challenging anything that mitigates labor's precarity—is a quintessentially neoliberal strategy, and all accelerate erosion of the autonomy that is the corporate capacity to practice institutional self-rule. Paradoxically, Moody's tells the academy's rulers they must muster the power necessary to respond with agility to the educational market's shifting imperatives, but it simultaneously undercuts that power by effectively dictating the constitution of the institutional order within which this capacity is to be exercised.

To illustrate, consider the following: In 2011, as state appropriations continued to decline, Moody's warned that net tuition revenue at Michigan State would become ever more crucial to maintaining its credit rating and, moreover, that a failure to increase that revenue could lead to a downgrade. Happily, though, Moody's also concluded that MSU is well positioned to generate that revenue because it has demonstrated greater "pricing flexibility" than have many public universities that are subject to stricter state-imposed restrictions on tuition increases.[33] Shortly thereafter, however, Moody's acknowledged that this extraction can be accomplished only if MSU's students are in fact able "to shoulder tuition increases."[34] Yet Moody's also expressed doubt about their capacity to do so because of the state's high unemployment rate, which means that their families now "face economic tightening."[35] In sum, Moody's informs MSU that its students must pay more even as it concludes that they are ill equipped to do so.

Within a neoliberal political economy, there are only so many possible solutions to this impossible dilemma. The assumption by students of still more debt represents an option that will always prove appealing in a financialized order that derives ever more profit from credit. However, should MSU or any other university go down this path, explain Rebecca Boden and Wilson Ng, we will be right to think of that debt as "a securitized income stream for universities to repay their borrowings. As such, students themselves become securitized assets, their interests now subservient to the need to ensure a steady income stream to satisfy lenders."[36] Students, on this account, are not those whom MSU educates but interest-paying debtors who do uncompensated work for the university by sustaining the confidence of Moody's risk analysts.

A perhaps more palatable strategy involves attracting more out-of-state students who can be charged higher tuition, as well as those whose families are wealthy enough to pay full freight. To lure and then reel in these customers as its rivals have done, Michigan State has undertaken major capital projects, including luxury dorms, state-of-the-art athletic facilities, and the like. To finance these endeavors, unsurprisingly, MSU has taken on still more debt. Servicing that debt, of course, cuts into the revenue available for annual operating budgets and so requires identification of additional sources of income, and that effectively brings us back to where we began.

This circle turns vicious when the distinction between debt and investment collapses as the assumption of debt becomes an investment in the academy's capacity to generate future tuition revenue. When that revenue is then employed to service this same debt, this serpent begins to gnaw at its own tail; and this auto-cannibalism reaches its absurd apogee when tuition revenue is pledged as collateral to secure still more debt but with the proviso that it will be forfeited should a college or university fail to pay its creditors.[37] Under these circumstances, it becomes difficult to say exactly what distinguishes the neoliberal academy from a Ponzi scheme that requires a steady stream of investors, including the clueless debtors MSU mispresents as students to keep it afloat.

There is little reason to think that higher education's fiscal plight has improved since the Roosevelt Institute published its 2018 study. Indeed, in 2020 Moody's upgraded its appraisal of the nonprofit higher education sector from negative to stable, only to reverse that assessment one year later.[38] Explaining this downgrade, among other factors, the agency pointed to the anticipated financial fallout from the COVID-19 pandemic, expected decreases in state appropriations for public institutions, uncertainty about the pace of economic recovery, and the so-called enrollment cliff that now bedevils colleges and universities, public as well as private, as they compete for a diminishing number of college-age students.

Given this ominous confluence, it's no surprise that Moody's 2021 report on the fiscal health of higher education included this cautionary note: "There is a rising risk that banks will pull back their exposure to the sector, which would leave many universities with fewer options to mitigate near-term operational stress."[39] If the for-profit financial sector concludes that investment in many colleges and universities is no longer worth the risk, or if lenders raise interest rates sharply to compensate for that risk, it is entirely reasonable to anticipate that the most vulnerable will go under. *Higher Ed Dive* should be commended, therefore, for the prescience it displayed in 2016 when it began to track closures, mergers, and acquisitions of US colleges and universities. Although this list's compilers insist that their aim is "not to create a death watch," it is not clear what renders that lengthening roster anything but an obituary for those entangled within financialized snares from which escape is no longer possible.[40]

Humpty Dumpty, Portfolio Manager

Moody's role at Michigan State and elsewhere indicates how the academy's capacity to act autonomously is qualified when it becomes an object of financial investment in the form of securitized debt purchased by others. But of course Michigan State is an investor in its own right, and, however counterintuitively, that too undermines its capacity to control its own destiny. Recall that the preamble to MSU's board bylaws affirms its commitment to the university's educational mission, and "to this obligation" the trustees "pledge themselves, separately and collectively, and the material and human resources over which they have been given direction." If the board is but a rubber stamp for decisions made by others, including those outside as well as within the university, this pledge will be evacuated of substantive meaning.

In 2015, Michigan State University created a new administrative position, that of chief investment officer, and its first occupant was a hedge fund manager. The primary responsibility of this officer is to oversee MSU's endowment. To assist in that effort, the board's investment policy provides for the appointment of additional officers, including investment "consultants," "managers," and "custodians." Collectively, the holders of these positions are required by this policy to invest university funds with an eye toward securing "maximum return with an acceptable degree of risk."[41] Their conduct is to be judged, in other words, not by how well their work contributes to MSU's educational mission but by how well the university's portfolio performs over time, as measured by its annual rate of return.

Formally, final authority over all major investment decisions remains with Michigan State's board. That body, however, acts on recommendations advanced by the chief investment officer on behalf of MSU's Investment Advisory Subcommittee. Kin to Purdue Global's advisory committee, the membership of this latter body includes four trustees but also an equal number of "external" members who, since its inception, have hailed from Goldman Sachs, Bank of America, J. P. Morgan Chase, and the like. Between 2008 and 2018, the Roosevelt Institute reports, the trustees unanimously approved every one of the seventy-one investment recommendations generated by this body, which meets behind closed doors. This remarkable record, the Roosevelt Institute surmises, indicates not that this subcommittee's counsel is always spot-on but, instead, that the members of Michigan State's governing board understand very little about what they invariably approve and so passively acquiesce to those who claim to know better.

Ignorance may be a necessary condition of this board's bliss, for only that enables its members to not know what they may not wish to learn. For example, Michigan State's substantial investment in Elliott Management Corporation binds the board to a hedge fund that, as of 2021, had over $48 billion in assets under its control. Elliott is best-known for gobbling up the stock of financially troubled companies with the aim of forcing them to implement drastic reductions—for example, laying off workers and curtailing investment in fixed capital—that will have the effect of generating short-term dividends for its shareholders. Much the same purpose animates Elliott's practice of buying the debt of distressed nations for pennies on the dollar and, that done, initiating litigation aimed at compelling governments to repay that debt in full and with interest. When states have proven recalcitrant, Elliott's well-heeled attorneys have sought and in some cases secured court orders authorizing it to seize government assets as collateral for unpaid debt, including, in the case of Argentina, its central bank reserves and pension fund assets. After Argentina's government failed to seal a deal with Elliott, the country defaulted on its debt, worsening a recession that had already caused massive unemployment and skyrocketing inflation. Facing a possible cutoff of the credit it could not do without, Argentina capitulated, and Elliott reaped an estimated 1,270 percent return on its initial investment.[42]

In the name of fulfilling their fiduciary obligations, Michigan State's trustees thus render the university financially dependent on Elliott's predatory exploitation of unknown others in dire straits. If this board were challenged to explain how that investment is consistent with MSU's egalitarian mission, and if they were candid, its members could concede that in the last analysis fulfillment of the university's purpose in East Lansing depends on the degradation of those elsewhere. This seems an unlikely prospect; and so, if pressed to justify its investments in Elliott's speculative ventures, MSU's board would most likely cite its obligation to maximize the university's endowment and so ensure "intergenerational equity" for subsequent generations of students. Even when assessed on its own terms, however, this argument is problematic: the firms managed by Elliott have in fact underperformed the S&P 500 every year since 2009, thus raising awkward questions about the expertise of the financial gurus before whom the board routinely genuflects.[43]

Moreover, noted a recent examination of Elliott's investments, as it plunders the companies it purchases, the consequences typically include the following: "debt increases, employment and wages fall, investment is reduced, and share buybacks increase, reinforcing the widespread critique of hedge funds as cash extractors that ultimately leave target companies smaller, weaker, and poorer."[44] In short, MSU's investment in Elliott contributes to the more pernicious effects generated by a neoliberal political economy, including the structural inequalities that render many students unable to attend MSU without assuming unsustainable debt. Armed with this fact, we should perhaps offer MSU's board this unappealing choice: Either this body can confess surrender of its decision-making powers to an advisory body whose ultimate accountability is not to those who attend MSU but to augmentation of the university's portfolio. Or alternatively, this body can reaffirm its powers and, having done that, confess to mismanagement of the resources entrusted to it. What MSU's board cannot credibly do is claim faithful discharge of the obligations imposed on it by the people of Michigan, as set forth in the constitution that is their instrument.

The COVID-19 pandemic has additionally complicated the capacity of governing boards at public as well as private institutions to affirm their fidelity to these duties. Fulfillment of their fiduciary responsibilities entails obligations to those who do the academy's productive work and so accomplish its educational end. To deny those obligations is to forget that boards are charged with stewarding not just the "material" but also the "human" resources that are this mission's necessary conditions. Yet as the AAUP explains in *COVID-19 and Academic Governance*, the pandemic provided convenient cover to many colleges and universities as they cut academic programs, slashed compensation and benefits, and, over the course of 2020 alone, terminated 650,000 employees, a majority of whom were adjunct faculty or service workers.[45]

At the same time, and chiefly as a result of investments in speculative financial ventures, the endowments of many colleges and universities saw remarkable gains. For example, the Massachusetts Institute of Technology reported that its endowment grew by 56 percent during the fiscal year ending in June 2021, whereas Dartmouth announced a 47 percent increase, the University of Minnesota 49 percent, Michigan State 42 percent, Yale 40 percent, and, bringing up the rear, Harvard an increase of just 34 percent.[46] These colleges and universities thus confronted an awkward public relations dilemma: Unless their rulers elect to echo the exhortation of the University of Colorado dean who, as I noted in the prologue, insisted that one should "never waste a good pandemic," how are they to explain the imposition of internal austerity measures even as their endowments boomed?

This apparent anomaly is easily resolved, however, if we think of these corporations not as the colleges and universities they claim to be but as financialized enterprises propelled by the imperative to accumulate. That reading enables us to understand why those that can afford to do so now appear to be animated not by an obligation to sustain the resources required to educate future generations of students but by the drive to boost their cumulative wealth. Only a conflation of the latter with the former can explain why these institutions now invest so heavily in financialized instruments that beckon with promises of extraordinary gain but also carry the risk of enormous loss.[47] Those investments are exceptionally volatile because they are exceedingly vulnerable to the vicissitudes of global capital markets. When governing boards cede control over the academy's assets to those who pretend mastery over these markets, they sacrifice the cause of higher education for a mess of speculative pottage.

Education's End

Within the American academy, the power to rule has been expropriated from those who, were this a member corporation, would be entitled to exercise its collective self-governance. Instead, as Texas Southern, the University of Tulsa, Princeton, the University of Montana, Michigan State, and others have illustrated, this power is now centralized within and monopolized by incorporated governing boards that are neither selected by nor accountable to those over whom that rule is immediately exercised.

As I have emphasized in this chapter, the powers of these external lay boards include that of determining how the academy's assets are to be employed. To the extent that the American academy has come to participate in specifically financialized capitalism over the course of the last four decades or so, those assets have become something other than what they once were. This property is not well understood on the model offered by John Locke, who in his *Second Treatise of Government* argued that the otherwise common goods of this world can become privately owned only when an individual, by incorporating labor within this or that, annexes some specific thing to itself. Nor can these assets be understood on the complementary model furnished by Blackstone, who as we saw in his *Commentaries* represented the right to property as the "sole and despotic dominion which one man claims and exercises over the external things of the world, in total exclusion of the right of any other individual in the universe."[48]

True, governing boards do still sometimes think of their ownership of the academy's assets in the terms provided by Locke and Blackstone, as the sign posted on UC Berkeley's perimeter suggests; and, granted, this construction may still bear some prima facie plausibility when we consider the academy's tangible assets, such as land, buildings, and equipment. This representation is anachronistic at best, though, when we attend to the academy's specifically financialized assets; for these assets are defined by their wholesale abstraction from the things Locke and Blackstone considered their own. That abstraction, as noted earlier, is accomplished by the securitization of illiquid assets and hence their conversion into so many highly liquid derivatives. As they circulate, "ownership" of these goods becomes inextricably intermediated within and by investment banks, credit rating agencies, brokerage houses, stock markets, and the like. Each of these parties, moreover, has interests of its own in the quest to accumulate capital; and so, today, the academy's autocrats stand as one competitor among many, all of whom aggressively seek to maximize their respective share of spoils created by the labor of others.

When the claim to "own" the academy's assets can no longer underwrite a claim to exercise dominion over their disposition, let alone to derive exclusive benefit from their employment, the power of governing boards to rule is hollowed out and so becomes ever more honorific. What distinguishes the specifically financialized academy from its predecessors, we might therefore say, is expropriation of the capacity to rule from its original expropriators. Or, alternatively, we might say that today fetishized capital assumes a life of its own and thereby dispossesses those who are legally constituted as the sole "members" of an academic corporation that, precisely because it is autocratically organized, cannot in fact be a member corporation. This, once more, is not to deny that the academy's rulers remain capable of great mischief, but it is to say that Humpty Dumpty's pretense to power is now proving to be just that.

On the one hand, as I will suggest in the epilogue that follows this chapter, dispossession of the academy's rulers is be welcomed, for it invites us to think anew about how we might best reconstitute the power of rule within US colleges and universities. On the other hand, should the academy's financialization remain unchecked and unchallenged, there is good reason to conclude that in time this will spell the end of any practice that can credibly be distinguished as higher education. To the extent that the reason of finance comes to prevail within the neoliberal academy, the conduct of free inquiry is absorbed within and displaced by a project of capital accumulation that has no end beyond itself; and that, recall, is to render education's reason mad.

To illustrate, consider the changing relationship between the academy and the goods on which the possibility of education's practice depends. Harvard's 1650 charter authorized the newly founded corporation's members to gather as needed for the purpose of "debating and concluding" all questions about how to allocate its assets. In conducting these deliberations, the charter made clear, the governing consideration must be "the use and behoof of the President, Fellows, scholars, and officers of the said College, and for all accommodations of building, books, and all other necessary provisions, and furnitures, as may be for the advancement of and education of youth, in all manner of good literature, arts, and science."[49] This charter thereby yokes Harvard's material assets to the concrete needs ("the use and behoof") of those who do the college's work, and that support is provided so that they in turn can better accomplish the corporation's substantive end ("the advancement and education of youth").

Now consider the recent revelation that Harvard and other wealthy colleges and universities are investing in Bitcoin and other cryptocurrencies (and that even those excluded from this privileged circle are now eagerly accepting donations in this form).[50] Bitcoin and its kin are perhaps the most sublime expression to date of a financialized order in which the imperative to accumulate is no longer grounded in use value geared to the satisfaction of palpable needs, whether that involves the production of goods or the provision of services. Although initially intended as bona fide currencies employable in purchasing commodities, cryptocurrencies are now chiefly so much speculative capital entirely delinked from the value of any tangible assets and so altogether ungrounded in the so-called real economy. These dematerialized creatures of the digital imagination, moreover, are backed neither by gold nor by any government's guarantee but merely by the open-source code that generates the digital record that is a blockchain. "Managed" by a decentralized network of high-performance computers, cryptocurrencies dispense with traditional intermediaries like banks and so, leaving aside the enormous amount of electricity they consume, fulfill neoliberalism's fantasy of financial transactions that flow free from any and all impediments in space and time. Thus emancipated, Bitcoin consummates the radically speculative nature of financialized reason insofar as its market value is based entirely in capitalized estimates of the income stream its tokens may (or may not) generate at some time in the future.

Within Bitcoin U, what was once called the "governance" of persons and things in the service of education's substantive good is displaced by the self-referential end we now call "capital fund management." This is what the Roosevelt Institute glimpses when it contends that Michigan State "is increasingly operating more as a company or financial corporation than as an institution providing a public good, that of higher education. Far from prioritizing equitable, accessible public education as its core mission, MSU today focuses on competing for students as consumers, engaging in risky borrowing practices, investing in financial strategies driven entirely by the purported bottom line, and decreasing the share of its revenues that should be spent on its core constituencies: students, faculty, and campus workers."[51] What is true of Michigan State is of course true elsewhere, and so we should not be surprised to learn, for example, that in 2014 Yale University paid about $480 million to private equity fund managers, while it spent less than half that amount on financial aid for its students.[52] Thomas Gilbert and Christopher Hrdlicka are therefore right on the money when, turning their attention to Yale's well-endowed neighbor to the north, they urge us to think of Harvard "as a tax-free hedge fund that happens to have a university."[53]

When capitalist values permeate the academy, Veblen insisted at the turn of the twentieth century, nothing will prove able to "stand scrutiny as a final term to this traffic in ways and means."[54] As that traffic becomes the stuff of neoliberal financial speculation, the wealthiest competitors in the higher education market will continue to display the symptoms of psychasthenia universitatis, but they will also begin to show telltale signs of the disorder the American Psychiatric Association calls "hoarding."[55] This malady appears as jealous retention of what these colleges and universities already have as well as an overweening obsession to get more. Arguably, only this can explain why in 2017 US university endowments earned on average a return of 12.2 percent, whereas the average payout rate from those endowments was just 4.4 percent. The bulk of investment income, in short, was shoveled back into endowments, where it then became available for reinvestment in the interest of still greater accumulation (minus of course whatever is extracted by capital management firms, whether external or in-house).[56]

As this example illustrates, it is not quite right to say that the academy's financialization entails an eclipse of its distinctive purpose by some other substantive end. Rather, the financialized academy becomes purposeless insofar as its end, like that of casino capitalism more generally, is its own self-reproduction and expansion. If it is to accomplish this end, Bitcoin U must mimic the strategies adopted by its for-profit counterparts not because its governing board must answer to shareholders but because the reason of financialized capitalism drives that board to conflate the academy's wealth with its well-being. We should not be taken aback, therefore, when even the richest colleges and universities oppose faculty and staff unions, adopt performance-based budgetary practices, replace tenure track with contingent appointments, and invest in hedge as well as private equity funds that are enormously risky but potentially quite lucrative. Each makes sense and indeed appears to be the only sensible option when the academy's assets are severed from their ground in and contribution to the concrete practices of educational inquiry and, instead, assume the form of so many free-floating speculative objects whose sole reason for being is to accumulate without end.

Nor should we be taken aback when we learn that universities and colleges are creating offshore shell companies to hide revenue that is generated via partnerships with private equity and hedge funds and so evade the Internal Revenue Service. This strategy will disturb us only if we persist in thinking that nonprofit colleges and universities are or should be governed by purposes that would otherwise call this scam into question. To his credit, Jim Hille, the chief investment officer of Texas Christian University, did what he could to disabuse us of this passé notion when he stated that the *only* question to ask about these so-called blocker corporations is "whether the expected return would offset the cost" of their creation and maintenance.[57]

Financialized reason stipulates that capital should always and only be invested where it will yield the highest rate of return. That in turn renders irrelevant and in time perhaps even unintelligible questions that might otherwise be posed about what happens to the academy when accomplishment of its goods becomes essentially dependent on the profit extracted by predatory financialized enterprises. Here, in Humpty Dumpty's dystopia, Montana's radical conflation of higher education and workforce training poses no troublesome issues because, after all, that *is* what education is. In the realm ruled by Humpty Dumpty, a deal like that between Princeton and Eli Lilly is unproblematic because we all understand that knowledge *is* so much cognitive capital and nothing but. So, too, when Humpty Dumpty's reason prevails, the marriage of Kaplan and Purdue raises no eyebrows, for the distinction between for-private and nonprofit enterprises no longer offers any purchase for challenging the latter's subsumption by the former. And, finally, when Michigan State pledges the entirety of its tuition revenue as collateral for debt whose repayment takes precedence over the cause of education, we occupants of Humpty Dumpty's kingdom will merely shrug our shoulders, for we understand that this is simply the cost of doing business.

Epilogue

Reenvisioning the Corporate Academy

> Nothing is so delightful as to incorporate.
>
> THE EARL OF SHAFTESBURY

Mrs. Partington's Broom

To explain why the academy cannot accomplish its ends absent a fundamental overhaul of its autocratic-capitalist form, in *The Goose-Step* Upton Sinclair invoked the tale of Mrs. Partington: when she "tried to sweep back the sea with her broom," she "was no more foolish than the college professor who imagines that he can have an institution with wealthy trustees dominating its financial existence, and preserve in that institution a real respect for the intellectual life, or a real democratic relationship between the trustees and their hired servants."[1]

Mr. Whittington is Mrs. Partington's descendant. In an essay published not long ago in the *Chronicle of Higher Education*, Keith Whittington offered advice about how best to secure the academy's fragile spaces of free inquiry. Governing board members are indispensable to this effort, Whittington argues, but their ability to assume the role required of them is uncertain at best. True, most governing board members "have a deep connection to and abiding affection" for the colleges and universities over which they preside.

But "it cannot be taken for granted that trustees will assume their office with a robust understanding of and appreciation for the core mission of a university" and still less with a commitment to the free inquiry that defines this mission. Indeed, Whittington admits, because so many trustees come to academic boards from capitalist firms in which employees can be disciplined for their utterances (leaving aside a few narrowly defined exceptions such as whistleblowing), we have good reason to anticipate that they will *not* grasp this principle and, indeed, may often endorse its violation. Whittington therefore recommends that all new trustees be encouraged to participate in orientation programs that invite them "to read about, think carefully about, and discuss the importance of principles and contours of academic freedom and free speech."[2]

This will not do. The problem to be fixed here is not first and foremost one of benighted trustees. Their capacity to contravene the academy's distinctive forms of freedom is a function of the offices they hold and the powers that define those positions. The danger Whittington identifies, in other words, is inherent within the constitutional structure of the American academy. Freedom of inquiry will never be secure so long as its conduct is located within corporations organized as hierarchical autocracies and based in capitalist employment practices. If domination is essentially baked into that structure, as it is, then programs designed to enlighten the uninformed cannot be anything but palliative.

Forever contrarian, Mr. Fish maintains that we have no need of Mrs. Partington's broom and so no need for the remedy commended by Mr. Whittington. In a 2007 essay, Stanley Fish argued that the constitution of rule within the academy is irrelevant to what takes place within it. Rejecting calls to reform the university on egalitarian principles, Fish contends that "questions of governance are logically independent of questions of mission" and hence, whether the academic constitution be organized democratically or autocratically, "good scholarship and good pedagogy . . . can flourish or fail to flourish in either."[3]

This argument is dewy-eyed and irresponsible. To see why it is the former, one need only consider the recent spate of cases in which presidents and/or governing boards have exercised their power to chastise and in some instances to discipline faculty members for utterances deemed unbecoming of a professor.[4] These sanctions cannot help but have a chilling effect on others who fear repercussions should their work stray too far from received orthodoxies. The comfortable assurance that such inquiry will go unpunished is a luxury good that cannot be afforded by those who, unlike

Fish, are unprotected by tenure, and that explains why his argument is irresponsible. Denying that the academy's form of rule matters, he dismisses as irrelevant the hard work required to sustain the places where the conduct of free inquiry, including his own, remains possible.

Nor, finally, will it do to call on faculty members, as Adrianna Kezar and her colleagues recommend, to "expand and substantiate shared governance models" as a way of securing "a democratically controlled workplace."[5] As I explained in my chapter on the AAUP, the appeal to shared governance represents not a challenge but an accommodation to an academy organized on antidemocratic principles. Until the autocratic constitution of the academy is directly confronted, the AAUP will continue to find itself in the implausible position of calling on trustees to reaffirm a commitment to shared governance even as the association struggles to navigate the seas that are now sweeping aside this practice and substituting rule by "unilateral fiat."

In 1926, one of the more astute contributors to the "professors' literature of protest," J. E. Kirkpatrick, published *The American College and Its Rulers*: "We are primarily concerned," explained Kirkpatrick, "with the long established and generally accepted academic constitution which removes from the campus responsibility for the conduct of the business of higher education and provides for an absolute government in an absentee lay board of trustees." Believing that "every device which a growing society adopts has only a temporary value and must sooner in turn give way to another," Kirkpatrick concluded that now is the time "to dispense with the office of lay trustee and director."[6]

Because the customary constitution of American colleges and universities serves the interests of economic and political elites, Kirkpatrick acknowledged that creation of an academy appropriate to a democracy will prove an uphill battle. But he also maintained that the weapons required to engage this battle need not be invented out of whole cloth, for the "tradition of the autonomous educational institution has continued to live throughout the period of lay domination." Kirkpatrick devoted much of his book, accordingly, to an examination of those "democratic stirrings" that have resisted the American academy's imperious form and proffered a very different vision of what it might yet become.[7]

In this book's closing pages, I aim to honor but also to build on the work of those whom Kirkpatrick celebrates. Although none are without defect, including but hardly limited to their failure to impeach established racial and gender hierarchies, these sources of inspiration include the tutors of colonial Harvard, who challenged appropriation of control over the college's affairs, chiefly by its overseers; the charter of William & Mary, which required that all governance powers be transferred to the new college's professors following its foundation; the "professors' literature of protest," which contested the university's subordination to an ascending class of industrial captains; and, yes, the AAUP, which, whatever its limitations, has accomplished much in its defense of academic freedom for more than a century.[8]

To contend that the academy's singular purpose cannot be realized within structures of power arranged autocratically is not to say that it should be organized in strict conformity to the principles and practices that define democratic rule: the scholarly community is not composed of so many equal citizens whose differences of opinion are to be resolved by simply counting heads. But this is to say that the academy, like a democracy, is predicated on the ideal of a self-governing community, and hence that neither requires an autocrat to impose and sustain its order through time. The academy is defined by its commitment to free inquiry and to a construction of inquirers as equal colleagues who adjudicate knowledge claims via persuasion supported by evidence. This norm cannot and will not be realized so long as the power of rule, whether exercised by means of command or contract or both, is monopolized by a head that remains unaccountable to the body it superintends.

Reconstituting the Academic Corporation

The argument foreshadowed in the preceding chapters suggests that the cure for what ails the academy is not a repudiation of its corporate constitution but, instead, that constitution's reconstruction. This is partly a matter of recovering elements of the corporate form that are forgotten when we academics respond with knee-jerk aversion to the very term *corporation*, thereby revealing that we too have been taken in by neoliberalism's ideological representation. If the salutary possibilities of the corporate form are to be fully realized, however, that form must also be radicalized by accentuating those elements that are at odds with the logic of private property and capitalist accumulation. Only when recovery and radicalization are threaded together can the idea of the corporation be turned against the academy's "corporatization" and toward a constitution of rule that is better suited to foster the free inquiry that undergirds the academy's pedagogical as well as its scholarly endeavors.

Toward that end, in what follows, I sketch two broad principles that are to guide the design of what I will christen "Commonwealth University" (or, as it is more familiarly known by its members, "CU"). This is not the place to offer a detailed blueprint of this constitution (whose specific design must in any event be left to those who are to fashion it via so much experimental practice). Instead, my aim is to ask, first, how this incorporated body is to organize the power of collective self-rule; and, second, how it is to manage the material conditions of this body's capacity to fulfill its educational and scholarly purposes. While I will present these principles separately, each is a necessary condition of the other's success, and it is their mutually complementary union that I mean to signal by employing the term *commonwealth*. I will close by explaining, quite briefly, why the achievement of Commonwealth University is not to be dismissed as a pipe dream.

Commonwealth University qua Republican Body Politic

Today we often hear calls to reject the academy's "privatization" and so recover higher education's standing as a uniquely "public" good. These appeals are parasitic on classical liberalism's categorical differentiation of the world into public and private spheres, and that is what renders them problematic. On the one hand, liberal political theory characteristically associates the public sphere with the state and, paradigmatically, with the forms of coercion it alone is authorized to exercise (for example, by arresting or executing persons). On the other hand, setting aside the household, liberal political theory typically associates the private sphere with the marketplace and hence with the sort of freedom it identifies with contractual exchange. As such, liberalism's distinction between public and private deflects our attention from the forms of coercion inherent within capitalist employment practices. These, recall, are the relations of power Elizabeth Anderson seeks to highlight by invoking what, from the standpoint of classical liberalism, is the oxymoronic category of "private government."

The nonprofit academy, whether public or private, is a site of private government. True, the academy is not a capitalist enterprise insofar as its purpose, in the judgment of the Internal Revenue Service, is not to maximize profit for its investors. But it is very much a capitalist enterprise in the way it structures employment, and that follows necessarily from construction of the academy's rulers as those who "own" the academy's resources and thus are exclusively positioned to hire those who do not. Organized in this manner, the American academy is a site of unfreedom. We will find it difficult to acknowledge this truth, however, so long as we continue to think in the terms provided by liberal political theory.

We are better equipped to render these relations of domination and subordination visible if, as preliberal representations of the corporation implied, we consider the incorporated academy neither as a public nor as a private entity but, instead, as a body politic that cannot be comprehended within the categories furnished by classical liberalism. The corporation, as I explained in chapter 3, is a body to which the state grants certain essentially political powers, including the power of self-governance and hence the authority to adopt, adjudicate, and enforce the laws that apply to those subject to their jurisdiction. As such, the corporation is independent of the state but not for that reason located within liberalism's private sphere.

If this power of corporate self-governance is organized autocratically, as the American academy is, this corporation's employees will be its subjects. If, however, this power is organized democratically, as the American academy is not, those who are now its subjects will become members identified by their title to take part in exercising the power of rule that each shares with all others. The category of membership thus becomes the common denominator and source of collective identity that displaces the inegalitarian relationship between employer and employee. That identity does not make power disappear within some idyllic home of happy harmony. But it does mean that conflict will no longer be structurally organized by the contractually mediated form of domination that is the commodification of wage labor within a capitalist economy. Nor will the relations among members be hierarchically arranged in accordance with the bureaucratized chain of command depicted in the organization chart I presented in chapter 1.

The conception of membership commended here entails a critique of our accustomed way of thinking about what a corporation is and hence what the academic corporation might be. Prior to the mid-nineteenth century, I also noted in chapter 3, the plural *they* was sometimes employed in reference to corporations. Use of this pronoun, which sounds odd to us today, indicates conceptualization of a corporation as an entity that *merges* multiple persons into a legally distinct entity but is not abstracted from these parties in the manner suggested by our now more familiar use of the pronoun *it*. This less familiar sense is what the English legal theorist, J. W. Smith, presupposed when in 1843 he insisted that the incorporated joint stock company consists of "several individuals, united in such a manner, that they and their successors constitute but one person in law, a person distinct from that of any of the members, *though made up of them all*."⁹ On this account, when recognized as a legal entity via conferral of a charter, persons form themselves into a corporation and, in the case of a specifically academic body politic, a *universitas magistrorum et scholarium* (a community of teachers and scholars) that is composed *by* but also *of* those who were not before but are now that corporation's members.

By way of contrast, the contemporary corporation, academic or otherwise, is most often figured as an impersonal entity anthropomorphized as a legal person standing apart from and above its members, and hence in a position to affirm interests, rights, and privileges of its own. That representation is possible only because the political capacities of its members have already been expropriated and reified into a noun-like entity that now confronts "its" employees or, better, its subjects. The specifically neoliberal corporation perfects this process of abstraction by folding "it" within circuits of immaterial financialized property that are said to obey the impersonal laws of capitalist markets but in fact advance the interests of self-satisfied plutocratic elites. Within this corporation, we can find no members *of* a body politic but only subjects employed *by* the detached rulers we call chief executive officers as well as their subordinates. This, as we saw in chapters 9 and 10, is also the fate of the contemporary American academy insofar as it assumes the form of a neoliberal corporation whose rule presents itself euphemistically as so much human resource management.

In the academy constituted as a member corporation, however, the power to rule is reappropriated as the academy is repoliticized not as an administrative bureau of the state but as a "little republic" whose powers afford it considerable autonomy from that state. Those who are "members" of Commonwealth University are entitled to call themselves such not because each is implicated within the nexus of economic contracts that the neoliberal confuses with a corporation. Rather, each can affirm this identity because all are eligible to take part in the exercise of corporate powers that are specifically political in nature.

As the logic of a member corporation requires, within Commonwealth University this body politic must operate in accordance with the principle of "one member, one vote" (unlike neoliberal shareholders, who typically have as many votes as they own shares). Moreover, to ensure accountability, those who hold office within CU, whether president, provost, or even trustee, must be subject to election and removal by the university's members. To check the exercise of arbitrary power, moreover, these officers must be bound by the republican rule of law and obligated to respect the norms of due process. Perhaps most important, because this is a necessary condition of higher education's capacity to flourish, CU's charter must guarantee the practice of free inquiry by, for example, expressly ensuring the right to dispute all claims to knowledge but also and more radically to contest the very criteria that at any given time determine what is to qualify as knowledge.

Commonwealth University is acephalous in the sense that it has no head akin to that found in the autocratic academy. Within CU, the academy's incorporated members must bear ultimate responsibility for fashioning the rules that specify how the power of rule is to be exercised, how disputes are to be adjudicated, and how competing interests are to be reconciled. Here, in other words, the fiduciary duty to secure the conditions necessary to education's end is no longer exclusively vested within an external elite composed of laypersons ill equipped to grasp that purpose. Instead, this duty is democratized insofar as it is distributed among all who share in the powers of collective self-governance. No rule or practice may be adopted, therefore, that would render any members subject to unaccountable domination. To do that would be to deprive those subjects of standing as members, thereby releasing them from any obligation to safeguard the conditions of free inquiry. Should this accountability be denied or neglected, the malady of the academy known as psychasthenia universitatis is sure to follow, since those stripped of power will soon require discipline (or, instead, an unending stream of enticements) to keep them in line.

Commonwealth University is substantially independent but never perfectly autonomous, and that is as it should be. Instead, CU is nested among corporations of diverse types, including the descendant of the corporation that is a republican government. As such, CU remains ultimately answerable to the people in their capacity as the sovereign author of its charter. But because that charter vests the "little republic" that is the academy with the powers, liberties, and immunities afforded to all corporations, this franchise possesses considerable power to guard against governmental encroachment. Yes, CU is obligated to act in accordance with the trust vested in its members, which is to cultivate our collective interest in free inquiry; and, yes, in the last analysis, that trust remains modifiable and even revocable by the people or their elected representatives. But that no more renders CU a "public" university (in the sense we intend today) than it renders CU a "private" university (in the sense we intend today). CU is neither public nor private, for its constitution eludes capture on the conceptual terrain provided by liberal political theory and hence the conventional typology I outlined in chapter 9. Instead, CU is a republican member corporation whose chartered purpose is to sustain the practice of free inquiry on behalf of the more comprehensive republican body politic of which it is a part.

Commonwealth University qua
Socialist Body Politic

As a corollary of its republican constitution, Commonwealth University must also assume the form of a socialist enterprise whose assets, owned by no one, are unavailable for appropriation as so much privatized property and hence insertion within capitalism's circuits of accumulation. This entails building on but also extending the insights of Cattell, Dewey, Veblen, and Sinclair, all of whom understood that no persuasive challenge to the academy's autocratic form can be advanced absent a broader critique of the economic regime within which it is situated.[10] I have already done that by arguing that the conduct of free inquiry cannot flourish when embedded within the relations of domination and subordination constitutive of capitalist employment practices. More needs to be said, though, about why knowledge's appropriation as private property transgresses the academy's promise as well as how CU remedies this violation.

Academic disciplines are socialist endeavors insofar as their epistemic fruits are necessarily collaborative productions. Until intersubjectively confirmed, a claim to knowledge is but a claim. This fact is institutionalized in the practice of peer review, as each candidate for the status of knowledge is subjected to analysis and critique by those qualified to do so. Absent such scrutiny, we may be in possession of faith, intuition, or opinion but not knowledge. Error is weeded out and knowledge secured by the practices of mutual inquiry among colleagues whose participation in this endeavor is grounded in familiarity with received but forever contestable norms of scholarly inquiry and the bodies of knowledge these practices have accumulated over time.

This unique way of substantiating the authority of claims that cannot be validated by means of tradition, fiat, market demand, charisma, or status is most familiar to us in the experimental inquiry of the natural sciences. But this practice also defines the social sciences and the humanities, although its specific methods vary from discipline to discipline. Consider, for example, an argument to the effect that American colleges and universities are structurally constituted as autocratic corporations and, in addition, that this constitution subverts the cause of higher education. Let us assume, moreover, that the author of this argument adduces considerable evidence, historical as well as contemporary, in its support. Once published, that argument will be subject to assessment by others who may contest, qualify, or, to the delight of its author, confirm its key claims as well as the evidence adduced in their support. Only *after* that process is substantially complete can we be confident that this author's argument, or what remains of it following critical examination, should be considered true.

Because that argument has now been reconstituted by the collective critical inquiry without which it cannot affirm the status of knowledge, it cannot be considered its author's exclusive creature or possession. To hold otherwise, to speak of knowledge as if it were individually created and hence subject to the prerogatives of private ownership, makes no more sense than to say the same of the goods produced by neoliberal capitalist corporations:

> Modern corporations—and the millions who participate in their activities worldwide and the many more millions who depend, directly and indirectly, on the success of those activities—are reflections and expressions of the general decline of production as a "truly 'private' economic activity" (quoting Joseph Schumpeter). They are aspects of the *socialisation* of production and of the growing economic interdependence that characterizes modern capitalism. Increasingly, our collective material fate is inextricably bound up with the use we make of corporate assets. It is arguable, therefore, that not only are corporate assets no longer private property, but that, as the product of the collective labour of many generations upon which we all depend, there are compelling grounds for designating them common property.[11]

Those who participate in producing these assets, Paddy Ireland concludes, are contributors to a fund of goods that would not exist absent the cooperative work that is the necessary condition of their creation, and the same, I maintain, is true of knowledge.

Scholarly inquiry is a distinctive form of work that over time generates what we might call a "cognitive commonwealth." One of the features that defines this commonwealth's goods, which distinguishes it from many others, is what economists call their "nonrivalrous" character. When I drink water from a glass, you cannot drink that same water, and so this good is rivalrous. Were knowledge akin to that water, my gain would come at your expense. However, when I share my knowledge with you, and you with me, we are both enriched. This, I take it, is essentially what Justice Brandeis was getting at when in 1918 he insisted that "the general rule of law is, that the noblest of human productions—knowledge, truths ascertained, conceptions, and ideas—become, after voluntary communication to others, free as the air to common use."[12]

Accordingly, should someone represent as "knowledge" something that has been removed from the epistemic commonwealth and rendered a rivalrous good via its privatization, we should respond by explaining that this misconstrues what in fact no longer qualifies as knowledge. Should I, for example, appropriate what belongs to this commonwealth and reconstitute that knowledge in the form of a textbook, I will thereby transform this good into a vendible commodity, which is a very different sort of thing. By the same token, should I uncritically employ the oxymoronic phrase "academic capitalism," you should be quick to tell me that I don't know what I am talking about. The category of "academic capitalism" appears coherent only because it masks the violation necessary to expropriation of the epistemic goods it represents as so many ownable objects. In order to become so much private property entitled to the liberal state's protection, like the pastures fenced in by the Enclosure Acts, these goods must be wrested from the social relations of production out of which they emerged and within which they would otherwise remain embedded. Only when removed from the epistemic commonwealth can they be reconfigured as the rivalrous entities presupposed by and necessary to the operation of a capitalist economy. Only then can their "owners" exclude others from access and, on that basis, claim sole title to whatever stream of benefits flows from these goods' transformation into the commodities that are the stuff of capital accumulation.

Within the academy, this dispossession was afforded its constitutional authorization when *Dartmouth* affirmed that the academy's tangible assets are so much private property effectively "owned" by a head severed from the depoliticized body it now rules. The neoliberal university consummates *Dartmouth*'s logic by extending this expropriation to knowing's intangible fruits via their commodification; and that offense is realized in the form of intellectual property law. That law is the principal means by which socially produced goods are reconstituted as something susceptible to private ownership claims as well as their protection by the state. If, therefore, access to knowledge is now something that is available to those who can afford it but denied to those who cannot, that is not because scarcity is inherent in knowledge's nature. Rather, that is so because the privatization of knowledge is enabled and enforced by means of patent, copyright, and other laws that restrict who may and who may not enjoy these epistemic goods as well as how much anyone must pay for that privilege. As these goods, now transmuted into commodities, become rivalrous, the epistemic commonwealth literally shrinks as socially produced goods are ripped from the context of their collaborative creation.

Commonwealth University challenges this expropriation by affirming its identity as a corporation that denies to anyone the right to extract this or that from its common pool of resources and then claim exclusive rights over disposition of that thing. To illustrate how CU does so, consider the following provision in Ohio's Revised Code regarding all public colleges and universities in that state: "All rights to and interests in discoveries, inventions, or patents which result from research or investigation conducted in any experiment station, bureau, laboratory, research facility, or other facility of any state college or university, or by employees of any state college or university acting within the scope of their employment or with funding, equipment, or infrastructure provided by or through any state college or university, *shall be the sole property of that college or university*." Here, setting aside this statute's misconstruction of the academy's members as employees, the Ohio legislature gets matters more right than wrong. It does so by affirming that the goods created by those who do the academy's productive work are not susceptible to ownership claims advanced by private individuals. This is the conclusion the statute correctly draws when it goes on to state: "No person, firm, association, corporation, or governmental agency which uses the facilities of such college or university in connection with such research or investigation and no faculty member, employee, or student of such college or university participating in or making such discoveries or inventions, shall have any rights to or interests in such discoveries or inventions, including income therefrom."[13] In sum, Ohio's academic corporations are the legal persons that "own" the goods collectively produced within them, and no one can claim otherwise as a preface to or pretext for expropriating and exploiting them for purposes of private gain.

Ohio's statute goes awry, however, when it authorizes the autocratic rulers of its public universities and colleges to carve out exceptions to these general provisions:

> As may be determined from time to time by the board of trustees of any state college or university, the college or university may retain, assign, license, transfer, sell, or otherwise dispose of, in whole or in part and upon such terms as the board of trustees may direct, any and all rights to, interests in, or income from any such discoveries, inventions, or patents which the college or university owns or may acquire. Such dispositions may be to any individual, firm, association, corporation, or governmental agency, or to any faculty member, employee, or student of the college or university as the board of trustees may direct.[14]

Here, eliding the contradictions internal to the category of "academic capitalism," the state of Ohio provides for the autocratic head of what cannot be considered a member corporation to claim exclusive authority over the academy's collectively produced goods; to disfigure those goods as so much privatized property; and, finally, to allocate to specific individuals the right to profit from their commodification.[15] That this right may sometimes be granted to certain of the academy's employees, including faculty, does not release them from their status as subjects; it merely renders them bribed.

At Commonwealth University, ownership of that which its members produce remains vested within the creature of law to which they collectively belong. CU's members no more own these assets than Ohio's trustees do, and so they too cannot treat these socialized goods as if they were so much alienable property to be trafficked in capitalist markets. As members, however, they retain the collective power to regulate disposition of this common wealth. That power cannot be conflated with the bundle of rights conventionally ascribed to private property owners, however, because this power remains grounded within the republican body politic constituted by its members. This of course does not guarantee that CU's members will make no ill-advised decisions about how best to make use of these goods. Nor does it presuppose that they are somehow especially virtuous and hence immune to the temptations of self-dealing. But it does ensure that what they collectively create will not come to oppose them as so much privatized property whose employment is dictated by those who are not this corporation's members.

The term *commonwealth* in this university's name signifies the reabsorption of expropriated private property within a corporation that is composed of its members but is not reducible to them, whether as individuals or as an aggregation of individuals. As such, CU must not be confused with, for example, the legally constituted form of association that is a partnership. Were CU that, title to its property would remain with the natural persons who are its unincorporated partners; and, were that so, each partner would retain the right to withdraw assets proportional to that party's initial investment. Were CU thus constituted, it would remain forever fragile because its individual investors can always cut and run whenever they are so moved.

CU's common wealth, by contrast, assumes the form of a nondivisible pool of resources. Because those resources are locked within this corporation and so shielded from private appropriation, the likelihood that this university will prove sustainable through time is considerably enhanced, as is its ongoing capacity to serve CU's chartered purpose. This renders CU quite unlike the neoliberal academy, which, best illustrated by Purdue Global, is in fact more akin to a legal partnership whose assets are so many rivalrous goods and whose participants struggle to wrest as much revenue as possible from one another. At CU, by way of contrast, democratic stewardship of goods held and regulated by its members in their corporate capacity replaces this contractually domesticated war of all against all.

Were this the appropriate time and place, I would now explain with some care why I believe that the two guiding principles of Commonwealth University, once conjoined, facilitate the promise of higher education, which is what the autocratic-capitalist academy so often thwarts. In lieu of that, at this juncture, I will merely submit that this corporation merits our consideration not in virtue of its democratic or socialist character per se but, rather, because its constitution opens the possibility of and may indeed act as a catalyst for decommodified forms of learning, educating, and knowing. Or, perhaps better, let us think of CU's constitution not as one that enables noncommodified inquiry but as itself an institutional articulation of knowledge-generating practices that elude the commodity form. Or, best of all, let's entertain the possibility that CU's corporate structure and these practices are mutually constitutive and hence that neither is cause and the other effect.

Commonwealth University envisions the practice of inquiry as one that is common to all its scholars, including faculty as well as those we now too neatly demarcate and designate as students. Here the commodity form does not dictate either's relationship to the academy, whether via the "private government" constituted by capitalist employment contracts or via the purchase of an education by means of tuition. Emancipated from that form, which is indispensable to the domination inherent within a capitalist political economy, these relationships become available for reconstitution in ways that better ensure (but never guarantee) the unique kind of freedom that is essential to fulfillment of the academy's end.

In its "1915 Declaration of Principles," the AAUP correctly insisted that the viability and vitality of the academic enterprise requires the form of freedom that enables and encourages unflinching criticism of the disciplinary truths we now take for granted but also received opinions, conventional practices, and all powers that be, whether located within or without the academy. If that freedom is to thrive, we must dismantle the vertical relations of unaccountable power that, today, give rise to psychasthenia universitatis among the dispirited. Or, to put this point in the affirmative, that freedom presupposes the horizontal relations of authority that govern a republican member corporation. So, too, this freedom requires an epistemic commons that defies capture by those who would reduce knowledge to so much cognitive capital, education to workforce training, and learning to the acquisition of credentials whose worth is measured by their exchange value in the occupational market. Each of these bastardizations assimilates what we mislabel "education" to ends other than its own and, specifically, those that define the project of capital accumulation within a neoliberal regime.

Achievement of this freedom requires the relative autonomy that accompanies Commonwealth University's constitution as a corporation. That corporation's powers enable it to stand not so much apart from but in an oblique relationship to the state that grants it corporate status but, by that very act, furnishes it with the capacity to frustrate its maker (as private for-profit corporations now do all too well). So positioned, as Cattell anticipated, CU harbors the potential to become a participant in broader democratic struggles against the forms of gendered, racialized, and socioeconomic exploitation with which neoliberal capitalism conspires. The conduct of inquiry within CU is not organized in accordance with the pricing mechanisms of the capitalist market, the managerial principles that inform hierarchically organized bureaucracies, or the coercive rule of law based in the state's monopolization of the means of legitimate violence. Grounded instead in the mutually reinforcing principles enumerated in this chapter, CU's very existence offers a standing critique of the relations of domination and subordination that prevail wherever and whenever forms of collective practice are ordered by these other methods.

Why I Am Not a Utopian (Except in the Best Sense of the Term)

No doubt, some of my readers will disparage Commonwealth University as utopian on the ground that it gestures toward a lotusland in which all competing interests and claims are happily resolved. But there is nothing about CU's republican constitution that presupposes or ensures that consensus rather than contestation will mark its governance. Indeed, if easy agreement on fundamental matters is routinely secured within CU, we will want to ask whether its members are failing in their fiduciary duty to practice the critical inquiry that is essential to the purpose for which this university is incorporated.

In leveling a charge of utopianism, however, perhaps my critics mean to disparage this project because it is quixotic or, like that of Mrs. Partington, because it is untethered from the world in which we now live. In fact, however, conditions conducive to the establishment of Commonwealth University are already immanent within this world, and that is so in several ways.

Perhaps the academic constitution we have inherited from colonial America made some sense in the absence of an established body of scholars, such as those at Oxford and Cambridge, in whom the powers of governance might be vested. Today, however, those in whom the law formally vests final authority to govern the academy's affairs are ever more akin to obsolescent relics whose claim to rule is routinely outstripped by forces over which they exercise ever less control. To lop off the head of this autocratic body politic is, therefore, to do no more than amputate a vestigial organ.

So, too, perhaps John Marshall's representation of Dartmouth College on the model of private property protected by the Constitution's Contract Clause made some sense in a predominantly agrarian order that had yet to realize the socialized nature of production, including the production of knowledge. Today, however, to allow the academy's autocrats to expropriate, privatize, and commodify the goods that comprise the commonwealth of knowledge is to wed a retrograde conception of property to an anachronistic representation of rule. Commonwealth University merely calls on us to replace this atavistic constitution with one better suited to the conduct of all work, including scholarly inquiry, in the twenty-first century.

For these reasons, Commonwealth University is not the neoliberal academy's antithesis and hence a possibility that can be realized only through a wholesale repudiation of the present. Yes, on my view, the promise of

American higher education has yet to be adequately accomplished and, yes, this promise will remain stultified so long as its practice remains circumscribed by an antidemocratic corporate form located within a capitalist political economy. My aim, though, is not to recover some precapitalist idyll when, as some would have it, education truly flourished. That fantasy is nothing but nostalgia for an ideal that never was, whereas CU's aim is to release the emancipatory potential that resides, albeit perversely so, within the present.

To do so, Commonwealth University embraces an institutional form, the corporation, that dominates today's political economy but urges us to disavow its neoliberal malformation. To set about doing so, we need only extend to the academy a possibility that the legal codes of most states already enable. California's statutory code, for example, provides for the constitution of what it calls "member-governed corporations," and it defines as a member "any person who, pursuant to a specific provision of a corporation's articles or bylaws, *has the right to vote for the election of a director or directors or on a disposition of all or substantially all of the assets of a corporation.* . . . 'Member' also means any person who is designated in the articles or bylaws as member and, pursuant to a specific provision of a corporation's articles or bylaws, *has the right to vote on changes to the articles or bylaws.*"[16] Available law, in short, already furnishes neoliberal academic corporations the statutory means to reconstitute themselves on nonautocratic foundations and in accordance with republican principles.[17]

By the same token, CU's establishment requires no revolutionary expropriation of the academy's expropriators. Instead, it merely calls on us to recall what has always been true of corporations: unlike an unincorporated partnership, an essential purpose of the corporate form is to secure collectivized resources within a legal artifact that is distinguishable from all natural persons, thereby immunizing those assets from private appropriation in the service of self-interested accumulation.[18] In this sense, the constitution of CU is fundamentally conservative, for it asks only that we remember a truth occluded by today's neoliberal ideologues.

What corporate law cannot furnish, though, is perhaps what we most sorely need: an enhanced capacity to reimagine an academy that now appears susceptible to nothing but tinkering around its margins. We see pinched imaginations on the part of perpetually anxious students preoccupied with securing whatever training will render them employable in a job market that ceaselessly redefines what is required to remain so. We see pinched imaginations on the part of faculty members who, in response to the latest encroachments of "corporatization," appear unable to articulate their grievances in anything other than the cramped and ultimately counterproductive rhetoric of "shared governance." And, of course, we see pinched imaginations on the part of governing boards whose trustees equate fulfillment of their fiduciary responsibilities with specifying the terms of the academy's envelopment within a neoliberal political economy.

If it is utopian to imagine an academy whose members are not subject to autocratic rule because they govern themselves, if it is utopian to imagine an academy in which employees are no longer subject to imperious employers because all are members of a corporate endeavor that has no place for either boss or hired hand, if it is utopian to imagine an academy in which free inquiry is no longer perpetually imperiled by a constitution of power that is antagonistic to its very possibility, then I happily plead guilty as charged.

Notes

A Prologue in the Form of a Puzzle

1   AAUP, *Special Report: COVID-19 and Academic Governance* (hereafter cited as *Special Report: COVID-19*), 2. For a more developed analysis of this report, see Kaufman-Osborn, "Shared Governance within the Autocratic Academy."

2   AAUP, *Special Report: COVID-19*, 3, 2.

3   AAUP, *Special Report: COVID-19*, 34, 37–38.

4   AAUP, *Special Report: COVID-19*, 40.

5   Even the most astute critics of US colleges and universities often overlook the academy's constitution in the form of a corporation. See, for example, Slaughter and Rhoades, *Academic Capitalism and the New Economy*: "Although colleges and universities are integrating with the new economy and adopting many practices found in the corporate sector, they are not becoming corporations" (26). To which the correct response is: they cannot *become* corporations because they already are and, in the United States, always have been.

6   Dewey, *The Public and Its Problems*, 183.

7   I recognize that the term *neoliberalism* and its derivatives are some of the slipperier terms in our contemporary political lexicon. The specific sense in which I employ these terms will become clearer in part IV. For now, suffice it to say that I mean to designate the form of contemporary capitalism that prevails in the United States today and so distinguishes it from, for example, merchant or industrial capitalism. I also recognize that the rise of authoritarianism around the globe, including within the United States, has persuaded some that the term *neoliberalism* is now an anachronistic descriptor. I understand the point, especially at the level of the national state, but I also believe that the forms of rationality and the practices constitutive of neoliberalism remain very much alive and well within the contemporary US academy.

8   Jastrow, "Academic Aspects of Administration," 326.

9   Hirji, "50 Emerging Technology Themes to Watch Out for in 2021."

10 As will become apparent in part IV, my argument about the role played by higher education within the capitalist political economy of the United States, especially since the late nineteenth century, is indebted to the work of Karl Marx. To his credit, Marx did not share the contemporary left's uncritical condemnation of the corporation. In volume 3 of *Capital*, he argued that the corporation is an inherently ambiguous institutional formation because it represents "the abolition of the capitalist mode of production within the capitalist mode of production itself, and hence a self-abolishing contradiction, which presents itself *prima facie* as a mere point of transition to a new form of production" (569). On this account, what Marx typically called the "joint stock company" presages the dissolution of private property insofar as "ownership," spread among a corporation's diverse shareholders, is effectively socialized. What Marx fails to understand, however, is that the publicly traded corporation does not distribute ownership among many. Rather, as I explain in chapter 3, the corporation dispossesses *all* owners by vesting its capital within an artificial person that is legally separate from all natural persons, including its shareholders. As such, the corporation collectivizes property in a way that is different from what Marx imagined; and, as I explain in the epilogue, that in part is precisely why I consider the corporation a viable institutional home for free inquiry.

11 Ahtone and Lee, "Ask Who Paid for America's Universities." For this project's results to date, see "Land-Grab Universities," *High Country News*, accessed July 26, 2022, https://www.landgrabu.org/. For an analysis of the University of North Carolina System's implication in slavery as well as its contemporary legacy, see Kaufman-Osborn, "How Not to Think about Institutional Racism."

12 Anonymous letter, in Cattell, *University Control*, 248.

13 Cattell, *University Control*, 62.

1. Imperious Regents and Disposable Custodians

1   Ellis, "This University's Board Now Has the Power to Fire Anyone."

2   Bylaws 1.2(c)(4), Board of Regents, Texas Southern University, adopted October 25, 2019, http://www.tsu.edu/about/board-of-regents/bor_bylaws06212013.pdf.

3   Ellis, "This University's Board Now Has the Power to Fire Anyone."

4   Ellis, "This University's Board Now Has the Power to Fire Anyone."

5   Board of Regents, Texas Education Code, sec. 106.11, accessed July 27, 2022, https://texas.public.law/statutes/tex._educ._code_section_106.11.

6   Bylaws 1.1, Board of Regents, Texas Southern University, accessed July 27, 2022, http://www.tsu.edu/about/board-of-regents/bor_bylaws06212013.pdf.

7   Bylaws 1.3, Board of Regents, Texas Southern University, accessed July 27, 2022, http://www.tsu.edu/about/board-of-regents/bor_bylaws06212013.pdf.

8   Although I will offer an alternative in chapter 9, the best-known scheme for classifying higher education providers remains the Carnegie Classification of Institutions of Higher Education, "Basic Classification Description." For another way of doing so, see Weiss, "Challenges and Opportunities in the Changing Landscape." Considering this plethora of institutional types, in an essay titled "Shock Wave II," Clark Kerr wondered whether the very category "higher education" misleads because it implies the existence of a unified genus when none in fact exists. On my view, contra Kerr, there is a denominator that is common to all, and that is the legal formation of American colleges and universities as autocratic corporations.

9   Kaplan and Lee, *The Law of Higher Education*, 21.

10   "An Act Relating to Dignity and Nondiscrimination in Public Education," Idaho Code, Title 33, Chapter 1, Section 33–138(2), accessed July 27, 2022, https://legislature.search.idaho.gov/search?IW_FIELD_TEXT =critical+race+theory&IW_DATABASE=idaho+statutes. The capacity of state legislatures to encroach on the internal affairs of public colleges and universities differs depending on, among other things, whether any given state constitution grants control over higher education to the legislative branch, as Idaho does, or, alternatively, establishes higher education as an independent constitutional department, as, for example, Montana does.

Article IX of Idaho's state constitution locates the responsibility for creating public institutions of higher education within the legislature and includes the following provision: "The regents shall have the general supervision of the university, and the control and direction of all the funds of, and appropriations to, the university, *under such regulations as may be prescribed by law*" (accessed July 27, 2022, https://legislature.idaho.gov/statutesrules /idconst/ArtIX/Sect10/, emphasis added).

Montana's first constitution, adopted in 1889, said much the same. However, in 1972, the state adopted a new constitution that located higher education under its own article (X) and granted its board of regents "full power, responsibility, and authority to supervise, coordinate, manage and control the Montana university system" (accessed July 27, 2022, https://courts.mt.gov /External/library/docs/72constit.pdf). How the constitution of Montana differs from that of Idaho explains why the former state's supreme court recently found unconstitutional a statute that overrode the Montana University System's policy that banned firearms from its campuses. See Board of Regents of Higher Education of The State v. State, 2022 MT 128 (Mont. 2022), accessed July 27, 2022, https://juddocumentservice.mt.gov /getDocByCTrackId?DocId=395212. In Idaho, given higher education's status within its constitution, it would be more difficult to affirm a comparable claim to institutional autonomy.

11   Of course, I recognize that the formal constitution of power does not exhaust
      the many informal ways that power is distributed and exercised within US
      colleges and universities. To see the point, one need only consider how struc-
      tures of gendered, racialized, and socioeconomic stratification do their work
      within the academy. Acknowledgment of that work does not compromise
      my representation of the American academy as an incorporated autocracy.
      Indeed, as I note in the next section, because most governing boards are so
      unrepresentative of the US population at large, it is more accurate to say that
      their formal powers are amplified by these officially unrecognized systems of
      domination and subordination and vice versa.

12   Anderson, *Private Government*, 42, 45.

13   Anderson, *Private Government*, 53–54.

14   Princeton University, "The Governing of Princeton University," 52. For
      Harvard's contemporaneous exploration of these same issues, see Harvard
      University, "The Organization and Functions of the Governing Boards and
      the President's Office." For another study that emerges out of the campus up-
      heavals of the 1960s but, unlike those of Harvard and Princeton, advances a
      radical democratic critique of, in this instance, Berkeley's received constitu-
      tion of rule, see Foote et al., *The Culture of the University*.

15   Princeton University, "The Governing of Princeton University," 51, 53.

16   Princeton University, "The Governing of Princeton University," 53–55.

17   Princeton University, "The Governing of Princeton University," 53, 56.

18   Princeton University, "The Governing of Princeton University," 60.

19   Legon and Chaffee, "Transforming Board Governance for the University of
      South Carolina System," 7, 1.

20   Legon and Chaffee, "Transforming Board Governance for the University of
      South Carolina System," 9.

21   Bevins et al., "Shaping University Boards for 21st Century Higher Education
      in the US." It is easy to find additional evidence to sustain the claim that,
      demographically speaking, boards are far less diverse than is the US popula-
      tion at large. See, for example, Whitford, "College Boards Are Still White and
      Male, Report Shows."

22   Scott, "Leadership Threats to Shared Governance in Higher Education," 2.

23   Mitchell and King, *How to Run a College*, 140.

24   For a helpful account of how American higher education reproduces en-
      trenched structures of inequality and domination, see Carnevale, Schmidt,
      and Strohl, *The Merit Myth*.

25   Legon and Chaffee, "Transforming Board Governance for the University of
      South Carolina System," 16.

26   Hofstadter and Metzger, *The Development of Academic Freedom*, 416.

27   AGB, *Statement on Board Responsibility for Institutional Governance*, n.p. The
      AGB's generalizations about the constitution of rule within American col-
      leges and universities apply best when considering boards that govern single

institutions. Although the AGB's basic characterization remains valid, the structure of governance is more complex when, for example, one considers system boards that coordinate multiple institutions, each of which may have its own board. For a discussion of diverse board types, see Longanecker, "The 'New' New Challenge of Governance by Governing Boards."

28   AGB, *AGB Board of Directors' Statement on the Fiduciary Duties of Governing Board Members*, 4, 6, 8.

29   AGB, *AGB Board of Directors' Statement on the Fiduciary Duties of Governing Board Members*, 2, 1 (emphasis added).

30   Legon and Chaffee, "Transforming Board Governance for the University of South Carolina System," 16.

31   Adam Smith, *An Inquiry into the Nature and Causes of the Wealth of Nations*, 700.

32   In their *Improving the Performance of Governing Boards*, Richard Chait and his coauthors say this about nonprofit governing boards in general: "After 10 years of research and dozens of engagements as consultants to nonprofit boards, we have reached a rather stark conclusion: *effective governance by a board of trustees is a relatively rare and unnatural act*. . . . Regrettably, most boards just drift with the tides. As a result, trustees are often little more than high-powered, well-intentioned people engaged in low-level activities. The board dispatches an agenda of potpourri tied tangentially at best to the organization's strategic priorities and challenges" (1). My research has given me little reason to doubt that this generalization applies equally well to the governing boards that rule America's colleges and universities.

33   Clancy, "November Board Update."

34   Clancy, "Building the Foundation for a Great Story," 2.

35   Fisher, "Tulsa Trustees Override Faculty." As it turns out, this blow did not in fact prove fatal. "True Commitment" was unceremoniously abandoned in 2020 and replaced by a new strategic plan that was approved by TU's board the following year. See Hindman, "Interdisciplinarity's Shared Governance Problem."

36   Clancy, "November Board Update."

37   Janet Levin, "The Academic Strategy for the University of Tulsa."

38   Article VI (Shared Governance), Constitution of the Faculty Senate, University of Tulsa, accessed July 27, 2022, https://35ht6t2ynxop1ztf96ih81r1 -wpengine.netdna-ssl.com/wp-content/uploads/2020/09/constitution-of-the -facultysenate-2018.pdf (emphasis added). For a response by AAUP members to the controversy at TU, see Hindman and Saylor, "A Crisis of Shared Governance at the University of Tulsa."

39   Howland, "Storm Clouds over Tulsa."

40   Howland, "Administrative Hardball at the University of Tulsa."

41   Howland, "Storm Clouds over Tulsa."

42   Howland, "Storm Clouds over Tulsa." For a later version of the argument advanced in "Storm Clouds over Tulsa," see Howland, "Corporate Wolves in Academic Sheepskins."

43 See photograph in Fisher, "How a Radical Restructuring Plan Fractured a Campus." Showing more tactical imagination than their instructors, as the controversy over "True Commitment" gained momentum, a group of students organized a mock funeral for the liberal arts that featured a coffin accompanied by fake headstones commemorating academic programs slated for elimination. See Vincent, "TU Is Becoming Something Other Than a Liberal Arts College."

44 For a hagiographic history of TU, see Logsdon, *The University of Tulsa.*

45 Office of the Secretary of State (Oklahoma), "Amended and Restated Certificate of Incorporation," University of Tulsa, last amended May 6, 1992. Available on request from the author.

46 Bylaws IV.3, Board of Regents, University of Tulsa, last amended September 25, 2018. Available on request from the author.

47 Bylaws V.3, Board of Regents, University of Tulsa. Available on request from the author.

48 This mission statement can still be found at, for example, "About the University of Tulsa," University of Tulsa, accessed August 26, 2022, https:// strategicplan.utulsa.edu/about-tulsa.html. TU's current mission statement is also so much pablum: "We are a student-centered research university that cultivates interconnected learning experiences to explore complex ideas and create new knowledge in a spirit of free inquiry. Guided by our commitment to diversity, equity, and service, we prepare individuals to make meaningful contributions to our campus, our community, and our world" ("Our Mission," University of Tulsa, accessed July 27, 2022, https://utulsa.edu/about/mission/).

49 Concerned Faculty of the University of Tulsa, "Request by the Faculty of the University of Tulsa for Legal Intervention by the Attorney General of Oklahoma," n.d., accessed July 27, 2022, https://docs.wixstatic.com/ugd/effbf7 _825a57acb6c34680adac993acd3bf1a5.pdf. For more on this legal complaint, see Knox, "U. of Tulsa Faculty to Ask Oklahoma's Attorney General to Halt Controversial Restructuring Plan."

50 On this point, see Oklahoma Statutes § 18-381.54 (General Powers): "Associations shall have the powers enumerated, authorized and permitted by this act and such other rights and powers as may be incidental to or reasonably necessary or appropriate for the accomplishment of the objects and purposes of the association" (accessed July 27, 2022, http://ok.elaws.us/os/18-381.54).

2. The Neoliberal Corporation Debunked

1 AAUP, *Special Report: COVID-19,* 3.

2 In this chapter, I focus on certain key features that distinguish the corporation from other types of institutional formations. Hence, here I gloss over distinctions that in later chapters will require delineation—for example, between for-profit and nonprofit corporations. In focusing on the specifically

neoliberal account, moreover, I fail to do justice to other accounts of corporations as well as their governance. While this renders my analysis partial in the sense of being incomplete, that limitation does not in my view invalidate any of the claims I make about the defects of the neoliberal representation.

3　Friedman, "The Social Responsibility of Business Is to Increase Its Profits."

4　In *Dodge v. Ford Motor Company*, 170 N.W. 668, 684 (Mich. 1919), the Michigan Supreme Court held that "a business corporation is organized and carried on primarily for the profit of the stockholders." Although he modified his views later in life, an early justification of something akin to the doctrine of shareholder primacy can also be found in Berle, *Studies in the Law of Corporation Finance*.

5　Hansmann and Kraakman, "The End of History for Corporate Law," 439.

6　Jensen and Meckling, "Theory of the Firm," 310 (emphasis in original). For a compressed intellectual history of this reading of the corporation, see Eisenberg, "The Conception That the Corporation Is a Nexus of Contracts, and the Dual Nature of the Firm," 820–22.

7　Easterbrook and Fischel, "The Corporate Contract," 1418.

8　Adam Smith, *The Wealth of Nations*, 13.

9　For just a few of the many excellent accounts of the harms wrought by neoliberal capitalism's corporations, see Barkan, *Corporate Sovereignty*; Duménil and Lévy, *The Crisis of Neoliberalism*; Kotz, *The Rise and Fall of Neoliberal Capitalism*; and Streeck, *Buying Time*.

10　Ciepley, "How America's Corporations Lost Their Public Purpose," 15.

11　For two excellent accounts of the ideological character of the neoliberal reading of the corporation, see Ireland, "Recontractualising the Corporation" and "Defending the Rentier."

12　Alchian and Demsetz, "Production, Information Costs, and Economic Organization," 777.

13　Easterbrook and Fischel, *The Economic Structure of Corporate Law*, 37.

14　Ireland, "Property and Contract in Contemporary Contract Theory," 483. Although they are its principal beneficiaries, for the most part, the neoliberal corporation's so-called owners are passive rentiers who need and most often do not know much if anything about the companies whose shares they hold. Moreover, should these corporations commit misdeeds by, for example, spilling enormous amounts of oil into the Gulf of Mexico, these shareholders will be relieved of any responsibility for these wrongs. From their vantage point, the beauty of the doctrine of limited liability is that it enriches shareholders while at the same time immunizing them from culpability and hence penalty for malfeasance as well as responsibility for whatever debts are incurred by the corporations they "own."

15　Stout, "The Corporation as Time Machine," 684.

16　Ciepley, "Beyond Public and Private," 146.

17　Dartmouth College v. Woodward, 17 U.S. 518, 636 (1819).

18 See Citizens United v. Federal Election Commission, 558 U.S. 310 (2010); and Burwell v. Hobby Lobby Stores, Inc., 573 U.S. 682 (2014).

19 Blackstone, *Commentaries*, 1:297.

20 Ciepley, "Our Corporate Civilization and Its Neoliberal Crisis," 4–5.

21 For more complete expositions of these claims, see Clarke, "The Contest on Corporate Purpose"; and Robé, "The Legal Structure of the Firm." For an account of the fiduciary responsibilities of for-profit board members, see the American Bar Association, *Model Business Corporation Act*, § 8.30.

22 See Revised Code of Washington 35A.11.010: "Each city governed under this optional municipal code, whether charter or noncharter, shall be entitled 'City of . . .' (naming it), and by such name shall have perpetual succession; may sue and be sued in all courts and proceedings; use a corporate seal approved by its legislative body; and, by and through its legislative body, such municipality may contract and be contracted with; may purchase, lease, receive, or otherwise acquire real and personal property of every kind, and use, enjoy, hold, lease, control, convey or otherwise dispose of it for the common benefit" (accessed July 28, 2022, https://app.leg.wa.gov/rcw/default.aspx?cite =35A.11.010).

23 "An Act to Establish an Institution of Learning in Walla Walla County," sec. 1, accessed July 28, 2022, https://www.whitman.edu/about/mission -constitution-and-bylaws/bylaws-and-charter.

24 For a helpful account of *quo warranto* and *ultra vires* proceedings, as well as an account of how they might be revitalized today, see Greenfield, "Ultra Vires Lives!"

25 For an excellent history of the origins and growth of general incorporation laws, see Hurst, *The Legitimacy of the Business Corporation in the Law of the United States*, 56–71.

26 For the statement to which this press release refers, see Business Roundtable, "Business Roundtable Redefines the Purpose of a Corporation."

27 On public benefit corporations, see Alexander, *Benefit Corporation Law and Governance*.

28 US Senate, *A Bill to Establish the Obligations of Certain Large Business Entities in the United States, and for Other Purposes*, S. 3348, 115th Cong., 2nd sess., introduced in Senate August 15, 2018, https://www.congress.gov/bill/115th-congress /senate-bill/3348/text.

3. Corporate Types

1 Francis Wayland, quoted in Lindsay, *Tradition Looks Forward*, 140.

2 For an overview of the historical lineage of these two types as well as their differences, see Ciepley, "Member Corporations, Property Corporations, and

Constitutional Rights." For a work that anticipates Ciepley's categorization of corporate types, see Tierney, *Religion, Law, and the Growth of Constitutional Thought*, especially 19–28.

3   Aquinas, "On Kingship, to the King of Cyprus," 205.

4   Ciepley, "The Anglo-American Misconception of Stockholders as 'Owners' and 'Members,'" 632.

5   Justinian, *The Digest of Justinian*, 3.4.1.

6   Ireland, "Capitalism without the Capitalist," 45.

7   Ciepley, "Is the U.S. Government a Corporation?," 418.

8   Ferdinand Maitland, introduction to *Political Theories of the Middle Ages*, xxx.

9   English East India Company, "Charter Granted by Queen Elizabeth to the East India Company," accessed July 28, 2022, https://en.wikisource.org/wiki/Charter_Granted_by_Queen_Elizabeth_to_the_East_India_Company.

10   Blackstone, *Commentaries*, 1:293.

11   Johnson v. M'Intosh, 21 U.S. (8 Wheat.) 543 (1823), 111–12.

12   "The Charter of Massachusetts Bay," accessed July 28, 2022, https://avalon.law.yale.edu/17th_century/mass03.asp.

13   "The Charter of Massachusetts Bay."

14   "Constitution of Massachusetts," accessed July 28, 2022, http://www.nhinet.org/ccs/docs/ma-1780.htm.

15   Ciepley, "Is the U.S. Government a Corporation?," 423. For an article that traces the abiding influence of the corporate form in Massachusetts, as company becomes colony and colony in turn becomes state, see Bowie, "Why the Constitution Was Written Down."

16   Locke, *Two Treatises of Government*, 331.

17   Madison, "The Federalist No. 49," 327–28.

18   Dixon et al. v. United States, case no. 3934 (Cir. Ct. D. Va. 1811).

19   Lieber, *Encyclopedia Americana*, 3:547.

20   Ciepley, "The Anglo-American Misconception of Stockholders as 'Owners' and 'Members,'" 632.

4. William & Mary Dispossessed

1   For helpful accounts of the history of rule within the American academy, see Herbst, *From Crisis to Crisis*; Duryea, *The Academic Corporation*; and Kirkpatrick, *Academic Organization and Control*.

2   Adam Smith, *The Wealth of Nations*, 120.

3   For a useful discussion of the internal politics of medieval European universities, see Ridder-Symoens, "Management and Resources." For an account of self-governance at the University of Paris specifically, see Post, "Parisian Masters as a Corporation."

4   Oxford and Cambridge Act (1571), accessed July 28, 2022, http://www
     .legislation.gov.uk/aep/Eliz1/13/29.

5   For a brief account of the internal governance of Cambridge during its early
     centuries, see Leedham-Green, *A Concise History of the University of Cambridge*,
     1–28. A more developed account can be found in Peacock, *Observations on the
     Statutes of the University of Cambridge*.

6   Morison, *The Founding of Harvard College*, 40. On the influence of Cam-
     bridge and Oxford on the founders and early governors of Harvard, see also
     Hofstadter and Metzger, *The Development of Academic Freedom*, 82–83; and
     Rudolph, *The American College and University*, 26–27.

7   In *From Crisis to Crisis*, Jurgen Herbst takes issue with the claim that Cam-
     bridge and Oxford provided the principal models for the organization of rule
     within early colonial colleges. Instead, he argues that it was the Calvinist
     model of church organization, which informed the colleges founded at Geneva
     (1559), Leyden (1575), and Edinburgh (1583), that was far more influential. By
     way of contrast, in his *The Founding of Harvard College*, Morison argues that its
     creators drew little or no inspiration from Calvinism or its Scottish variant in
     particular: "There was very little intercourse of any kind between Scotland
     and New England until late in the seventeenth century, and their two
     schools of Protestant theology hardly became aware of one another until the
     debates of the Westminster Assembly disclosed their differences in matters
     of polity" (129). As will become clear in this chapter and the next, on my
     reading, Morison is more persuasive on this question.

8   "The First Charter of Virginia" (April 10, 1606), accessed July 28, 2022,
     https://avalon.law.yale.edu/17th_century/va01.asp.

9   "The Second Charter of Virginia" (May 23, 1609), accessed July 28, 2022,
     https://avalon.law.yale.edu/17th_century/va02.asp#1.

10   "The Third Charter of Virginia" (March 12, 1611), accessed July 28, 2022,
     https://avalon.law.yale.edu/17th_century/va03.asp.

11   "An Ordinance and Constitution of the Treasurer, Council, and Company
     in England, for a Council of State and General Assembly" (July 24, 1621),
     accessed July 28, 2022, https://avalon.law.yale.edu/17th_century/va04.asp.

12   Tyler, *Williamsburg*, 110.

13   Canby, "A Note on the Influence of Oxford University upon William and
     Mary College in the Eighteenth Century."

14   College of William & Mary, "The Charter, the Transfer," 3, 6, 7.

15   College of William & Mary, "The Charter, the Transfer," 6, 8, 9, 39, 19. In this last
     provision, we see traces of medieval understandings that sometimes regarded the
     nation as a body politic constituted as an incorporated concatenation of subordi-
     nate corporations, some but not all of which were granted the privilege of formal
     political representation. As one would expect, William & Mary was divested of
     this right when Virginia's new constitution, based on the principle of popular
     sovereignty exercised by individual citizens, was adopted in 1776.

16   College of William & Mary, "The Charter, the Transfer," 3, 4, 6, 7, 8, 10.

17   Hofstadter and Metzger, *The Development of Academic Freedom*, 133.

18   College of William & Mary, "The Charter, the Transfer," 13.

19   Blair and Fouace, "The Statutes of the College of William and Mary."

20   For more detailed accounts of these violations, see Herbst, *From Crisis to Crisis*, 55–61; and Hofstadter and Metzger, *The Development of Academic Freedom*, 130–34.

21   I abstract this account of the events that transpired between 1756 and 1758 from the more detailed version found in Morporgo, *Their Majesties' Royall Colledge*, 122–27.

22   William & Mary College, "A Statute for the Better Government of the College."

23   Horrocks et al., "Journal of the President and Masters of William and Mary College," 83, 84, 85, 87.

24   Jefferson, "A Bill for Amending the Constitution of the College of William and Mary."

25   Bracken v. Visitors of William and Mary College, 7 Va. 573 (1790) at 11.

26   *Bracken*, 7 Va. at 28.

27   *Bracken*, 7 Va. at 14, 15.

28   *Bracken*, 7 Va. at 21.

29   *Bracken*, 7 Va. at 19, 21–22.

30   *Bracken*, 7 Va. at 20–22. For Blackstone's account of offices as estates, see *Commentaries*, 1: sec. 5.

31   *Bracken*, 7 Va. at 21.

32   *Bracken*, 7 Va. at 26.

33   For the text of the 1906 statute, see College of William & Mary, "The Charter, the Transfer," 44–45.

34   Hofstadter and Metzger, *The Development of Academic Freedom*, 134.

35   See Hofstadter and Metzger, *The Development of Academic Freedom*, 134.

5. "The College of Tyrannus"

1   Morison, *The Founding of Harvard College*, 179.

2   Morison, *The Founding of Harvard College*, 168.

3   Morison, *The Founding of Harvard College*, 193.

4   Morison, *The Founding of Harvard College*, 228.

5   Morison, *The Founding of Harvard College*, 234.

6   Fahs, "In the School of Tyrannus."

7   Morison, *The Founding of Harvard College*, 241.

8   *Massachusetts Bay Records*, quoted in Morison, *The Founding of Harvard College*, 326.

9   Hofstadter and Metzger, *The Development of Academic Freedom*, 127.

10   Hofstadter and Metzger, *The Development of Academic Freedom*, 123.

11   "The Harvard Charter of 1650," Harvard University Archives, accessed July 29, 2022, https://www.colonialsociety.org/node/396.

12   "The Harvard Charter of 1650." Anticipating the tax-exempt status of contemporary nonprofit colleges and universities, the charter also stipulated that the property and revenue of the college, up to a limit of £500 per year, shall "be freed from all civil impositions, taxes, and rates." The charter, incidentally, also provided that the "president, fellows, and scholars, together with the servants, and other necessary officers to the said president or college" be exempt from taxation; and, moreover, that these parties be "exempted from all personal civil offices, military exercises, or services."

13   "The Harvard Charter of 1650."

14   The text of this amendment can be found in Morison, *Harvard College in the Seventeenth Century*, 11–12 (emphasis added).

15   "The Harvard Charter of 1650."

16   A thorough account of these governance struggles can be found in Siegel, "Governance and Curriculum at Harvard College in the 18th Century."

17   For an overview of Harvard's governance struggles during this period, see Morison, *Harvard College in the Seventeenth Century*, 489–537. For the charters proposed in 1672, 1692, 1696, 1697, 1699, and 1700, see Quincy, *The History of Harvard University*, 1:592–608.

18   For the text of the Court's declaration, see Quincy, *The History of Harvard University*, 1:159.

19   For a careful review of the Sever controversy, see Siegel, "Governance and Curriculum at Harvard College in the 18th Century," 42–60.

20   Ware et al., *To the Reverend and Honorable the Corporation of Harvard University*, 10, 20.

21   Morison, *Harvard College in the Seventeenth Century*, 21.

22   Ware et al., *To the Reverend and Honorable the Corporation of Harvard University*, 8.

23   Sever and Welsteed, *The Memorial of Nicholas Sever and Wm. Welsteed*, 235.

24   Ware et al., *To the Reverend and Honorable the Corporation of Harvard University*, 27.

25   Norton, *Speech Delivered before the Overseers of Harvard College*, 22.

26   Sever and Welsteed, *The Memorial of Nicholas Sever and Wm. Welsteed*, 230.

27   Everett, *A Letter to John Lowell*, 98, 100, 101.

28   Norton, *Speech Delivered before the Overseers of Harvard College*, 24.

29   Sever and Welsteed, *The Memorial of Nicholas Sever and Wm. Welsteed*, 236, 229–30.

30   Sever and Welsteed, *The Memorial of Nicholas Sever and Wm. Welsteed*, 231.

31   Norton, *Speech Delivered before the Overseers of Harvard College*, 25, 24.

32   "The Harvard Charter of 1650"; Norton, *Speech Delivered before the Overseers of Harvard College*, x.

33   "The Harvard Charter of 1650."

34   Ware et al., *To the Reverend and Honorable the Corporation of Harvard University*, 2.

35   "The Harvard Charter of 1650."

36   Everett, *A Letter to John Lowell*, 42 (emphasis added).

37   Sever, "Tutor Sever's Argument," 55.

38   Norton, *Remarks on a Report of a Committee of the Overseers of Harvard College*, 5, 6.

39   Everett, *A Letter to John Lowell*, 48.

40   Ware et al., *To the Reverend and Honorable the Corporation of Harvard University*, 6.

41   Ware et al., *To the Reverend and Honorable the Corporation of Harvard University*, 25.

42   Norton, *Speech Delivered before the Overseers of Harvard College*, 16.

43   *Statutes and Laws of the University in Cambridge, Massachusetts*, secs. 12, 13.

44   *Statutes and Laws of the University in Cambridge, Massachusetts*, secs. 12, 14, 21.

45   Norton, *Remarks on a Report of the Committee of the Overseers of Harvard College*, xiv, xxiii.

46   *Statutes and Laws of the University in Cambridge, Massachusetts*, secs. 16, 18 (emphasis added).

47   *Statutes and Laws of the University in Cambridge, Massachusetts*, sec. 63.

48   Quoted in Ware et al., *To the Reverend and Honorable the Corporation of Harvard University*, 21.

49   Ware et al., *To the Reverend and Honorable the Corporation of Harvard University*, 9.

50   Everett, *A Letter to John Lowell*, 50.

51   Although I end my tale here, cessation of the mid-1820s dispute did not bring to a halt controversy about Harvard's governance and, more particularly, the appropriate role of the faculty in institutional rule. Indeed, as late as 1940, in an essay titled "Non-resident Government at Harvard," the Cambridge Union of University Teachers echoed its seventeenth- and eighteenth-century predecessors when it declared that "Harvard, like most American colleges and universities, is a very model of undemocratic administration, that the Faculty has no responsibilities and certain academic privileges, but no real power, except the right to recommend or suggest, and that the autocratic powers of the President are derived from an absentee, self-perpetuating government, the Corporation, of which the faculty members are servants and employees" (1).

6. The Marshall Plan

1   Webster, "Peroration, the Dartmouth College Case."

2   "Dartmouth College Charter," accessed August 1, 2022, http://www .dartmouth.edu/trustees/docs/charter-2010.pdf.

3   Occom to Wheelock, July 24, 1771, quoted in Newman, "Indigeneity and Early American Literature."

4   "Dartmouth College Charter."

5   Yale Corporation, "Charter and Legislation," accessed August 1, 2022, https:// www.yale.edu/sites/default/files/files/University-Charter.pdf.

6   Hofstadter and Metzger, *The Development of Academic Freedom*, 137.

7   "Dartmouth College Charter."

8   "Dartmouth College Charter."

9   "Dartmouth College Charter."

10   For a detailed account of the events leading up to *Dartmouth*, as written by
     the college's principal librarian, see Morin, "Will to Resist: The Dartmouth
     College Case." For a helpful history of *Dartmouth*'s proceedings in state and
     federal court, see Stites, *Private Interest and Public Gain*.

11   See Dartmouth's website for its self-congratulatory reading of *Dartmouth*:
     "The case is considered to be one of the most important and formative docu-
     ments in United States constitutional history, strengthening the Constitution's
     contract clause and thereby paving the way for American private institutions
     to conduct their affairs in accordance with their charters and without in-
     terference from the state" (accessed August 1, 2022, https://home.dartmouth
     .edu/life-community/explore-green/history-traditions). For Harvard's equally
     sanitized version of the history of its governance struggles, see "Leadership and
     Governance," Harvard University, accessed August 1, 2022, https://www.harvard
     .edu/about/leadership-and-governance/. And for William & Mary's airbrushed
     account of its origins, see "About W&M," William & Mary, accessed August 1,
     2022, https://www.wm.edu/about/history/index.php.

12   Frederick Hall to Nathaniel Shattuck (April 28, 1804), quoted in Stites, *Pri-
     vate Interest and Public Gain*, 7.

13   Stites, *Private Interest and Public Gain*, 10–11.

14   "Dartmouth College Charter."

15   Wheelock and Parish, *Sketches of the History of Dartmouth College*, 39, 86, 53, 88.

16   Dartmouth College, *A Vindication of the Official Conduct of the Trustees of Dart-
     mouth College*, 79, 34, 33.

17   Wheelock and Parish, *Sketches of the History of Dartmouth College*, 87.

18   Wheelock, quoted in Stites, *Private Interest and Public Gain*, 16.

19   Wheelock and Parish, *Sketches of the History of Dartmouth College*, 87.

20   Plumer, quoted in Herbst, *From Crisis to Crisis*, 236; Plumer, quoted in White-
     head, *The Separation of College and State*, 216.

21   Jefferson, quoted in Herbst, *From Crisis to Crisis*, 236. In arguing that corpora-
     tions enable concentrations of private power that are at odds with the repub-
     lican commitment to popular sovereignty, Plumer participated in a much
     broader anticorporation movement that saw its greatest strength during the
     first half of the nineteenth century. For a review of this movement, see Peter
     Hall, *The Organization of American Culture, 1700–1900*, 95–124.

22   For this bill's complete text, see "Act of the Legislature of June 27, 1816,"
     in Farrar, *Report of the Case of the Trustees of Dartmouth College*, 18–22. This
     compendium contains multiple documents from this case, including but
     not limited to the relevant legislative acts, oral arguments presented before
     the New Hampshire Superior Court as well as the US Supreme Court, and,
     finally, the opinions of the justices in *Dartmouth*.

23   Blackstone, *Commentaries*, 1:471.

24   "Dartmouth College Charter."

25   "Dartmouth College Charter."

26   Blackstone, *Commentaries*, 1:324.

27   Mr. Holmes, "Arguments in the Supreme Court of the United States," in Far-
      rar, *Report of the Case of the Trustees of Dartmouth College*, 286.

28   Mr. Bartlett, "Arguments in the Superior Court of New Hampshire," in Far-
      rar, *Report of the Case of the Trustees of Dartmouth College*, 204.

29   William Richardson, "Opinion of the Superior Court of New Hampshire," in
      Farrar, *Report of the Case of the Trustees of Dartmouth College*, 232.

30   Mr. Sullivan, "Arguments in the Superior Court of New Hampshire," in Far-
      rar, *Report of the Case of the Trustees of Dartmouth College*, 86.

31   Mr. Sullivan, "Arguments in the Superior Court of New Hampshire,"
      73–74.

32   Opinion of the court (C. J. Richardson), Superior Court of New Hampshire,
      65 New Hampshire Reports 624 (1817), in Farrar, *Report of the Case of the Trust-
      ees of Dartmouth College*, 220.

33   Trustees of Dartmouth College v. Woodward, 17 U.S. 518, 627 (1819).

34   *Dartmouth*, 17 U.S. at 627, 643–44, 653.

35   Mr. Mason, "Arguments in the Superior Court of New Hampshire," in Farrar,
      Report of the Case of the Trustees of Dartmouth College, 38.

36   For an overview of these debates, see Newmyer, "Justice Joseph Story's Doc-
      trine of 'Public and Private Corporations,'" 839–40.

37   I thank David Ciepley who, in private correspondence, first called my atten-
      tion to Marshall's confusion of the logic of a corporation with that of a trust.
      For his reading of *Dartmouth*, see Ciepley, "Governing People or Governing
      Property?"

38   Trustees of Dartmouth College v. Woodward, 17 U.S. 518, 636–37 (1819).

39   *Dartmouth*, 17 U.S. at 654.

40   "Dartmouth College Charter."

41   Mr. Smith, "Arguments in the Superior Court of New Hampshire," in Farrar,
      Report of the Case of the Trustees of Dartmouth College, 116.

42   Webster, "Arguments in the Supreme Court of the United States," in Farrar,
      Report of the Case of the Trustees of Dartmouth College, 261.

43   Trustees of Dartmouth College v. Woodward, 17 U.S. 518, 642 (1819).

44   *Dartmouth*, 17 U.S. at 634.

45   *Dartmouth*, 17 U.S. at 654. By way of contrast, in his concurring opinion,
      Justice Story argues that trustees as individuals do in fact possess a property
      claim to their positions and hence can seek a judicial remedy if deprived of
      that property: "Each Trustee has a vested right, and legal interest, in his of-
      fice, and it cannot be divested but by due course of law" (705).

46   Webster, "Arguments in the Supreme Court of the United States," in Farrar,
      Report of the Case of the Trustees of Dartmouth College, 259.

47   Trustees of Dartmouth College v. Woodward, 17 U.S. 518, 703 (1819).

48   Blackstone, *Commentaries*, 1:304.

49   Although Blackstone's identification of ownership with dominion over
      "external things" prevented him from appreciating this properly, in a cap-
      italist economy, private property is not so much a thing or a constellation
      of things as it is a "bundle of rights." For example, to affirm that property is
      "private" is to say it is rivalrous—that is, that only a single owner may possess
      rightful title to it any moment in time. This is different from, for example,
      the English feudal conception that represented the Crown as the sole party
      entitled to legal ownership of the realm's landed property (*dominium directum*)
      but granted qualified usage rights to others absent full legal title (*dominion
      utile*). However, once the Crown's dominion was wrested from the monarch
      and relocated in the property owners imagined by John Locke, the rights
      attributed to these proprietors came to include, among others, the exclu-
      sive right to hold, sell, rent, or transfer property to another party and, even
      more important, the right to exclude all others from access to, use of, and/or
      benefit from it.

50   Trustees of Dartmouth College v. Woodward, 17 U.S. 518, 679–80 (1819).

51   Webster, "Arguments in the Supreme Court of the United States," in Farrar,
      Report of the Case of the Trustees of Dartmouth College, 269.

52   When it serves his purposes, Webster represents faculty positions as free-
      holds (see, for example, Webster, "Arguments in the Supreme Court of the
      United States," in Farrar, *Report of the Case of the Trustees of Dartmouth College*,
      269–72). Webster does so here to bolster his claim that the state of New
      Hampshire violated the rights of faculty when it enlarged the size of Dart-
      mouth's corporation, thereby reconstituting the body that has the authority
      to hire and fire them. Webster does not invoke this category, however, to
      affirm the right of faculty to be protected against arbitrary dismissal by Dart-
      mouth's trustees.

53   Blackstone, *Commentaries*, 1:300.

54   Trustees of Dartmouth College v. Woodward, 17 U.S. 518, 676 (1819) (Story, J.,
      concurring).

55   Webster, "Arguments in the Supreme Court of the United States," in Farrar,
      Report of the Case of the Trustees of Dartmouth College, 249.

56   *Dartmouth*, 17 U.S. at 675. Justice Story draws the same conclusion: "As
      founder, too, Dr. Wheelock and his heirs would have been completely
      clothed with the visitatorial power; but the whole government and control,
      as well of the officers as of the revenues of the College, being with his consent
      assigned to the Trustees in their corporate character, the visitatorial power,
      which is included in this authority, rightfully devolved on the Trustees"
      (681).

57   *Dartmouth*, 17 U.S. at 681 (Story, J., concurring).

58   With respect to judicial review of exercises of visitatorial authority, the
      principal precedent cited in *Dartmouth* is *Philips v. Bury*, 90 Eng. Rep. 1294
      (1694). The ruling in this case denied that a professor expelled by a visitor
      from Exeter College could appeal to the courts, for a visitor is authorized to
      remove a university employee "where ever he seeth cause" (1302).
59   AAUP, *Special Report: COVID-19*, 37.
60   Carroll, *Through the Looking-Glass*, 110–11.

7. Psychasthenia Universitatis

1   Tiede, *University Reform*, 24.
2   *Minutes of the Trustees of Columbia University* (March 5, 1917), quoted in Hof-
      stadter and Metzger, *The Development of Academic Freedom*, 498.
3   Nicholas Butler, "Commencement Day Address" (June 6, 1917), quoted in
      Hofstadter and Metzger, *The Development of Academic Freedom*, 498.
4   Julius Kahn to Butler (August 27, 1917), quoted in Hofstadter and Metzger,
      The Development of Academic Freedom, 501.
5   Jastrow, "Academic Aspects of Administration," 326.
6   For helpful accounts of anticorporate sentiment as well as the restrictions
      on corporate power adopted by many states, especially during the first half
      of the nineteenth century, see Speir, "Corporations, the Original Under-
      standing, and the Problem of Power"; and Novak, "The American Law of
      Association."
7   For this charter's text, see Pennsylvania Railroad, *Charter and Supplements of
      the Pennsylvania Railroad Company*.
8   Some early and mid-nineteenth-century companies departed from this "one
      member, one vote" rule but, in an effort to forestall emergence of a pluto-
      cratic governing elite, limited the votes apportioned to any given shareholder
      to a certain number or to a certain proportion of the total number of votes
      cast. For an account of these diverse practices, see Dunlavy, "From Citizens
      to Plutocrats," especially 72–79.
9   For a very helpful account of these transformations within nineteenth-
      century railroad companies, see Roy, *Socializing Capital*, 83–97.
10   Hofstadter and Metzger, *The Development of Academic Freedom*, 308.
11   Metzger, *Academic Freedom in the Age of the University*, 30.
12   Barrow, *Universities and the Capitalist State*, 36–37.
13   For careful accounts of these new universities, see Geiger, *The History of
      American Higher Education*, 269–333; and Thelin, *A History of American Higher
      Education*, 110–54, 205–59.
14   Cooke, *Academic and Industrial Efficiency*, 36.
15   Cooke, *Academic and Industrial Efficiency*, 24.

16   Romeo and Tewksbury, "You Can't Trust the Businessmen on the Board."

17   Veblen, *The Higher Learning in America*, 49nf.

18   Cattell, *University Control*, 17.

19   For a table Cattell produced to summarize his respondents' assessment of his proposal, see *University Control*, 23. Many of those sympathetic to Cattell's proposal suggested modest modifications regarding, for example, the specific composition of the corporation he commended, the precise division of labor between the faculty and that corporation's trustees, the role of the faculty in appointing their colleagues, and so on. Those more hostile often rejected the very premises on which his proposal was founded: "I am not optimistic . . . about the ability of academic men to organize their own government. I think that the specialist in science or literature prefers to have somebody develop the methods of scientific organization and relieve him of the necessity of considering these matters" (116). This sort of skepticism led others to draw conclusions like this: "I am one of those hopelessly antiquated or reactionary few who believe in the beneficent autocrat theory" (284). Or, more pithily: "The more I see of democracies, the more I come to believe in a limited monarchy" (89).

20   Paton, "University Administration and University Ideals," 442. For an early discussion of this "nervous disease," see Coriat, "Psychasthenia," in *Abnormal Psychology*, 273–97. On Coriat's account, the symptoms of psychasthenia include "obsessions of sacrilege, crime, disgrace of self and body"; "mental agitations, such as manias of interrogation, doubt, precision, precaution, repetition, conjuration, and arithmetical manias"; "motor agitations and tics"; and "emotional agitations, which comprised the various phobias or fears." To remedy these symptoms, Coriat recommends baths, electroshock therapy, and the consumption of potent drugs.

21   Creighton, "The Government of American Universities," 397.

22   Cattell, quoted in Tiede, *University Reform*, 24.

23   Stratton, "Externalism in American Universities," 430.

24   Munroe, "Closer Relations between Trustees and Faculty," 464.

25   Munroe, "Closer Relations between Trustees and Faculty," 464.

26   Stratton, "Externalism in American Universities," 428–29.

27   Stratton, "Externalism in American Universities," 426.

28   Kirkpatrick, "The Why of Academic Unrest," 53; Cattell, "Concerning the American University," 423; Anonymous letter, in Cattell, *University Control*, 163.

29   Stratton, "Externalism in American Universities," 428.

30   Stratton, "Externalism in American Universities," 426.

31   Stratton, "Externalism in American Universities," 429.

32   Stevenson, "The Status of the American College Professor," 388.

33   Cattell, *University Control*, 35.

34   Anonymous letter, in Cattell, *University Control*, 248.

35   Munroe, "Closer Relations between Trustees and Faculty," 464; Stevenson, "The Status of the American College Professor," 380.

36   Munroe, "Closer Relations between Trustees and Faculty," 464.

37   Sinclair, *The Goose-Step*, 24.

38   Sinclair, *The Goose-Step*, 23-24.

39   Jastrow, "The Administrative Peril in Education," 338; anonymous letter, in Cattell, *University Control*, 311; Stratton, "Externalism in American Universities," 434; Jastrow, "The Administrative Peril in Education," 326-27.

40   Jastrow, "The Administrative Peril in Education," 327.

41   Jastrow, "The Administrative Peril in Education," 327.

42   Leighton, "University Government," 370.

43   Munroe, "Closer Relations between Trustees and Faculty," 468.

44   Jastrow, "The Administrative Peril in Education," 332.

45   Jastrow, "The Administrative Peril in Education," 340.

46   Jastrow, "The Administrative Peril in Education," 340-41.

47   Stratton, "Externalism in American Universities," 433.

48   Stratton, "Externalism in American Universities," 435.

49   Veblen, *The Higher Learning in America*, 162-63.

50   Veblen, *The Higher Learning in America*, 162, 156.

51   Veblen, *The Higher Learning in America*, 90.

52   Jastrow, "The Administrative Peril in Education," 337.

53   Jastrow, "The Administrative Peril in Education," 324-25.

54   Sinclair, *The Goose-Step*, 383.

55   Sinclair, *The Goose-Step*, 384.

56   Veblen, *The Higher Learning in America*, 156-57.

57   Cattell, *University Control*, 31.

58   Jastrow, "The Administrative Peril in Education," 328 (quoting an editorial titled "The Progress of Science" and published in the *Popular Science Monthly*, January 1911, 78.

59   Creighton, "The Government of American Universities," 394.

60   Ladd, "The Need of Administrative Changes in the American University," 351.

61   Jastrow, "The Administrative Peril in Education," 337.

62   Jastrow, "The Administrative Peril in Education," 331.

63   Stevenson, "The Status of the American College Professor," 329.

64   Paton, "University Administration and University Ideals," 448.

65   Jastrow, "The Administrative Peril in Education," 328 (quoting without citation an editorial published in *The Dial*).

66   Munroe, "Closer Relations between Trustees and Faculty," 466; Stratton, "Externalism in American Universities," 427; Cattell, *University Control*, 39.

67   Stratton, "Externalism in American Universities," 427.

68   Jastrow, "The Administrative Peril in Education," 337.

69   Creighton, "The Government of American Universities," 394.

70   Jastrow, "The Administrative Peril in Education," 330.

71   Stratton, "Externalism in American Universities," 437.

72   Cattell, "Concerning the American University," 423.

73   Veblen, *The Higher Learning in America*, 231.
74   Jastrow, "The Administrative Peril in Education," 329; Jastrow, "The Academic Career as Affected by Administration," 565–66.
75   Veblen, *The Higher Learning in America*, 212.
76   Chapman, "Professorial Ethics," 459.
77   Chapman, "Professorial Ethics," 460.
78   Pritchett, "Shall the University Become a Business Corporation?"
79   Cattell, *University Control*, 32.
80   Veblen, *The Higher Learning in America*, 75.
81   Veblen, *The Higher Learning in America*, 103, 90.
82   Veblen, *The Higher Learning in America*, 76.
83   Veblen, *The Higher Learning in America*, 200.
84   Anonymous letter, in Cattell, *University Control*, 233.
85   Veblen, *The Higher Learning in America*, 139, 173, 177.
86   Veblen, *The Higher Learning in America*, 172.
87   Veblen, *The Higher Learning in America*, 227, 229.
88   Veblen, *The Higher Learning in America*, 227, 224.
89   Cattell, *University Control*, 17–18.
90   Cattell, *University Control*, 62.
91   Lawton, "The Decay of Academic Courage," 397.
92   Creighton, "The Government of American Universities," 400.
93   Creighton, "The Government of American Universities," 395.
94   Cattell, *University Control*, 18.
95   Cattell, "Concerning the American University," 422; Cattell, *University Control*, 29.
96   Cattell, *University Control*, 18.
97   Jastrow, "The Administrative Peril in Education," 335n5.
98   Anonymous letter, in Cattell, *University Control*, 285.
99   Cattell, *University Control*, 19.
100   Cattell, *University Control*, 20–21.
101   Creighton, "The Government of American Universities," 399–400.
102   Jastrow, "The Administrative Peril in Education," 319.
103   Cattell, *University Control*, 20.
104   Jastrow, "The Administrative Peril in Education," 334.
105   An American Professor, "The Status of the American Professor," 423.
106   Cattell, *University Control*, 35.
107   Anonymous letter, in Cattell, *University Control*, 137.
108   Cattell, *University Control*, 21.
109   Cattell's respondents employ language drawn from diverse theoretical traditions in talking about the foundation of legitimate authority within the academy. For example, some define that authority in the discourse of modern liberalism—that is, as an extension to higher education of social contract theory's maxim that no authority deserves obedience unless rooted

in consent of the governed. Others construe this assent in the vernacular of conservatism—that is, as a restoration to their rightful owners of powers illegitimately usurped by overlords whose day has come and gone. And some, like Cattell, regard this authority as a fulfillment of radical democracy's commitment to egalitarian empowerment. Each vernacular, though, affords legitimacy to those who, today, have no recognized claim to authority.

110 Cattell, "A Program of Radical Democracy," 614.

111 Veblen, *The Higher Learning in America*, 88.

8. "Shared Governance" as Placebo

1 Hockett and Howland, "How to Resist a Corporate Takeover of Your College."

2 My understanding of the history of modern professions is especially indebted to Abbott, *The System of Professions*; Freidson, *Professionalism*; and Larson, *The Rise of Professionalism*.

3 Committee of the Corporation and the Academical Faculty, "Reports on the Course of Instruction in Yale College," accessed August 4, 2022, https://www.higher-ed.org/resources/Yale/1828_curriculum.pdf.

4 For one of the better accounts of the birth of the American research university, see Veysey, *The Emergence of the American University*.

5 Geiger, *The History of American Higher Education*, 315. For an account of the university's emerging monopoly over the training of doctors and lawyers, see also 516–19.

6 Brint, *In an Age of Experts*, 23.

7 See American Medical Association, "Constitution and Bylaws" (January 2020), https://www.ama-assn.org/system/files/2019-12/ama-constitution-and-bylaws.pdf. The situation of attorneys is a bit more complicated insofar as it is individual state bar associations that specify the conditions of admission and regulate professional conduct. That said, the basic principles governing member corporations remain intact.

8 Larry G. Gerber, *The Rise and Decline of Faculty Governance*, 166.

9 Witmer, *The Nearing Case*, 29, 25.

10 In his introduction to Veblen's *The Higher Learning in America*, Richard Teichgraeber suggests that publication of *University Control* served "as the catalyst for the founding of the American Association of University Professors" (12). For Cattell's call to create a national association, see "University Control," in Cattell, *University Control*, 61.

11 For a good account of academic populism, see Scott M. Gerber, *The University and the People*.

12 "The Report of the Working Men's Committee," in Commons et al., *A Documentary History of American Industrial Society*, 5:98–99.

13   Cattell, "The 'Policies' of the Carnegie Company," 22. Perhaps this is the place to acknowledge my own ambivalence toward unionization and hence collective bargaining as a response to the contemporary crisis of the academy. So long as the academy is predicated on capitalist employment practices, this strategy makes considerable sense. Unionization, however, does not seek to overcome the inherently antagonistic relationship between employer and employee. Instead, this strategy presupposes the capitalist political economy I want to call into question and then seeks to ameliorate the imbalance of power between those who sell their labor in return for a wage and those who are in a position to make that purchase. In this sense, unionization is akin to the AAUP's "accommodationist" strategy, as outlined in this chapter, for it takes this structural antagonism as a given and then seeks to temper its more egregious excesses. Call me naive if you will, but this book is predicated on the belief that the work of the academy will best thrive when founded on a common purpose shared by those who are not employers and employees but joint members of a collective enterprise.

14   Dewey, "Why I Am a Member of the Teacher Union," 4.

15   Lovejoy, "Annual Message of the President."

16   Dewey, "The American Association of University Professors: Introductory Address," 149.

17   Barrow, *Universities and the Capitalist State*, 174.

18   To see these linkages spelled out in more detail, see Larry G. Gerber, "Professionalization as the Basis for Academic Freedom and Faculty Governance" and "'Inextricably Linked.'" As a rule, within this book, I appeal not to "academic freedom" but, instead, to "free inquiry." Here's why: On the AAUP's construction, academic freedom assumes several forms, each of which is grounded in the professional identity of the professoriate. For example, affirmation of academic freedom constitutes a negative claim against interference by those who do not have the expertise claimed by professionals, as certified by their receipt of advanced degrees. Academic freedom also asserts an affirmative claim to be able to set one's own intellectual agenda and to share the fruits of inquiry as one thinks best.

    But as I have just noted, on the AAUP's account, the practice of academic freedom is only ensured by the institution of tenure and the (relative) security from retaliation it provides. If that is so, then the wholesale collapse of tenure over the course of the past half century means that academic freedom is now a luxury that can only be exercised by a privileged minority.

    We cannot respond to this difficulty by affirming the centrality of free speech to the work of the academy, for the claim to free speech is rooted in First Amendment guarantees afforded to persons not qua professionals but in their capacity as citizens. Perhaps, therefore, we should now insist that free inquiry is essential to the academy, which I believe is so, and that its conduct must be guaranteed to all even if tenure is eradicated altogether.

19   AAUP, "1915 Declaration of Principles," 6.

20   AAUP, "1915 Declaration of Principles," 6.

21   Seligman, "Preliminary Report of the Joint Committee," 380. This report, which provided the foundation for the AAUP's "1915 Declaration of Principles on Academic Freedom and Academic Tenure," was adopted by the Joint Committee on Academic Freedom and Tenure and prepared on behalf of the American Economic Association, the American Sociological Association, and the American Political Science Association.

22   AAUP, "1915 Declaration of Principles," 6.

23   AAUP, "1915 Declaration of Principles," 4.

24   AAUP, "1915 Declaration of Principles," 5.

25   Seligman, "Preliminary Report of the Joint Committee," 380.

26   AAUP, "1915 Declaration of Principles," 9, 8.

27   AAUP, "1915 Declaration of Principles," 8.

28   AAUP, "1915 Declaration of Principles," 8, 9.

29   Leighton, "Report of Committee T," 19.

30   Leighton, "Report of Committee T," 23.

31   Leighton, "Report of Committee T," 29, 30.

32   Leighton, "Report of Committee T," 32.

33   Leighton, "Report of Committee T," 26, 25, 34.

34   AAUP, "Statement on Government of Colleges and Universities," 117.

35   Mortimer and Sathre, *The Art and Politics of Academic Governance*, 22.

36   Leighton, "Report of Committee T," 17–18.

37   AAUP, "Statement on Government of Colleges and Universities," 119.

38   AAUP, "Statement on Government of Colleges and Universities," 118.

39   Leighton, "Report of Committee T," 19, 28.

40   AAUP, "Statement on Government of Colleges and Universities," 120.

41   AAUP, "Statement on Government of Colleges and Universities," 119, 120.

42   One might argue that the conservatism of the 1966 "Statement" is a function of its joint composition by three associations and hence the AAUP's need to attenuate its principles in the service of crafting a document acceptable to all. I find this implausible since, in 1962, the AAUP issued its own statement of principles regarding shared governance, and these do not differ materially from those advanced in the 1966 joint document. See AAUP, "Faculty Participation in College and University Governance." For an account of the composition of the 1966 "Statement," see Larry G. Gerber, *The Rise and Decline of Faculty Governance*, 95–100.

43   For a more detailed account of the emergence and ultimate failure of the professoriate qua profession, see Kaufman-Osborn, "Disenchanted Professionals."

44   "Mission," AAUP, accessed August 4, 2022, https://www.aaup.org/about /mission-1.

45   For a quick summary of these changes in the composition of the academic labor force, see Bowen and Tobin, *Locus of Authority*, 152–53. For a more

detailed account, see Finkelstein, Conley, and Schuster, *The Faculty Factor*, especially 57–66. For the most recent data available at the time of this writing, see AAUP, "The Annual Report on the Economic Status of the Profession, 2021–22."

46 Morson and Schapiro, "The Future of Higher Education in the United States (and the World)," 160.

47 American Federation of Teachers, *An Army of Temps*.

48 Standing, *The Precariat*; Kezar, DePaola, and Scott, *The Gig Academy*.

49 US House Committee on Education and the Workforce, "The Just-in-Time Professor," 1, 32.

50 The bifurcation I note here does not do justice to additional stratifications internal to the class of contingent faculty. There are significant differences, for example, between the situation of full-time contingent faculty on multiyear contracts and part-time contingent faculty on contracts that are renewed, if at all, on a term-to-term basis. Were we to incorporate these inequalities within the pyramidal structure of authority I drew in chapter 1, the academy's quasi-feudal distribution of power would become even more evident.

51 Joseph Schwartz, "Resisting the Exploitation of Contingent Faculty Labor in the Neoliberal University," 516.

52 On the demographics of the contemporary American faculty, see Finkelstein, Conley, and Schuster, *The Faculty Factor*, especially 66–84.

53 AAUP, "One Hundred Years. One Faculty."

54 Larry G. Gerber, *The Rise and Decline of Faculty Governance*, 8.

55 Leighton, "Report of Committee T," 38, 47.

56 Sabine, "The Place and Function of Faculties in University and College Government," 142.

57 Larry G. Gerber, *The Rise and Decline of Faculty Governance*, 59. "In sum, in 1940 the typical American college or university still did not make available means for faculty to communicate directly with their governing board or to have any formal role in the selection of a president, dean, or department head and provided for faculty consultation on appointments, promotions, dismissals, and budgets only through department heads or chairs" (79).

58 Larry G. Gerber, *The Rise and Decline of Faculty Governance*, 6.

59 AAUP, "Report of the Survey Subcommittee of Committee T," 73.

60 I draw these criteria principally from Freidson, *Professionalism*, passim.

61 Larry G. Gerber, *The Rise and Decline of Faculty Governance*, 82.

62 AAUP, *Special Report: COVID-19*, 2.

9. Outsourcing Self-Governance

1 California Constitution, Article IX (Education), Section 9(f), accessed August 8, 2022, https://leginfo.legislature.ca.gov/faces/codes_displaySection .xhtml?lawCode=CONS&sectionNum=SEC.%209.&article=IX.

2   Wood, "Introduction: The Emergence of the Public-Private Distinction in Early America."

3   Article III, Sections 1 and 2, Constitution of the State of Montana (1889), accessed August 8, 2022, http://www.umt.edu/media/law/library /MontanaConstitution/Miscellaneous%20Documents/1889_const.pdf.

4   Article XI, Section 1, 11, Constitution of the State of Montana (1889).

5   Article XII, Section 2, Constitution of the State of Montana (1889).

6   "An Act to Establish, Locate, Maintain, and Govern the University of the State of Montana," in *Laws, Resolutions and Memorials of the State of Montana* (1893), 174.

7   "An Act to Establish, Locate, Maintain, and Govern the University of the State of Montana," 174.

8   Article X, Section 1, 10, Constitution of the State of Montana (1972), accessed August 8, 2022, https://courts.mt.gov/portals/189/library/docs /72constit.pdf.

9   Article X, Section 9, Constitution of the State of Montana (1972).

10   Article VIII, Section 5, Constitution of the State of Montana (1972) (emphasis added).

11   "The Montana University System-Mission," University of Montana Catalog (2018–19), http://archive.umt.edu/catalog/18-19/administration/musmission /index.html (emphasis added).

12   Marcus, "One State Uses Data about Job Needs to Help Decide What Colleges Should Teach."

13   National Governors Association, *A Governor's Action Guide.* To see how other states have moved in much the same direction, see Thompson, "Kentucky Colleges Are Going Beyond Teaching Students the Soft Skills Employers Want"; and Natalie Schwartz, "Nevada Governor Shifts Focus on Community College Split to Workforce Development."

14   Gary Hall, *The Uberfication of the University.*

15   Hirji, "50 Emerging Technology Themes to Watch Out for in 2021."

16   National Governors Association, *A Governor's Action Guide,* 3.

17   Marx, *Capital,* vol. 1, chap. 28; National Governors Association, *A Governor's Action Guide,* 19, 7.

18   National Governors Association, *A Governor's Action Guide,* 12.

19   Busteed, "Is It a School or a Workplace?"

20   Internal Revenue Service, Exemption Requirements—501(c)(3) Organizations, accessed August 8, 2022, https://www.irs.gov/charities-non-profits/charitable -organizations/exemption-requirements-section-501c3-organizations.

21   Princeton University, *The Charters and By-Laws of the Trustees of Princeton University,* 12. This charter was replaced by a slightly amended version two years later, and it is from the 1748 version that I quote.

22   Office of the President, Princeton University, accessed August 8, 2022, https://president.princeton.edu/vice-president-and-secretary/board-trustees.

23   Fields v. Trustees of Princeton University, Tax Court of New Jersey (April 1, 2015), complaint at 3.

24   Knapp, "Princeton University Is Sued by Borough Residents over Tax-Exempt Buildings."

25   *Fields*, Tax Court of New Jersey, complaint at 7.

26   Seltzer, "Deferring a Key Battle for Wealthy Universities."

27   *Fields*, Tax Court of New Jersey, complaint at 19.

28   *Fields*, Tax Court of New Jersey, complaint at 22.

29   Seltzer, "Deferring a Key Battle for Wealthy Universities."

30   Mulvaney, "Princeton Univ. Denied Attempt to Dismiss Another Lawsuit Challenging Tax-Exempt Status."

31   Anne Levin, "Witherspoon-Jackson Joins Lawsuit against University over Payment of Taxes."

32   D'Elia, "Bill That Could Block Citizens' Rights to Challenge Tax Exemptions."

33   For an excellent account of how intangible goods such as knowledge become legally coded as private property and hence wealth, see Pistor, *The Code of Capital*.

34   My understanding of academic capitalism is especially informed by Slaughter and Leslie, *Academic Capitalism*; Slaughter and Rhoades, *Academic Capitalism and the New Economy*; and Berman, *Creating the Market University*.

35   Megosh et al., "H. Private Benefit under IRC 501(c)(3)," 150.

36   Eli Lilly, Annual Report (2008), Form 10-K, Securities and Exchange Commission, 6, accessed August 8, 2022, https://www.sec.gov/Archives/edgar/data/59478/000095015209001897/c49534e10vk.htm.

37   Eli Lilly, Annual Report (2008), Form 10-K, Securities and Exchange Commission, 6.

38   Ollwerther, "Trial Centers on Patent of Drug That Funded Chemistry Building."

39   For a more recent example of the same unholy alliance, this time involving an alliance of universities and pharmaceutical companies to block the federal government from seeking to reduce the price of certain very expensive drugs, see Basken, "US Universities Fight Potential Biden Move on Drug Patents."

40   "Patent Rights in Inventions Made with Federal Assistance," 35 U.S.C. § 200, Legal Information Institute, Cornell Law School, accessed August 8, 2022, https://www.law.cornell.edu/uscode/text/35/200.

41   Pusser, Slaughter, and Thomas, "Playing the Board Game," 769.

42   If space permitted, I would also discuss Grand Canyon University. Whereas Purdue Global involves the purchase by a public university of certain assets owned by a for-profit corporation, Grand Canyon involves the conversion of a for-profit enterprise into a nonprofit university. For an account of Grand Canyon's mutation, see Carey, "The Creeping Capitalist Takeover of Higher Education." Also worth a careful look is Arizona State University's now revoked deal with Zovio; see Natalie Schwartz, "University of Arizona Global Campus Terminates Contract with Zovio."

43 "An Act Donating Public Lands to the Several States and Territories Which May Provide Colleges for the Benefit of Agriculture and the Mechanic Arts," *United States Statutes at Large*, July 2, 1862 (12 Stat. 503), accessed August 8, 2022, https://memory.loc.gov/cgi-bin/ampage?collId=llsl&fileName=012/llsl012.db&recNum=534 (emphasis added).

44 Indiana General Assembly, *Laws of the State of Indiana* (1865).

45 "Graham Holdings Company Reports 2018 and Fourth Quarter Earnings," Graham Holdings, February 25, 2019, http://www.ghco.com/news-releases/news-release-details/graham-holdings-company-reports-2018-and-fourth-quarter-earnings.

46 Purdue University Global, "About Purdue University Global," accessed August 8, 2022, https://www.purdueglobal.edu/about/about-purdue-global/.

47 Mulhere, "Purdue University Just Bought a Major For-Profit College for $1."

48 Fain, "Alternative Credentials on the Rise."

49 Seltzer, "Birth Dearth Approaches."

50 For a helpful account of different ways of structuring public-private partnerships in higher education, see Busta, "Colleges Look to Public-Private Partnerships for Help with Sustainability."

51 Shireman, quoted in Fain, "Purdue's Global Arrival."

52 Amended and Restated Articles of Incorporation of Purdue Global University, Inc. (as amended through February 13, 2018), sec. 3.01, 8.02(b), 8.01, accessed August 8, 2022, https://www.purdueglobal.edu/faculty/articles-of-incorporation-pg-may-2018.pdf.

53 "Postsecondary SEI Affiliated Public Institution," Indiana Code § 21-7-13-26.5, accessed August 8, 2022, http://iga.in.gov/legislative/laws/2020/ic/titles/021#21-7-13-26.5.

54 Amended and Restated Articles of Incorporation of Purdue Global University, Inc., sec. 6.01.

55 Bylaws of Purdue University Global, Inc., sec. 2.02, accessed August 8, 2022, https://www.purdueglobal.edu/faculty/bylaws-purdue-university-global.pdf.

56 Frederic Maitland, "The Crown as Corporation," 131, 140.

57 Bylaws of Purdue University Global, Inc., secs. 2.02, 3.01.

58 Amended and Restated Articles of Incorporation of Purdue Global University, Inc., sec. 7.01.

59 For the distinction between these two types of constraint, see Shireman, "How For-Profits Masquerade as Nonprofit Colleges."

60 "Transition and Operations Support Agreement," Section 2.1, Exhibit 10.1 (March 22, 2018), Form 8-K, Graham Holdings Company, filed with the Securities and Exchange Commission on March 22, 2018, accessed August 8, 2022, https://content.edgar-online.com/ExternalLink/EDGAR/0000950157-18-000360.html?hash=0c3e4f97e7d969ee749def075e5617098ea3bf8a163fd6ad57b786e197cb55ed&dest=EX10-1_HTM#EX10-1_HTM.

61 "Transition and Operations Support Agreement," sec. 3.2(c), 3.2(d).

62 "Transition and Operations Support Agreement," sec. 2.5(d) (emphasis added). The power of Purdue Global's board to govern the university is additionally constrained by contractual terms that specify what is and is not subject to modification. Recall that the board is authorized to make, modify, and amend the bylaws that govern Purdue Global. That may be, but an exhibit attached to the "Transition and Operations Support Agreement" expressly states that no party to this contract may assign its rights or delegate any of its obligations to another without the "express prior written consent of each other Party to this Agreement, *except that Contributor [Kaplan] may assign this Agreement to another entity owned, directly or indirectly, by Graham Holdings Company*" (sec. 20.6).

63 Criteria for Accreditation, Higher Learning Commission, accessed August 8, 2022, https://www.hlcommission.org/Policies/criteria-and-core-components .html.

64 "Transition and Operations Support Agreement," exhibit F, sec. 3.2(c).

65 "Transition and Operations Support Agreement," sec. 14.2(b).

66 Shireman, "Can Purdue Create a 'Public' University Controlled by Investors?"

67 "Transition and Operations Support Agreement," sec. 3.2.

68 "About Purdue University Global."

69 Shireman, "How For-Profits Masquerade as Nonprofit Colleges." For a skeptical reading of Purdue Global's qualification for tax-exempt status as a nonprofit, see Shireman, "How Purdue Global Got Its IRS Stamp of Approval."

70 Amended and Restated Articles of Incorporation of Purdue Global University, Inc., sec. 8.02 (a).

71 The Carnegie Classification of Institutions of Higher Education (updated 2018), accessed August 8, 2022, carnegieclassifications.acenet.edu.

10. "Humpty Dumpty Sat on a Wall . . ."

1 "Encouragement of Education," Article VIII, Section 1, Constitution of Michigan of 1963, accessed August 10, 2022, http://www.legislature.mi.gov /(S(kaid313x2gr33vmnsae10vn4))/mileg.aspx?page=getObject&objectName =mcl-Constitution-VIII.

2 Preamble, Bylaws, Board of Trustees, Michigan State University, accessed August 10, 2022, https://trustees.msu.edu/bylaws-ordinances-policies/bylaws /preamble.html.

3 Banerji, Kennedy, and Sengal, "The Financialization of Higher Education at Michigan State University." See also Granville, Miller, and Mishory, *Michigan's College Affordability Crisis*.

4 Johnson, "Michigan's Average Student Debt Rose $10K in a Decade."

5 Article VIII, Section 5, Constitution of Michigan of 1963; Preamble, Bylaws, Board of Trustees, Michigan State University.

6   Greenwood and Scharfstein, "The Growth of Finance," 3.

7   Krippner, "The Financialization of the American Economy," 179–80.

8   Marx, *Capital*, 3:599.

9   As of 2021, the top 10 percent of Americans own 70 percent of all wealth, with the top 1 percent owning half of that, whereas the bottom 50 percent own a mere 2 percent. See Bucholz, "The Top 10 Percent Own 70 Percent of Wealth."

10 For a very helpful diagram that charts the "organizational forms of financial intermediation in US higher education," see Eaton, *Bankers in the Ivory Tower*, 23.

11 Hanson, "Average Cost of College and Tuition."

12 For an analysis of the relationship between institutional and student debt, see Eaton, *Bankers in the Ivory Tower*, 114–17.

13 See Lundy, "How Institutional Debt Became the Other Educational Debt Crisis"; and Seltzer, "Debt Strategies Help Colleges Navigate Pandemic but Carry Risk."

14 Chung and Korn, "Bond Boom Comes to America's Colleges and Universities." For more about higher education's turn to debt, see Eaton et al., "Borrowing against the Future."

15 Olsen, "MSU Board of Trustees Approves $500M 'Century Bond' to Advance Excellence and Impact."

16 Colomer, "Michigan State's Gymnastics Sex Abuse Scandal Triggers a Downgrade."

17 Korn and Belkin, "Michigan State to Fund $500 Million Sex-Abuse Settlement through Bonds." This, by the way, does not include the $64 million in legal bills stemming from the Nassar case or the more than half a million dollars paid to a public relations firm that tracked social media activity about the university during its negotiations with the survivors' attorneys.

18 Colomer, "Michigan State Wraps Up Settlement Bonds amid Continued Scandal Challenges."

19 Associated Press, "MSU Board Unanimously Votes to Approve $500M Settlement," June 22, 2018, https://www.wilx.com/content/news/Michigan-State-board-to-consider-payout-to-Nassar-victims-486238801.html.

20 Guzman, "Michigan State Cuts Faculty Wages amid Coronavirus Budget Implications."

21 Ellis, "Michigan State Needed Dining-Hall Workers."

22 Eaton and Gibadullina, "The Social Circuitry of High Finance," 11. For earlier studies of what are sometimes called "trustee/corporate board interlocks," see Slaughter and Rhoades, *Academic Capitalism and the New Economy*, 233–55; and Pusser, Slaughter, and Thomas, "Playing the Board Game."

23 Jenkins, "The Wall Street Takeover of Nonprofit Boards," 48.

24 United Campus Workers Colorado, "Questionable Decisions," 26.

25 Massachusetts State College Building Authority, Financial Statements (June 30, 2019 and 2018), 15, https://www.mscba.org/docs/114_MSCBAFY2019AuditedFinancialStatements.pdf.

26   Schirmer, "It's Not Just Students Drowning in Debt."

27   Schirmer et al., "American Universities Are Buried under a Mountain of Debt."

28   Moody's Investor Service, "Higher Education Methodology" (August 4, 2021), 24, https://www.moodys.com/researchdocumentcontentpage.aspx?docid =PBM_1257002. For my purposes, Moody's can stand in for all credit rating agencies that assess colleges and universities, including Standard and Poor's as well as Fitch.

29   Moody's Investor Service, "Higher Education Methodology," 8, 16, 12, 18, 31, 17.

30   Moody's Investor Service, "Higher Education Methodology," 20.

31   Moody's Investor Service, "2021 Outlook Negative as Pandemic Weakens Key Revenue Streams" (December 8, 2020), https://www.moodys.com /researchdocumentcontentpage.aspx?docid=PBM_1251126.

32   Schirmer, "It's Not Just Students Drowning in Debt."

33   Moody's Investor Service, "Moody's Affirms Michigan State University's Aa1, Aa1/VMIG1, and P-1 Ratings" (February 24, 2011), https://www.moodys.com /research/MOODYS-AFFIRMS-MICHIGAN-STATE-UNIVERSITYS-Aa1 -Aa1VMIG1-AND-P-1-Rating-Update—RU_16837887.

34   Moody's Investor Services, "Moody's Affirms Michigan State University's Aa1, Aa1/VMIG1, and P-1 Ratings" (May 1, 2012), https://www.moodys.com /research/MOODYS-AFFIRMS-MICHIGAN-STATE-UNIVERSITYS-Aa1 -Aa1VMIG-1-AND-P-Rating-Update—RU_900338880.

35   Moody Investor Services, "Moody's Assigns Aa1 Rating to Michigan State University's $187.8 Million General Revenue Bonds, Series 2013A" (March 22, 2013), https://www.moodys.com/research/Moodys-assigns-Aa1-rating-to -Michigan-State-Universitys-1878-million-New-Issue—NIR_901084283.

36   Boden and Ng, "Exploiting the Exploitable," 45.

37   Meister, "They Pledged Your Tuition."

38   See Moody's Investor Service, "Research Announcement: Moody's-Outlook for US Higher Education Sector Changed to Stable from Negative on Steady Revenue Gains" (December 10, 2019), https://www.moodys.com/research /Moodys-Outlook-for-US-higher-education-sector-changed-to-stable—PBM _1207036; and Moody's Investor Service, "2021 Outlook Negative as Pandemic Weakens Key Revenue Streams."

39   Moody's Investor Service, "2021 Outlook Negative as Pandemic Weakens Key Revenue Streams."

40   "A Look at Trends in College Consolidation since 2016," *Higher Ed Dive*, updated December 7, 2021, https://www.highereddive.com/news/how-many -colleges-and-universities-have-closed-since-2016/539379/. For the tale of a college that dug itself a debtor's hole from which it could not climb out, see Bauman, "The Money Pit." For a more general account of the cottage industry of speculators on higher education's future, see Carlson, "The Oddsmakers of the College Deathwatch."

41 "Investment Policy," Board of Trustees, Michigan State University, accessed
    August 10, 2022, https://trustees.msu.edu/bylaws-ordinances-policies/policies
    /01-07-01.html.

42 Kolhatkar, "Paul Singer, Doomsday Investor."

43 Communications Workers of America and SOC Investment Group, "Activist
    Hedge Fund Risks to Pension Funds," 7.

44 Communications Workers of America and SOC Investment Group, "Activist
    Hedge Fund Risks to Pension Funds," 7.

45 Kroger, "650,000 Colleagues Have Lost Their Jobs."

46 Gandel, "Big University Endowments Make Billions in Returns in a Bumper
    Year." See also Hogan, "The Triumph of the Money Managers"; Whitford,
    "Endowments Skyrocket for the Wealthiest Colleges"; and Whitford,
    "Endowment Returns Tumble."

47 On average, Hedge Clippers tell us in "Endangered Endowments," those
    who manage university endowments invest nearly 20 percent of available
    resources in hedge funds, with some reaching as high as 40 percent in this
    single asset class.

48 Blackstone, *Commentaries*, 1:304.

49 "The Harvard Charter of 1650." For a fascinating account of Harvard's
    financial affairs during the seventeenth century, see Foster, *"Out of Smalle Be-
    ginnings."* As Foster explains, during the seventeenth century, students would
    sometimes pay their tuition not with money but with so-called "commodity
    money" or "country pay," which included corn, wheat, livestock, and, in at
    least one instance, shoes. By the end of that century, Harvard had begun to
    rely more heavily on bonds and mortgages as sources of revenue; but, even
    then, the college could not be said to possess investable "capital" since, as a
    rule, expenses were incurred only as income was received.

50 Ma and Simauchi, "Harvard Management Company Has Invested in Bitcoin
    since 2019." See also Whitford, "Your Crypto Made This Possible."

51 Banerji, Kennedy, and Sengal, "The Financialization of Higher Education at
    Michigan State University," 24.

52 Hogan, "The Triumph of the Money Managers."

53 Gilbert and Hrdlicka, "A Hedge Fund That Has a University." In his *Ivory
    Tower Tax Haven*, Charlie Eaton reminds us that the "capital growth strategy"
    adopted by many colleges and universities in recent decades is much en-
    hanced by the nonprofit academy's tax-exempt status. That status effectively
    transforms these colleges and universities into tax havens "supported by a
    triple tax break: 1) a tax deduction for donors to the endowment; 2) a tax
    exemption for investment income from the endowment, and 3) a tax exemp-
    tion for interest on municipal bonds used in place of capital expenditures
    from endowments" (5–7).

54 Veblen, *The Higher Learning in America*, 76.

55 Fleischer, "Stop Universities from Hoarding Money."

56   Bird-Pollan, "Taxing the Ivory Tower," 112–13.

57   Saul, "Endowments Boom as Colleges Bury Earnings Overseas."

Epilogue

1   Sinclair, *The Goose-Step*, 457.

2   Whittington, "Free Speech Is a Core Tenet of the Academy."

3   Fish, "Shared Governance," 13, 11.

4   For an account of recent cases, see Quintana, "Under Fire, These Professors
      Were Criticized by Their Colleges."

5   Kezar, DePaola, and Scott, *The Gig Academy*, 152, 158.

6   Kirkpatrick, *The American College and Its Rulers*, 96, 97, 98.

7   Kirkpatrick, *The American College and Its Rulers*, 54, 195.

8   As noted in my acknowledgments, I draw additional inspiration from con-
      temporary experiments to reconstitute the academy outside the United
      States. Here I think especially of Spain's Mondragón University (https://www
      .mondragon.edu). For a helpful account of Mondragón's constitutional
      structure, see Wright, Greenwood, and Boden, "Report on a Field Visit to
      Mondragón University." Also worthy of note is the Co-operative College's
      ongoing work to found the United Kingdom's first cooperative university.
      For a good introduction to this project, see Neary and Winn, "Beyond Public
      and Private." Finally, for an account of a domestic experiment aimed at re-
      constituting an established university on democratic principles, see Edel, *The
      Struggle for Academic Democracy*, and especially Edel's summary of the bylaws
      adopted to govern New York's city colleges in the late 1930s (261–68).

9   J. W. Smith, *A Compendium of Mercantile Law*, 81 (emphasis added). On this
      point, see Ireland, "The Corporation and the New Aristocracy of Finance," 67.

10   For a brief but helpful comparison of the social democratic commitments of
      these four figures, see Barrow, *Universities and the Capitalist State*, 174–77.

11   Ireland, "Company Law and the Myth of Shareholder Ownership," 56.

12   International News Service v. Associated Press, 248 U.S. 215, 250 (1918)
      (Brandeis, J., dissenting).

13   "Rights to and Interests in Discoveries, Inventions or Patents," Ohio Revised
      Code, Section 3345.14, accessed August 2022, https://codes.ohio.gov/ohio
      -revised-code/section-3345.14 (emphasis added).

14   Ohio Revised Code, Section 3345.14.

15   See Ohio Revised Code, Section 3345.14(D)(1): "Notwithstanding any
      provision of the Revised Code to the contrary, including but not limited to
      sections 102.03, 102.04, 2921.42, and 2921.43 of the Revised Code, the board of
      trustees of any state college or university shall adopt rules in accordance with
      section 111.15 of the Revised Code that set forth circumstances under which
      an employee of the college or university may solicit or accept, and under

which a person may give or promise to give to such an employee, a financial interest in any firm, corporation, or other association to which the board has assigned, licensed, transferred, or sold the college or university's interests in its intellectual property, including discoveries or inventions made or created by that employee or in patents issued to that employee."

16 "Nonprofit Corporation Law," California Civil Code Section 5056, accessed August 8, 2022, https://law.justia.com/codes/california/2013/code-corp/title-1 /division-2/part-1/section-5056/ (emphasis added).

17 For an example of an academy formally constituted in accordance with the principles of a republican member corporation, see the charter of Gold-smiths College in England (accessed August 11, 2022, https://www.gold.ac .uk/governance/charter/) as well as the statutes that govern this academy (accessed August 11, 2022, https://www.gold.ac.uk/governance/statutes/). As of this writing, there is considerable controversy about whether the leaders of Goldsmiths have violated the democratic promise embedded within its governing documents (see, for example, the "Collective Change State-ment" [August 25, 2020], https://we-are.gold/2020/08/25/collective-change -statement/).

18 Inspired principally by the work of Elinor Ostrom (see, for example, Ostrom, *Governing the Commons*), there is now a considerable body of literature that asks how institutions might best be organized if their aim is to preserve what she calls "the commons." For a helpful discussion of the relationship between "common-pool resources" and the corporate legal form, see Deakin, "The Corporation in Legal Studies," especially 57–59, and "The Corporation as Commons."

Bibliography

AAUP (American Association of University Professors). "1915 Declaration of Principles on Academic Freedom and Academic Tenure." In *Policy Documents and Reports*, 11th ed., 3–19. Baltimore, MD: Johns Hopkins University Press, 2015.

AAUP (American Association of University Professors). "The Annual Report on the Economic Status of the Profession, 2021–22" (June 2022). https://www.aaup.org/sites/default/files/Annual-Report-on-the-Economic-Status-of-the-Profession-2021-22.pdf.

AAUP (American Association of University Professors). "Faculty Participation in College and University Governance: Statement of Principles Approved by the Council." *AAUP Bulletin* 48, no. 4 (December 1962): 321–23.

AAUP (American Association of University Professors). "One Hundred Years. One Faculty" (2015). Accessed July 10, 2022. https://www.aaup.org/sites/default/files/files/One%20Faculty%20Principles(1).pdf.

AAUP (American Association of University Professors). "Report of the Survey Subcommittee of Committee T." *Bulletin of the American Association of University Professors* 57, no. 1 (March 1971): 68–124.

AAUP (American Association of University Professors). *Special Report: COVID-19 and Academic Governance*. Washington, DC: American Association of University Professors, 2021. https://www.aaup.org/special-report-covid-19-and-academic-governance.

AAUP (American Association of University Professors). "Statement on Government of Colleges and Universities." *Policy Documents and Reports*, 11th ed., 117–29. Baltimore, MD: Johns Hopkins University Press, 2015.

Abbott, Andrew. *The System of Professions: An Essay on the Division of Expert Labor*. Chicago: University of Chicago Press, 1988.

"An Act to Establish, Locate, Maintain, and Govern the University of the State of
Montana." In *Laws, Resolutions and Memorials of the State of Montana*. Butte City,
MT: Inter Mountain, 1893. https://www.umt.edu/research/ORSP/propdev
/budgetinfo/Charter%20U%20of%20M.pdf.

AGB (Association of Governing Boards of Universities and Colleges). *AGB
Board of Directors' Statement on the Fiduciary Duties of Governing Board Members*.
Washington, DC: Association of Governing Boards, 2015.

AGB (Association of Governing Boards of Universities and Colleges). *Statement on
Board Responsibility for Institutional Governance*. Washington, DC: Association
of Governing Boards, 2010.

Ahtone, Tristan, and Robert Lee. "Ask Who Paid for America's Universities."
New York Times, May 7, 2020. https://www.nytimes.com/2020/05/07/opinion
/land-grant-universities-native-americans.html.

Alchian, Armen A., and Harold Demsetz. "Production, Information Costs, and
Economic Organization." *American Economic Review* 62, no. 5 (1972): 777–95.

Alexander, Frederick H. *Benefit Corporation Law and Governance*. Oakland, CA:
Berrett-Koehler, 2018.

American Bar Association. *Model Business Corporation Act, 2016 Revision*. Accessed September 30, 2021. https://www.americanbar.org/content/dam/aba
/administrative/business_law/corplaws/2016_mbca.authcheckdam.pdf.

American Federation of Teachers. *An Army of Temps: AFT Adjunct Faculty Quality of
Work/Life Report*. Washington, DC: American Federation of Teachers, 2022.
https://www.aft.org/sites/default/files/qualitylifereport_feb2022.pdf.

An American Professor. "The Status of the American Professor." *Educational Review*
16 (December 1898): 417–34.

Anderson, Elizabeth. *Private Government: How Employers Rule Our Lives (and Why We
Don't Talk about It)*. Princeton, NJ: Princeton University Press, 2017.

Aquinas, Thomas. "On Kingship, to the King of Cyprus." In *Aquinas: On Law,
Morality, and Politics*, 2nd ed., edited by William P. Baumgarth and Richard J.
Regan, 203–10. Indianapolis: Hackett, 2002.

Banerji, Aman, Brigid Kennedy, and Ademali Sengal. "The Financialization
of Higher Education at Michigan State University." Roosevelt Institute,
2018. https://rooseveltinstitute.org/wp-content/uploads/2020/07/RN
-Financialization@MSU-201804.pdf.

Barkan, Joshua. *Corporate Sovereignty: Law and Government under Capitalism*.
Minneapolis: University of Minnesota Press, 2013.

Barrow, Clyde W. *Universities and the Capitalist State: Corporate Liberalism and the
Reconstruction of American Higher Education, 1894–1928*. Madison: University of
Wisconsin Press, 1990.

Basken, Paul. "US Universities Fight Potential Biden Move on Drug Patents."
Times Higher Education, April 7, 2022.

Bauman, Dan. "The Money Pit: How One University Drowned Itself in Red Ink."
Chronicle of Higher Education, March 18, 2022. https://www.chronicle.com/
article/the-money-pit.

Berle, Adolf, Jr. *Studies in the Law of Corporation Finance.* Chicago: Callaghan and Company, 1928.

Berman, Elizabeth Popp. *Creating the Market University: How Academic Science Became an Economic Engine.* Princeton, NJ: Princeton University Press, 2012.

Bevins, Frankki, Jonathan Law, Saurabh Sanghvi, and Rachel Valentino. "Shaping University Boards for 21st Century Higher Education in the US." McKinsey & Company, November 12, 2020. https://www.mckinsey.com/industries /public-and-social-sector/our-insights/shaping-university-boards-for-21st -century-higher-education-in-the-us.

Bird-Pollan, Jennifer. "Taxing the Ivory Tower: Evaluating the Excise Tax on University Endowments." *Pepperdine Law Review* 48, no. 4 (2021): 101–28.

Blackstone, William. *Commentaries on the Laws of England in Four Books.* 4 vols. Philadelphia: J. B. Lippincott, 1893.

Blair, James, and Stephen Fouace. "The Statutes of the College of William and Mary, Codified in 1736." *William & Mary Quarterly* 22, no. 4 (1914): 281–96.

Blumenstyk, Goldie. "Arizona State Will Create a For-Profit Spinoff to Court Students in the Work Force." *Chronicle of Higher Education*, March 19, 2019. https://www.chronicle.com/article/Arizona-State-Will-Create-a/245929.

Boden, Rebecca, and Wilson Ng. "Exploiting the Exploitable: The Financialization of Students in English Universities." *Tiedepolitiikka* 46, no. 2 (2021): 45–51.

Bowen, William G., and Eugene M. Tobin. *Locus of Authority: The Evolution of Faculty Roles in the Governance of Higher Education.* Princeton, NJ: Princeton University Press, 2015.

Bowie, Nikolas. "Why the Constitution Was Written Down." *Stanford Law Review* 71, no. 6 (2019): 1397–1508.

Brint, Steven. *In an Age of Experts: The Changing Role of Professionals in Politics and Public Life.* Princeton, NJ: Princeton University Press, 1994.

Bucholz, Katharina. "The Top 10 Percent Own 70 Percent of Wealth." *Statista*, August 31, 2021. https://www.statista.com/chart/19635/wealth-distribution -percentiles-in-the-us/.

Business Roundtable. "Business Roundtable Redefines the Purpose of a Corporation to Promote 'an Economy That Serves All Americans.'" 2019. Accessed September 27, 2021. https://www.businessroundtable.org/business-roundtable -redefines-the-purpose-of-a-corporation-to-promote-an-economy-that-serves -all-americans.

Busta, Hallie. "Colleges Look to Public-Private Partnerships for Help with Sustainability." *EducationDive*, October 19, 2019. https://www.educationdive.com/news /plugging-in-colleges-seek-partners-to-help-reach-energy-goals/564868/.

Busteed, Brandon. "Is It a School or a Workplace?" *Forbes*, October 21, 2021. https://www.forbes.com/sites/brandonbusteed/2021/10/21/is-it-a-school-or-a -workplace/?sh=288d70f33237.

Cambridge Union of University Teachers. "Non-resident Government at Harvard." *Bulletin of the Cambridge Union of University Teachers* 2, no. 4 (1940): 1–4.

Canby, Courtlandt. "A Note on the Influence of Oxford University upon William and Mary College in the Eighteenth Century." *William & Mary Quarterly* 21, no. 3 (1941): 243–47.

Carey, Kevin. "The Creeping Capitalist Takeover of Higher Education." *Highline*, April 1, 2019. https://www.huffpost.com/highline/article/capitalist-takeover-college/.

Carlson, Scott. "The Oddsmakers of the College Deathwatch." *Chronicle of Higher Education*, January 31, 2020. https://www.chronicle.com/article/the-oddsmakers-of-the-college-deathwatch/.

Carnevale, Anthony P., Peter Schmidt, and Jeff Strohl. *The Merit Myth: How Our Colleges Favor the Rich and Divide America*. New York: New Press, 2020.

Carroll, Lewis. *Through the Looking-Glass*. New York: H. M. Caldwell, 1913.

Cattell, James McKeen. "Concerning the American University." In *University Control*, 405–24. New York: Science Press, 1913.

Cattell, James McKeen. "The 'Policies' of the Carnegie Company." *School and Society* 9 (January 4, 1919): 10–23.

Cattell, James McKeen. "A Program of Radical Democracy." *Popular Science Monthly*, January–June 1912, 606–15.

Cattell, James McKeen. *University Control*. New York: Science Press, 1913.

Chait, Richard P., Thomas P. Holland, and Barbara E. Taylor. *Improving the Performance of Governing Boards*. Phoenix: Oryx, 1996.

Chapman, John Jay. "Professorial Ethics." In *University Control*, by James McKeen Cattell, 453–61. New York: Science Press, 1913.

Chung, Juliet, and Melissa Korn. "Bond Boom Comes to America's Colleges and Universities." *Wall Street Journal*, December 26, 2020. https://www.wsj.com/articles/bond-boom-comes-to-americas-colleges-and-universities-11608978781.

Ciepley, David. "The Anglo-American Misconception of Stockholders as 'Owners' and 'Members': Its Origin and Consequences." *Journal of International Economics* 16 (2020): 623–42.

Ciepley, David. "Beyond Public and Private: Toward a Political Theory of the Corporation." *American Political Science Review* 107, no. 1 (2013): 139–58.

Ciepley, David. "Governing People or Governing Property? How *Dartmouth College* Assimilated the Corporation to Liberalism by Treating It as a Trust." SSRN, March 2, 2021. https://papers.ssrn.com/sol3/papers.cfm?abstract_id=3796298.

Ciepley, David. "How America's Corporations Lost Their Public Purpose, and How It Might Be (Partially) Restored." *Accounting, Economics and Law* 10, no. 3 (2020): 1–25.

Ciepley, David. "Is the U.S. Government a Corporation? The Corporate Origins of Modern Constitutionalism." *American Political Science Review* 111, no. 2 (2017): 418–35.

Ciepley, David. "Member Corporations, Property Corporations, and Constitutional Rights." *Law and Ethics of Human Rights* 11, no. 1 (2017): 31–59.

Ciepley, David. "Our Corporate Civilization and Its Neoliberal Crisis." Institute for Advanced Study, School of Social Science. Occasional Paper 56 (2016): 1–22. https://www.sss.ias.edu/sites/sss.ias.edu/files/papers/paper56.pdf.

Clancy, Gerard. "Building the Foundation for a Great Story and a Greater Commitment at the University of Tulsa." University of Tulsa Strategic Plan, 2017–22. Accessed January 27, 2020. https://35ht6t2ynxop1ztf96ih81r1 -wpengine.netdna-ssl.com/wp-content/uploads/2017/12/utulsa-strategic-plan -2017-10-12.pdf.

Clancy, Gerard. "November Board Update." University of Tulsa, November 7, 2019. https://utulsa.edu/november-board-update-november-7-2019/.

Clarke, Thomas. "The Contest on Corporate Purpose: Why Lynn Stout Was Right and Milton Friedman Was Wrong." *Accounting, Economics and Law* 10, no. 3 (2020): 1–46.

College of William & Mary. "The Charter, the Transfer. Acts, 1888 [and] 1906." *Bulletin of the College of William & Mary* 6, no. 3 (1913): 1–52.

Colomer, Nora. "Michigan State's Gymnastics Sex Abuse Scandal Triggers a Downgrade." *Bond Buyer*, May 3, 2018. https://www.bondbuyer.com/news /michigan-states-gymnastics-sex-abuse-scandal-triggers-a-downgrade.

Colomer, Nora. "Michigan State Wraps Up Settlement Bonds amid Continued Scandal Challenges." *Bond Buyer*, February 12, 2019. https://www.bondbuyer .com/news/michigan-state-wraps-up-nasser-settlement-bonds.

Commons, John R., Ulrich Bonnell Phillips, Eugene Allen Gilmore, Helen L. Sumner, and John B. Andrews, eds. *A Documentary History of American Industrial Society*. New York: Russell and Russell, 1958.

Communications Workers of America and SOC Investment Group. "Activist Hedge Fund Risks to Pension Funds: The Case of Elliott Management." September 2021. https://cwa-union.org/sites/default/files/activist_hedge _fund_risks_to_pension_funds_case_of_elliot_mgt_sept_2020_socig_and _cwa.pdf.

Cooke, Morris Llewellyn. *Academic and Industrial Efficiency: A Report to the Carnegie Foundation for the Advancement of Teaching*. New York: Carnegie Foundation for the Advancement of Teaching, 1910.

Coriat, Isador H. *Abnormal Psychology*. London: William Rider & Son, 1911.

Creighton, J. E. "The Government of American Universities." In *University Control*, by James McKeen Cattell, 393–404. New York: Science Press, 1913.

Dartmouth College. *A Vindication of the Official Conduct of the Trustees of Dartmouth College*. Concord, NH: G. Hough, 1815.

Deakin, Simon. "The Corporation as Commons: Rethinking Property Rights, Governance and Sustainability in the Business Enterprise." *Queen's Law Journal* 37 (2012): 329–81.

Deakin, Simon. "The Corporation in Legal Studies." In *The Corporation: A Critical, Multi-disciplinary Handbook*, edited by Grietje Baars and Andre Spicer, 47–63. Cambridge: Cambridge University Press, 2017.

D'Elia, Gianluca. "Bill That Could Block Citizens' Right to Challenge Tax Exemptions of Universities, Hospitals and Other Nonprofits Still Awaits Assembly Approval." *Planet Princeton*, December 9, 2017. https://planetprinceton.com /2017/12/09/bill-that-could-block-citizens-right-to-challenge-tax-exemptions -of-universities-hospitals-and-other-nonprofits-still-awaits-assembly-approval/.

Dewey, John. "The American Association of University Professors: Introductory Address." *Science*, January 29, 1915, 147–51.

Dewey, John. *The Public and Its Problems*. Athens, OH: Swallow Press, 1954.

Dewey, John. "Why I Am a Member of the Teacher Union." *American Teacher* 12 (1928): 3–6.

Duménil, Gérard, and Dominique Lévy. *The Crisis of Neoliberalism*. Cambridge, MA: Harvard University Press, 2011.

Dunlavy, Colleen A. "From Citizens to Plutocrats: Nineteenth-Century Shareholder Voting Rights and Theories of the Corporation." In *Constructing Corporate America: History, Politics, Culture*, edited by Kenneth Lipartito and David B. Sicilia, 66–93. Oxford: Oxford University Press, 2004.

Duryea, Edwin. *The Academic Corporation: A History of College and University Governing Boards*. New York: Falmer, 2000.

Easterbrook, Frank H., and Daniel R. Fischel. "The Corporate Contract." *Columbia Law Review* 89, no. 7 (1989): 1416–48.

Easterbrook, Frank H., and Daniel R. Fischel. *The Economic Structure of Corporate Law*. Cambridge, MA: Harvard University Press, 1991.

Eaton, Charlie. *Bankers in the Ivory Tower: The Troubling Rise of Financiers in US Higher Education*. Chicago: University of Chicago Press, 2022.

Eaton, Charlie. *The Ivory Tower Tax Haven*. Berkeley, CA: Haas Institute for a Fair and Inclusive Society, 2018. https://belonging.berkeley.edu/sites/default/files /hier_ed_tax_haven_april_18.pdf.

Eaton, Charlie, Cyrus Dioun, Daniela García Santibáñez Godoy, Adam Goldstein, Jacob Habinek, and Robert Osley-Thomas. "Borrowing against the Future: The Hidden Costs of Financing U.S. Higher Education." *Debt and Society*. Institute for Research on Labor and Employment, University of California at Berkeley, 2014. http://debtandsociety.ucmerced.edu/publication/borrowing _against_the_future/.

Eaton, Charlie, and Albina Gibadullina. 2020. "The Social Circuitry of High Finance: Universities and Intimate Ties among Economic Elites." Research and Occasional Paper Series 11.20, UC Berkeley Center for Studies in Higher Education, Berkeley, CA. https://cshe.berkeley.edu/sites/default/files/publications /rops.cshe.11.2020.eatongibadullina.socialcircuitry.9.23.2020_0.pdf.

Edel, Abraham. *The Struggle for Academic Democracy: Lessons from the 1938 "Revolution" in New York's City Colleges*. Philadelphia: Temple University Press, 1990.

Eisenberg, Melvin A. "The Conception That the Corporation Is a Nexus of Contracts, and the Dual Nature of the Firm." *Journal of Corporation Law* 24, no. 4 (1999): 819–36.

Ellis, Lindsay. "Michigan State Needed Dining-Hall Workers. So It Asked the Faculty and Staff to Volunteer." *Chronicle of Higher Education*, October 20, 2021. https://www.chronicle.com/article/michigan-state-needed-dining-hall-workers-so-it-asked-the-faculty-and-staff-to-volunteer.

Ellis, Lindsay. "This University's Board Now Has the Power to Fire Anyone—'Even Down to the Janitor.'" *Chronicle of Higher Education*, February 3, 2020. https://www.chronicle.com/article/This-University-s-Board-Now/247957.

Everett, Edward. *A Letter to John Lowell*. Boston: Oliver Everett, 1824.

Fahs, C. Ramsey. "In the School of Tyrannus." *The Crimson*, October 30, 2014. https://www.thecrimson.com/article/2014/10/30/in-the-school-of/.

Fain, Paul. "Alternative Credentials on the Rise." *Inside Higher Ed*, August 27, 2020. https://www.insidehighered.com/news/2020/08/27/interest-spikes-short-term-online-credentials-will-it-be-sustained.

Fain, Paul. "Purdue Acquires Kaplan University to Create a New Public, Online University under Purdue Brand." *Inside Higher Ed*, April 28, 2017. https://www.insidehighered.com/news/2017/04/28/purdue-acquires-kaplan-university-create-new-public-online-university-under-purdue.

Fain, Paul. "Purdue's Global Arrival." *Inside Higher Ed*, March 7, 2018. https://www.insidehighered.com/news/2018/03/07/accreditor-backs-purdue-university-global-more-profits-seek-convert-or-sell.

Farrar, T. *Report of the Case of the Trustees of Dartmouth College against William H. Woodward: Argued and Determined in the Superior Court of Judicature of the State of New-Hampshire, November 1817: and on Error in the Supreme Court of the United States, February 1819*. Portsmouth, NH: John Foster, and West Richardson and Lord; Boston: J. J. Williams, 1819.

Finkelstein, Martin J., Valerie Martin Conley, and Jack H. Schuster. *The Faculty Factor: Reassessing the American Academy in a Turbulent Era*. Baltimore, MD: Johns Hopkins University Press, 2016.

Fish, Stanley. "Shared Governance: Democracy Is Not an Educational Idea." *Change* 39, no. 2 (March–April 2007): 8–13.

Fisher, Lauren. "How a Radical Restructuring Plan Fractured a Campus and Fueled a No-Confidence Vote." *Chronicle of Higher Education*, November 14, 2019. https://www.chronicle.com/article/How-a-Radical-Restructuring/247542.

Fisher, Lauren. "Tulsa Trustees Override Faculty to Uphold Academic-Restructuring Plan with Sweeping Cuts." *Chronicle of Higher Education*, November 7, 2019. https://www.chronicle.com/article/Tulsa-Trustees-Override/247504.

Flaherty, Colleen. "Barely Getting By." *Inside Higher Ed*, April 20, 2020. https://www.insidehighered.com/news/2020/04/20/new-report-says-many-adjuncts-make-less-3500-course-and-25000-year.

Fleischer, Victor. "Stop Universities from Hoarding Money." *New York Times*, August 19, 2015. https://www.nytimes.com/2015/08/19/opinion/stop-universities-from-hoarding-money.html.

Foote, Caleb, Henry Mater, and Associates. *The Culture of the University: Governance and Education.* San Francisco: Jossey-Bass, 1968.

Foster, Margery Somers. *"Out of Smalle Beginnings . . .": An Economic History of Harvard College in the Puritan Period (1636–1712).* Cambridge, MA: Harvard University Press, 1962.

Freidson, Eliot. *Professionalism: The Third Logic.* Chicago: University of Chicago Press, 2001.

Friedman, Milton. "The Social Responsibility of Business Is to Increase Its Profits." *New York Times,* September 13, 1970. https://www.nytimes.com/1970/09/13 /archives/a-friedman-doctrine-the-social-responsibility-of-business-is-to.html.

Gandel, Stephen. "Big University Endowments Make Billions in Returns in a Bumper Year." *New York Times,* October 15, 2021. https://www.nytimes.com /2021/10/15/business/university-endowments.html.

Geiger, Roger. *The History of American Higher Education.* 2nd ed. Princeton, NJ: Princeton University Press, 2015.

Gerber, Larry G. "'Inextricably Linked': Shared Governance and Academic Freedom." *Academe* 87, no. 3 (2001): 22–24.

Gerber, Larry G. "Professionalization as the Basis for Academic Freedom and Faculty Governance." *Journal of Academic Freedom* 1 (2010): 1–26.

Gerber, Larry G. *The Rise and Decline of Faculty Governance: Professionalization and the Modern American University.* Baltimore, MD: Johns Hopkins University Press, 2014.

Gerber, Scott M. *The University and the People: Envisioning American Higher Education in an Era of Populist Protest.* Madison: University of Wisconsin Press, 2011.

Gilbert, Thomas, and Christopher Hrdlicka. "A Hedge Fund That Has a University." *Wall Street Journal,* November 13, 2017. https://www.wsj.com/articles/a -hedge-fund-that-has-a-university-1510615228.

Granville, Peter, Kevin Miller, and Jen Mishory. *Michigan's College Affordability Crisis.* Washington, DC: Century Foundation, 2019. https://production-tcf.imgix .net/app/uploads/2019/09/09095321/Michigan_final3.pdf.

Greenfield, Kent. "Ultra Vires Lives! A Stakeholder Analysis of Corporate Illegality (with Notes on How Corporate Law Could Reinforce International Law Norms)." *Virginia Law Review* 87, no. 7 (2001): 1279–379.

Greenwood, Robin, and David Scharfstein. "The Growth of Finance." *Journal of Economic Perspectives* 27, no. 2 (2013): 3–28.

Guzman, Wendy. "Michigan State Cuts Faculty Wages amid Coronavirus Budget Implications." *State News,* June 23, 2020. https://statenews.com/article /2020/06/michigan-state-cuts-faculty-wages-amid-coronavirus-budget -implications.

Hall, Gary. *The Uberfication of the University.* Minneapolis: University of Minnesota Press, 2016.

Hall, Peter Dobkin. *The Organization of American Culture, 1700–1900: Private Institutions, Elites, and the Origins of American Nationality.* New York: New York University Press, 1984.

Hansmann, Henry, and Reinier Kraakman. "The End of History for Corporate Law." *Georgetown Law Journal* 89, no. 2 (2001): 439–68.

Hanson, Melanie. "Average Cost of College and Tuition." Education Data Initiative. Last updated November 15, 2021. https://educationdata.org/average-cost-of-college.

Harvard University. "The Organization and Functions of the Governing Boards and the President's Office." University Committee on Governance, March 1971. https://files.eric.ed.gov/fulltext/ED051755.pdf.

Hedge Clippers. "Endangered Endowments: How Hedge Funds Are Bankrupting Higher Education." *Hedge Papers*, no. 25 (2016). https://hedgeclippers.org/wp-content/uploads/2016/02/HP25.pdf.

Herbst, Jurgen. *From Crisis to Crisis: American College Government (1636–1819)*. Cambridge, MA: Harvard University Press, 1982.

Hindman, Matthew Dean. "Interdisciplinarity's Shared Governance Problem." *Academe* 107, no. 4 (2021). https://www.aaup.org/article/interdisciplinarity%E2%80%99s-shared-governance-problem#.YkxarOjMKUk.

Hindman, Matthew Dean, and Ryan Saylor. "A Crisis of Shared Governance at the University of Tulsa." *Academe Blog*, May 3, 2019. https://academeblog.org/2019/05/03/a-crisis-of-shared-governance-at-the-university-of-tulsa/.

Hirji, Rahim. "50 Emerging Technology Themes to Watch Out for in 2021." *LinkedIn*, December 30, 2020. https://www.linkedin.com/pulse/50-emerging-technology-themes-watch-out-2021-rahim-hirji.

Hockett, Jeffrey, and Jacob Howland. "How to Resist a Corporate Takeover of Your College." *Chronicle of Higher Education*, July 16, 2020. https://www.chronicle.com/article/how-to-resist-a-corporate-takeover-of-your-college.

Hofstadter, Richard, and Walter Metzger. *The Development of Academic Freedom in the United States*. New York: Columbia University Press, 1955.

Hogan, Dennis M. "The Triumph of the Money Managers: Universities Impose Cutbacks One Day and Reap Endowment Windfalls the Next." *Chronicle of Higher Education*, October 25, 2021. https://www.chronicle.com/article/the-triumph-of-the-money-managers.

Horrocks, James, John Camm, Emmanuel Jones, and Josiah Johnson. "Journal of the President and Masters of William and Mary College." *William & Mary Quarterly* 5, no. 2 (1896): 83–89.

Howland, Jacob. "Administrative Hardball at the University of Tulsa." James G. Martin Center for Academic Renewal, May 8, 2019. https://www.jamesgmartin.center/2019/05/administrative-hardball-at-the-university-of-tulsa/.

Howland, Jacob. "Corporate Wolves in Academic Sheepskins, or, A Billionaire's Raid on the University of Tulsa." *The Nation*, June 18, 2019. https://www.thenation.com/article/archive/higher-education-corporate-takeover-kaiser-university-of-tulsa/.

Howland, Jacob. "Storm Clouds over Tulsa." *City Journal*, April 17, 2019. https://www.city-journal.org/university-of-tulsa.

Hurst, James Willard. *The Legitimacy of the Business Corporation in the Law of the United States, 1780-1970*. Charlottesville: University Press of Virginia, 1970.

Indiana General Assembly. *Laws of the State of Indiana, Passed and Published, at the Forty-Third Regular Session of the General Assembly*. Indianapolis: Indiana Legislative Council, 1865. https://hdl.handle.net/2027/uc1.aa0003060795.

Ireland, Paddy. "Capitalism without the Capitalist: The Joint Stock Company Share and the Emergence of the Modern Doctrine of Separate Corporate Personality." *Journal of Legal History* 17, no. 1 (1996): 41-73.

Ireland, Paddy. "Company Law and the Myth of Shareholder Ownership." *Modern Law Review* 62, no. 1 (1999): 32-57.

Ireland, Paddy. "The Corporation and the New Aristocracy of Finance." In *Multinationals and the Constitutionalization of the World-Power System*, edited by Jean-Phillippe Robé, Antoine Lyon-Caen, and Stéphane Vernac, 53-98. New York: Routledge, 2016.

Ireland, Paddy. "Defending the Rentier: Corporate Theory and the Reprivatisation of the Public Company." In *The Political Economy of the Company*, edited by John Parkinson, Gavin Kelly, and Andrew Gamble, 141-73. London: Bloomsbury, 2001.

Ireland, Paddy. "Property and Contract in Contemporary Contract Theory." *Legal Studies* 23, no. 3 (2003): 453-509.

Ireland, Paddy. "Recontractualising the Corporation: Implicit Contract as Ideology." In *Implicit Dimensions of Contract: Discrete, Relational, and Network Contracts*, edited by David Campbell, Hugh Collins, and John Wightman, 255-88. London: Bloomsbury, 2003.

Jastrow, Joseph. "Academic Aspects of Administration." *Popular Science Monthly*, October 1908, 326-39.

Jastrow, Joseph. "The Academic Career as Affected by Administration." *Science*, April 13, 1906, 561-74.

Jastrow, Joseph. "The Administrative Peril in Education." In *University Control*, by James McKeen Cattell, 315-48. New York: Science Press, 1913.

Jefferson, Thomas. "A Bill for Amending the Constitution of the College of William and Mary, and Substituting More Certain Revenues for Its Support." June 18, 1779. https://founders.archives.gov/documents/Jefferson/01-02-02-0132-0004-0080.

Jenkins, Garry W. "The Wall Street Takeover of Nonprofit Boards." *Stanford Social Innovation Review* (Summer 2015): 46-52.

Jensen, Michael C., and William H. Meckling. "Theory of the Firm: Managerial Behavior, Agency Costs and Ownership Structure." *Journal of Financial Economics* 3, no. 4 (1976): 305-60.

Johnson, Mark. "Michigan's Average Student Debt Rose $10K in a Decade." *Lansing State Journal*, December 9, 2019. https://www.lansingstatejournal.com/in

-depth/news/2019/10/10/student-loan-debt-average-michigan-state-university
-western-um-ferris-recession/3788129002/.

Justinian. *The Digest of Justinian*. Edited by Alan Watson. Philadelphia: University of Pennsylvania Press, 1985.

Kaplan, William A., and Barbara A. Lee. *The Law of Higher Education*. 5th ed., Student Version. San Francisco: Jossey-Bass, 2014.

Kaufman-Osborn, Timothy V. "Disenchanted Professionals: The Politics of Faculty Governance in the Neoliberal Academy." *Perspectives on Politics* 15, no. 1 (March 2017): 100–115.

Kaufman-Osborn, Timothy V. "How Not to Think about Institutional Racism." *Inside Higher Ed*, June 23, 2022. https://www.insidehighered.com/views/2022 /06/23/racism-was-baked-unc-governance-beginning-opinion.

Kaufman-Osborn, Timothy V. "Shared Governance within the Autocratic Academy." *Inside Higher Ed*, October 22, 2021. https://www.insidehighered.com /views/2021/10/22/shared-governance-fatally-flawed-opinion.

Kerr, Clark. "Shock Wave II: An Introduction to the Twenty-First Century." In *The Future of the City of Intellect*, edited by Steven Brint, 1–19. Stanford, CA: Stanford University Press, 2002.

Kezar, Adrianna, Tom DePaola, and Daniel T. Scott. *The Gig Academy*. Baltimore, MD: Johns Hopkins University Press, 2019.

Kirkpatrick, John Ervin. *Academic Organization and Control*. Yellow Springs, OH: Antioch, 1931.

Kirkpatrick, John Ervin. *The American College and Its Rulers*. New York: New Republic, 1926.

Kirkpatrick, John Ervin. "The Why of Academic Unrest." *School and Society* 10, no. 237 (July 1919): 52–53.

Knapp, Krystal. "Princeton University Is Sued by Borough Residents over Tax-Exempt Buildings." *Times of Trenton*, April 15, 2011. https://www.nj.com /mercer/2011/04/residents_challenge_status_of.html.

Knox, Liam. "U. of Tulsa Faculty to Ask Oklahoma's Attorney General to Halt Controversial Restructuring Plan." *Chronicle of Higher Education*, August 22, 2019. https://www.chronicle.com/article/u-of-tulsa-faculty -to-ask-oklahomas-attorney-general-to-halt-controversial-restructuring -plan/.

Kolhatkar, Sheelah. "Paul Singer, Doomsday Investor." *New Yorker*, August 20, 2018. https://www.newyorker.com/magazine/2018/08/27/paul-singer -doomsday-investor.

Korn, Melissa, and Douglas Belkin. "Michigan State to Fund $500 Million Sex-Abuse Settlement through Bonds." *Wall Street Journal*, June 22, 2018. https://www.wsj.com/articles/michigan-state-to-fund-500-million-sex-abuse -settlement-through-bond-offering-1529679986.

Kotz, David M. *The Rise and Fall of Neoliberal Capitalism*. Cambridge, MA: Harvard University Press, 2017.

Krippner, Greta R. "The Financialization of the American Economy." *Socio-economic Review* 3, no. 2 (2005): 173–208.

Kroger, Dennis M. "650,000 Colleagues Have Lost Their Jobs." *Inside Higher Ed*, February 19, 2021. https://www.insidehighered.com/blogs/leadership-higher -education/650000-colleagues-have-lost-their-jobs.

Ladd, George T. "The Need of Administrative Changes in the American University." In *University Control*, by James McKeen Cattell, 349–69. New York: Science Press, 1913.

Larson, Magali Sarfatti. *The Rise of Professionalism: Monopolies of Competence and Sheltered Markets*. New Brunswick, NJ: Transaction, 2013.

Lawton, William Cranston. "The Decay of Academic Courage." *Educational Review* 32 (1906): 395–404.

Leedham-Green, Elisabeth. *A Concise History of the University of Cambridge*. Cambridge: Cambridge University Press, 1996.

Legon, Richard, and Ellen Chaffee. "Transforming Board Governance for the University of South Carolina System." University of South Carolina, January 24, 2020. https://sc.edu/about/offices_and_divisions/faculty _senate/faculty-toolbox/documents/facsen_meetings/2020-02-28_agb _report.pdf.

Leighton, Joseph A. "Report of Committee T on Place and Function of Faculties in University Government and Administration." *Bulletin of the American Association of University Professors* 6, no. 3 (March 1920): 17–47.

Leighton, Joseph A. "University Government." *Educational Review* 60 (December 1920): 363–75.

Levin, Anne. "Witherspoon-Jackson Joins Lawsuit against University over Payment of Taxes." *Town Topics* 70, no. 14 (April 6, 2016). https://issuu.com /witherspoonmediagroup/docs/town_topics_4-6-16.

Levin, Janet. "The Academic Strategy for the University of Tulsa." Presentation to University of Tulsa Faculty and Staff. April 11, 2019. https://utulsa.edu /truecommitment/academicstrategy/.

Lieber, Francis, ed. *Encyclopedia Americana*. Philadelphia: Carey and Lea, 1830.

Lindsay, Julian Ira. *Tradition Looks Forward: The University of Vermont: A History, 1791–1904*. Burlington: University of Vermont and State Agricultural College, 1954.

Locke, John. *Two Treatises of Government*. Edited by Peter Laslett. Cambridge: Cambridge University Press, 1988.

Logsdon, Guy William. *The University of Tulsa*. Norman: University of Oklahoma Press, 1977.

Longanecker, David A. "The 'New' New Challenge of Governance by Governing Boards." In *Governance and the Public Good*, edited by William G. Tierney, 127–55. Albany: State University of New York Press, 2006.

Lovejoy, Arthur. "Annual Message of the President." *Bulletin of the American Association of University Professors* 5 (November–December 1919): 29–31.

Lundy, Kasia. "How Institutional Debt Became the Other Educational Debt Crisis." EY-Parthenon, 2020. https://www.ey.com/en_us/strategy/looming-educational-debt-crisis.

Ma, Virginia L., and Devin A. Simauchi. "Harvard Management Company Has Invested in Bitcoin since 2019, per Report." *Harvard Crimson*, January 27, 2021. https://www.thecrimson.com/article/2021/1/27/hmc-buying-bitcoin/.

Madison, James. "The Federalist No. 49." In *The Federalist*, by Alexander Hamilton, John Jay, and James Madison. New York: Modern Library, 1960.

Maitland, Ferdinand William. Introduction to *Political Theories of the Middle Ages*, by O. Gierke, vii–xlv. Cambridge: Cambridge University Press, 1951.

Maitland, Frederic. "The Crown as Corporation." *Law Quarterly Review* 17 (1901): 131–46.

Marcus, Jon. "One State Uses Data about Job Needs to Help Decide What Colleges Should Teach." *Hechinger Report*, November 8, 2018. https://hechingerreport.org/one-state-uses-data-about-job-needs-to-help-decide-what-colleges-should-teach/.

Marx, Karl. *Capital*. 3 vols. London: Penguin, 1981.

Megosh, Andrew, Larry Scollick, Mary Jo Salins, and Cheryl Chasin. "H. Private Benefit under IRC 501(c)(3)" (2001). Internal Revenue Service. Accessed August 15, 2022. https://www.irs.gov/pub/irs-tege/eotopic01.pdf.

Meister, Bob. "They Pledged Your Tuition: An Open Letter to UC Students." Council of UC Faculty Associations, n.d. Accessed April 23, 2021. https://cucfa.org/news/2009_oct11.php.

Metzger, Walter P. *Academic Freedom in the Age of the University*. New York: Columbia University Press, 1955.

Mitchell, Brian C., and W. Joseph King. *How to Run a College*. Baltimore, MD: Johns Hopkins University Press, 2018.

Morin, Richard M. "Will to Resist: The Dartmouth College Case." *Dartmouth Alumni Magazine*, April 1969, 2–44.

Morison, Samuel Eliot. *The Founding of Harvard College*. Cambridge, MA: Harvard University Press, 1963.

Morison, Samuel Eliot. *Harvard College in the Seventeenth Century*. Cambridge, MA: Harvard University Press, 1936.

Morporgo, J. E. *Their Majesties' Royall Colledge: William and Mary in the Seventeenth and Eighteenth Centuries*. Washington, DC: Hennage Creative Printers, 1976.

Morson, Gary Saul, and Morton Schapiro. "The Future of Higher Education in the United States (and the World)." In *The Fabulous Future? America and the World in 2040*, edited by Gary Saul Morson and Morton Schapiro, 155–73. Evanston, IL: Northwestern University Press, 2015.

Mortimer, Kenneth P., and Colleen O'Brien Sathre. *The Art and Politics of Academic Governance*. Lanham, MD: Rowman & Littlefield, 2007.

Mulhere, Kaitlin. "Purdue University Just Bought a Major For-Profit College for $1. Here's Why." *Money*, April 27, 2017. http://money.com/money/4757972/purdue-university/.

Mulvaney, Nicole. "Princeton Univ. Denied Attempt to Dismiss Another Lawsuit Challenging Tax-Exempt Status." *Times of Trenton*, February 12, 2015. https://www.nj.com/mercer/2015/02/princeton_university_loses_2011_lawsuit_challengin.html.

Munroe, James P. "Closer Relations between Trustees and Faculty." In *University Control*, by James McKeen Cattell, 462–73. New York: Science Press, 1913.

National Governors Association. *A Governor's Action Guide to Achieving Good Jobs for All Americans*. Washington, DC: National Governors Association, 2019. https://www.nga.org/center/publications/good-jobs-for-all-americans-governors-guide-2/.

Neary, Mike, and Joss Winn. "Beyond Public and Private: A Framework for Co-operative Higher Education." *Open Library of the Humanities* 3, no. 2 (2017). https://olh.openlibhums.org/article/id/4443/.

Newman, Andrew. "Indigeneity and Early American Literature." *Oxford Research Encyclopedia of Literature*, February 27, 2017. https://oxfordre.com/literature/view/10.1093/acrefore/9780190201098.001.0001/acrefore-9780190201098-e-141.

Newmyer, R. Kent. "Justice Joseph Story's Doctrine of 'Public and Private Corporations' and the Rise of the American Business Corporation." *DePaul Law Review* 25, no. 4 (1976): 825–41.

Norton, Andrews. *Remarks on a Report of a Committee of the Overseers of Harvard College, Proposing Certain Changes: Relating to the Instruction and Discipline of the College; Read May 4, 1824, and to Be Taken into Consideration June 1, 1824*. Cambridge, MA: Hilliard and Metcalf, 1824.

Norton, Andrews. *Speech Delivered before the Overseers of Harvard College, February 3, 1825, in Behalf of the Resident Instructors of the College*. Boston: Cummings, Hilliard, & Co., 1825.

Novak, William J. "The American Law of Association: The Legal-Political Construction of Civil Society." *Studies in American Political Development* 15, no. 2 (2001): 163–88.

Ollwerther, W. Raymond. "Trial Centers on Patent of Drug That Funded Chemistry Building." *Princeton Alumni Weekly*, October 13, 2010. https://paw.princeton.edu/article/trial-centers-patent-drug-funded-chemistry-building.

Olsen, Dan. "MSU Board of Trustees Approves $500M 'Century Bond' to Advance Excellence and Impact." *MSU Today*, December 17, 2021. https://msutoday.msu.edu/news/2021/msu-board-of-trustees-approves-$500M-century-bond.

Ostrom, Elinor. *Governing the Commons: The Evolution of Institutions for Collective Action*. 1990. Reprint, Cambridge: Cambridge University Press, 2015.

Paton, Stewart. "University Administration and University Ideals." In *University Control*, by James McKeen Cattell, 439–52. New York: Science Press, 1913.

Peacock, George. *Observations on the Statutes of the University of Cambridge*. London: J. W. Parker, 1841.

Pennsylvania Railroad (and Pennsylvania). *Charter and Supplements of the Pennsylvania Railroad Company: With the Acts of Assembly and Municipal Ordinances Affect-*

ing the Company; Together with the By-Laws of the Board of Directors. Philadelphia: Crissy & Markley, 1859.

Pistor, Katharina. *The Code of Capital: How the Law Creates Wealth and Inequality.* Princeton, NJ: Princeton University Press, 2019.

Post, Gaines. "Parisian Masters as a Corporation, 1200–1246." *Speculum* 9, no. 4 (1934): 421–45.

Princeton University. *The Charters and By-Laws of the Trustees of Princeton University and the Rules of Order of the Board.* Princeton, NJ: Princeton University Press, 1906.

Princeton University. "The Governing of Princeton University: Final Report of the Special Committee on the Structure of the University." April 1970. https://files.eric.ed.gov/fulltext/ED040657.pdf.

Pritchett, Henry S. "Shall the University Become a Business Corporation?" *Atlantic Monthly*, September 1905, 289–99.

Pusser, Brian, Sheila Slaughter, and Scott L. Thomas. "Playing the Board Game: An Empirical Analysis of University Trustee and Corporate Board Interlocks." *Journal of Higher Education* 77, no. 5 (2006): 747–75.

Quincy, Josiah. *The History of Harvard University.* Vol. 1. Cambridge, MA: Harvard University Press, 1860.

Quintana, Chris. "Under Fire, These Professors Were Criticized by Their Colleges." *Chronicle of Higher Education*, June 28, 2017. https://www.chronicle.com/article/Under-Fire-These-Professors/240457.

Ridder-Symoens, Hilde De. "Management and Resources." In *A History of the University in Europe*, vol. 2, edited by Hilde De Ridder-Symoens, 154–209. Cambridge: Cambridge University Press, 1996.

Robé, Jean-Philippe. "The Legal Structure of the Firm." *Accounting, Economics and Law* 1, no. 1 (2011): 1–86.

Romeo, Nick, and Ian Tewksbury. "You Can't Trust the Businessmen on the Board." *Chronicle of Higher Education*, June 30, 2020. https://www.chronicle.com/article/you-cant-trust-the-businessmen-on-the-board-of-trustees.

Roy, William G. *Socializing Capital: The Rise of the Large Industrial Corporation in America.* Princeton, NJ: Princeton University Press, 1997.

Rudolph, Frederick. *The American College and University: A History.* Athens: University of Georgia Press, 1990.

Sabine, G. H. "The Place and Function of Faculties in University and College Government." *Bulletin of the American Association of University Professors* 24, no. 2 (February 1938): 141–50.

Saul, Stephanie. "Endowments Boom as Colleges Bury Earnings Overseas." *New York Times*, November 8, 2017. https://www.nytimes.com/2017/11/08/world/universities-offshore-investments.html.

Schirmer, Eleni. "It's Not Just Students Drowning in Debt. Colleges Are Too!" *The Nation*, November 20, 2020. https://www.thenation.com/article/society/student-debt-university-credit/.

Schirmer, Eleni, Jason Thomas Wozniak, Dana Morrison, Rich Levy, and Joanna Gonsavles. "American Universities Are Buried under a Mountain of Debt." *The Nation*, April 15, 2021. https://www.thenation.com/article/activism /universities-student-debt-reveal/.

Schwartz, Joseph. "Resisting the Exploitation of Contingent Faculty Labor in the Neoliberal University: The Challenge of Building Solidarity between Tenured and Non-tenured Faculty." *New Political Science* 36, no. 4 (2014): 504–22.

Schwartz, Natalie. "Nevada Governor Shifts Focus on Community College Split to Workforce Development." *Higher Ed Dive*, April 29, 2021. https://www .highereddive.com/news/nevada-governor-shifts-focus-on-community -college-split-to-workforce-develo/599326/.

Schwartz, Natalie. "University of Arizona Global Campus Terminates Contract with Zovio." *Higher Ed Dive*, August 1, 2022. https://www.highereddive.com/news /university-of-arizona-global-campus-terminates-contract-with-zovio/628603/.

Scott, Robert A. "Leadership Threats to Shared Governance in Higher Education." *Journal of Academic Freedom* 11 (2020): 1–17.

Seligman, Edwin. "Preliminary Report of the Joint Committee on Academic Freedom and Tenure." *American Political Science Review* 9, no. 2 (1915): 374–81.

Seltzer, Rick. "Birth Dearth Approaches." *Inside Higher Ed*, December 15, 2020. https://www.insidehighered.com/news/2020/12/15/more-high-school -graduates-through-2025-pool-still-shrinks-afterward.

Seltzer, Rick. "Debt Strategies Help Colleges Navigate Pandemic but Carry Risk." *Inside Higher Ed*, March 11, 2021. https://www.insidehighered.com/quicktakes /2021/03/11/debt-strategies-help-colleges-navigate-pandemic-carry-risk.

Seltzer, Rick. "Deferring a Key Battle for Wealthy Universities." *Inside Higher Ed*, October 21, 2016. https://www.insidehighered.com/news/2016/10/21/princeton -settlement-leaves-door-open-future-tax-exemption-challenges.

Sever, Nicholas. "Tutor Sever's Argument (August 23, 1723)." *Massachusetts Historical Society* 50, no. 5 (1878): 54–67.

Sever, Nicholas, and Wm. Welsteed. *The Memorial of Nicholas Sever and Wm. Welsteed, Resident Fellows of Harvard College, to His Excellency the Governor and the Honorable and Reverend the Rest of the Overseers of the Said College*. In John Ervin Kirkpatrick, *Academic Organization and Control*, 227–36. Yellow Springs, OH: Antioch, 1931.

Shireman, Robert. "Can Purdue Create a 'Public' University Controlled by Investors?" Century Foundation, August 6, 2018. https://tcf.org/content /commentary/can-purdue-create-public-university-controlled-investors/.

Shireman, Robert. "How For-Profits Masquerade as Nonprofit Colleges." Century Foundation, October 7, 2020. https://tcf.org/content/report/how-for-profits -masquerade-as-nonprofit-colleges/.

Shireman, Robert. "How Purdue Global Got Its IRS Stamp of Approval." Century Foundation, December 19, 2019. https://tcf.org/content/commentary/purdue -global-got-irs-stamp-approval/.

Shireman, Robert. "Purdue University Is a For-Profit College Masquerading as a Public University." Century Foundation, August 6, 2018. https://tcf.org /content/commentary/purdue-university-global-profit-college-masquerading -public-university.

Siegel, Thomas Jay. "Governance and Curriculum at Harvard College in the 18th Century." PhD diss., Harvard University, 1990.

Sinclair, Upton. *The Goose-Step: A Study of American Education*. Rev. ed. Los Angeles: Self-published, 1923.

Slaughter, Sheila, and Larry L. Leslie. *Academic Capitalism: Politics, Policies, and the Entrepreneurial University*. Baltimore, MD: Johns Hopkins University Press, 1997.

Slaughter, Sheila, and Gary Rhoades. *Academic Capitalism and the New Economy*. Baltimore, MD: Johns Hopkins University Press, 2004.

Smith, Adam. *An Inquiry into the Nature and Causes of the Wealth of Nations*. Edited by Edwin Cannan. New York: Modern Library, 1937.

Smith, J. W. *A Compendium of Mercantile Law*. 3rd ed. London: Saunders & Benning, 1843.

Speir, Ian. "Corporations, the Original Understanding, and the Problem of Power." *Georgetown Journal of Law and Public Policy* 10, no. 1 (2012): 115–83.

Standing, Guy. *The Precariat: The New Dangerous Class*. London: Bloomsbury, 2011.

Statutes and Laws of the University in Cambridge, Massachusetts. Cambridge, MA: Harvard University Press, 1826.

Stevenson, John J. "The Status of the American College Professor." In *University Control*, by James McKeen Cattell, 370–92. New York: Science Press, 1913.

Stites, Francis N. *Private Interest and Public Gain: The Dartmouth College Case, 1819*. Amherst: University of Massachusetts Press, 1972.

Stout, Lynn A. "The Corporation as Time Machine: Intergenerational Equity, Intergenerational Efficiency, and the Corporate Form." *Seattle University Law Review* 38 (2015): 684–723.

Stratton, George M. "Externalism in American Universities." In *University Control*, by James McKeen Cattell, 425–38. New York: Science Press, 1913.

Streeck, Wolfgang. *Buying Time: The Delayed Crisis of Democratic Capitalism*. 2nd ed. Translated by Patrick Camiller and David Fernbach. London: Verso, 2017.

Thelin, John. *A History of American Higher Education*. Baltimore, MD: Johns Hopkins University Press, 2011.

Thompson, Aaron. "Kentucky Colleges Are Going Beyond Teaching Students the Soft Skills Employers Want." *Higher Ed Dive*, May 14, 2021. https://www .highereddive.com/news/kentucky-colleges-are-going-beyond-teaching -students-the-soft-skills-employ/599751/.

Tiede, Hans-Joerg. *University Reform: The Founding of the American Association of University Professors*. Baltimore, MD: Johns Hopkins University Press, 2015.

Tierney, Brian. *Religion, Law, and the Growth of Constitutional Thought, 1150–1650*. Cambridge: Cambridge University Press, 1982.

Tyler, Lyon Gardiner. *Williamsburg: The Old Colonial Capital*. Richmond, VA: Whittet and Shepperson, 1907.

United Campus Workers Colorado. "Questionable Decisions: A Review of the University of Colorado's Budget Choices and Priorities." May 2021. https://static1.squarespace.com/static/5e94bc1433df04324f00395d/t /60ad644155862a47666ba656/1621976142732/202105_UCWCOReport_QD.pdf.

US House Committee on Education and the Workforce. "The Just-in-Time Professor: A Staff Report Summarizing eForum Responses on the Working Conditions of Contingent Faculty in Higher Education" (2014). http://democrats -edworkforce.house.gov/imo/media/doc/1.24.14-AdjunctEforumReport.pdf.

Veblen, Thorstein. *The Higher Learning in America: A Memorandum on the Conduct of Universities by Business Men*. Baltimore, MD: Johns Hopkins University Press, 2015.

Veysey, Laurence R. *The Emergence of the American University*. Chicago: University of Chicago Press, 1965.

Vincent, Samantha. "TU Is Becoming Something Other Than a Liberal Arts College." *Tulsa World*, April 20, 2019. https://www.tulsaworld.com/news/tu-is -becoming-something-other-than-a-liberal-arts-college/article_6622b066 -654e-50d0-a065-d5db597e565f.html.

Ware, Henry, Levi Hedge, John S. Popkin, Sidney Willard, John Farrar, Andrews Norton, Edward Everett, George Otis, and James Hayward. *To the Reverend and Honorable the Corporation of Harvard University*. Cambridge, MA: Harvard University Press, 1824.

Webster, Daniel. "Peroration, the Dartmouth College Case." March 10, 1818. https://www.dartmouth.edu/~dwebster/speeches/dartmouth-peroration .html.

Weiss, Daniel H. "Challenges and Opportunities in the Changing Landscape." In *Remaking College*, edited by Rebecca Chopp, Susan Frost, and Daniel H. Weiss, 25–40. Baltimore, MD: Johns Hopkins University Press, 2014.

Wheelock, J., and E. Parish. *Sketches of the History of Dartmouth College and Moors' Charity School, with a Particular Account of Some Late Remarkable Proceedings of the Board of Trustees, from the Year 1770 to the Year 1815*. Accessed August 15, 2022. https://catalog.hathitrust.org/Record/007693695.

Whitehead, John S. *The Separation of College and State*. New Haven, CT: Yale University Press, 1973.

Whitford, Emma. "College Boards Are Still White and Male, Report Shows." *Inside Higher Ed*, December 2, 2021. https://www.insidehighered.com/news/2021/12 /02/new-report-shows-slow-diversification-college-boards.

Whitford, Emma. "Endowment Returns Tumble." *Inside Higher Ed*, February 19, 2021. https://www.insidehighered.com/news/2021/02/19/college-and -university-endowments-post-worst-returns-five-years.

Whitford, Emma. "Endowments Skyrocket for the Wealthiest Colleges." *Inside Higher Ed*, October 1, 2021. https://www.insidehighered.com/news/2021/10/01 /wealthy-colleges-see-double-digit-returns-fiscal-2021.

Whitford, Emma. "Your Crypto Made This Possible." *Inside Higher Ed*, May 24, 2021. https://www.insidehighered.com/news/2021/05/24/colleges-line-accept -bitcoin-cryptocurrency-donations.

Whittington, Keith. "Free Speech Is a Core Tenet of the Academy. College Trustees Really Ought to Know That." *Chronicle of Higher Education*, December 5, 2018. https://www.chronicle.com/article/Free-Speech-Is-a-Core-Tenet-of /245264.

Wilder, Craig Steven. *Ebony and Ivy: Race, Slavery, and the Troubled History of America's Universities.* New York: Bloomsbury, 2013.

William & Mary College. "A Statute for the Better Government of the College, Ordained in a Meeting of the Visitors and Governors on September 14, 1763." In *The Fulham Papers at Lambeth Palace Library*, vol. 14, edited by William Wilson Manross. London: Lambeth Palace Library, n.d.

Witmer, Lightner. *The Nearing Case.* New York: B. W. Huebsch, 1915.

Wood, Gordon. "Introduction: The Emergence of the Public-Private Distinction in Early America." In *The Public and the Private in the United States*, edited by Hitoshi Abe, Hiroko Sato, and Chicko Kitagawa Otsuru, 1–12. Osaka: Japan Center for Area Studies, 1999.

Wright, Susan, Davydd Greenwood, and Rebecca Boden. "Report on a Field Visit to Mondragón University." *Learning and Teaching* 4, no. 3 (Winter 2011): 38–56.

zunguzungu. "Breaking Trust: The Past and Future of the University of California" (2011). Accessed October 16, 2020. https://zunguzungu.wordpress.com/2011/12 /08/breaking-trust-the-past-and-future-of-the-university-of-california/.

Index

Academic and Industrial Efficiency (Cooke), 142–43

academic capitalism, 213–16, 267

academic freedom, 174–79, 192–93, 258, 294n18

academic governance: AAUP 1920 report on, 178–81; AAUP/ACE/AGB joint statement on, 181–84; antidemocratic nature of, 8, 18; autocratic rule in, 12–18, 59–60; as capitalist autocracy, 16–18; Cattell's proposed democratization of, 156–61; class, race, and gender stratification in, 6, 21–22, 276n11, 276n21; college president's role in, 148–50; Commonwealth University and, 269–72; COVID-19 pandemic impact on, 1–4; in Dartmouth case, 105–6, 124–29; external lay governing boards and, 22–24, 63; faculty status in, 24–29, 89–92, 143, 150–53; financialization of contracts, ruling capacity undermined by, 198, 214–16, 223–28; at Harvard University, 83–84, 86–87, 89–92, 101–4; historical influences on, 47–48; institutional debt and fiscal problems and, 239–46; investment strategies as part of, 246–49, 251–54, 303n53; at Michi-

gan State University, 232; at Montana State University, 208–9; at Princeton University, 18–21, 214–16; at Purdue Global University, 219–29; pyramidal structure of, 13–16, 129–30; reform proposals for, 255–58; undermined by financialized contractual agreements, 198, 214–16, 223–28; at William & Mary College, 68–80. See also autocratic rule; shared governance

academic practices, commodification of, 5–6

accommodationist strategy, AAUP adoption of, 173, 294n13

Accountable Capitalism Act, 45–46

accreditation, 224

Aculon, 211

adjunct faculty, proliferation of, 185–87

Afran, Bruce, 210–13

Ahtone, Tristan, 7

Alchian, Armen A., 34–35

Alimta, 211, 214

Amazon, 205

American Association of State Colleges and Universities, 218

American Association of Universities, 166

business practices, proposed adoption by universities of, 153–55

Business Roundtable, 45

"Business Roundtable Redefines the Purpose of the Corporation to Promote an Economy That Serves All Americans," 45

Butler, Nicholas, 135

Calvinism: as organizational model for American universities, 282n7; vocational view of labor and, 169–70

Cambridge Union of University Teachers, 285n51

Cambridge University: corporate constitution of, 63–66, 80; governance of, 145, 156, 270; influence on Harvard of, 66, 83–87, 96–97, 282n7

canon law, 49–50

Capital (Marx), 274n10

capital fund management, 252–54

capitalism and capital accumulation: AAUP challenges to, 174–78; academic capitalism, 213–16; academic governance and maximization of, 5–6, 16–18, 147–48, 153–55, 274n10; employment contracts and, 15–18; financialization of, 233–36; government role in, 218; higher education as tool for, 147–48, 153–55; impact of *Dartmouth* case on, 137–41; medieval guilds and, 164–65; neoliberal economics and, 36, 192–93, 203–9, 234–36; nonprofit corporations and, 24; ownership in, 37–38; Populist criticism of, 172; professionalism and, 165–68, 193. *See also* financialized capitalism; neoliberalism; property rights

Carlyle, Thomas, 148

Carnegie, Andrew, 139

Carnegie Classification of Institutions of Higher Education, 229, 275n8

Carnegie Foundation, 135, 142, 153

Catholic Church, property law and, 49–50

Cattell, James McKeen, 135–37, 144, 153, 156–62, 172–73, 179, 263, 269, 290n19

Chait, Richard P., 277n32

Chapman, John Jay, 136

charters of incorporation: for Cambridge and Oxford universities, 65–66; for colonial trading companies and unincorporated partnerships, 53–55; as contracts, Marshall's interpretation of, 118–23; *Dartmouth* case implications for, 115–23, 177–78; for Dartmouth College, 107–9, 116; for Harvard, 85–92, 95–104, 124, 146–47, 251, 284n12, 303n49; for Michigan State University, 231; for Princeton University, 209–10; for Purdue University, 216–17; state charters in post-Revolutionary America and, 55–58; state modification of in *Dartmouth* case, 115–17; for University of Montana, 203–4; for University of Tulsa, 27; for Virginia Company, 67–68; for William & Mary College, 69–74, 76–80. *See also* corporations; trusts

Christian theology, monarchical absolutism, 49

Chronicle of Higher Education, 11, 25, 143, 216, 255–56

Ciepley, David: on corporation as model for republican constitutions, 57–58; on corporations as franchises, 42; on corporations vs. trusts, 287n37; on member corporations, 50–52, 59; on property corporations, 48–50, 59; on shareholder primacy, 34, 39

cities, incorporation of, 43–44, 280n22

Citizens United v. FEC, 41

civil corporations, Blackstone's definition of, 115, 122

Clancy, Gerard, 25

classical curriculum, 165–66

class stratification, professionalization mythology and, 184–87, 296n50

Cleveland, Grover, 203

cognitive capital, 6

cognitive commonwealth, 265

Cold War, research and development projects and, 190–93

colonialism: corporate structure and, 52–55, 82; governance in Massachusetts and, 55–58, 87–88; Harvard University and, 85; higher education and, 200–202

Columbia University, 135–36

Commentaries (Blackstone), 115, 125, 250

Committee T on the Place and Function of Faculties in University Government and Administration (AAUP), 179–80, 183, 188

Commonwealth of Massachusetts, founding instruments of, 57

Commonwealth University: non-utopian nature of, 269–72; as republican body politic, 259–63; as socialist enterprise, 263–69

community colleges, 191–93, 229

Concerned Faculty of TU, 27, 109

constitutions: corporate charters as origin of, 55–58; of Michigan, 231; of Montana, 203–5

consumer satisfaction, higher education reforms linked to, 147–48

contingent faculty positions, rise of, 185–87, 206–7, 296n50. *See also* at-will employment

Contract Clause (US Constitution), 120–23, 129, 138, 270

contracts: college charters defined as, in *Dartmouth* case, 119–23; employment contracts, 128; erosion of corporate powers by, 197–98; nexus of contract model of corporations, 31–36; Purdue-Kaplan joint operating agreement as, 220, 226–29; state authorization of, 40–43

"Contribution and Transfer Agreement" (Kaplan Inc. and Purdue Global University), 217, 220

Cook, Tim, 38

Cooke, Morris, 142–43, 147, 153

Co-operative College, 304n8

corporate governance: academic reconstruction of, 258–59; directors as fidu-

ciaries in, 43–46; impact of *Dartmouth* case on, 137–41; industrialization and transformation of, 137–41; neoliberal representation of, 4–6, 273n7, 278n2; property vs. member corporations, 48–52

corporations: in ancient Rome, 64; Blackstone's typology of, 115–16; Cambridge and Oxford universities as examples of, 65–66; challenges to neoliberal form of, 43–46; as colonial charter template, 55–58; colonial trading companies as, 52–55; for-profit structure, consolidation of, 137–41; governance powers eroded by contract, 197–98, 226–28; in-house "universities" at for-profit, 189–90, 208, 219; limited liability of, 38–39, 279n14; medieval models of, 52, 64–65; member vs. property corporations, 48–52; neoliberal theory and, 31–43; powers granted by state to, 16, 28, 40–43, 46; as state constitution template, 55–58. *See also* charters of incorporation; *specific types of corporate structure*

corporatization: *Dartmouth* case and, 106; higher education's alleged conquest by, 1–6, 25–27, 30–31, 106, 136–37, 187–88, 190–92, 226, 258–59, 271–72, 273n5; shared governance rise and fall and, 187–93. *See also* academic capitalism

COVID-19 pandemic: academic governance and impact of, 1–4, 248–49; financial impact on higher education of, 245–46; impact at Michigan State University of, 238

credentials: online universities' provision of, 219; professionalism linked to, 166–67; as skills indicator, 206–7. *See also* professionalism and professionalization

credit rating agencies: higher education debt burden and, 242–46; scoring system for colleges and universities, 242–43

Creighton, J. E., 136
critical race theory, bans on teaching
   of, 15
cryptocurrencies, college and university
   investment in, 251–54

Dartmouth College: consolidation of
   trustee power at, 129–32; endowment
   at, 249; faculty status in *Dartmouth*
   case, 126–29; founding of, 106–7;
   hybrid corporate structure of, 124–26;
   incorporation of, 107–9; More's Indian
   Charity School and, 106–7; republican
   challenge to governance of, 109–14;
   website of, 286n11. See also *Trustees of
   Dartmouth College v. Woodward*
debt: academic governance and impact
   of, 239–49; fiscal crisis in higher
   education and, 216–19; student debt,
   explosion of, 219, 232, 237; universities'
   assumption of, 237–39
"Declaration of Principles on Academic
   Freedom and Tenure, 1915" (AAUP),
   174–78, 190, 269, 295n21
democratization: Cattell's commitment
   to, 156–62; Commonwealth University
   vision of, 261–62; shared governance
   and, 179–84
Demsetz, Harold, 34–35
deprofessionalization, 190–93
deregulation, neoliberal economics and,
   36, 233
derivatives market, proliferation of,
   234–36, 250
Dewey, John, 3–4, 174–75, 263
Digest (Justinian), 50–51
digital badging system, 207
disciplinary associations, emergence of,
   171
discovery doctrine, 55
Disney Corporation, "university" in,
   219
Dodd-Frank Act, 233
Dudley, Joseph, 88–89
Dunster, Henry, 83, 85–86

Easterbrook, Frank, 31–32, 34
East India Company (England), 54
Eaton, Charlie, 303n53
Eaton, Nathaniel, 83
*Ebony and Ivy: Race, Slavery, and the
   Troubled History of America's Universities*
   (Wilder), 7
ecclesiastical corporations, Blackstone's
   definition of, 115
economic inequality: neoliberal economics and, 34–36, 234–36, 301n9; within
   professoriate, 186–87
educational policies: AAUP governance
   framework for, 179–84; effects of credit
   ratings on, 242–46; workforce training
   and, 205–6, 226–27
eduplyment, 6, 206–9
eleemosynary corporations, 115, 122,
   126
Eli Lilly, 211–16, 254
Eliot, Charles, 103–4
Elizabethan statutes, Cambridge and
   Oxford universities and, 66
Elliott Management, 247–49
employment contracts, 128. *See also* at-will
   employment
Enclosure Acts, 240–41, 265
Encyclopedia Americana, 58
endowments at colleges and universities, 230, 249–54, 303n47. *See also*
   investment strategies of colleges and
   universities
equal protection guarantees, corporations and, 139
equity, faculty-founded startups as source
   of, 215–16
Etaphase, 211
Europe: corporation structure and commerce in, 52, 235; universities in, 64–65,
   124, 156
Everett, Edward, 97
experimental method, emergence of,
   169–70
experts and expertise, mythology of
   professionalism and, 169–70

external lay governing boards (colleges and universities): at Dartmouth College, 108–9; faculty subordination to, 145–48; fiduciary duties of, 22–24, 84; financialized capitalism and composition of, 239–46; Harvard faculty protests against, 92–97; Harvard's adoption of, 90–92; justification of, attempts at, 18–21; at Michigan State, 247–49; at University of South Carolina System, criticism of, 21–22; at William & Mary College, 22–24

Fable of the Bees (Mandeville), 53–54
Facebook, "university" at, 219
faculty: AAUP Declaration of Principles (1915) for, 174–78; academic governance and role of, 24–29, 89–92, 143, 150–53, 257–58, 296n57; Cattell's analysis of, 135–36, 156–61, 290n19; college presidents and, 149–50; compensation for, 99–101, 128, 160–61; *Dartmouth* case and role of, 105–6, 126–29; declining tenure status for, 184–87; gatekeeper role of, 167–68; Harvard overseers-faculty conflict, 89–104, 144, 152–53, 285n51; Populist movement and, 172–74; postwar labor market and, 191–93; professionalization of, 170–74; professors' literature of protest and, 136–37; property rights to content of, 143; psychasthenia universitatis and role of, 150–53; shared governance and, 13, 174, 178–84, 187–92; at William & Mary, visitors-faculty conflict, 71–74, 76–80, 144. *See also* contingent faculty positions, rise of; professors' literature of protest; *specific colleges and universities*
Farmers' Alliance, 172
"Federalist 49," 57
Federalists, 201
Federal Reserve, 218
fellows: at Cambridge University, 65–66; at Harvard University, 86–87, 89–92, 95–101, 144

Fellows Orchard (Harvard University), property dispute over, 99–100
fiduciary duties: AAUP template for, 177; AGB conception of, 22–23; capitalist employment contracts and, 128; of college and university trustees, 29, 43, 240; democratization within member corporations, 51, 262; Michigan State trustees' breach of, 247–48; Princeton trustees' violation of, 210; of Purdue Global's governing board, 228; within trusts, 121; Tulsa University trustees' contravention of, 27–29
financialized capitalism: college and university debt and, 236–39; college and university investment and, 246–49; history of, 233–36; impact on colleges and universities of, 236–39, 249–54; mission of higher education subordinated to, 253–54; property reconfiguration at colleges and universities and, 249–53. *See also* investment strategies of colleges and universities
Fischel, Daniel R., 31–32, 34
Fish, Stanley, 256
Flynt, Henry, 89–90
Forell, E. V., 172
for-profit colleges and universities, 189–90, 199–202, 219
for-profit corporations: academic governing board members drawn from, 23–24; ascendancy in nineteenth century of, 137–41; nonprofit universities' agreements with, 211–16
Fouace, Stephen, 72, 76
Founding of Harvard College, The, 282n7
franchises, corporations as, 42–43, 56, 80, 98, 116, 200–202
freeholds, faculty appointments and, 79, 127–28
free market fundamentalism, neoliberal economics and, 34–35. *See also* market forces
free speech, academic freedom and, 294n18
Friedman, Milton, 31, 43, 46

Geiger, Roger, 166

gender inequality, higher education's re-
inforcement of, 21–22, 257, 269, 276n11

general incorporation statutes, rise of,
44–45, 138

genocide, academic governance and
complicity in, 67–69

George III (king of England), 107, 115–16,
121

George Kaiser Family Foundation, 27

Gerber, Larry, 168–70, 187–93, 294n18

German models of universities, 166

GI Bill of 1944, 191, 237

Glass-Steagall Act, 233

Goldman Sachs, 234, 247

Goldsmiths College, 305n17

Google, 205

*Goose-Step: A Study of American Education,
The* (Sinclair), 136, 255

governing boards. *See* external lay governing boards (colleges and universities)

"Governing of Princeton University,
The" (1970), 19–21

*Governor's Action Guide to Achieving Good
Jobs for All Americans, A*, 206

Graham Holdings Company, 217, 225

Grand Canyon University, 298n42

Grange movement, 172

Great and General Court of Massachusetts Bay, 82–83, 86–87, 88–90, 95–97,
200

Great Recession of 2007–9, 218, 236

Greenwood, Robin, 233–34

guilds, modern professionalism and,
164–66

Hall, Gary, 206

Hansmann, Henry, 31, 45

Harlan, John Marshall, 139

Harvard, John, 83

Harvard University: Cambridge as
model for, 66, 83–87, 282n7; competing charters for, 87–89; early history
of, 63–64, 82–84; endowment at, 249;
expropriation of faculty powers at,

97–104, 251, 303n49; incorporation of,
84–87, 284n12, 303n49; revolt of tutors
at, 89–92, 285n51; tutors' governance
credo at, 92–97. *See also* overseers,
Harvard board of

Hechinger Report, 205

Heisenberg, Werner, 223

Henry III (king of England), 65

Herbst, Jurgen, 282n7

higher education: autocratic rule in,
59–60; classification of, 198–202, 229,
275n8; corporate governance in, 1–7;
financialized capitalism and, 236–39;
fiscal crisis and debt burden in, 218–19,
237–39; as human capital generator,
205–9; industrial approach to reform
of, 142–43; justification for autocracy
in, 18–22; medieval universities, 64–65;
Montana constitution and, 204–9;
nonprofit institutions of, 15–16; postwar expansion of, 190–93; proposed
taxonomy for, 229–30; systemic violence and role of, 7; white male domi-
nance of governing boards in, 21–22;
workforce polarization in, 186–87.
See also educational policies; *specific
colleges and universities*

Higher Education Act of 1965, 191,
237

Higher Learning Commission, 224

*Higher Learning in America: A Memorandum
on the Conduct of Universities by Business
Men, The* (Veblen), 136, 143–44, 153–55,
293n10

Hille, Jim, 253–54

Hobby Lobby. See *Burwell v. Hobby Lobby*

Hockett, Jeffrey, 163–64

Hoffman, Christian Balzac, 172

Hofstadter, Richard, 22, 71, 81, 84, 107–8

Hough, Samuel, 83

House Bill 377 (Idaho), 15, 275n10

Howland, Jacob, 26–27, 163–64

"How to Resist a Corporate Takeover of
Your College" (Hockett and Howland),
163

Ladd, George, 136
land grant universities: formation of, 142, 216, 231; modern professionalism and, 166, 190–93
Law of Higher Education, The (Kaplan and Lee), 14–15
lay corporations, Blackstone's definition of, 115
Lee, Barbara A., 14–15
Lee, Robert, 7
legal profession, faculty as gatekeeper for, 167–68
Legge, William, 107
Leighton, J. A., 179
Leslie, Larry, 213
Leverett, John, 88–90
Levin, Janet, 26
liberal arts colleges: classification of, 191–93; financial elites on boards of, 240
liberalism, 33, 42, 201–2, 219–20, 259–60
licensing agreements, between nonprofit and for-profit corporations, 211–13
Lieber, Francis, 58
lifelong learning programs, 207
limited government, American ideal of, 58–60
limited liability doctrine, shareholder protection and, 38–39
Locke, John, 57, 250
Lovejoy, Arthur, 173
Lumina Foundation, 205

Madison, James, 57
Maitland, Frederic, 222
Mandeville, Bernard, 53–54
market forces: corporations and, 31–33; higher education reforms and, 26–29, 147–48, 243–46; neoliberal economics and, 34–36; workforce training and, 25, 206–9
Marshall, John: Bracken defended by, 75–77; on corporations, 52–53, 55, 57–58, 158; *Dartmouth* case and, 4–5, 41, 118–23, 126–29, 131–32, 201

Marx, Karl, 193, 207, 233–36, 274n10
Mary (queen of England), 72
Massachusetts Bay Colony, 56, 88
Massachusetts Bay Company, 56, 115
Massachusetts Bay Province, 88
Massachusetts Constitution (1780), 200
Massachusetts Institute of Technology, 249
Massachusetts regional state universities, debt burden of, 241
Mather, Cotton, 83
Mather, Increase, 88
McDonald's, "university" in, 219
McKinsey and Company, 21–22
Meckling, William H., 31
medical profession, faculty as gatekeeper for, 167–68
medieval universities: corporate model and, 57, 64–65, 124; governance of, 145, 156; roots of tenure in, 127
member corporations, 48, 50–55; colonial trading companies as, 52–55, 141–43; Commonwealth University as, 260–63, 271–72; constitutional republics as, 58–60; Dartmouth's hybrid status as, 124–26; for-profit corporations as, 139–40; Harvard as, 87, 92–97, 124; medieval model of, 57; modern professions as, 164–68; state charters in post-Revolution America and, 55–58, 282n15; Virginia Company as, 67–68; William & Mary as, 69–71
memorial petitions: by Harvard tutors, 89–90; by William & Mary president and masters, 74–75
Metzger, Walter, 22, 71, 81, 84, 107–8
Michigan State University: endowment of, 249; fiscal crisis and debt burden of, 238–39; founding of, 231; governance at, 6; investment-debt circle at, 245–46, 301n17; investment management at, 246–49, 252–54; municipal bond issue at, 231–32, 241; subordination to credit agencies at, 239–46; trustees' violation of fiduciary duties at, 231–32

Microsoft, 205
Mitchell, Brian, 21
Modern Language Association, 171
Mondragón University (Spain), 304n8
Montana Constitution (1889), 203
Montana Constitution (1972), 204
Montana State University: constitutional
  reform of governance at, 204–5, 275n10;
  elimination of distinction between
  education and skills training at, 205–7;
  founding of, 202–4; subordination to
  imperatives of capital accumulation
  at, 207–8
Montana State Workforce Innovation
  Board, 205
Moody's Investor Service, 238, 242–46
More, Joshua, 106–7
Morison, Samuel Eliot, 66, 83, 88–89, 92,
  282n7
Morpurgo, J. E., 73
Morrill Act of 1862, 7, 142, 216
Motoaka (Pocahontas), 69
Motorola, "university" at, 219
municipia (municipality), member corpo-
  rations and, 50–52
Munnings, George, 82
Munroe, James, 136

Nassar, Larry, 238–39, 301n17
Nation, The, 26
National Governors Association report,
  205–7
national professional associations, creation of, 168
Navigation Acts, 88
Nearing, Scott, 170–71
neoliberalism: challenges to corporations
  based on theory of, 43–46; characterization of corporations by, 31–33, 37–43,
  226–27; Commonwealth University as
  antithesis to, 270–72; concept of, 192,
  273n7; *Dartmouth* case as forerunner of,
  119; financialization in relation to, 233–
  36; history of, 233–36; incorporation
  statutes and role of, 138–39; intellectual

property law and, 266; pernicious and
  ideological consequences of, 33–36;
  privatization and, 202; public-private
  distinction and, 201–2; tax evasion by
  corporations and, 218; taxonomy of
  higher education and, 229–30; tenured
  faculty's displacement by contingent
  appointments and, 192–93
New Hampshire state government:
  Dartmouth dispute and role of, 111–17,
  128–29, 288n52; Supreme Court ruling
  of violations by, 119–23
nexus of contracts: corporations as, 31–36;
  incoherence in theory of, 37–43
nondistribution rule, 24
nonprofit colleges and universities: classification of, 15–16, 199–202; credit ratings
  for, 242–46; fiscal crisis of, 219; as private
  government, 259–60; Purdue Global as
  for-profit/nonprofit hybrid, 216, 219–20;
  tax-exempt status of, 199, 209, 284n1
nonresidential rule over colleges and
  universities, at Harvard, 93–97
Norton, Andrews, 101–2

Occom, Samson, 107, 116
offshore shell companies, universities'
  and colleges' creation of, 253–54
Ohio Revised Code, 266–67, 304n15
O'Keefe, Pat, 238–39
Omnibus Statehood Bill, 203
"One Faculty" campaign (AAUP), 187
online higher education courses, 217–19
Orthobond, 211
Ostrom, Elinor, 305n18
overseers, Harvard board of: code of statutes (1825) adopted by, 102–4; establishment of, 87–92, 97–101, 107, 130, 202;
  expropriation of faculty powers by,
  101–4. *See also* Harvard University
ownership: capitalist representation
  of, 263–68; financialized capitalism's
  reconfiguration of, 251–53; neoliberal
  concept of, 37–43; property corporations and, 49

res publica (public concerns), 51

Revolutionary War, post-Revolution corporate structures and, 55–58, 116–17, 145–46, 200–201

Rhoades, Gary, 213

Rise and Decline of Faculty Governance, The (Gerber), 168–69, 187–93

Robie, Thomas, 89–90

Rockefeller, John D., 139, 166

Roman law, origins of corporations within, 49–52

Roosevelt Institute, 231, 247, 252

Sabine, George, 188

Sanders, Bernie, 7

Santa Clara County v. Southern Pacific Railroad Company, 138–39

Scharfstein, David, 233–34

Schirmer, Eleni, 241–42

Schurman, Jacob Gould, 136

Schwarz, Joseph, 187

science, mythology of professionalism and role of, 169–70

Scott, Robert, 21

Second Treatise of Government (Locke), 57, 250

Securities and Exchange Commission (SEC), 214

self-governance: Commonwealth University proposal and, 260–63; corporate practice of, 41–43, 197–98; *Dartmouth* case and issue of, 122–26; evolution of professionalism and, 164–68; at Harvard, 84–87, 95–101; at Oxford and Cambridge Universities, 66; state powers and, 203; at William & Mary, 69–72. *See also* member corporations; republican corporate structure

senate (university), Cattell's proposals for, 159–61

Sever, Nicholas, 89–90, 92–97, 108

"Shall the University Become a Business Corporation?" (Pritchett), 153

shared governance: AAUP advocacy for, 174, 178–81; AAUP attenuation of,

181–84; academic workforce polarization and, 186–87; accommodationist strategy and, 173–74; COVID-19 pandemic and threats to, 1–4; faculty role in, 13, 24–29, 89–92, 143, 150–53, 168–70, 257–58, 296n57; flaws of, 163–64, 272; rise and decline of, 187–93

shareholder primacy doctrine: asset lock-in and, 39; consequences of, 34–36; early forms of, 289n8; financialization of capitalism and, 234–36; incoherence in theory of, 37–43, 279n14; member corporations and, 139–40; neoliberal principle of, 31–33; Purdue Global University–Kaplan Inc. partnership and, 224–29

Sherman Antitrust Act of 1890, 147

Shireman, Robert, 220, 225–27

"Shock Wave II" (Kerr), 275n8

Shurtleff, Roswell, 111

Sinclair, Upton, 136, 146–47, 255, 263

Sketches of the History of Dartmouth College, 1770–1815 (Parish), 112–13

Slaughter, Sheila, 213

slavery: college and university complicity in, 68–71; higher education's dependence on, 7

Smith, Adam, 24, 32, 64

Smith, J. W., 261

Smith, John, 111

socialization of corporate property, 39–40, 46; Commonwealth University proposal and, 263–69. *See also* property rights

Special Report: COVID-19 and Academic Governance (AAUP), 1–4, 30, 129, 184, 248–49

staff, academic governance and role of, 13

Stanford, Leland, 166

Stanford University, 158

"Statement on Governance of Colleges and Universities" (AAUP, ACE, and AGB) (1966), 181–84, 189–93, 295n42

state-university relations: corporate charters in post-Revolution America and, 55–58, 116–17; corporations' dependence on, 40–43, 46, 138–41; *Dartmouth* dispute and role of, 111–23, 128–32; economic conditions and, 218–19; federal funding for higher education and, 191–93; Michigan State University and, 231; Montana constitution on, 203–9; neoliberal economics and, 202; Omnibus Statehood Bill and, 203; private, nonprofit colleges and, 214–16; Purdue University and, 216; William & Mary College and role of, 75–81, 282n15

Stevenson, John, 136

stipend, Harvard faculty compensation as, 96, 100–101

Story, Joseph, 126, 130–31, 287n45, 288n56

Stout, Lynn, 39

Strada Education Network, 205

Stratton, George, 136

student debt, growth in, 219, 232, 237, 244–46

student-hour (credit hour), establishment of, 142–43

Tag Optics, 211

tax evasion by corporations, 218

tax-exempt charitable organizations: colleges and universities as, 209–16, 303n53; Princeton's status challenged, 209–16; Purdue Global University status as, 224–25

taxonomy of higher education: alternative version of, 229–30; conventional version of, 198–99; *Dartmouth* case and revision of, 200–201; neoliberal reconstruction of, 202

Taylor, Francis, 142

Taylor, John, 77–80, 81

teaching hospitals, emergence of, 167

tenure: AAUP advocacy for, 174–78; elimination of, 2–4, 17, 184–87, 192–93; faculty push for institutionalization of,

143; medieval roots of, 127–28; proposed reforms of, 159–61

Terrell, Wesley G., 11

Texas Christian University, 253–54

Texas Southern University, 11–12, 28, 43, 47, 73

Thatcher, Margaret, 52, 233

trading companies, contractual agreements in, 52–55, 141–43, 227–28

"Transition and Operations Support Agreement" (Kaplan Inc. and Purdue Global University), 217, 223–26, 300n62

"True Commitment" plan (University of Tulsa), 25–29, 163–64, 277n35, 278n43

trustees: AAUP on role of, 180–84; autocratic rule by, 11–18; caricature of faculty by, 150–53; Cattell on role of, 156–57; *Dartmouth* case and role of, 111–14, 116–18, 126–32; Dartmouth College opposing boards of, 109–10; at Harvard University, 83–87, 97–104; at Michigan State University, 247–49; at Montana State University, 203–5, 208–9; as philistines, characterization of, 145–48; at Princeton University, 209–10; at Purdue Global University, 220–28; at South Carolina University System, 21–22; at University of Tulsa, 24–29; Veblen's criticism of, 143–44; at William & Mary College, 69–75, 78. *See also* academic governance

Trustees of Dartmouth College v. Woodward: academic governance issues and, 105; at-will employment and legacy of, 170; Dartmouth's transformation into property corporation and, 124–26; external lay governing boards and, 63–64; faculty power expropriated by, 76, 126–29; for-profit corporations encouraged by, 4–5, 137–41; Marshall's ruling in, 4–5, 41, 118–23; New Hampshire's defense against suit, 115–18; prerogative power of board affirmed by, 129–32, 289n58; private property rights and, 48, 105–6,